KARL RAHNER
IN DIALOGUE

KARL RAHNER IN DIALOGUE

CONVERSATIONS AND INTERVIEWS

1965–1982

Edited by Paul Imhof
and Hubert Biallowons

Translation edited by Harvey D. Egan

CROSSROAD · NEW YORK

1986
The Crossroad Publishing Company
370 Lexington Avenue, New York, N.Y. 10017

Originally published as
Karl Rahner im Gespräch, Band 1: 1964–1977
© 1982 by Kösel Verlag GmbH & Co., München
Karl Rahner im Gespräch, Band 2: 1978–1982
© 1983 by Kösel Verlag GmbH & Co., München

Translation © 1986 by The Crossroad Publishing Company

Library of Congress Cataloging in Publication Data

Rahner, Karl, 1904–1984
Karl Rahner in dialogue.

Translation of: Karl Rahner im Gespräch.
1. Rahner, Karl, 1904–1984—Interviews.   2. Catholic
Church—Doctrines.   3. Theology, Doctrinal.
I. Imhof, Paul.   II. Biallowons, Hubert.   III. Egan,
Harvey D.   IV. Title.
BX4705.R287A342513   1986   230'.2   86–8972
ISBN 0-8245-0749-5

Interviews 2 ("Questions about Today's Church and World"),
5 ("The Church's Responsibility for the World"), and
32 ("Karl Rahner at 75 Years of Age") have been reprinted
with permission of America Press, Inc., 106 West 56th Street,
New York, NY 10019. © 1965, 1970, and 1978. All rights
reserved.

CONTENTS

v

Part IV : THE CHURCH IN A PERIOD OF TRANSITION:
Interviews 1980–1982

TRANSLATION EDITOR'S PREFACE

Shortly before Father Karl Rahner, S.J., died on March 30, 1984, I had just finished reading *Karl Rahner im Gespräch*, two volumes of his television, radio, and newspaper interviews from 1964 to 1982.[1] Although I had seen and heard some of these interviews during my doctoral studies under Rahner in Germany, the reading of all these interviews in a short interval of time had a tremendous effect upon me.

First, these interviews reminded me of how lively, direct, homey, and simple Rahner had been in his doctoral seminars and in the Christology course he taught with Wilhelm Thüsing, a New Testament exegete at the University of Münster. The Rahner who lectured and the Rahner who wrote difficult theological essays receded into the background. Rahner the pastoral theologian and popularizer took center stage. Here appeared the Rahner who listened to the catechism of the heart and who spoke directly and effectively to this heart.

Second, as someone who has been reading Rahner for over twenty years and teaching his thought for over ten, these interviews struck me as the easiest and best introduction to Karl Rahner's world of thought for the average person. These interviews reveal much about Rahner the man, the Jesuit, the priest, the Christian, and the theologian. They likewise communicate in relatively straightforward language an excellent cross section of his speculative, pastoral, practical, spiritual, and ecumenical ideas. A few even provide an easy access to the philosophical underpinnings of his theology.

Third, these interviews also intensified an ever present awareness of how indebted to him I am for my own theological and spiritual life.

The reader can grasp through these interviews both Rahner's architechtonic, holistic grasp of the faith and the way he applies this unified vision to a vast range of issues as they arose in the important twenty-year period following the Second Vatican Council. Rahner's awesome mastery of the Church's tradition and his unusual sensitivity to the "signs of the times" permeate these

---

1. A third volume, largely composed of interviews from 1983 and 1984, has been published under the title *Glaube in winterlicher Zeit: Gespräche mit Karl Rahner aus den letzten Lebensjahren*, ed. Paul Imhof and Hubert Biallowons (Düsseldorf: Patmos Verlag, 1986).

interviews. They reflect both Rahner's and the Church's identity-in-transformation over the years.

So, I was eager to make these interviews accessible to Rahner's already wide American audience. I cannot recommend this American volume strongly enough to those teaching introductory courses in Rahner or to those merely interested in easy access to the thinking of the Father of Roman Catholic theology in the twentieth century.

After much urging from a few friends, I decided to organize a team of translators from the many Rahner experts in the United States. A team effort would reduce the time required for translating. Also, the interview nature of the material lends itself to such an approach.

The Germans have a custom of presenting a person celebrating some special occasion with a *Festschrift*, an honorary publication written by others. In a small way this volume of Rahner's interviews translated by former Rahner students or Rahner enthusiasts serves to commemorate the death of this great man approximately two years ago.

The reader should note that some interviews of the original two-volume German edition were not translated and a few have been presented in abridged form. I did not see a need for translating interviews that dealt with specifically German church problems that lack wider application. And Rahner did repeat himself on occasion in the German interviews.

Finally, I am most grateful to Father George W. Hunt, S.J., editor of *America* magazine, for permission to use *America*'s translation of interviews 2, 5, and 32. I also wish to thank the many Rahner scholars throughout the United States who directly and indirectly contributed to this American translation. But I want to thank in a special way Father Joseph Donceel, S.J., of Fordham University. Fortunately he was the first person I called about this project and within a few weeks he had already translated several interviews. The project was off the ground. Furthermore, Father Donceel should likewise be thanked for the number of years he has spent making the best of European thought available to American scholars through his numerous translations and publications.

Harvey D. Egan, S.J.

EDITORS' PREFACE[1]

Anyone who knows Karl Rahner knows that he blooms in conversation. Here the "lecturing professor" recedes into the background, while what is really at issue comes into the limelight in an understandable and nontechnical way. In spontaneous dialogue even the most difficult theological questions become interesting and colorful. Moreover, the dialogue-partner, the one seeking God—even if for the moment the *explicit* question of God is not at issue for this person—becomes the focal point. "Not the theological drama, but the person of today in his own self-understanding, is Rahner's theological starting point. To be sure, one often hears the complaint that Rahner is difficult to understand. His terminology and style of thinking place unreasonable demands on the average Christian."[2] He has even been called a "theological atomic physicist."[3]

The interviews in these volumes aid us to understand the "difficult Rahner." He makes important basic concepts and thoughts from his overall theology clear by using the language of daily speech. These interviews offer a new and relatively easy entrance into Rahner's anthropology and theology—in fact, even to theological questions in general. At the same time, they are an introduction to practical and speculative theology. Readers will find in them theological views personally useful for guiding themselves in these confusing times in Church and society.

Karl Rahner, the Christian, the theologian, the philosopher of religion—in dialogue. Quantitatively speaking, Rahner used the interview forum more and more in his later years as the medium for his theological output. Questions and answers become an inextricable pattern for Karl Rahner's theological

1. A conflation and slight emendation of the two prefaces found in *Karl Rahner im Gespräch, Band 1: 1964–1977* and *Band 2: 1978–1982*, edited by Paul Imhof and Hubert Biallowons (Munich: Kösel Verlag, 1982 and 1983)—Harvey D. Egan.
2. Karl-Heinz Weger, *Karl Rahner: Ein Einführung in sein theologisches Denken* (Freiburg i. Br.: Herder, 1978), p. 4. This section is not found in the English translation, *Karl Rahner: An Introduction to His Theology*, tr. David Smith (New York: Crossroad, 1980). See also: Herbert Vorgrimler, *Karl Rahner: His Life, Thought, and Works*, tr. Edward Quinn (Glen Rock, N.J.: Paulist Press, 1966), and idem, *Understanding Karl Rahner: An Introduction to His Life and Thought*, tr. John Bowden (New York: Crossroad, 1986).
3. See interview no. 34, p. 204

3

thinking. Of course, not all these interviews can be compared to a Platonic dialogue. At times, however, many readers may become aware of certain similarities so that this association will not appear completely arbitrary. It is not fortuitous that Karl Rahner expresses himself as a theologian in dialogue. That is to say, dialogue is and remains the basic way theological convictions and contents are mediated. In fact, the spoken word belongs to and constitutes Jesus' gospel itself.

Jesus himself transmitted his gospel in a question and answer format. It is a basic way of his own self-communication. And in him you find God's very own self-communication. "Through Jesus Christ, crucified and risen, the victorious self-communication of God, established by God himself, has been manifested as victorious, as eschatological, as definitively final."[4] Jesus Christ is God's Word, the Logos who has appeared. This Word continues to be effective. In the course of history the formulations of individual dogmas that brought the content of faith to term arose through a process of dialogue and discussion. Today, too, is the living word of God—irrevocably linked with Jesus Christ himself—transmitted in dialogue with Holy Scripture and the Church's tradition. From that springs the Church's living tradition and a pastorally relevant theology. Certainly, an abiding difference, a clearly unbridgeable chasm, remains between spoken and written theology. Still, the written word becomes more important the more it succeeds in approximating the spoken word. Yet, this requirement for a living theology is remarkably fulfilled by these published Rahner interviews.

Hence, Karl Rahner's practical suggestions and theological thinking become more accessible and more easily understood in his interviews than in his imposing, systematic writings. In the lively give-and-take of an interview, Rahner masterfully succeeds in transmitting the "categorical," that is, the concrete aspect of his transcendental, metaphysical thought. Without this concrete aspect theology remains all too often pale and lifeless.[5] Many of his dogmatic and pastoral principles become clear through his use of concrete examples. Also, Rahner does not hesitate to express his own opinions pointedly.

These collected interviews show clearly that Rahner sought dialogue with all sorts of people: believers, unbelievers, young people, experts, journalists, publishers, politicians, and church officeholders. To put it another way,

4. Karl Rahner, "The Church's Redemptive Historical Provenance from the Death and Resurrection of Jesus," in *Theological Investigations XIX*, tr. Edward Quinn (New York: Crossroad, 1983), p. 30.

5. For a brief treatment of the "categorical" and "transcendental" aspects of Rahner's theology, see the foreword by Harvey D. Egan, S.J., in C. Annice Callahan, R.S.C.J., *Karl Rahner's Spirituality of the Pierced Heart: A Reinterpretation of Devotion to the Sacred Heart* (Lanham, Md.: University Press of America, 1985), pp. iv–viii.

Rahner sought dialogue with people whose questions and problems offered him the very opportunity to select his themes and theological replies. Again and again, he sought living contact with the world.

These interviews are a key to Rahner's thinking, an essential element of his autobiography in which he takes a position, in which he communicates his world view and himself. At the same time, these collected interviews are an authentic commentary from a witness of our age—an era whose basis will shape the future. Moreover, these volumes contain material important not only for Rahner's biography but also and especially for the timeliness and significance of their content.

The people who interviewed Rahner provided the catalyst for these dialogues (and his approximately four thousand publications). They present an excellent cross section of his thinking on the "anonymous Christian," liberation and political theology, birth control, the saints, ecumenical questions, afterlife, resurrection, revolution, papal infallibility, the future of Christianity, the peace movement, the Church's practical life—to name but a few. The attentive reader will notice that over the course of time Rahner's views changed with regard to individual questions, although—but also precisely because—his architechtonic view of the faith remained unchanged.

Rahner's readiness ever to enter into dialogue with his age's "topic of the day" resulted both in this topic influencing Rahner's theology and in this topic being influenced by his theology. Yet his willingness to expose himself even to banal, annoying, and hostile questions and to appear in the glare of ecclesiastical and secular society brought him not only respect but also much hostility. Despite much annoyance and many disappointments, Rahner's resolute sympathy with and compassion for a great variety of people made him someone with whom one could meaningfully remain in dialogue. Rahner's humane, priestly concern for others overflows into explicit dialogues that advise and assist others. An essential aspect of his compassion—his readiness to dialogue —is definitely oriented toward persons and their concerns.

Rahner communicated not merely his ideas but also gave others the freedom to express themselves in personal dialogue. He often works like a spiritual father or like an understanding confessor who evokes from people what is really in their hearts. This brings about what inextricably belongs to all priestly activity, Rahner's, too: a sacrament. The proclamation of the word and sacramental activity are the two sides of priestly existence. On July 26, 1982, Rahner concelebrated Mass with his Jesuit brothers in celebration of his fiftieth anniversary as a priest. On this occasion, the archbishop of Freiburg, Dr. Oskar Saier, in whose diocese Rahner was born and raised, wrote to him: "Through your research and teaching scholarly theology has received a new impetus, which was and will be rich in blessings for the encounter of the Church and the world. Many seekers, not only in Germany but also in the whole world, have been enriched and inspired by your theological contributions for the Church and its mission in our time." Trusting in God's grace, Rahner entered the Jesuits some sixty years ago on April 20, 1922. He never regretted that step. "We must love Jesus in the unconditional acceptance of his life's fate as our own norm of existence, in order to experience serenely and joyously our own existence as finally redeemed."[6]

The editors wish to thank—also in Father Rahner's name—his various interviewers who made their material readily available. Their questions, follow-up questions, and ideas contributed much to the spontaneity, liveliness, and simplified precision of Rahner's "spoken theology." Most of the TV and radio interviews were obtained from the Karl Rahner archives in Innsbruck.

We would also like to thank the numerous men and women of TV and radio whose help made many of these interviews accessible for the first time, namely: Dr. Ernst Emrich and Mr. Hans-Jörg Xylander of Radio Bavaria; Dr. Heinrich Büttgen, Dr. Edgar Lersch, and Dr. Ulf Sharlau of South-German Radio, Stuttgart; Dr. Erika Ahlbrecht-Meditz, Mr. Norbert Sommer, and Mr. Frank-Rainer Huck of Radio Saarland; Mrs. Liselotte Braun, Mrs. Hanneliese Niggemeyer, and Mr. Helmut Schwarz of West-German Radio, Cologne; Dr. Michael Albus and Mr. Joachim Krischer of West Germany's Channel 2; Mr. Christian Modehn of RIAS, Berlin; Dr. Anton Fellner and Dr. Oskar Schatz of Radio Austria; and Father Reinhold Iblacker, S.J., of the Communications and Media Institute at the Jesuit Philosophate in Munich. Our thanks likewise go to Mrs. Annegret Biallowons of Krailling, to Mrs. Elizabeth Meuser, and Mrs. Michaela Reuther of Munich for helping with the typing, proofreading, and the like.

We would like to thank in a special way Dr. Christoph Wild for his initiative. He not only broke new publishing ground with these volumes but also he augmented Karl Rahner's bibliography. We also want to thank Dr. Bogdan Snela, who suggested this book, for his work both as publisher's reader and for his critical editorial help.

We attempted to preserve as much as possible the conversational tone of the interviews. Still, redactional emendations were occasionally introduced. These and other emendations were approved by Karl Rahner.

One final word: That Karl Rahner found an answer to many of the classical

6. Karl Rahner, "What Does It Mean Today to Believe in Jesus?" *Theological Investigations XVIII*, tr. Edward Quinn (New York: Crossroad, 1983), p. 156.

theological questions provides the meaningful background for the many answers given in these interviews. With ever-new formulations he sought to answer not only individual questions but also the basic question: In what does a Christian believe? What does the core conviction of many Christians mean that Christianity is ultimately not a matter of revealed dogmas that one holds as true—and which indeed must not contradict reason—but is the basic mystery of the incarnate God in Jesus Christ?

The Christian's fate is rooted in Jesus' resurrection. To continue to proclaim Jesus' history, to proclaim the gospel, to be prepared to make a defense to any one who calls upon the Christian for the hope that is in him (1 Pet. 3:15) are essential theological tasks. Karl Rahner has dedicated himself to these tasks in this volume. What he wrote in a fictitious address by Ignatius of Loyola to today's Jesuits is the motto of his own toil: ". . . since the actual form of the papacy remains subject, in the future too, to an historical process of change, your theology and ecclesiastical law has above all to serve the papacy as it will be in the future, so that it will be a help and not a hindrance to the unity of Christendom. In addition, . . . try to evolve a theology which can touch the ear and heart of people today. But the point of departure and the end of your theology, which even today should have the courage to be genuinely systematic, remains Jesus Christ, the Crucified and Risen Lord. He is the triumphant promise made by the incomprehensible God to his world. He and not some spiritual fashion or other which is here today and gone tomorrow is your beginning and your end."[7]

Paul Imhof, S.J., and Hubert Biallowons
Munich, April 20 and October 30, 1982

Translated by Harvey D. Egan, S.J.
Boston College

---

7. Karl Rahner, S.J., and Paul Imhof, S.J., *Ignatius of Loyola*, tr. Rosaleen Ockenden (Cleveland: Collins, 1979), p. 32.

Part I

ON THE SECOND VATICAN COUNCIL

INTERVIEWS 1965–1972

1 · A Theologian at Work

Interview with Patrick Granfield, Washington, D.C. (October, 1965)

Father Rahner, you have often been called the "theologian of liberty" because of your frequent writings on that subject. Do you consider this your greatest contribution to theology?
By no means. It is true that I have written on the theological dimensions of liberty, but I have also written on many, many other subjects. I must say in all modesty that some of my other writings have greater value for theology than my work on freedom.

What would you consider your most important writings?
I have written on the Trinity, Christology, and many other questions dealing intimately with almost every aspect of dogmatic theology. So far I have not written a complete dogmatic treatise for seminaries, except for the notes that I use in my courses on dogmatic theology at Innsbruck. Nearly all the things I have written are shorter commentaries or essays on specific points of dogmatic theology. Yet all of these are of equal if not of greater value than my work dealing precisely with religious liberty.

I am also editor of *Lexikon für Theologie und Kirche* along with Josef Höfer. The new edition of this theological encyclopedia will consist of ten large volumes, and I have written many of the articles on dogmatic problems. I have also written *Dictionary of Theology*,[1] in which I presented in a condensed version the whole field of dogmatic theology. Then there is my work, *Hearers of the Word*,[2] which presents the necessary speculative background for fundamental theology. There I discuss the transcendental structure of the human person insofar as his internal spiritual nature is open to divine revelation. I have also written a book on the theory of knowledge according to Saint Thomas. All of these works are much more important than my writings on religious liberty.

You have written over three hundred articles and several books. Do you have any special system or method that enables you to produce so much?
I have not written so much when you consider the works of Saint Thomas, Suarez, and others. I have no special method. I just sit down and write. Some days I write nothing.

1. Karl Rahner and Herbert Vorgrimler, *Dictionary of Theology* (New York: Crossroad, 2nd ed., 1981).
2. Tr. Michael Richards (New York: Herder and Herder, 1969).

11

Spirit in the World[3] *was your first book and perhaps your most controversial one. Could you tell us how you came to write it?*
Spirit in the World is a study of Saint Thomas's ontology of knowledge. Originally, it was conceived as a doctoral dissertation at Freiburg. However, at that time the Nazis were in power and, for reasons too complicated to explain here, I was unable to do my thesis under Heidegger. Instead, I worked under the Catholic Professor M. Honecker who was teaching philosophy at the state university at Freiburg. Professor Honecker rejected the thesis, because he felt that I had incorrectly interpreted the doctrine of Saint Thomas too much according to modern philosophy (Heidegger's ideas in particular) and the fundamental tenets of German idealism. But I am convinced that my interpretation is correct. If one analyzes Saint Thomas in proper perspective, it is quite clear that he is a *penseur moderne*. There is certainly a conformity, affinity, and correspondence between the modern method of proceeding and that problem which may be called transcendental. Even in the work of Saint Thomas this can be found. To grasp that fact is very important for any genuine, mutual understanding of the modern concept of man and the Thomistic concept of man.

Spirit in the World *has been the subject of much discussion over the years. Father C. Ernst, O.P., who translated Volume I of your* Theological Investigations *questions the foundational principle of your theory, namely:* "Knowledge is the being-present-to-itself *of Being, and this being-present-to-itself is the* Being *of any entity." This, he feels, is unacceptable in terms of the Thomistic thesis that our ontological knowledge of reality is derived from our experience of the world. How would you answer this objection?*
First of all, I would like to say that Father Ernst is a good friend of mine. In fact, he has just recently agreed to be the English co-editor of *Sacramentum Mundi*,[4] a Catholic theological lexicon that has not yet been published. (The other English co-editor is a young Dominican Father Kerr.) So there is no question here about an attack on my theological or philosophical ideas.
Now about the objection. I think that the ideas expressed in *Spirit in the World* are truly Thomistic. But certainly this question has been freely discussed among Catholic theologians. The interpretation I have given is not mine alone; the whole school of recent German philosophical thought holds this. For example, Max Müller, Father Lotz, the late Gustav Siewerth, and

---

3. Tr. William Dych (New York: Herder and Herder, 1968).
4. Karl Rahner, Cornelius Ernst, and Kevin Smyth, *Sacramentum Mundi: An Encyclopedia of Theology*, 6 volumes (New York: Herder and Herder, 1968).

other scholars find no difficulty in this opinion. Of course, it has to be correctly understood. We are not pure *esse*. We are a composite, a mixture of act and potency, if we want to use the classic terms. *Beisichsein* (being-present-to-itself) has, even in us, some element of potentiality. Every being, inasmuch as it is in act, is present-to-itself. In as much as *I am*, I am present-to-myself. This thesis is certainly Thomistic; it is a metaphysical thesis that is not immediately experiential. If Father Ernst says that knowledge in the Thomistic view must be understood as an a posteriori knowledge, then I would say with Saint Thomas that while I receive individual species from things coming to me in an a posteriori way, I also have a light of the *intellectus agens*. And if we try to interpret metaphysically the image of the light of the *intellectus agens* then it appears as nothing other than a dynamic, transcendental, and intellectual element in being itself.

It is well known that Heidegger influenced you greatly. What was the precise form of this influence?
For two years after my ordination I studied philosophy under Martin Heidegger at the University of Freiburg. I attended his lectures and his philosophical seminars. We still see each other occasionally. However, it was thirty years ago that I was a student. One may perhaps say that it is not specific doctrines that I have taken from Heidegger, but rather a style of thinking and of investigating which has proved most valuable. This may be described as a method or approach by which one does not examine dogmatic truths *merely* as evidence derived from the positive sources, but one seeks to construct a synthesis. One takes the various dogmatic propositions and reduces them to certain fundamental principles. In that way an internal, coherent body of dogmatic truth is established. The modern person is thus able to perceive the order and harmony in the mysterious truths of the Church and Christianity. The modern person no longer is satisfied with taking a collection of the truths and various opinions that are proven in Denzinger and thinking no more about it. Rather, he or she looks for some synthetic idea, even though it might be quite simple, to organize the immense material of Christian dogma. Once this is achieved, other specific truths are able to be understood as obvious and necessary consequences of the principal idea.

What other philosophers influenced you?
I must mention Père Rousselot and Joseph Maréchal of Louvain, for both of them exercised a great influence on my philosophy.
Certainly, while Maréchal influenced me, it cannot be said that my philo-

sophical ideas were completely and adequately determined by him. There were many other profound influences that help elaborate and at times transform what Maréchal said. But the initial, truly philosophical insight was given to me by Maréchal. His book, *Le point de départ de la métaphysique*, especially *Cahier V*, influenced me greatly when I was younger.

One must not forget Father Erich Przywara. For the Catholics of Germany in the twenties, thirties, and forties he was considered one of the greatest minds. He had a great influence on all of us when we were younger. He is now seventy-five, but is quite sick and can barely write.

What of Blondel?

His influence was more indirect than the others. Every man lives in a specific intellectual atmosphere and is influenced by many things without actually realizing it. I can say that I was not a dedicated reader of Blondel, even though I do accept some of his opinions. Robert Scherer, a friend of mine who lives in Freiburg, translated the works of Blondel into German. But objectively I am not able to say that Blondel exercised any great, direct, and immediate influence on me that I am aware of.

Contemporary European theology is characterized by its involvement in modern philosophy. What is the origin of this new approach?

The mutual relationship between modern philosophy and Thomistic thought was initiated by Blondel, Maréchal, Sertillanges, Rousselot, and Hans Urs von Balthasar. One might also mention Heidegger, Max Scheler, Siewerth, and Müller. These men do not form a school in the proper sense of the word, since they profess widely differing views. However, they do share one thing in common. They agree that we must be receptive to modern philosophy without considering it absurd or as something to be opposed and criticized. What is needed is a trusting colloquium between traditional scholastic philosophy and modern philosophy. This is necessary if, on the one hand, we are to be of our time and speak the language that people today must speak if they are to understand themselves and others. On the other hand, we do not want to lose the true riches of tradition.

Max Müller, Gustav Siewerth, Father Lotz, and I have all written on Saint Thomas. We four were disciples of Heidegger, and yet it is clear from our writings that we have a great admiration for Saint Thomas. If someone would accuse us of not being Thomists, I would reply that I know of no one who can state precisely who is a Thomist and who is not. I am not being indiscreet when I say that the young Dominican priests at Walberberg esteem my writings very highly. In fact, there is a Dominican priest from Walberberg who is studying under me at Munich. Afterwards he will be a professor at the Dominican college at Walberberg. The sterile and narrow brand of traditional Thomistic philosophy is found practically nowhere in Germany or in France.

Do you think that is true in America also?
I do not know. I am not qualified to judge. Yet, I would say that the tendency is certainly along these same lines.

Throughout the history of Christian theology there have appeared various schools of thought. What value do these have for contemporary man?
The Suarezian, Thomistic, and Scotistic schools are traditional. They have their great riches, but they also have their lacunae. Today they are no longer living or life-giving. For that reason they belong to history, not to the present. Our contemporary needs are different. There is no reason to establish determined schools of thought, closed systems that are carefully distinct from one another. Such schools are not needed now, nor will they be in the future. There will always be various tendencies, preoccupations, and stimuli that develop from the different aspects of the intellectual world. Thus, some will be influenced by orthodox existentialism, others will proceed according to the Thomistic method, and still others will attempt to construct a new system, as for example, Father Lonergan and Father de Finance at the Gregorian University in Rome.

You have written somewhere that the renewal of Christian thought began with the philosophers?
Yes, the revitalization of Christian thought began in philosophy rather than in theology. From the time of Modernism to the present, there has been a slow but steady progress in philosophy, but the same is not true in theology. But now there are signs that progress in fundamental theology as well as in dogmatic theology is beginning. I am not talking here about the development in biblical and patristic theology that has made such great strides. I think that today speculative theology must and can be renewed. It is not a question of mere speculation, but of what answer we are to give to our modern world. For example, we say that the foundation of our faith can be summarized in the phrase: "the Word became flesh." Now how can we present this to modern, technical, and scientific persons so that they may believe it? This is a difficult task, but, above all, a possible task.

What is being done in Germany to facilitate the renewal of speculative theology?
Permit me to name two theologians who are representative of this new
spirit in Germany. One is my friend Bernhard Welte who is professor of religion in the theological faculty at the Catholic University at Freiburg-im-Breis-
gau. The other is my former student and friend, Johannes Baptist Metz who is
professor of fundamental theology at Münster. These men are representative
of, I will not say, a school, but of a mentality that is becoming quite common
in Germany. It is not universal in Germany, since there are some who follow
the more traditional way of teaching dogmatic theology. We must approach
the modern mentality with a simple trust and reason philosophically and theologically in such a way that it means something for the people of our age. We
belong to this generation, too, and so should avoid any Catholic intellectual
ghetto. It is our duty to speak with scientists, Marxists, non-Christian philosophers, existentialists, and those in America and England who may be called
logical positivists. For too long we have been negligent in this area. I believe
that philosophy and Christian theology must do more than has been done
even in Germany in establishing a sincere and open dialogue with others.
There is an immense field of work ahead for us; for too long we have remained
secure in our home, and we were wrong in doing so. There is more to do than
simply to keep our Catholics simple and pious as they were in kindergarten
and in primary school. We have to enter into battle, or rather into an open and
honest dialogue with non-Christians. An outstanding example of this occurs in
Germany at the Paulus Gesellschaft, where annually about two hundred professors of science, philosophy, and theology meet and discuss common problems.

*In view of the contemporary movement to establish a rapport between theology and
modern philosophical thought, can we still correctly speak of theology as a deductive
science?*
There is no doubt that Saint Thomas developed a theology according to a
notion of science that is not completely accepted today. Personally, I have a
great aversion to the dogmatic positivism that flourished in Catholic schools
during the last century. For example, if you wanted a course on the seven sacraments, you were told to use Denzinger. This was a disease that theology had
contracted. Yet, while I detest dogmatic positivism, I am a great lover of speculative theology, which, if you wish, you may call deductive theology. But
that is not a good word to use, since it poorly describes its function.
   Theology necessarily desires to arrive at some knowledge of the intimate
connection between all truths revealed by God. Single propositions cannot be

correctly understood unless seen in the context of the whole. I think an example will illustrate what I mean. The infallibility of the magisterium can only be understood according to Christian eschatology. What answer do you give when one asks if there was an infallible magisterium in the Old Testament? Why did not God, for the salvation of the Israelites, institute some supreme authority or perhaps a special assembly of rabbis? This would have been most useful and almost necessary, since Vatican I teaches that God must reveal himself if we are to know him and natural truths as well without any error. Yet we know for a fact that there was no infallible magisterium in the Old Testament. If we tell modern persons that what God did not do in the Old Testament he did in the New Testament by his grace, they will ridicule us. What we must do is explain *why* we now have an infallible magisterium. I have not the time now to explain fully, but what we must do is to show how this doctrine belongs to the history of salvation and the eschatological situation. This will be of great importance to explain even to Protestants why God instituted an infallible magisterium in the New Testament. Protestants don't believe this and it is not enough to cite text after text, because other exegetes come along and say that these texts can be interpreted in a different way. Therefore, you must explain a specific point of dogma, whatever this may be, from the coherence and totality of the Christian message. This kind of theology is not the formal, deductive kind that follows Aristotelian logic. Yet it is speculative theology that seeks a simple internal principle and through it sees the unity of all dogmatic thought. This is the work that today demands our attention.

Granted that theology must avoid an exaggerated positivistic approach, can we say that the primary end of theology is contemplation of truth?
No. The salvation of man is the primary end. Truth is the intrinsic constitutive element of this salvation; the possession and contemplation of truth are so close that we should not separate them. Christ and the Church preach the good news of the gospel to men and women. This preaching that God wants us to receive is not complete unless some reflection accompanies it. There has to be some systematic reflection on that word in which we hear from God about God and even about ourselves. Because there is a kerygma, then there must be reflection about the kerygma, and that we call theology. The kerygma differs from theology, but there is a mutual relationship involved. Thus, theology can be considered a reflective science, as something secondary that is derived from the kerygmatic words of God, of the Church, and of Christ. Theology can be distinguished from the kerygma, but it must serve the kerygma. The same thing can be said of attempting to define love and charity. One must give great

attention to his or her own practice of love and charity. Subtle contemplation is not necessarily loving contemplation. The ancient debates on the primacy of the intellect and the primacy of the will seem to me to be foolish and obsolete. In the last analysis, we cannot truly know God unless we know him as the one who speaks the Word and who breathes love, the Holy Spirit. Likewise, we cannot be known except through this mutual compenetration of love and knowledge. Both demand each other. As long as I am a *viator* then I must seek that truth that leads to my salvation. Here on earth all reflective knowledge of God's truth that we call theology must be directed toward the salvation of human beings and nothing else.

You once wrote that "the strictest theology . . . is itself in the long run the most kerygmatic." Would you please comment on this?

Father Lakner and others at Innsbruck attempted to establish a theology called kerygmatic that would exist side by side with that theology that we call scientific, university, and academic. This I do not agree with. I believe that this attempt, while done in all good will, was false. The most scientific theology is the most kerygmatic and vice versa. If we really want to make certain elements and truths of our faith relevant to the modern mentality so that it may understand them, then, above all, we have to ask highly scientific and profound dogmatic questions.

Do you agree with those who call your theological approach anthropocentric?

I suppose one could characterize my theology that way. However, to call my theology anthropocentric can easily be misunderstood by those who say that this is in opposition to theocentric theology. Such an interpretation is foolish. There is in modern philosophy a valid development from a cosmic philosophy to a more anthropological philosophy. My friend and student, Johannes-Baptist Metz, has written a small book, *Christliche Anthropozentrik*, in which he explains the metaphysical speculative anthropocentrism of Saint Thomas. He considers Thomas and not Descartes the first modern anthropocentric philosopher.

If human beings in their concrete and historical essence cannot be described unless we say that they are those to whom God, as uncreated grace, communicates existence, then we cannot speak of them without speaking also of God. We are not able to understand what God is except by referring to the infinite transcendentality of human beings themselves. God is not like other beings, but the inscrutable principle of being. It is not possible to go into the whole philosophy of this now, but I must insist that the true understanding of the nature and existence of God cannot be properly grasped by us unless we develop a transcendental, categorical philosophy. This transcendental philosophy is at the same time a description of ourselves insofar as we are spiritual beings. What is a spiritual being? I would say that it is that being that, by tending to God and transcending all limits of determined being, possesses itself. Thus you see that in the last analysis, philosophically and theologically, anthropocentrism and theocentrism are the same. How can a Christian speak adequately of God unless he or she speaks also of human beings? The Word made flesh is and remains the eternal and infinite man so that you cannot know God as he is unless you think of him at the same time as God made man. Thus, you cannot have a full theology unless you consider its anthropological aspects. If you wish to speak accurately of God, then you must speak of human beings. Likewise, you cannot investigate the depths of our nature, unless you say that we are those beings whom God has created and conserves in existence.

One could, then, correctly call your theology incarnational?
Yes. Certainly. Christology, theology, and anthropology are so intimately connected that it would help bring out the true idea of anthropocentric theology to call it incarnational.

Père Congar seems to insist that theology belongs to priests. Thus he writes: "The laity, . . . can bring a wealth to the Church. . . . But they never handle theology like priests, they have never quite the same contact with the Church's traditions. . . . Theology properly so called is preeminently a clerical, priestly, learning." Do you agree with this?
I do not know the full context of Père Congar's remarks, but if I must judge by what you have quoted, I would say that it cannot be true. The layperson must save his or her soul also. Why must we say that laypersons are less intelligent than we priests? Today's laypersons are looking for a relationship between their faith and their whole intellectual life. In many cases, perhaps in most, they need more theology than the simple pastor or chaplain who teaches children. If Einstein were a Catholic you could not say that he would be like any ordinary layman or pious housewife. Certainly not! That would be impossible, since he would have established a dialogue between his Christian faith on the one hand and his scientific knowledge on the other. If he had done that he would have contributed a profound understanding to theology. In the end, he would have known more theology than is generally given to our seminarians. It is true that the priest, by reason of his office, is necessarily directed to theology. But the layperson for other reasons, practically might have the same interest. Both should be equally interested in theology.

Your influence in the Second Vatican Council was considerable. What do you think . . .

Excuse me, but I must say that I did not exercise any great influence at the Council. To say anything else is just not true. There were so many *periti* and collaborators at the Council that no one, except the pope himself and the moderators, could be said to influence the Council in any significant way. It is true that I attended almost all of the meetings of the Theological Commission and that I collaborated with the other theologians. As you know the most important schemata of this commission were on the Church and revelation. I was a member of certain subcommissions that worked on these, but my contribution was not great.

What of the schema on religious liberty?

I did not see the schema on religious liberty that was prepared in the secretariat of Cardinal Bea, since I was not a member. I did discuss the matter in the beginning with some of the bishops, with Bishop de Smedt for example. Yet, in the second and third sessions of the Council, I was for the most part absent from Rome. I did not get to Rome for the third session till the end of October, and I had to leave after a short time to return to Munich for my classes. Practically, I had little to do with this schema. I heard some of the debates on this schema, I talked with some of the Spanish bishops, and I saw the *relatio* of Father De Broglie, professor at the Institut Catholique at Paris. For the most part I was a spectator. I have written some things on the subject, *Free Speech in the Church*, 1959, and something on the concept of tolerance in *Theological Investigations* II (pp. 235–263), but I don't think these had a great influence in the writing of the schema on religious liberty.

Did you not talk to many of the bishops at the Council?

Occasionally, I had conferences with the German, Brazilian, and Spanish bishops. These were friendly meetings during which we discussed some of the problems connected with the various schemata. In my opinion, Msgr. Gerard Philips, professor of dogmatic theology at Louvain, must be given great credit for his work as secretary of the Theological Commission. With the exception of the bishops themselves, Monsignor Philips did more than anyone else in preparing the schema on the Church. One must also mention Father Congar, Father Grillmeier, Father Otto Semmelroth and many, many others who were very active and influential in the commission meetings.

What do you think is the greatest benefit for theology that has come from the Council?

The Council is the beginning, not the end. It is an inauguration of a tendency, not its completion. I think that this can be easily seen in the Council debates on the Church, the bishops, the lay apostolate, and so on. I am convinced that we theologians in the next ten years have to give careful thought to these and other truths. Much more than we have so far. We must rethink the problems of the existence of God and the possibility of God realizing himself in us. We must concentrate on making the doctrines of grace and the Incarnation something meaningful for modern people. These problems are important objectively, and also they are not without a pastoral or kerygmatic dimension. Theologians have an immense amount of work to do in the years that are ahead.

Would you say that theologians in the past have often misunderstood their task?
One could say so. Not long ago I saw a list of writings put out by the Academia Mariana in Rome. I think it said that over one hundred volumes have been written on Mariology since the war. This is good—*De Maria numquam satis.* ("One can never say enough about Mary") But it seems to me today that we have greater problems facing us that concern the basic preaching of Christian truth. We have not the time to spend on writing thick volumes on the minute subtleties of Mariology. I can also honestly say that I cannot understand why the Institute of Josephology was established in Canada. We don't have time for these kinds of things, if we see the world as it really is. I am not sure of America, but in Europe perhaps only 20 percent of those who are Catholic in origin really believe in God and Christ. We must do something other than discuss pious subtleties. We must find out how we can make the doctrine of the Incarnation intelligible for a person who knows only dialectical materialism. How can we make the existence of God reasonable for such a person? It is not enough to say: "Well we have the five proofs of Saint Thomas. Read that and that's all you need."

What do you think of the traditional division between fundamental theology and dogmatic theology?
I think that there must be a greater interpenetration, a greater reciprocity between the two. As it stands now we are not too successful. In traditional fundamental theology we say that we must first prove that God revealed himself to us, but we say nothing about *what* God revealed. This should not continue. An abstract and formalistic concept of revelation should not be the object of proof. Today's person wants to know some of the things God has revealed about himself before making an act of faith. The modern person

wants to learn from you about God in order to determine whether revealed truth is credible and existentially acceptable. For that reason I think that there should be a fundamental, basic discipline that combines the nucleus of dogmatic truth along with the proof that these things have been revealed by God. Unless I can first give some introductory notions of God and human beings and show how these ideas necessarily fit into an anthropological metaphysics, modern persons will say that they can never believe that God became man. A mere a prioristic proof has no force. They are arguments that do not convince. Thus, we have the doctrine of the Protestant exegetes who argue that Jesus did not appear to be the Son of God, but that this doctrine was developed slowly, evolving from the so-called communitarian theology.

In conclusion, Father Rahner, would you like to give a few words of advice to students of theology?

Students of theology should have a holy abnegation in their study of theology. Zealously and courageously they must give themselves to theology without a false preoccupation concerning their future ministry. They must study theology as much as they can—even scholastic and abstract theology—and realize that whatever they learn can later, in some way, be used profitably. Professors of theology must study ceaselessly and teach a theology that corresponds to the inner needs of their students and of modern men and women. Theology must be so presented that it encourages a genuine dialogue between the best of traditional thought and the exigencies of today.

Translated by Patrick Granfield, O.S.B.
The Catholic University of America

2 · Questions about Today's Church and World

Interview with Eugene C. Bianchi, for *America* magazine
New York (June 12, 1965)

The last session of Vatican II promulgated the Dogmatic Constitution on the Church. As a theologian who played a prominent role there, how would you view the relationship between pope and bishops implied in collegiality?

Of course, we recognize that the dogmatic teaching of Vatican I about the papacy stands beyond question. We should acknowledge, however, that full and supreme ecclesiastical authority is also vested in the episcopal college joined to the pope. This was explicitly discussed even at Vatican I, and today Vatican II expressly proclaims it. Also, the authority of the college of bishops is not delegated to them by the pope, even though he can decide who will become a bishop. For according to the Constitution on the Church, the college of bishops has authority by divine right, that is, as legitimate successors to the apostolic college.

Many questions remain open, of course. For example, the college of bishops under certain circumstances can exercise its supreme collegial office even outside a general council. But how and when this actually happens are questions open to study. Another debatable point concerns our understanding of the relation between pope and bishops, when the pope exercises his authority in a way that is *juridically* independent of the episcopal college—as, for example, when he teaches *ex cathedra*. Must we not say that even in this situation the pope always acts in accord with the faith of the Church and as head of the college of bishops?

I personally think that the pope always acts as head of the episcopal college, even when this activity is not *juridically* verifiable, as it would be, for example, in an ecumenical council. I am certainly not saying that the pope must consult each individual bishop before he defines something. But I do say that in a given historical situation the pope may have a *moral*, not *juridical*, obligation to consult with the episcopate. Both Pius XII and Pius IX have, in fact, done this.

Father Rahner, what is your view on the discussion about the Church's position on marriage and family limitation?

I am no moral theologian. But I do not believe that either in *Casti Connubii* or in Pius XII's teaching on the subject we have absolutely formal and irreformable doctrine. I personally think that a clarification of doctrine in this area is possible and desirable. This does not mean that everything contained in what Pius XI

23

and Pius XII said has now suddenly become untrue. Rather, it seems to me that a further development of our teaching on sex and marriage can have great practical significance. Of course, you know that the pope has appointed a sizable commission to study questions related to birth control. It consists of medical experts, social scientists, theologians, and some married couples. How much time it will require, what it will come up with, I don't know.

In your book Nature and Grace[1] *you discussed the role of the individual conscience in difficult moral decisions. Would you like to say something about the formation of the Christian conscience?*

Well, first of all, we never have an ethical situation in which it is suddenly made clear that the Church knows nothing about the objectively true ethics involved, and that thus each person must form his or her conscience entirely alone. Any such situation-ethic is naturally un-Catholic. But it can certainly happen that a concrete case may be of such complexity that the Church can only refer to various principles involved. Then the Church must say: "I cannot tell you from these principles what you should do here and now. You yourself must work it out with God and your conscience."

For example, if President Kennedy had come to Pope John with the question: "Should I as a Christian cut back the production of nuclear weapons, or should I extend their production?" In such a complex and vastly important moral issue, I do not believe that the Church could give a definite answer. The pope would have had to say to Mr. Kennedy: "We're sorry. You should take into consideration such and such principles, but what follows from them as far as this concrete decision is concerned, you have to decide for yourself."

Often it is not easy to determine the relationship between general norms taught by the Church and the morally correct action or decision in a person's particular circumstances.

Of course, an individual is not free to do whatever he or she wants in the face of an unambiguously clear divine or ecclesiastical moral law. Individuals cannot rightly resort to a kind of situation-ethic that allows them to make a moral decision while prescinding totally from universal norms taught by the Church. In other words they should try to inform their consciences adequately about ethical norms, taking account also of the particular circumstances surrounding their decision.

But it must be pointed out that the individual is a unique spirit-person. And

---

1. *Nature and Grace: Dilemmas in the Modern Church* (New York: Sheed and Ward, 1964).

within the morally permissible, he or she has the right and the duty to make choices that cannot be directly governed by the Church's laws. A large part of a Christian's religious life is outside the official juridical life of the Church. What Christians read and think, what vocations they choose, and so on, are left to their own decisions. They must therefore face up to decisions that imply an imperative for themselves; very often they cannot take shelter behind the moral rulings of the Church. They must realize that moral theology, necessary as it is, is still no substitute for the gift of discernment of spirits.

A man or woman can, indeed, misuse the Church as a teaching community if either abdicates his or her own responsibility to decide before God with Christian freedom. Such persons resemble ecclesiastical collectivists, who mistakenly think they are saved by being freed *from* themselves—by a Church supposedly relieving them of the burden of taking initiative and making mature moral decisions *for* themselves.

For such initiative to flourish creatively in the Church, Father, would not a wide scope of freedom of thought and action have to be encouraged in the Church?
Well, there are always a few ecclesiastical nonconformists who resort to protest at all times for reasons of temperament or style. They call this freedom, when, in truth, it is only conformity to the latest vogue. But I do believe that the opposite fault also exists among religious leaders and among the laity. There is too little understanding that it is not only possible, but also helpful, for Christians to hold different opinions and to express them in the Church. People are not un-Catholic because they affirm that everything at official, clerical levels is not splendid.

Of course, most people would admit that free public opinion has a place in the Church. But is the recognition of this principle carried out sufficiently in practice? Do we appreciate it enough that only in an environment of freedom can individuals become Christians and Christians become persons? Do we really understand and act on that venerable maxim: "In necessary things, unity; in doubtful things, liberty"? For in the long run, a unity of many individuals, a unity that is truly personal and responsible, can come about only if the second part of the maxim is taken seriously.

In schema 13, the Council is considering the relations between the Church and the world. In what sense are the Church and the world irreconcilable? And in what sense does grace penetrate the whole created order?
It seems to me that, up to now, schema 13 has not pursued these basic questions with enough precision, and has gone ahead as though these fundamental

issues were clear and resolved. Now there is, of course, a compenetration of grace and a redeemed world. The world, none the less, remains always sinful.

But besides this dialectic of the world as matter for grace and the world as sinful and thus grace-resisting, another problem enters our theological consciousness today, perhaps for the first time. Let's call it the new worldliness of the world. In the past, a people's possibilities in the world were, for the most part, static, fixed in a given dimension. Consequently, they needed only to consider how and in which morally correct ways they might do what was in general to be done in every case: for example, beget children, plant fields, raise cows, sell milk, and so on. But now we have something very new: a world mostly subject to our design and fashioning. Of course, this world is under the law of Christ. But I cannot deduce from Christian principles alone what ought to be done; in other words, there arises the worldliness of a world made by ourselves and this cannot be derived directly as a necesary conclusion of the Christian ethic.

For example, I am always surprised to see how little the official Church and other Christians have considered the moral implications of space travel. Christians seem to say: since we have the capacity and the know-how to probe the farthest reaches of space, why not do it? But we must still ask ourselves whether it is not moral vulgarity of a low order to pour out so many billions to send people to the moon, while at the same time we are faced with worldwide hunger. I don't mean to prejudge this particular issue. But as Christians we have to confront a dynamic world, which potentially contains tendencies that are really un-Christian. I do, of course, concede that we are not obliged to give an unequivocal yes or no to this dynamic society solely on the basis of Christian principles. Rather, I am questioning our attitude as Christians. Are we only to trail along in the wake of this or that technological development, and accept it unthinkingly? This seems to be what often happens. Or do we still have a Christian power of decision, which, although it cannot be derived simplistically from abstract principles, can none the less influence history?

You spoke of a new worldliness of the world. Could you explain this a little more?
Well, we might look at it another way by saying that the Church today lives as a minority community in a diaspora situation. The Church is no longer limited to one culture and one historical sphere, in which she is the unquestioned leader and ruler, as in the Middle Ages. Today, the realms of politics, technology, and culture enjoy an autonomy of their own. On the other hand, the Church has actually become worldwide, and the histories of separate peoples have merged into one single history of humankind, as perhaps never

before. Thus, today the Church is seen more fully as a pilgrim community bearing its message in a diaspora of scientific, intellectual, and historical values.

But the fact that we are in a diaspora situation is not a cause for dismay and a discouraged hankering after a past age. It is something that, on the basis of our faith, we should have expected within the history of salvation. The loss of the Church's medieval dominance in cultural life was something to be theologically expected. And this is true even though the ensuing schism, apostasy and de-Christianization involved human guilt inside and outside of the Church. For God works out his plan within the very context of our sinfulness.

But the more important point is that the medieval form became impossible when the West became an integral part of world history. And furthermore, the medieval pattern was in many ways more a fact of cultural history than of theological necessity. Thus, the Church today must carry out her mission in a world that has politically, intellectually, and scientifically come of age. We Christians should not be downhearted because we are a minority on the world scene. The Church's missionary dimension, though it needs to be reexamined and adapted, should be dynamic and optimistic without worrying overly much about membership statistics.

Perhaps Augustine's thought about church membership can help us overcome our tendency toward defeatism in the diaspora situation: Many whom God has, the Church does not have, and many whom the Church has, God does not have. After all, there is grace outside the Church. Of course, we pray and work that God will have pity on all, and bring all to himself.

What are some implications for the Christian of the modern Church's life in a diaspora situation?

Well, for one thing, the Christian will receive little or no support from institutional morality, public opinion, and custom. Christianity, as a way of life, ceases to be a religion into which one is simply born and henceforth takes for granted. It becomes a religion of personal choice, a faith option constantly renewed in a challenging and perilous atmosphere.

Much of the scientific and cultural riches of the age, will not be specifically Christian. Yet Christians must learn to appreciate these values for their own intrinsic merit, if they would carry out their vocations in the world. The pilgrim Church of the diaspora will have to be a Church with a dedicated and active laity. This laity will need to be conscious of being itself the Church, and not simply an object to be looked after and directed by the clergy. Christians will have to be open to the non-Christian world, and not seal themselves off in a comfortable ghetto, which they mistake for the kingdom of Christ.

Coming to terms with the reality of the diaspora situation may require the Church to relinquish certain works that she alone performed in early times. Today these are adequately provided for by civic society. But curtailing some activities, the Church will be able to concentrate her limited energies on her more directly religious and moral tasks.

In this time of renewal, we are witnessing in a particularly vivid way the tension between the institutional and the charismatic in the Church. How do you understand this tension?

Everything genuinely institutional in the Church is at one and the same time a furthering, a facilitating, of the charismatic and an obstacle to the charismatic. Consider a concrete example. A particular religious order is still carrying on the charismatic ideal of its founder. If this order had not been founded (thus institutionalized), there would not have been so many men and women in history who in some measure realized the order's ideal in their lives. On the other hand, it is clear that the institutionalization of any religious order leads to a considerable amount of compromise, callousness, and fossilization. This is true, not only of religious congregations but of all ecclesiastical institutionalization. There is no facile solution for this problem. We must, however, learn to cope with a living tension between a historical, institutional expression of a charismatic ideal and a kind of relaxation of that institutionalization. Such relaxation gives broader scope for the original charisms to become evident.

When we consider that the Holy Spirit operates not only downward, as it were, through the official hierarchy, but also through charismatic gifts in the People of God, can we rightly speak of a certain democratic element in the Church?

Although authority in the Church derives from above, divinely willed dualism of charism and office permits us to see in the Church something in the nature of a democracy—the opposite of a totalitarian system. A democracy, of course, is not ultimately constituted by the fact that everyone possesses a ballot. But rather, it is a society where no single authority holds all the power, where there is a plurality of really distinct powers, so that the individual is protected from the exercise of excessive authority.

Now, the Church's constitution is "undemocratic," because her office and authority, being founded directly on God himself, have, in their own domain, a final jurisdiction. There is no absolute right to resistance or need for it in this area, because God guarantees that the authority will not abuse its formal right in a completely decisive way. But, on the other hand, there is not in the Church any absolute monopoly of real power at any one point—as, for example, in her hierarchy. Such a monopoly would be contrary to the very nature and purpose of the Church as embodied in her ministry itself. For this ministry does not aim at gathering to itself all real influence. It sets limits to itself, and this limitation allows due scope to charismatic forces of a nonofficial kind. We know that the Spirit also operates directly in the People of God.

Therefore the Church is a hierarchical system, but only because its summit is God. And the Church is likewise a community in which power and authority are distributed, and thus it is a kind of democracy, though of its own special kind.

Translated by Eugene C. Bianchi
Emory University

3 · Priesthood, Celibacy, and Marriage

Interview with Gerhard Eberts, Olten (September 22, 1968)

Professor Rahner, celibacy directly concerns only a small part of the faithful. Yet this way of life, sponsored by the Church, intrigues many people, Christians and non-Christians. Next to the pill no topic has provoked so many emotional discussions. How do you explain this?
Good Catholics are interested in the celibacy of the Latin diocesan clergy. This is natural. These are their priests, and it is not strange that their way of life interests Catholics. Where this interest is shared by non-Catholics, I am afraid that it contains an element of snobbishness. Why should they worry about it? We understand that they are interested in the problem of the pill. But who worries whether John Jones gets married or not, or that he is looking for his sixth divorce? Not only have Catholics to do with priests they know;

they may have a son who is thinking of becoming a priest. No wonder then that they are interested in the problem of celibacy.

Quite often we hear people say that celibacy is that precept of the Church that is not anchored in the Bible, and that, for this very reason, it is the more urgently insisted upon by the Church.

There is something like renouncing marriage for the sake of the kingdom of heaven, for the sake, as Paul says, of a total dedication to Christ, that is undoubtedly taught by Scripture. Whether Scripture teaches that diocesan priests should live in celibacy is quite another question. Let me answer right away: No, Scripture never mentions anything of the kind. This does not, however, decide the question whether there are not serious reasons why the Church may want to entrust the priesthood, as a service to human beings in the name of God, only to those who can also assume the celibate way of life. This question is not mentioned in Scripture. The times were not ripe for it. But this silence does not imply a rejection of celibacy, if one admits that there might exist a real charismatic vocation to renounce marriage. And I remain convinced that this may be found in Scripture.

The theologians of Munich have recently spoken with a great majority (94 percent) for voluntary celibacy, although in his encyclical Paul VI was opposed to this. What should we think of this vote? Is it justified, or is this some incipient rebellion?

There is no doubt that the Church has the duty to pay serious attention to this event and keep in mind the following principle: If the Church does not find a sufficient number of diocesan priests without giving up celibacy, she would in that case (not yet demonstrated) have to give it up. On the other hand, I do not believe whether or not to keep celibacy can be decided in the Church by ballot of this kind: first, because the problem of such democratic voting within the Church is a theological problem; next, because we must not forget that democratically reached majorities do not necessarily choose the best course; finally, because the priesthood is not something that everyone, who feels inclined to it, has a right to demand from the Church.

If somebody does not want to assume celibacy, is this a sufficient reason for denying him ordination to the priesthood?

We suppose that there exists a meaningful convergence between celibacy and a priestly vocation—in which a man should be radically free, beyond possible family ties, for the service of others. If there exists such an inner meaningful, even if not necessary, connection between celibacy and priestly service, it seems to me that the Church is allowed to decide whether she will grant the priesthood only under the condition of celibacy. We must, however, keep in mind what we said before, that the Church has to see to it that there is a sufficient number of priests. This duty takes precedence over the possibility of imposing celibacy upon the clergy.

Would a dwindling number of priests be the only legitimate reason why the Church might drop celibacy? Might there not be other grounds, deriving from present-day circumstances, for instance, that too much is being demanded of priests?

Where the priest performs his duty and the Church hers in order to make possible a kind of life that is meaningful and not overburdened, it is doubtful whether too much is really demanded of priests. However, should it become evident that, with a few exceptions, that is actually the case, we would, of course, have to say: Nobody, not even the Church, has a right to demand so much of her priests. And the Church would have to give up celibacy.

In connection with Humanae Vitae *the objection has been made that this encyclical is onesidedly clerical. Married priests would have spoken differently; they would not have reached the conclusions that Pope Paul VI reached.*

This is obviously false, since quite a number of priests who favor celibacy hold other opinions on this point than Paul VI. This does not help us decide which of the two opinions is the right one. But it is clear that living in priestly celibacy does not lead one necessarily to a conservative position on the question of the pill. We might even defend the opposite position. He who has nothing to do with the whole affair is the most objective observer.

What positive reasons might most strongly induce the Church to hold on to celibacy?

We should in this case also seriously take into account what Holy Scripture says—and not only in cases that suit us. There are instances where one remains unmarried for the sake of the kingdom of heaven. Secondly, to give up for the love of God, in a personal relation to Jesus Christ, for one's whole life, such a lofty value as marriage is a concrete and shining act of faith in eternal life. For if such are not the reasons for this choice, the decision is sheer nonsense, human self-destruction. On the other hand, I would say that if such a way of life were to disappear totally in the Church—I mean the Church as a whole—the Church would be a social institution that has properly nothing to do with faith in eternal life, in the living God, in the unspeakable mystery of grace (that cannot be measured with human yardsticks).

You speak of giving up, of renouncing. That sounds as if only those who look for the cross, for suffering and difficulties, can be happy. . . .

To claim that abnegation for its own sake is the only way of practicing faith, hope, and charity would be—if you allow me such a jump—"Buddhistic" negativism. But those who contract marriage are not looking for the cross (which all of us have to accept eventually). They are looking for an immediate, authentic, and noble fulfillment of their lives that is to some extent still unconnected with their hope of eternal life. At any rate, they are not intending abnegation directly in itself. The sacrament of marriage is not an immediate sign of it.

What are those in charge—the heads of seminaries, the bishops, and so on—doing to make it easier for celibates to assent meaningfully to their form of life?

We can at least say that efforts are being made to provide a meaningful and genuine foundation for celibacy, one that is independent of unconscious Manichean tendencies. That is evident from the many meetings of the spiritual advisers and of the leaders of our seminaries. Efforts are being made to keep the unfit out of the priesthood and also to provide meaningful and bearable alternatives for those who find out too late that they have chosen a wrong career.

Church authorities have forbidden a monastery in Mexico to use psychotherapeutic methods to weed out unsuitable candidates. What is the Church's attitude toward psychotherapy?

When an abbot, as in Mexico, wants to push everyone through the mill of a complete psychoanalysis, and the Church tells him that this is utter nonsense, I consider that the Church acted wisely. It is too easy to develop an exaggerated opinion of what psychoanalysis can do. However, when a gifted man wishes to become a priest, but turns out to need a certain amount of psychotherapy, the Church has no objection to such a procedure. There can be no doubt that some Church leaders still harbor unconscious and false misgivings against psychotherapy. But there is no general prohibition of psychotherapeutic treatment.

More than ever priests have to work together with lay people. This must increase their feeling of loneliness. How do you think the rectory of the future should look?

I cannot say much about this. But if, as for instance in Württemberg, the younger priests prefer to do their work not in a single parish—even though such an administrative division may remain useful—but in a district, as a team of priests, the possibility arises for some common life, as secular priests, without anything conventlike—the possibility at least for a larger brotherly community. This new conception of the priestly ministry, which may well be unavoidable in the future, may to some extent take care of such difficulties. I do not deny that the problem of loneliness will nonetheless stay with us. But where is the person who is not lonely deep down? How many people, even in married life, have experiences of a basic loneliness?

Suppose that a priest has remained celibate for, say, twenty years and then, as the saying goes, "quits." Has this priest bungled his life? Do the years of faithful service no longer count in the eyes of God?

We do not know how almighty God judges a life. Of course I would tell that American Jesuit provincial who quit his charge at the age of fifty-six: You have to live up to the inner law that made you set out; you cannot give it up. He may in people's eyes have "quit," but nobody knows what this really means.

I am thinking of the twenty-five years during which he has honestly toiled and worked for the Church. . . .

This brings up a difficult theological problem. We cannot imagine that, when God settles the final account of a life, he simply adds the items and says: At the end, you were a rascal but before that you were a decent fellow, so the average is good. For a Christian it is obvious that things do not work out that way. On the other hand, a priest must consider the possibility that he may, around the end of his life, destroy his whole life, also in the eyes of God. We have to do here with human and theological problems that are ultimately insoluble, because our Christian faith tells us that we do not judge ourselves but that God judges us.

Unconsciously, in many allocutions at ordinations and first Masses, an idea was at work that we might put in words as follows: The priest is too good for marriage. Young clerics bluntly object to this. That is why they get rid of clerical dress, scoff at clerical titles, and so on. They also refuse to look different from their peers with whom they went to school or to college.

The lifestyle of priests is strongly influenced by the law of history. Priestly formation can and should be different from what it used to be. It seems obvious to me that a priest will always be a priest, hence that his function and his lifestyle will differ from those of other church members. But I feel that it becomes gradually more obvious that a priest cannot imagine that he is too good for marriage. Nobody is too good for marriage, but marriage is so good that it makes sense to forego it.

In connection with celibacy one speaks of a crisis of the priestly profession. Is that justified?

It is clear that where a priest begins to have doubts about his priestly task the problem of celibacy arises in a wholly new and also unsolvable way. But as a Catholic Christian one cannot hold that the priestly function could now or in the future totally disappear from the Church. If the social prestige that used to help the priest to some extent in the past disappears today, so that the priesthood has to be lived in a much more radical way, this is all for the better.

Translated by Joseph Donceel, S.J.
Fordham University

4 · The Birth Control Encyclical

Interview with the *Spiegel* correspondent Inge Cyrus and the *Spiegel* editor Werner Harenberg, Hamburg (September 23, 1968)

Professor Rahner, the pope has said no to the pill. A very great number of Catholics have protested. What has decreased now, the pope's authority or the pill's use?

Sociologically speaking, I believe that the use of the pill has not decreased. That is a fact that should be soberly admitted. It is naturally another question whether the prestige—or whatever you call it—of the pope and of the institution which he represents has really diminished. What does it mean that someone's prestige has diminished? Is the prestige of an institution's authority diminished when that institution clashes with a very great number of people?

Of course. No?

Certainly, but one could also hold the opposite view. An institution that has lost the courage to assert itself against the majority would basically have already abdicated its authority. At most it would find itself to be only a loud-speaker for public opinion, but unable to influence it by its own independent position.

Do you think with many other theologians that the pope's strong stand against public opinion demonstrates the strength of the Church?
Yes, I think so. On the other hand, one might object that a proof of such courage should be given when the situation justifies it.

Naturally.
And this is then the really decisive question: Is the pope, in fact, from the point of view of Christian ethics, right or wrong?

What is your opinion? Do you side with the pope or with what is probably the majority of Catholics?
Well, you are asking me a question that drives me at once into a most complex situation. That is your right, of course. The situation is this: I will have great trouble explaining to you and to the readers of this interview why my position is so complicated, why I must hem and haw. My position may look more diplomatic than it really is and than it is really meant to be.

Start hemming.
On the one hand, as a very normal Catholic, I am obliged to attach great importance to the position of the highest authority in the Catholic Church, presented in this encyclical. On the other hand, I also have the right and the duty not to consider such a position simply and absolutely the last word, but to give it more thought and eventually to reach my own personal position, assumed on my own responsibility.

Which side do you lean to?
Even after this pontifical declaration I would rather think that the approval of the pill (to put it so clumsily) would not conflict with the essential Catholic conception of sexuality. However, I cannot say either that this is my solid, my clear, my unequivocal conviction. Do *you* know so precisely who is right?

Do not many people know it?
Almost everybody seems to know it, whether they are for or against it. It belongs to our human situation that in practical matters we must decide 100 percent, even when the arguments stand as 51 to 49. Those who do not see

this are basically unable to have a voice in such discussions. Yet today those who feel that way are considered stupid, cowardly, diplomatic.

Granted that on the topic "pope and pill" both sides have decided 100 percent, have assumed a radical position, the encyclical hardly gives the impression that for the pope himself the arguments stood for many years at 51 to 49, that he himself has hesitated for years.

But consider also the other side. There have been wildly emotional protests. Does that mean that the defenders of the pill are right? I cannot see that.

When you yourself today weigh the arguments, may we presume that you would not have decided like the pope?

I would probably have left the question open. But let me insist right away: I am not absolutely certain that this position would, in fact, objectively and unequivocally have been the right one.

Do you claim that all Catholics have the right to go on reflecting on the content of the encyclical, putting off their own decision and eventually deciding against the encyclical?

Obviously. I refer to the declaration of the German bishops that came out before the encyclical, and that simply stated obvious principles of church doctrine. The gist of it is that an authentic declaration of the magisterium, that does not intend to be definitive, is a doctrine that challenges a Catholic in conscience, but leaves room for further discussion, and a further decision even of the individual conscience.

But Paul VI, like Pius XII formerly, has certainly wished to put an end to the discussion and not to stir it up.

I do not quite agree with you. Of course, an authentic declaration of the magisterium is a declaration that intends to be right and to be accepted. As a Catholic one cannot simply say that nothing has changed. Yet the declaration is made explicitly or implicitly with the reservation of possible modifications, so that an absolute end to every discussion is simply not intended.

Meanwhile, things have come to pass where the pope can no longer put an end to the discussion, even if he wanted to. Recently, at the Katholikentag *in Essen, a resolution against the encyclical passed by almost five thousand votes against only a few dozen. What do you think of this reaction?*

I make a distinction between two things. It is important for the Church's leaders to know what the faithful really think and feel. They do not always know this too well. And at times they may be quite wrong on this score. To this extent this protest possesses a certain theological importance about which I will say no more here. On the other hand, where truth is at stake, such balloting must be handled very soberly and very prudently.

Maybe because such a group is not representative?
Not only for that reason. Look, let me put it very bluntly and clearly. I am quite anxious to say this in the present connection. Suppose you drum together a few thousand Catholics and you harangue them with a fiery speech in the style of some modern theologians: Jesus Christ has not risen from the dead; that is a pious fairy tale. Next you poll these Catholics and you discover that twenty-five hundred among them hold that Jesus Christ has not risen from the dead, while only five hundred continue to believe this. In that case as a Catholic I would still have to say: These twenty-five hundred may still be Catholics sociologically, but in reality they no longer are. The Church is represented by the other five hundred.

Do you not oversimplify? The resurrection is a dogma, while no dogma is involved in the pill.
Sure, there are differences. I wanted only to point out that, according to our Catholic conception of the Church, a show of hands like the one at the *Katholikentag* does not constitute the ultimate norm.

Since we are speaking of a majority, is it really true, what Pope Paul VI has asserted in his message to the German Katholikentag *about the reaction to his encyclical: "The predominant majority of the Church has accepted our word with agreement and obedience . . ."?*
I must say that I do not exactly know according to what criteria or norms . . .

The pope has made sure of the majority?
Yes. If one considers how the bishops of the world have reacted, one may conclude that this statement is true. If he meant the mind of the majority of Catholics, then I too would be unable to say how this majority was ascertained, even though one should not take as a starting point the mind of the German, the Dutch, or the North American Catholics.

There are undoubtedly some important facts that have led us and also others, later on, to the conclusion, and a valid conclusion, that the pope has acted against the Cath-

olic Church. The majority of the commission that the pope himself had convoked disagreed with him. The majority of the bishops that have spoken of this topic at the Council or later, disagreed with him. The majority of the moral theologians, at least in German speaking countries, hold an opinion that differs from his. The practice in the confessional, as is now openly admitted, was different from what it should be according to the encyclical. The married life of most Catholic couples probably contradicts the pope's demands. One might also mention the results of questionnaires and other data.

This calls for quite a number of remarks. First, I do not believe that, from the point of view of Canon Law, the pope has acted against the decisions of the Second Vatican Council. You know, of course, that many a theologian believes that the pope has offended against the doctrine of collegiality of Vatican II.

Professor Rahner, the collegiality of the pope and the bishops is the idea, developed by you, that the Church should, even must be directed by the pope in communion with the bishops.

Even Vatican II has explicitly granted the pope the possibility of deciding the way he has done.

Did you not, like many others, have the impression during the Council that the assembly of bishops had decided to leave the faithful free about birth control and that it is especially through the intervention of the pope that such a decision has been prevented?

That is a question that can ultimately not be answered in a really historical way. It is certain that at the Council the pope insisted on prudence and declared that he wished to give further thought to this question and decide by himself. But who will demonstrate that the Council did not agree with this? The fact that many bishops favored freedom of choice does not demonstrate this.

Has this pope, as it were, not acted in an even more uncollegial way than either Pius IX or Pius XII? In 1870 the first Pius pushed through, at the First Vatican Council, the dogma of the infallibility of the pope; and Pius XII proclaimed the dogma of the bodily Assumption of Mary. But beforehand, both Piuses had made sure of the consent of the bishops, while Paul VI has neither consulted nor informed the bishops.

But there is a very great difference between a pope who decides *ex cathedra*, that is, proclaims a dogma, and a pope, like Paul VI, who makes known an authentic but revisable doctrine.

For the theologian this difference is clear. But the simple Catholic feels that birth control has more to do with his life than a dogma about Mary and should therefore be considered equally important.

Yes, and that is why I might say that, although the pope formally had the right to proceed as he did, it is quite another question whether it was desirable or, in fact, justified to proceed in this way. I do not really know how to answer this second question. I might only say in all sincerity that I would really have wished that the pope's way of proceeding in this affair had been more collegial.

What is the theological meaning of the fact that the pope's decision notoriously contradicts the practice of most Catholics?

Here I must first ask: Are you so sure that this contradiction exists? In most countries the pill is not yet a real problem. This should make us very prudent. But suppose things were as you say. Can the average practice of the people of a certain Church not be false? Take, for instance, the polls that the *Spiegel* has conducted about the attitude of many Catholics with respect to the dogmas of their Church.[1] Should it appear that 60 percent doubt the belief in the eternal life of the individual, I would have to say as a Catholic that I regret that it is so, but that changes nothing of the fact of the dogma of the Church.

Is this case not the same as that of the resurrection? For the doctrine of eternal life the daily life of Catholics can have no normative influence. But when the majority of Catholics uses methods of birth control that the pope forbids . . .

Take another doctrine that is a church dogma: the indissolubility of marriage. Should it be established that 60 percent of Catholics do not accept this, nothing again would be changed. Of course, here too the case is different. About birth control we have an authentic, but revisable doctrine and a practice that conflicts with it, at least in many countries. And with regard to such a doctrine an opposed practice means of course, even theologically, more than in the other case. Obviously, this has to be granted. But I would add, this belongs to the situation which we have to bear and endure as Catholic Christians and theologians.

Is it still possible, when we consider this discrepancy between doctrine and life, to go on saying that the faithful—as the Council required—respectfully acknowledge the supreme magisterium and obey its directives?

In the presence of a revisable, even though authentic doctrine, Catholics

1. "Was glauben die Deutschen?" feature story in *Der Spiegel* 52/1967.

who do not accept it can have in fact two different critical attitudes. They may say off the bat that they do not care at all what Rome has to say; such an attitude would not be Catholic. Yet this authentic, albeit revisable doctrine does not demand that the Catholic accept it as a final decision. Catholics who react to such a church doctrine with reservations and further questions, while also paying serious attention to it, do not disagree with the Council's demand which you have quoted.

You consider that a Catholic woman may take the pill, yet after careful considera- tion believe that she obeys the pope?
Yes, this woman may subjectively hold this opinion. Whether she is ob- jectively right is another question.

But for this woman and for the Church it would be sufficient that she have this subjective opinion?
Yes.

And in the confessional this woman must not make sure as often as possible that her opinion is right?
No. She does not have to return to this point in every confession. When I am personally convinced, according to my subjective and never-to-be-overruled conscience, that I have acted in the right way, then what I have done is no matter for confession.

And how should confessors behave? Should they ask women whether they use the pill?
I believe—but this is only my own private opinion—that, when the confes- sor prudently may suppose that the penitent has a peaceful and certain con- science, he should not ask her.

Father Rahner, we have the impression that many ideas and prejudices that many people believed to belong to the past have been revived by the encyclical: that the pope decides autocratically as secular monarchs used to do; that the Catholic Church is alienated from the world; that her priests must be hypocritical; that the Jesuits obey blindly. We have examples to prove it.
There can be no doubt that such prejudices have revived. But one may wonder whether a repressed but still active prejudice is better than one that erupts openly.

For example, many people believed that the Jesuits no longer blindly obeyed the pope. You and other members of the Order during the last years have contributed so many new ideas to the Church, even against the opposition of the authorities, that one no longer considered the Jesuits a blindly obedient bodyguard of the Holy Father, but the vanguard of the Church.

If it is as you say, why would there now have been any change?

Your General, Pedro Arrupe, has told all Jesuits that they should do their utmost in order to "enter into the ideas of the encyclical and help others to understand it." All right. But then he goes on about the encyclical and the Jesuits. "These ideas may at first not have been his own, but he will discover that they are right and forego his own!" The general knows this before the Jesuits have started to read! And he continues: "No fear should prevent us then"—when this process of unlearning is over—"eventually to make publicly known that we have changed our opinion."

I would say: Here the general wants to say only what I said before: Study the encyclical, take it seriously. If, as a result of this . . .

But he does not say "if." Should he have said "if," things would look different. But now he orders the Jesuit to make the pope's position his own.

No, no. I reject this interpretation as positively false. The general can, must even, to my mind, consider the possiblity that a Jesuit, even after doing what he is told to do, maintains his former conviction and acts accordingly.

Formerly, we used to think about the Catholic Church: One man, the pope, decides, and all others have to obey.

Whoever interprets the encyclical correctly cannot submit it as proof for this opinion, because it is not an absolute and definitive decision but, if you like, a provisional one that should and must fight it out with each individual's conscience.

Must it not make a false impression on outsiders when priests are now obliged to speak and to act differently according to where they happen to be. I mean, in the pulpit they may not criticize the encyclical, but they may do it in the parish hall or at the Katholikentag. *And as for the bishops, the simple Catholics will not find out from their parish bulletin that, for instance, Cardinal Döpfner held and maybe continues to hold another opinion than the pope.*

Well, they may and should know about this. But there is quite a difference between the proclamation of the gospel from the pulpit and discussions in the parish hall or elsewhere. That is evident.

But when the pope appeals to divine right, is a priest not allowed to criticize this from the pulpit?

It seems to me that in this concrete case there is no objection, if the situation is objectively and calmly explained to the faithful.

May the Catholics who sit in the church hear, then, that the man in the pulpit has another opinion about this point than the pope?

I believe they may. Provided that the priest endeavors at the same time to explain to the faithful the seriousness and importance of such an authentic doctrinal pronouncement.

Whoever has enjoyed a solid education, listens attentively, and knows how to read a bit between the lines finds a way or a way out. Is this not unfair with regard to the simple faithful who take the pope literally? Is it not an injustice so to help the clever and to leave the simple folk with upset consciences?

You know, there exists naturally, if you allow a bit of jargon, a certain global moral instinct that can operate and does operate, at least for the subjective moral life of a Christian, without any need for that instinct to be reflected upon and put into words. That is even typical of the so-called nonintellectuals.

Really?

They may think as follows: Even if I take the pill, I keep a friendly relation to almighty God. They will also have the required good subjective conscience, although attained with less reflection than the educated Catholic. Nevertheless, I do not deny that there are difficulties in the line which you mentioned.

Many partisans of the encyclical seem to be not only alienated from the world, but downright hostile to the world. Jan Visser, a theology professor in Rome, a Dutchman, was asked over German television whether "the Church would also accept a hopeless overpopulation of the world in order to defend her traditonal doctrine." Whereupon Visser answered: "Yes. If she really is convinced that this is God's law, I would think so. Righteousness must prevail, even should the world perish."

I believe that this . . .

Visser.

. . . this professor Visser has been tricked into a situation that I can only consider unreal. You might as well ask me: What would you do if the pope defined *ex cathedra* 2 x 2 = 5? I would simply answer: That would mean the end of the Church and I leave the Catholic Church. I can say this honestly and without any reservation. But it stands to reason that I should also say that such things do not happen.

An especially difficult chapter is the question of the Holy Spirit. Paul VI appeals to the fact that for his decision he enjoyed the help of the Holy Spirit.
But he does not say thereby that this decision is infallible, neither does he say that it would not subjectively be possible for a Catholic who wishes to remain Catholic to reach a different subjective decision in conscience.

It has nevertheless shocked some Catholics: If one can even discuss against the Holy Spirit, what is left?
Basically the pope has only said: It belongs essentially to the Holy Spirit to intervene in the decisions of the magisterium. Yet when a decision is revisable, as the one we are speaking of, and if it turned out—I say, if—that it should indeed be revised, hence, if it appears later to have been erroneous, it is of course clear that, in fact, the Holy Spirit had no part in it. When Galileo was forced to recant, the Holy Spirit had no part in this decision. We have by now become aware of this.

So the pope's opinion that he was assisted by the Holy Spirit is also revisable?
Yes. Naturally, decisions exist that can be and ought to be revised, in which I can still discover and accept a certain timebound or historical significance, when I see later that they have not hit the nail on the head. There are such things in life. In your own life you can certainly say that this or that which you have done in the past was, on second thought, false. Yet you may add that in some way or other it made sense in your life. Despite its objective erroneousness it has had a positive meaning.

Sure. But does this happen in the Church too?
Of course. Many decisions of the Pontifical Biblical Commission in the early twentieth century were, as we know now, objectively false. They have nevertheless had some providential significance: against a blindly raging rationalism that threatened to tear up Holy Scripture. This may also happen nowadays. Thus it may be that the pope's decision is false in itself, in its proper material substance, and that nonetheless one may say later on: Thank God that the Church has resisted a wild hedonism in the line of sex. One can really not act as if in this respect everything were in order and as if the pope were only the wicked killjoy of a lofty sexual morality.

Nobody speaks that way.
O yes, some do.

Who, for instance.
Read many of the letters to the editor that you have printed in the *Spiegel*, where having-fun-doing-it is touted as the adequate norm of morality, as if there were no ethical principles in the domain of sex.

May we return once more to the assistance of the Holy Spirit, since the situation obviously looks unclear and almost hopeless for many a Catholic? The pope himself says that he has enjoyed the assistance of the Holy Spirit. Theologians say that an error is not excluded, quite a number even consider it probable or even certain. So here the Holy Spirit allows at least the possibility of an error. But when a dogma is proclaimed it is precisely this Holy Spirit who excludes the possibility of an error. How and where should the line be drawn. And who draws it?
For the Catholic understanding of faith, which many people, of course, do not share, it is indeed certain that in the case of real irrevocable definitions of the Church the Holy Spirit prevents any real error. According to the doctrine of the Church, a definition must be so stated that it is unequivocally certain that the magisterium requires in an unrevisable way the faith assent of Catholics. So where this intention is not mentioned, only a revisable doctrine is presented.

To the Catholic who is convinced that in the encyclical on birth control the pope has erred, who gives the guarantee that this pope or another pope does not also err when he defines a dogma? Only his faith?
The conviction based on faith that the Church of Christ would cease to exist if she were to introduce an error into the. midst of her own existence. In that case, the Church as Christ's community of faith would, according to Catholic doctrine, cease to exist, and the Catholic is convinced by his or her faith that this cannot happen and that this community of faith as such cannot perish.

You have developed a series of arguments in your books in order to explain the dogma of the pope's infallibility. If we may oversimplify it—to the point perhaps of falsifying it: A decision of the pope should come only at the end of a development, when in the Church a common conviction has already developed about a truth of the faith, when the pope therefore proclaims solemnly only what has already become obvious. Does this apply only to a dogma and not also to other decisions of the magisterium? Otherwise, you would have been refuted by the encyclical on birth control.

First, this agreement should not be understood too much on the model of a democratic majority. Yet I would agree basically that the ideas which you have roughly exposed should be restricted to the proclamation of dogmas. You see, this distinction occurs also in human life. There are human convictions that are final, radical, definitive basic decisions, and there are opinions that are valid while yet leaving open a further spiritual development toward another opinion. Something similar happens also in the Church. That I must love my neighbor is a basic decision of my life. That is quite different from whether I think that employees should have a say in management.

Is it realistic when you and other Catholic theologians emphasize the provisional and revisable nature of this encyclical? On the contrary, is it not more realistic to insist that alongside Pius XI and Pius XII this is now the third pope who proclaims this doctrine, and that it looks less revisable than ever?

No. Take the example of the prohibition of interest. It involved a longer-lasting negative attitude, adopted by a still greater number of popes than in the present case, where the Holy See has for thirty to thirty-five years adopted this position toward birth control. When we consider greater lengths of time, things may look different.

Professor Rahner, we thank you for this interview.

Translated by Joseph Donceel, S.J.
Fordham University

5 · The Church's Responsibility for the World

Interview with William V. Dych, S.J. for *America* magazine,
New York (October 31, 1970)

Father Rahner, it is almost five years now since the end of the Second Vatican Council. Looking back from this vantage point, what do you see as the major accomplishment of the Council, and its real significance for the Church today?

I think that what the Council accomplished more than anything else was to give the Church the courage to face the modern world in a way that was not true before the Council. Comparing the Church before and after Vatican II, I see a real movement away from a more negative, defensive attitude toward a more open and positive attitude. This, I think, was a real accomplishment, and one that has much significance for us today.

Where do you see this more positive attitude manifest?

I see it manifest, for example, in a positive appreciation of modern culture and of modern science and technology, in an awareness of the fact that the Church has something to learn from modern methods of scientific investigation. I see it manifest also in an awareness of specifically contemporary problems facing mankind today, of the Church's involvement in these problems, and of her responsibility in helping to find solutions to them. The Second Vatican Council's *Gaudium et Spes* (The Church in the Modern World) represents the first time that the contemporary situation of humankind was described in an official church document of such high authority.

If you can remember back to your own personal hopes and expectations of the Council, were they realized or were they disappointed?

I would say that, given the situation of the Church at the time of the Council, the Council fulfilled what anyone could have *reasonably* hoped for at that particular time. However, in assessing the success of the Council or the lack of it, it is necessary to bear in mind the distinction between two very different movements that were set in motion by the Council, and to assess them accordingly.

Which two movements do you mean?

I mean, first of all, that there were certain movements which the Council Fathers quite consciously intended to set in motion, for example, a reform of

46

the liturgy, an adaptation of religious orders, and an introduction of collegiality into the government of the Church, and so on. These things the Council Fathers saw as definite goals to be achieved by the Council. But there were, secondly, other movements which the Council Fathers did not intend, but *de facto* were set in motion by the Council's discussions and deliberations. Many of these movements neither were nor could have been successfully completed by the Council itself, and even today, five years later, are just in their beginnings.

Could you give some examples of this?

The Council certainly opened the way for a much deeper and much more radical questioning of some very central issues than was either foreseen or intended by the Council Fathers. Take for example, the whole question of the existence and nature of God and how we are to understand his relationship to the *present* world—a question which comes up in many different forms, for example, in the question of horizontalism and verticalism, and the question of the relationship of the love of God and neighbor. One does not find these questions discussed in the conciliar texts themselves. But *de facto* they have become central questions for theology, and theology has to have the courage to face them as deeply and as radically as they demand.

Such questioning, of course, always brings many dangers, but also brings much promise. In many other areas, too, the Council has opened up far more radical questions than it either foresaw or intended. This is the kind of movement I mean when I say that it was begun by the Council, but neither was nor could have been settled by the Council itself. The same is true in practical as well as in theoretical matters. I see the same kind of movement in an increased awareness of the church's responsibility for and obligations to the contemporary world. In such matters as peace and war, racial equality, underdeveloped and underprivileged peoples, and the Church's critical function in society, there are movements at work in the Church which go far beyond what was foreseen and intended by the Council.

What do you see as the still unattained goal of the Council with regard to the movements that you have been describing?

I would see as the goal toward which the Church and the Church's theology have to strive the realization of a more living and vital unity between what I called the horizontal and the vertical dimensions, that is, between the Christian's relationship to God and his relationship to the world. To put the same thing another way, we have to come to see much more clearly than before that a more radical spirituality today brings with it a more radical responsibility for the world, and vice versa, that a more radical responsibility for the world must be accompanied by a more radical spirituality. We must come to see both poles as a unity rather than as alternatives. To reach this goal we still have a long way to go, both in theory and in practice.

As a result of these various movements in the five intervening years since the Council, has the situation of theology and of a theologian like yourself changed since the time of the Council?

The situation of theology has certainly changed since the Council. I would say that during Vatican II the central issue was ecclesiology, which is not the case today.

What do you think is the central issue facing theologians today?

I would express it very briefly and very simply by saying: God . . . in Jesus Christ . . . in one's neighbor. We must work out the relationship between these three in the life of the Christian, and express it in terminology that is intelligible today.

In this case how would you describe the shape that theology will have to take in the future?

Before giving my own views on the shape that theology will take in the future, I must begin with the reservation that in a very real sense the future of theology, like the future of the Church, is ultimately unknown to us today, and this is true not only in fact, but also in principle. For God in his Spirit is the Lord of the Church's history and of theology's history, and we can neither control nor predict this future. The fact that the Church and its theology have an essence or a permanent identity that abides through history does not remove them from history, for it is in and through history that their growth and development must take place.

I think that the practical consequence of this is that neither theologians nor the magisterium should be too concerned about steering or controlling the future development of theology. If they were, there would be the danger of theology falling into a kind of ideological sclerosis in its own self-understanding, a self-understanding which must rather be open to change and growth and development. If, despite this reservation, I do talk about the future of theology, my views also represent to some extent, of course, my own personal wishes and preferences. But there is nothing wrong with wishing, and usually it is more sensible than prophesying.

Bearing all of this in mind, I would state as the basic principle that will be at work in the future development of theology—or as the basic trend that theology will follow in the future—the following: The Church's theology in the future will become ever less the theology of a particular, culturally regional society as it has been in the past. In other words, the theology of the Church (or churches) will become the theology of a world-Church, but a theology which cannot base itself upon some particular culture. For this world-Church will be everywhere (although in very different degrees) a diaspora Church which will have to maintain itself by its own strength and power within an (at best) neutral, secular world. This situation is partially present already, and it can only be expected to increase, and it will greatly influence the future shape of theology.

Could you specify some of the characteristics of a theology that would develop in such a situation?

I would mention what I consider to be four such characteristics:

1) This theology will be a pluralistic theology, rather than a single, homogeneous theology for the entire Church. If the Church wants to be universal in more than a geographical sense, and if it wants to remain true to its missionary task of relating itself genuinely to the plurality of cultures in the world—a plurality which varies not only from one geographical region to another, but also within the same geographical region—then we will have to have a plurality of theologies. Such a pluralism can express the riches and the universality of the Church. This pluralism, of course, raises new questions about the relationship of theology to the magisterium and to the common creed of the Church, questions which we cannot go into here, but such a pluralism in no way implies anarchy in theology.

2) This theology will be more immediately missionary and mystagogical than in the past. For with Christian faith losing its social basis and support and becoming more a faith that is rooted in the personal decision and conviction of the individual, theology will have to serve this faith in a new way. By mystagogical I mean bringing the *fides quae* or what we believe into the closest possible unity with the *fides qua* or the act of faith itself, and thus showing what the tenets of faith actually mean for the individual and for society.

3) This theology, then, will have to be demythologizing. This word, of course, has acquired many connotations in recent years, but I am using it in the perfectly orthodox sense of transposing and expressing Christian faith in such a way that it can really be assimilated by contemporary people. We are and shall always be bound to tradition, of course, but the tradition is the beginning, not the end of theology.

4) Finally, I think that this theology will be more transcendental, by which I mean that it will bring out more clearly the role of the knowing subject in all of our objective knowledge, including our knowledge via faith and theology.

A theology that has the four characteristics that I have just mentioned would also, of course, be more ecumenical, and be more directly related to the contemporary world than has been true in the past.

How will this theology be related to what has been the Church's theology in the past?

I would describe this relationship by saying that theology in the future, proceeding from the ground of the *practical* reason, will express the doctrines of the old theology of the theoretical reason in such a way that the theological as such will become a principle of action.

How would you describe the role or function of this theology in the total life of the Church?

I think that the function of theology in the life of the Church lies in the service that it can and must perform for the Church's mission to preach the gospel of Jesus Christ in the present age. This function has two aspects: Theology must help the preacher preach the gospel in such a way that it can really be understood and assimilated today; and theology also has a critical function, and I see this critical function to lie especially in preventing the Church in its preaching or in its practice from becoming a ghetto or a sect within the contemporary world. The Church is, and will become more so, a "little flock," a diaspora Church in a secular world, but this is something altogether different from developing the mentality of a sect, which makes its social ineffectiveness and impotence into an ideal and into a sign of its own election. It is against the danger of this mentality that theology in its critical function must struggle.

Do you see signs of this danger in the Church today?

I would say that the dangers of a false adaptation of the Church to the modern world, or of falling into a purely secular humanism—which are real dangers in the Church's attempt to open itself outwards to the modern world—can invite as a defensive reaction the opposite danger, namely, to turn inwards and to make the Church a closed sect in the sense that I have described.

What kind of practical steps could the Church take to avoid either danger in relating or adapting itself to the modern world?

I would mention four such practical steps that strike me at the moment as being important:

1) There is the very practical problem of communications within the Church. We need more and better channels of communication between officials and members of the Church and much more *mutual* trust on both sides.

2) We need the formation of communities within the Church that are really living and vital communities, communities that lead a truly charismatic Christian life that is more than just pentecostal enthusiasm.

3) The offical Church must have the courage to demand of its members something more in the way of service to the contemporary world and its pressing needs. I mean by this really concrete demands, and not just the preaching of abstract ideals, which are true, but, so long as they remain abstract, cause no one any trouble.

4) We need, too, a renewal of the religious orders, a renewal that is such that the contemporary world can really see and hear in them the radical demands of the Sermon on the Mount. It is this kind of renewal, and not a rush to be stylish, that will enable the religious orders to perform their mission in the modern world.

The new papal theological commission will be holding its second meeting very shortly in Rome. Do you think that it has a significant role to play in the various problems we have been discussing?

I think that the commission could play such a role given the right circumstances. Contrary to my own views, some think that the commission should devote itself to what amounts to practically the whole of theology. I think that the commission would be far more effective if it devoted its time and energies to a limited number of questions which could really be mastered by a relatively small commission, but which, nevertheless, have great practical significance for the life of the Church.

The commission should not try to accomplish what could only be accomplished at best by the whole of Catholic theology. For the commission to select such limited, concrete questions presupposes, of course, that the pope and the bishops really do want to learn something new about particular, concrete problems that we are facing at the moment, and are not of the opinion that we already have clear solutions to these problems. Up until now official Rome has not yet given the impression that it really does want to hear something from the commission.

Could you give some examples of the practical questions that you thnk could and should be taken up by the commission?

There are many such questions, and among them I would include such questions as: When *exactly* must the Church consider a marriage indissoluble? What should be the Church's concrete attitude and behavior with regard to different kinds of remarriages, that is, remarriages which have resulted from differing circumstances? The question of infant baptism deserves some attention today. There are the various questions that would be treated in a theology of revolution. There are questions of a more theological kind with regard to priestly celibacy that are still open today. I would also like to discuss how we are to interpret theologically the status of those people who belong to a particular religious denomination, including the Catholic Church, for purely historical and socioreligious reasons, and not for theological reasons. There are, for example, people who hate the pope, and people who love the pope, and do this for purely historical reasons, not for really religious or theological reasons.

You were speaking earlier, Father Rahner, of pluralism or diversity in theology and in the Church. On your several visits to the United States, have you noticed any differences between the German and the American churches?

A European, of course, would notice many differences in the typical American style of life, but prescinding from these externals, I have the impression that before the Council the American Church was more conservative than the German Church. Today, however, I find the willingness and readiness to change in all areas greater in the American Church than among us. That brings with it many risks and dangers, but also brings great promise.

What is your opinion of what is called the "underground church" in the United States?

If "underground church" means that communities of believers can exist in the Church which are not identical with the local parish and which are not immediately and directly instituted by the hierarchy, then I think that such communities are legitimate and could have a positive meaning and importance for the Church. I spoke earlier of the need for such communities. If "underground church" means a community that consciously separates itself in heresy or schism from the Church of the pope and the bishops, at least in practice—then I think that such a community should be condemned. Even in the latter case, however, such a community poses the question to the bishops whether they really leave enough room for the free sway of the Spirit and his charisms in the Church. Whether the so-called underground church in the United States falls into the one category or the other is for Americans to decide, not me.

Does the same phenomenon exist in Germany?
The closest parallel that I know of in Germany is a group here in Munich which is striving for what it calls an "integral" Christian life. By this they mean an attempt at a radical Christianization of life in all its aspects, a kind of lay religious order. I am not familiar enough with either group to know how similar they are.

One final question. You began by speaking of a more positive and open attitude toward the contemporary world as a major accomplishment of the Second Vatican Council. Given this attitude, how would you express the mission which the Church has in this world?
I would begin by clarifying what the word *Church* means in your question. We tend to think automatically that it means the official, hierarchical Church, and so we tend to ask what mission *they* have in the world. But I do not think that much can be expected if the question is asked in this sense.

We Christians have to begin to realize that *we* are the Church, and from this point of view your question is asking: What must *I* do in my concrete situation, myself as an individual and in community with others, so that the Spirit of Christ in *me* and in *us* can overcome in the contemporary world the non-spirit of egoism and hatred—of the quest for power, of the use of violence, of skepticism about the meaning and value of life—and overcome the nonspirit of a false secularism, which is without the worship of God and without ultimate hope? This is the mission of the Church, that is, *our* mission, in the contemporary world.

When enough Christians begin to ask the question in this way, and honestly begin to seek an answer, then the mission of the Church in the contemporary world is not only a mission of awesome scope and frightening responsibility, but also a mission of great hope and great promise.

Translated by William V. Dych, S.J.
Fordham University

6 · The Feast of All Saints: The Communion of Saints

Interview with Eberhard Kuhrau on West-German Radio (WDR),
Cologne (November 1, 1970)

Professor Rahner, as professor you teach Catholic dogma—a very abstract and demanding discipline—and at the same time you have always taken seriously your duties as a priest in the Jesuit order. You have never limited yourself to academic theology. Does the feast of All Saints still have a meaning in your eyes?

I'd have to say, with proper care and caution, that while I wish it were meaningful for my whole Christian and religious life, nevertheless I can't claim personally a great enthusiasm for this feast. It would be religious hypocrisy to say I did. However, I would say that I judge the total possibilities of a spiritual life to be wider, greater, and deeper than what I personally can immediately experience at any one time. This is why it is right for the Church to set down this feast as an official sign of her religious life. It says, in effect, "Pay attention, here is a religious dimension you can experience or study." And in this sense, despite my own spiritual poverty, I celebrate this feast with a proper and authentic conviction and with a sincere effort to discover and experience its truth and reality.

The truth and reality that we encounter in the saints could perhaps be described as threefold: The saints are models for us and offer us new effective possibilities of both religious and secular lifestyles. They also intercede for us. Finally, they function as guardians. While I can find much in the first function, namely, the saints as models —for example, I can easily imagine people being inspired by a Francis of Assisi, or someone like Father Delp—the other two meanings cause me difficulty.

I believe we can best understand the second and third functions, or the second and third aspects of Christian or Catholic devotion to the saints, by concentrating on the first and trying to understand it, namely, that the saints are religious models. I mean we are all one in being human. The most important things in our lives as a whole, and thus also the most important things in the lives of the saints, take place in encounter with others: with a loving mother, with a father who is present to and gives himself for his family, or perhaps with a politician who truly uses his or her life unselfishly for others. These are only a few examples. But the things that strike me as an individual are even clearer in the lives of the saints as models. They are effective models for each individual—of faith in Jesus Christ, of how to be immediately present to the unspoken mystery of God. This is what "saint" means: those who give us as

54

individuals an example to follow. That there are always new models through-out history, in new times and circumstances, shows us the meaning of Christianity as love of God and neighbor. This much is self-evident. They show us how to begin anew. You said that you could more easily relate to this aspect of saints. I would simply say: When a Christian is convinced that such a life of faith, of radical hope, and love goes beyond death and does not collapse into nothingness, when it is believed that these people, whom we call saints, are permanently valid examples of people who remain before God and have found fulfillment in God, then I already have the grounds for the second and third aspects of the meaning of the cult of the saints, which initially caused you difficulty.

This is good. But let's concentrate a moment on the "model" function. Let's suppose that the meaning of honoring saints lies in what you described. But then shouldn't it be made more evident in the practice of canonization which virtues the Church considers important for the twentieth century? Doesn't the fact that mainly celibates are saints leave the impression that one can only be a saint by remaining unmarried?

Naturally, the process of canonization and the ecclesiastical procedures of advancing someone toward sainthood are subjected somewhat to chance and whim. From a great throng of people, whose Christian lives gave the impression that they were, let's not say saints, but at least outstanding Christians, this or that person is selected. It is normal that this process happens according to the style and world view of each time. However, the result of this is that because of the circumstances there will be models of our time who would not have been seen as exemplary in an earlier period. On the other hand, many who were canonized previously and are saints for us have become uninteresting. Furthermore the conditions and procedures of canonization in the Roman Catholic Church are long and drawn out, which causes a certain time lag.

What would you say about the virtues needed in today's world that are meaningful for Christians?

Naturally, it's hard to say, because it varies according to countries, social class, and degree of education. For example, a poor woman who cares for her children, who leads an exemplary Christian life, could also play a real role today in the heavenly court of the saints. One can also assume that there should be politicians today who lead a model Christian life. There should be saints who demonstrate what a critical, sociopolitical commitment is. In any case, we should see that the center of such lives reveals a relationship to God in faith, hope, and love.

May I now ask you very directly, would a person like Camillo Torres be a good example of a saint?

Of course I can't answer this question directly since I don't know the precise details of Torres's life. However, I can imagine that he could be someone who for certain people convincingly demonstrated an absolute love of God and neighbor in his political commitment. Without knowing his life, however, the following would be important, since it pertains to being a model: Was he truly human, yet in a way that was more than just typical? This would be necessary for canonizing a saint in particular circumstances. For example, I knew Father Rupert Mayer, who courageously stood up to the Nazis. I was a good friend of Alfred Delp, whom you mentioned. I don't know whether these men, despite their great achievements as humans and as Christians, are canonizable for that reason. For me, however, this doesn't make any difference in the end. I may even treasure those people who don't fit the official categories more than those—some pious American nun, for instance—who have been canonized.

Doesn't the problem start with the juridical decision that this person is holy? Although this may not imply that others are not also holy, nevertheless doesn't the juridical declaration of sainthood cause problems?

Yes, certainly, there are problems with this practice, and I hope in a foreseeable future these procedures will be modified, so that, for example, outstanding men and women will also be recognized and honored, even in the Church's worship—especially people from particular regions in particular churches, who would not be of interest to other churches because of the particularity of their lives. In this way, I think the official Church could better correspond to concrete realities.

What is your opinion on the theological background the Church uses in recognizing saints? What do they mean for us? Why are they so important as to be mentioned in the creed?

The expression "saint" of course receives its meaning from the New Testament, where it refers to all true believing, hoping, and loving Christians whose lives are lived by the grace of God and whose whole existence is hidden in a hopeful love of God, and from this interior attitude they radically love their neighbors. Thus all who live this way are saints according to the biblical, as well as the theological sense. This is why even Catholic scholastic theology still speaks of "sanctifying grace" and holds that each person who has not absolutely rejected God possesses this sanctifying grace by the help of God. However, there are also others whose lives manifest a saintliness in, as it were, an empirical sense. But the overall answer to your question is that when we speak of the holy Church, when we celebrate the feast of All Saints, when on this feast we read the text of Revelation that speaks of a great host of saints, which no one can number, who sit before the throne of the lamb, this means all who have been saved and have found their final destiny by means of God's grace. This wider sense of saint, which *also* refers to officially recognized saints, is the more central and decisive one.

How would you give this expression a content? Aren't "those who appear before the throne of the lamb" or "the host of those saved" mythical images? Or, at least expressions that are very difficult to interpret?

The first thing I would say is that today the word *saint* should be shelved and its intended meaning expressed in a simpler, but also truer and more radical way. There are people who leave us with the impression that they have spent their whole lives, with all their disappointments and absurdities, for the love of neighbor, and in this love of neighbor they have reached the final mystery called God who must support this love. Where selfless love occurs in daily life; where people die devoutly, patiently, and hopeful of an absolute meaning, despite all the absurdities of existence; where people do the simplest tasks of their daily lives without an egoistical turning in on themselves—there is God and his grace. This is what sainthood means. The word could quietly be abandoned, since it seems to imply something out of the ordinary, which does not pertain to everyday, reasonable people. Normally today people have more important things to do than pietistically "care for their souls" to bring joy to the "dear Lord." Such representations of sainthood no longer stir people to holiness, and therefore it would perhaps be good on the feast of All Saints to speak of sainthood without using the word.

. . . About a saintliness then that is not officially recognized or termed as such, but that perhaps must remain unrecognized and unrecognizable?

Yes, this is correct. There are not only "unknown soldiers" but also "unknown saints," that is, men and women who, I would almost say, have so forgotten themselves that they suffer the fate of remaining unrecognized by others. However, in this seeming anonymity they manifest such a radical selflessness that it should be identified. Maybe the exceptions should be those whom the Church officially declares saints—while all are really saints who are so selfless and who do their duty in such an unnoticeable way that people think they are only doing their duty. This selfless fulfillment of duty of real saints manifests nothing out of the ordinary, but is done simply, without hope of thanks or reward. When one of these people does stand out, however, and we designate him or her as a saint, this is justifiable and meaningful, yet a secondary event in the communion of saints.

Nevertheless, the difficulty remains, even more so when you define things in this way, namely, that it is especially the unrecognized. Thus you would be advocating a Church of saints who cannot be "empirically" indicated.

Naturally, you have to understand what I was saying correctly. You see, this idea of anonymous saints does not refer to a type of people who have protected themselves in advance, as it were, from the judgment of history and thus, in a false sense, wanted to be among the "little" people. Nor does it mean those who are unremarkable and involve themselves in as few things as possible, or who refuse to take upon themselves any great responsibilities and do not have the courage to blame themselves for anything. But wherever life openly offers a great challenge or an absolute commitment, there too is an occasion for a holy life. Therefore, do not misunderstand what I said before. If this is properly understood, why shouldn't Christianity recognize such people as exemplary? It happens in all churches. Although his Church has no canonization process, this happened to Friedrich Bodelschwingh (†1910), a Lutheran minister known for his work with the poor. This is how a person like Martin Luther King is recognized. Whether we can call Camillo Torres a saint—to return to your example—I don't know. But why not? The Church has always been open to recognizing such people everywhere. It should realize this. But if you exaggerate the anonymity of the true Christian, you are perhaps unwittingly encouraging "pseudo-littleness"—the kind of person who cannot stomach responsibility, especially public responsibility. That would not be right.

A great statesman, a poor mother who cares for her children, both can lead exemplary Christian lives and can perhaps play a role in the public worship of the Church. Naturally, the question you posed in the beginning, whether and in what sense such "saints" can intercede for us, has not yet been answered. Should I say a few words about it now?

Yes.

The first thing I would say is that here too, according to Catholic teaching on sainthood and on the communion of saints or the cult of saints, they are not to be considered as a "board of appeals" or as a special intervention process, where they would be involved in running messages to the throne of God, messages that otherwise would not arrive there. I would say that the language concerning the intercession of the saints means nothing else than that their lives, accepted now by God where we all belong together in the community God loves, are meaningful for me—and not just as secular lives, but as lives related to God. I don't stand alone before God, although I am absolutely individual before God and God's grace, but I belong to others. Each person is meaningful for another. Praying to someone to intercede for me thus means nothing else than saying in prayer that the other is significant for me, in a way known finally only by God and only when I stand before God.

Translated by James V. Zeitz, S.J.
Marquette University

7 · Speaking about the Meaning of Life with Young People

Interview with the editors of *Zeitschrift des KSJ-Schwaz*, Widum (1971)

Father Rahner, how do you explain that almost forty percent of polled young people do not believe in life after death?
It seems to me that three reasons are responsible for this: (1) Young people do not yet have a real experience of eternity, of our need and our hope that a life for which we are freely responsible may contain something which is really forever. (2) Public opinion no longer helps young people by pointing out and correctly explaining the experience of eternity implicit in their exercise of responsibility. (3) Religious instruction and church homilies speak too much about life eternal in a language that makes this truth of our faith sound like mythology. But I cannot show this here in detail.

Why can so few of these young people tell us whether their life has a true meaning?
When a young person has not yet had the experience that a freely assumed responsibility in unselfish loving service of others makes us happy, provided, of course, that this life of responsible unselfishness leads up to definitive liberation and not into nothingness, that youngster cannot discover a real meaning for life. He or she does not yet have the experience of life itself, nor its correct and clear interpretation through the message of the gospel.

Do you believe that the teaching of religion in the high schools no longer lives up to the demands of our time?
The teaching of religion in the high schools suffers, of course, without being *itself* responsible for it, from the general difficulties that the Christian message has making itself understood in today's terms. This translation of the Christian message that we need badly today is difficult, takes time, but is not impossible. Moreover, the success or failure of religious instruction will depend to a great extent on the personality of the teacher. A teacher who is fully alive, who keeps abreast of the questions of our time, who keeps on learning anew, who prays, who renews his or her belief daily, putting trust in God's grace ("Lord, I believe, help my unbelief"), such a teacher will succeed. It stands to reason that this success will always be only partial. Such was also the fate of Jesus, and it is the fate of every truth that tries to express ultimate concerns.

Why do young people feel so little for the sacrifice of the Mass? Why do so many of them not go to church? What should be changed?
Understanding the sacrifice of the Mass is not the start, but almost something like the maturity of a Christian conception of life. Hence, we should not require or expect too much from youngsters. The celebration of the Eucharist should be organized in such a way that young people can really feel involved in it. The Mass should not be understood as a reserved, sacral domain in a profane world, like an island in the sea. The Mass should be understood as the explicit coming-to-awareness of this tremendous drama, full of guilt and grace, that unfolds in the whole of world history, therefore also in our times and in our own life. It assumes a meaning, it peaks in that death in which Jesus, in the incomprehensibility of his death, surrendered in total confidence to the mystery of forgiving love, to the mystery we call God. We do not always dwell at the core of our incomprehensible being, we stay on the surface, we are exiled to humdrum, bustling daily life. Yet once in awhile, we too are thrown into the mystery of guilt, death, forgiveness, and unfathomable freedom that issues from God into the midst of our life.

And this is the mystery that we should also allow to engulf us in the holy celebration of the Lord's death.

Translated by Joseph Donceel, S.J.
Fordham University

8 · The Church's Duty to Change

Interview with Klaus Wrobel, Nürnberg (December 24, 1971)

Father Rahner, I remember something you said to the effect that if we do not keep moving, we will soon be the rear guard. You were speaking of the Catholic Church. My question is: Moving to where?
This implies a double question. It concerns the situation within the Church as well as the relation between Church and society. Both are naturally connected.

Let us first consider the relation of the Church to society. What does this mean today?
It means this: announcing the gospel in a way adapted to our time, as a service to be rendered to society. The gospel message is extremely rich. It must forever be presented in a way adapted to the historical situation. Today we live in the time of rationality, of new scientific knowledge, of new social demands in a society of huge masses of people.

The demand for democratization, for instance?
Yes, growing democratization obliges the proclamation of the gospel to proceed in ways that were hitherto not so well known.

And what function does God have in this modern world?

The gospel message will always refer to the supreme unreachable mystery that we call God. But we have to explain this in a wholly new way to people.

So we have to speak of God in a way that differs from the way of earlier times?

When we speak of God we should take more clearly into account the rationality of modern man. Hence, the need of a certain amount of demythologization.

Yet in spite of demythologization God remains a transcendent "metaphysical" reality.

Yes, the vertical dimension in Christian faith must be kept, precisely as the living foundation of a Christian relation to the world. That is why Christians naturally have the duty to change the world: They must work for more justice and more freedom. But this task comes to them from God. Christians should be neither innerworldly utopians, who have broken away from God, nor reactionary conservatives who say, "Mine is the sound world that must be maintained." Both of them do away with God.

So authentic Christianity includes the will for social changes?

It is only through the will for necessary social changes that people can really aim their hope toward the absolute future that is God. Otherwise, the idea "God" is nothing more than the people's opium.

In that case the Christian can also not reject revolution?

Christian moral theology does not have to reject revolution in principle. But two things must be kept in mind. It is difficult to separate revolution from evolution; revolution should not mean violence.

But revolution includes the possibility of violence.

Yes, but we should not paint the idea of violence with too black colors. My definition is: There is revolution where a social group considerably modifies social relationships, without being able to appeal to rules that are honestly accepted in this society.

Once more: Is such a modification desirable when it includes violence?

To a certain extent, force is brought into play everywhere in the world, even in evolutions. If careful deliberation shows a reasonable relationship between more freedom and justice and the means required for these, then it may happen that even a violent revolution makes sense.

The Church, the official Church is still strongly tied to capitalism. But this is not a necessity that follows from the gospel.

There are certainly several kinds of economic systems that may, within certain limits, be accepted by Christians.

That smacks of neutrality in the Church. Should the Church also not be an innovating force for social changes?

Christians should be such an innovating force, even where the official Church rightly remains neutral. Christians themselves must develop their own conceptions about society.

Even when these conceptions contradict a papal encyclical?

This too does not have to be always unconditionally excluded. In the Catholic Church there is something like a built-in nonconformism against the system. When the pope does not define, I must do my own thinking.

Can a Christian be a Marxist?

What do you mean by "Marxist"? That must first be made clear before we can answer the question. It is evident that a Christian cannot embrace an ideology that opposes basic Christian values. But must I as a Christian, for instance, be opposed unconditionally to the public ownership of basic industry? The Council explicitly allows social and political solutions that may be debated among Christians. At any rate, in such matters nobody can appeal to the Church's authority for a solution.

Something that certain groups repeatedly have done in the past.

Of course. Some groups in society easily get a hearing. Yet despite all differences, the Christian faith is always shared by all.

Christmas means that God has victoriously and irreversibly inserted himself into the world and its history as absolute future. Their course can no longer go totally wrong. True, there is no straight development, but the end result is positive. The individual life passes through death into eternal life. In this optimism all disasters can be assimilated.

In part of the younger generation there emerges for the time being a spontaneous and unexpected return toward God and the gospel. The so-called Jesus movement. Is this a positive development or only a faddish form of flight from the world?

I cannot yet sufficiently evaluate the whole phenomenon. On the one hand, I fear that some are scared by the hard struggle with the world and run therefore to Jesus; on the other, I find the inspiration behind the movement splendid.

But the Church keeps her distance?
It is remarkable that even nowadays Jesus quite often seems to bring his liveliest ideas to people without the help of the Church.

Translated by Joseph Donceel, S.J.
Fordham University

9 · What Do I Mean When I Say: I Say Something?

Interview with Marietta Peitz and Karl Weich on West Germany's Channel 2 (ZDF), Mainz (April 4, 1971)

At the common synod of the Catholic dioceses in January of this year, in the Würz-burg cathedral, in the midst of a debate on procedual matters, a theological debate burst out. It showed clearly that, when Christians get together, although they profess the same faith, they hold quite divergent opinions. The same concepts cover contents that are by no means understood in the same way.
The conservative canon lawyer Heinrich Flatten, from Bonn, claimed that there was no room in the Church for Catholic Christians who say that they no longer be-lieve that Jesus Christ is Son of God and has risen from the dead, and deny the Virgin Birth and the indissolubility of marriage. In speaking this way, Flatten has practi-cally repeated an utterance of Cardinal Joseph Höffner of Cologne. But what is the use, so objects Karl Rahner, professor of dogmatic theology in Münster, what is the use of simply referring people to the doctrinal statements of the Church, of quickly solving today's problems by simply quoting some doctrinal statements? The Church's

dogmas too should be rethought ever anew and replaced in the total context of the life of today's people.

. . . The occasion for this short program and for the series that is to follow is the Würzburg synod. It reminded us that there are certain doctrines of faith with which we cannot tamper. I have said that this was quite obvious, but that I felt that many of these doctrines need a certain amount of rethinking, because it is not so clear what they really mean. Now this simple declaration has provoked, beside many positive reactions, some very violent protests too. Thus I read in a letter I received: "It is more than time that you began to hold your tongue. Otherwise, what you have been saying and writing for so many years may no longer be considered true. It would be too bad if the utterances of the mature man lost their importance because of senile behavior that smacks of puberty." And another one writes in connection with my Würzburg talk: "Well, you improvised, without notes, you were probably rather tired; otherwise, you would not have let your tongue run away with you. I suppose that you look back with regret upon this derailment, because a derailment it was."

Well, whether it was a derailment is the question that stands in the background of today's and of the following discussions. It cannot be denied that even in the domain of faith there are statements about which we can and should ask: What do I mean properly when I say this or that? So this basic question should be our topic today: that every human word and every human statement that we utter is understood only from out of a wider context. This applies also to the statements of our faith.

Father Rahner, can you perhaps give an example of what you mean?
Here is an extreme example. When I say, as a Catholic Christian and theologian, that there are three persons in God, I would almost bet my life that what normal Christians have in mind when they hear this is quite different from what they should think according to theology and the authentic doctrine of faith.

May I be allowed to suggest that you give us first a profane example before you bring up a theological one?
There are, of course, many statements that are very easy to understand, because the concrete context in which they are spoken is obvious for speaker and hearer. Thus when I say in the sauna that it is hot enough, another man who is there too will understand right away the words as I meant them. But when, for instance, I say that I am sad, then what is meant by sadness is a very

obscure thing. When a young child says: I am sad because mommy does not buy me some ice cream, this sadness means evidently something quite different from that of a woman who says: I am infinitely sad because my husband died in the war.

May I interrupt, Father Rahner, you say that we have to do here with two different degrees of sadness and that they must be seen in their context in order to understand that the mother's sadness is other than the child's. Yet is the sadness for the moment not the same for the child as for the woman, whether it refers to some ice cream, a deceased spouse, or a broken family? Is this not an existential sadness, whose reason we see only from without?

The child thinks that she is as unhappy because she has no idea of a deeper, more radical sadness, of a sadness that more intensely shakes up the whole person than the one she experiences at the moment. Later, however, she will discover that the tears she shed as a child are, after all, the expression of a very peripheral event in her life. We see this because the "blubbering" is followed very quickly by a smiling, happy face.

So I believe that in the profane domain too there are statements and words whose meaning is extraordinarily complex, that must therefore be more exactly interpreted, before we can say that we have understood them. There are, of course, things that belong, as it were, to the physical-biological domain of the person, words that are, as it were, signals within this biological domain. But words such as joy, sadness, justice, freedom, responsibility, love—all of them are words that we believe we understand very easily. In reality, they are words that open unexpected vistas when we begin to become more precisely aware of their meaning.

I might perhaps return again to the example of the child. The child says: I am sad. The mother says: I am sad. Yet what separates both of them is in reality a different experience, or a sum of experiences. When you say now: Happiness, friendship, love are wholly other things having an enormous background that we can hardly measure, you mean that here we simply get lost in a mystery of the person and this person's experience, both inexhaustible for us.

I mean really that there are ideas that basically evade every adequate definition. There may be in mathematics, perhaps also in physics—I am afraid that my knowledge of it is insufficient—concepts whose content can be set down with 100 percent accuracy, although even this, when we carefully read the theory of science (for instance, about the field of mathematics) does not seem to be 100 percent true. At any rate, there are many human concepts that refer to an experience that every person has, each in his or her own way, that can never be made fully conscious. Some perhaps in a very primitive way, others in a very profound way. Some as youngsters, others as old, prudent, mature persons who are not far from death. That is why such concepts—I am not speaking of theological concepts yet—are concepts about which we can always ask the simple question: What do I really mean when I say joy, peace, love, justice, responsibility, and so on?

Does the sum of human experiences produce some kind of "approximate value" for the truth of a word, if you will?

I would not simply say that a statement would automatically be false just because it does not explicate the entire sum of experience that may stand behind a word. But we are speaking now of a difficult and obscure question that is again becoming quite controversial among Catholic theologians.

May I once more return to the child. You say that she is sad, without really having any experience of sadness.

The child has experience, she is really sad. She cries, she may feel depressed. So she has a certain experience and she expresses it. But the mother uses the same word and lo, we tend to believe that it means the same thing. But in reality quite different experiences and very different contents of the same word may stand behind such statements.

Is the mother's word "truer"?

I would say that it contains more truth, deeper truth, hence deeper reality. The child is quite right, when she says that she is sad. She does not make a false statement. But she utters what we might call a thin, shallow, relatively empty statement.

If we apply this to the question from which we started, the Würzburg controversy, this means: If I simply repeat the traditional statements of faith, I am not yet sure that the fullness of later experience has entered into them.

Yes, naturally. Suppose you say God, Trinity, grace, love, eternity, survival after death, and a thousand other such theological words. What do people imagine under these words? That is the real problem. They may think that they have correctly understood a word. They may have correctly understood part of it, like the child, who has also correctly grasped part of sadness in the experience of her life. But the child has, as it were, not truly penetrated into the endless depth and width of such an idea. Something similar, even to a much greater extent, occurs naturally in theology. And that is why the simple conclusion that I draw from this is stubbornly to emphasize that in theology we should ever ask anew: What do I properly mean, when I say something with certain words?

Father Rahner, how do you go about this?

Now you are, of course, asking a question for which a general procedure is very difficult to provide, for the simple reason that the several concepts of which we are speaking are themselves so different. Thus freedom and responsibility are more familiar to people, their experience and their life, than when I speak of God, Trinity, grace, Holy Spirit, and so on. Hence, different theological words require naturally, as it were, different procedures. Yet one might mention a certain basic procedure that would prescribe this: In order to know what is meant by a certain theological word or statement, one should first go back to the original human experience that underlies the words,and then in a second step see the word in question in the total context of other theological utterances.

Are there words that do not have to be examined in this way. Are there, as it were, sacrosanct statements that may not be questioned?

No, I would say that the most fundamental statements or words must be investigated the most thoroughly. For example, there does not exist for Christian theology a more fundamental word than the word *God*. But whoever imagines that one has only to use this word to know at once exactly what is meant by it is quite wrong! One forgets the watchword: Reflect upon what you really mean when you say this or that! So there are no taboo words that may not be examined in this way.

Was this not the heart of your controversy in Würzburg?

I would not lightly accuse my highly esteemed opponents of this. But in the letters that I have received and that protest against my statement, it seems quite obvious to me that there are enough people and Christians among us who believe that as soon as one has uttered a certain statement all questions have been answered, so that such a statement, so clear to people, must be ruthlessly defended.

If I understand your correspondents correctly, they say that Professor Rahner does not respect a certain statement, therefore he destroys the thing.

That is precisely the misunderstanding to which I am exposed. I accept this statement. But at the same time, I tell not only the others but even myself that eventually I must find out much more precisely what is meant by this statement. Thus I accept the statement that a Christian, sacramental marriage is indissoluble. But when is marriage a Christian marriage? What does it presuppose? And so on. These are items that are not at once fully obvious; neither has official theology given them sufficient thought. Of course, these questions have been the object of much reflection. The whole of theology is always asking what is properly meant by this or that word: by indissoluble marriage, by Holy Spirit, by grace, by freedom, by responsibility, and so on. But the process of reflection is never and can never be at an end.

I can imagine somebody saying that when we give up this solid starting point of a traditional statement, such as, "you shall not dissolve marriage," or "God lives and exists in our life," we are at sea, we have no more certitude, the situation becomes unbearable.

First, to put it quite bluntly, I would say: If we are honest, all of us are at sea! Next I must add: There always are some unshaken certitudes that, at the same time, strangely enough turn questionable! Take a statement like the one that tells us to love our neighbor. This is undoubtedly a statement that requires continually a great amount of thought. Nevertheless, I do not consider it a statement about which I should expect that, as soon as I begin to think it over, I would conclude that it would be sheer folly to love one's neighbor.

In other words: We are at sea, yet we are quite sure that we will never drown.

Yes, I would say: We may be at sea, but there are always planks around to hold on to.

Do you believe, Father Rahner, that every person has an original religious experience? What does a person who claims to be an atheist do, for instance, with a statement such as Jesus is God?

We can, of course, not yet examine to what extent such single statements can be understood and assimilated. But basically I would say that deep down all persons have a religious experience. Whether they are aware of it, whether it is intense, whether they explicitly call it religious are quite other questions. To my mind, all those who have once had the experience of responsibility, of genuine love, of the inability to run away from their responsibility, have basically had a religious experience, whether they are aware of it or not.

Does this not amount to a very clever way of lumping people together? I mean:

Somebody experiences responsibility, absolute love, friendship, and then you come sneaking in and you say that this is religious; this person has had a religious experience.

I answer with an opposite question: Is it possible to face other people without in a certain sense interpreting them, rather than simply accepting their own self-interpretation as they offer it to us? To my mind, this does not happen. I necessarily interpret all people, I arrange them, if you want, in some way in the system of my own experience and basic convictions. I do not expect them to buy these from me on the spot. But will today's atheist not likewise claim, as he or she interprets me, that I am an old-fashioned man, tied down by traditional taboos? The atheist must do this if he or she is an atheist, on the one hand, and pays any attention to me, on the other. As I said, the atheist interprets me and I interpret the atheist to some extent, and we are absolutely unable to avoid it.

So interpreting—in our case, the interpretation of friendship, of love, of absolute responsibility as religious experience—means seeing a certain situation through one's own spectacles?

Yes, but I would claim: through spectacles through which we see what is really given.

But outside one's own head and eyes there is nothing to see with, so that the result may eventually be corrected?

Counterquestion: Does there exist in the world a court of appeals that can relieve a human being of the final interpretation of the meaning of existence? Second question: Can I forego an interpretation of the meaning of life simply because there is no such court of appeals? I would say: You definitely cannot do that, for the moment you live, by really loving and by really taking responsibility upon yourself, there you have already accepted—even if perhaps only in a very unreflective manner—a certain interpretation of the meaning of your life.

Is there nothing left then that may, from tradition, from history, from experience, from knowledge be considered certain?

First, I would say: My own interpretation, for which ultimately I alone am responsible, may nonetheless, at the same time, be backed up by the traditional interpretation of existence. When, for instance, I feel that Beethoven's Ninth Symphony is a magnificent artistic creation, I believe that I can also vindicate this evaluation myself. Quite another question is whether I would have reached it if society and tradition had not readied the way for me. But we must now return to our real theme: What do I mean when I say this or that? A first general answer to this question would be: Reduce these statements to an original religious experience. And view them at the same time in the context of the whole Christian faith. In this way, in our further conversations we might also take a few of these statements and inquire: What do I actually mean when I say this or that? Only by using this method will we find out if it works.

Translated by Joseph Donceel, S.J.
Fordham University

10 · What Do I Mean When I Say: God Speaks?

Interview with Marietta Peitz and Karl Weich on West Germany's Channel 2 (ZDF), Mainz (May 16, 1971)

We have received about two hundred letters since our last interview. On the one hand, a great number of them agreed with us; they tell us that a great vacuum has been filled and invite us to continue. Next comes a series of letters of a more general nature, about questions that do not come under our theme. Then come questions about our topic, developing it further. Also requests for copies of the talk. However, we also have a large pile of worried negative reactions. They refer especially to the statement: "In fact, all of us are at sea." Father Rahner.

I cannot, of course, repeat my whole last talk, of which this statement was but a short recapitulation. The only thing I want to make clear is that when I said: "In fact, all of us are at sea," I wanted after all only to say that every statement made by people presupposes that, in their own mind, many things are given and somehow understood of which they are not yet aware, to which they have not yet given any thought. Thus when one makes such a statement, one necessarily faces new questions. In this sense, as Christians and non-Christians, we may say that we are all at sea. That means that our efforts to understand how we live, what we think, what we are, are a task that never ends, that we must forever shoulder again.

What do I mean when I say: God speaks? That is the question, Father Rahner, that you have chosen as today's topic—the theme of revelation. Why have you chosen this problem from among so many important theological topics? Is it your "favorite theological hobby," if I may say so? Or is it because this speaking by God has become for today's person especially unintelligible, hard to grasp, perhaps even boring?

I would say that there are many reasons, and all of them cannot, of course, demonstrate that this was the topic we had to choose. One has to choose a topic out of an endless mass of them. If one thinks that this topic is certainly important, that it raises special difficulties for the modern mind, I feel that the choice is amply justified. Of course, one could say that, before one asks what is properly meant by God's revelation, one might also inquire: Is there anything like God? Do we have any kind of necessary relation with him? Is there necessarily in the human person an original experience of God, conscious or unconscious? Yet we may also, it seems to me, start with the topic we have chosen today.

What does revelation mean, Father Rahner?

I must first remark that by revelation we intend to understand that which the Christian religion, Christian theology understands by it. So we must naturally distinguish what we mean from a "natural" knowledge of God deriving from the world, as God's creature. Moreover, we mean something that is not identical with every conceivable experience of God. But we mean a real self-communication of God to humankind, in what we call the "words of the prophets," the "words of Scripture," the "doctrine of the Church." All these utterances present themselves with the claim that they are the word of God. We ask therefore how we must more precisely conceive of this revelation of God, so that it may still be a believable reality for us nowadays.

God speaks. Undoubtedly, this means something that comes to us, as it were, from God himself. Now what meaning should such an idea have for us? We cannot evade this question. A "speaking" God, who doesn't "click" for me, is really of no use.

Of course, when I know who is really meant by the word *God*, whom I have to think under this word, it is naturally obvious that his speaking has a meaning for me. Concretely, if a God speaks to me, who is for me the first origin and the ultimate reality, toward whom the whole history of the world is directed, it is evident that this has for me a fundamental meaning. The same obviousness results also from what Christianity understands explicitly as word of the self-revealing God. When God says that he gives himself to us with his own, infinite, eternal glory and reality; when God says that he himself will be our final end, an end for which the whole of created reality strives; when he says that he wishes to be the one who sanctifies us, who forgives, it is, of course, quite evident that, if God has really said this, it is of the utmost importance for our own life.

All of us have at some time during our religion classes heard that God speaks to a person, and the latter then comes to us as a messenger. Does the New Testament too oblige us to think of revelation in this way?

There exists a traditional image of revelation that we must call to mind, so that we may ask: (1) How does that image look? (2) What difficulties do we have when we try to make it our own? But then the question arises: Can one not—without denying that there does exist this personal revelation of God—get another idea of revelation, so that it may be easier for us today to accept what is meant? It seems to me that I may describe the traditional conception of revelation in the following way: In a certain sense, there is a profane world that is, as it were, self-contained with its nature and its activity. And then the living God arrives at some clearly set-off single point of its history, intervenes in this profane history, chooses certain individuals, who are then called prophets, and imparts certain statements to these prophets. The latter experience these statements as imparted to them by God. They pass them on to other people and finally they prove that they themselves have been sent by God through what we usually call miracles.

Summarizing we may say: Typical of the traditional idea of revelation is that it occurs only now and then, at some definite points in history. That is where we may wonder whether this is the way we have to think of a divine revelation that undoubtedly occurs.

And why not?

Several reasons militate against this way of conceiving revelation. I cannot now develop all of them in detail, yet I would like to say something about the difficulties that occur to the modern mind with regard to this conception of revelation.

First, one might point out, precisely as a Christian theologian, that in this conception grace in the strict sense, the grace of faith, is not required.

Father Rahner, excuse me. What is meant by the "grace of faith" in this context?
Well, Christian theology and the Christian doctrine of the Church say that people can believe only with a special help from God within themselves, in the depths of their conscience. That is called grace and without this grace authentic faith is impossible.

And to what extent is this grace of faith overlooked in the above conception?
It is overlooked because one may conceive of a divine revelation that needs no grace. The prophet is inspired by God; he makes known to us certain statements that God has put into him; he demonstrates them through what we call miracles. In this case, it is enough for me to listen to what the prophet says, and I have the right and the duty to accept as true what he says, simply on account of the miracles he has wrought.

Yet Christian doctrine says that the grace of faith is needed. But in the above conception one does not see for what purpose this grace is absolutely necessary.

Pardon me, if I interrupt you. Does this grace of faith exist also outside the Christian religion for the traditional conception as explained by you?
Yes, certainly. The Second Vatican Council has explicitly insisted that faith can exist —and faith in this truth revealed by God in Christianity—also outside Christianity and that God can communicate himself, as the Council put it, "in a way that he alone knows" to these persons so that they may accept God's message in faith. So it is impossible to deny that through such a faith imparted by God's grace he can save a person even outside what we call official, confessional, institutional Christianity.

Does this mean that there is revelation also outside Christian religion, and that this may be explained in the traditional doctrine?
In the traditional doctrine the thing becomes very difficult. It is impossible to know exactly from where revelation may come to the person who finds salvation outside Christianity. One explanation speaks of a primordial revelation made in paradise that would have been transmitted in some remarkable way. Others say that, by default of all other means, God may move a single individual to the assent of faith by means of some heavenly illumination.

We have now been speaking quite a while of the difficulties of the traditional familiar conception. How then do you envisage another conception?

May I first once more briefly point out a more fundamental difficulty of this traditional conception? Even when he claims that his statements are God's own words, the prophet has, of course, in his consciousness, nothing but human contents of consciousness. Naturally, he cannot compare the contents of his consciousness with what, if I may speak this way, is present in the thought of Almighty God. For of this divine knowledge he has only that which is given in human statements in his own consciousness. Hence derives a basic difficulty in this traditional conception, namely: How do these contents enter the prophet's consciousness at all?

But how are we to get out of these difficulties?

To my mind it is possible today, while starting from the traditional Christian doctrine of grace, to present a hypothetical interpretation of God's revelation that overcomes this conception of revelation as happening only now and then. Of course, there is no obligatory doctrine within Catholic theology about this topic. Every theologian constructs a system that he or she deems most acceptable, and at his or her own risk and peril. This goes without saying.

So we wonder now: How can we conceive of this?

I would say that what we call God's grace is primarily something that means basically the self-communication of God in the depth of the person's spiritual existence. Now this self-communication is not something that, in the course of human history, happens only here and there sporadically, in the so-called prophets. Or that happens perhaps only in those who listen to this word of the prophets. But it is something that is, as a matter of course, given always and everywhere to all human beings, whether they freely accept or reject it. I might say that God is the innermost dynamism of the world and of the person's spirit. Even where persons give it no thought, even when they cannot express it at all, the grace of this self-communication of God is, as a matter of course, given in their spiritual reality. And this is the most fundamental, the most original element of what we call revelation.

You just said "the grace of God's self-communication." Could you explain what you mean by this through some simple example?

Can you realize that all human beings, whether they are aware of it or are quite unable to tell it to themselves, possess an innermost ultimate dynamism of their spiritual existence? Can you realize that human beings, when they act, when they love, when they think correctly, when they search, when they inquire, when they act freely and responsibly, are ultimately intending the ineffable, unfathomable mystery that we call God? And when this innermost dynamism, inserted by God's self-communication in the midst of spiritual existence, is a dynamism toward God's immediacy—even when God is not only as it were the asymptotic point . . .

"Asymptotic point," Excuse me. What do you mean by this?
Do you know what a movement toward an end is? Now, when this end remains forever that which is never reached, but only that which, through its attraction, keeps the movement going, but in such a way that one never gets there, then we would have an asymptotic goal. Now, according to Christian revelation, God is not only the eternally distant One who puts the world in motion and keeps it moving. He is also the one who has made himself the end of the world, an end that can actually be reached in immediacy. And when he communicates himself in this way to the world, we have exactly that which Christianity means when it speaks of supernatural grace, of divinization of the world, of indwelling of the Holy Spirit, and so on.

As I try to follow you, I must say that I understand very well that God is present in all impulses and movements of this world and of the human spirit. But when I wish to speak of revelation, God should somewhere show himself, "make himself heard." How does he make himself heard? Can you explain this to us as clearly as possible?
We must, of course, make an important distinction here. There is, on the one hand, the experience of this innermost dynamism of our spirit, which we call God. That experience is a grace; it may be unconscious; it may never be able to reach consciousness. And on the other hand, there is our reflective awareness of this innermost communication of the spirit. We also meet such distinctions elsewhere. There is love, there is responsibility, there is freedom, and other experiences. And, there is reflective awareness of such spiritual realities, in which these original spiritual realities are put into words. I believe that we said a few things about this last time. Therefore, we may say: When and where this innermost self-communication of God, which is already revelation, is wholly and correctly reflected in consciousness, and is objectivated in words, there we have that which one calls—I might say—in the common (and correctly common) theological sense revelation. It has always a double component: the original self-communication of God and at the same time the reflective awareness of this original self-communication as it occurs in the history of humankind—of course not only individually, but also collectively.

Where in the model that you develop does Jesus of Nazareth belong for us Christians?

Before I can answer this question I must say that the reflective awareness of this original revealing self-communication of God is not the product of mere introversion. It occurs in concrete, historical, human experiences. People do not experience what love is, what responsibility is, by sitting and asking themselves in some psychological introspection: Who am I really? They make this experience of freedom, of responsibility, of love in concrete life, in their concrete activity, in their concrete historical reality. So when I ask: Where in their history do human beings make, with the absolute certitude of faith, the experience that God has actually promised himself to them in his grace, and that this self-pledging of God is irreversibly and victoriously given to humankind, then to this question a Christian answers: I make this experience in Jesus Christ, he who was crucified and rose from the dead. That is where I encounter the person in whose reality, in whose history, in whose actuality, in whose self-interpretation is really experienced that the innermost dynamism in me is really authentic, that it is reliable, that it is not a mere fiction of the mind. Therefore, in the concrete historical experience of Jesus Christ the innermost revelation of God's grace is experienced as undeniably certain and as irrevocable.

That means that in his destiny I read what is for me the word of God.

Yes, but a word of God that has already as a matter of course been addressed to me by what I call grace, so that by now historical experience and the innermost dynamism of human beings toward God meet each other and confirm each other. From this unity of the historical experience of Jesus Christ and of the innermost experience of grace emerges then what we call God's revelation accepted in faith in the full sense of the word.

Father Rahner, I have a few difficulties with Christ in your schema. Hitherto we heard only that God is in the world and speaks through humankind's history and experience. Yet the traditional conception holds that Christ comes from outside as a messenger in the world. Are you combining two schemata?

No, I do not have two schemata. For God's grace in the world, a grace that is always there, has a history, a real history. That means it has very definite and varying stages and strives for a final peak, in which this innermost dynamism of the world is historically realized. In that respect, Christ is, to my mind, the one who comes from the innermost center of the world and who is at the same time, the one in whom the innermost center of the world is experienced. In that respect, I can also, of course, ever again see him as the one who has been given to the world by the gift of God's grace. But undoubtedly, Christ is the one who is the fullness of time and also the fullness of revelation history. That is why he has a prehistory that is also already the history of God's grace.

That means, if I understand you correctly, that he is fully present in your schema, not only as prophet but also as redeemer.

Certainly, I have not been able to develop here in every respect that which the Christian believes about Jesus Christ. That would be too much for half an hour. Obviously I may ever say anew—I must say this—that for me as a Christian God's revelation to the world is given and made believable through the fact that I have the experience of Jesus Christ, that I find him in my history, and that I experience him as worthy of belief in his word and message.

Translated by Joseph Donceel, S.J.
Fordham University

11 · What Do I Mean When I Say: Jesus Is God?

Interview with Marietta Peitz and Klaus Breuning on West Germany's Channel 2 (ZDF), Mainz (September 19, 1971)

May I begin by interrupting you, Father Rahner? I believe that today you intend to treat a very central question of Christianity. If I have correctly understood the letters commenting on the last program, they seem occasionally to sniff a bit of heresy. May I ask you very clearly and distinctly what is the meaning of the topic for you about which you intend to speak today: What do I mean by Jesus is God?

When I say Jesus is God, I mean and believe quite exactly what this statement says and should say. Of course, as a Christian and a rational, thinking man, I must try to find out what is properly meant by the statement. When I do this and try to say what I understand by the statement, and, when, in so doing, I do not merely repeat the formulas, then, of course, I will necessarily utter things that may smack of heresy for a listener. That is a fate which one cannot avoid. It seems to me that, as long as one utters such an interpretation openly and honestly, within the Church, as long as one is not, as a result, openly or implicitly disowned by the magisterium of the Church, so long one has a right to be convinced that one's own interpretation and the official faith may co-exist in a meaningful and friendly way.

Does this mean, when you speak of the topic Jesus is God, you do not offer your own interpretation, but you try to interpret the traditional doctrine of the Church?
Of course, I try to interpret the traditional doctrine of the Church and nothing else. I do not want to "sell" my opinion, but to say what the Church teaches. But I can do this only by trying to explain this statement Jesus is God and to defend it against misunderstandings. And this, of course, is done unavoidably at my own risk and peril.

But before you make this decisive statement Jesus is God, you will first as a theologian, and also to prevent misunderstandings, as clearly or even more clearly have to say Jesus is man.
That goes without saying. It is impossible to understand correctly the statement Jesus is God unless one has grasped and is convinced that Jesus is a true, genuine, real man. What we call the humanity of Jesus is not merely a mannequin, is not merely a puppet, is not merely a costume in which Almightly God walks in the world. That is more or less, if I am not mistaken, how Goethe put it. No, this person Jesus is truly a man with body and soul, hence with a wholly created reality. He is a man who has a human, subjective consciousness, who stands with this subjective consciousness before the incomprehensibility of God, who stands actively as against this God, as is also the case with us. He is a man who prays, who stands undeniably before the question of the conformity of his human reality and of his human will with the will of God, who must be obedient or who is tempted, and so on.

But Jesus' God is the Old Testament God?
Certainly. It goes without saying that when Jesus speaks of God his Father, he means the God whom his listeners know from the Old Testament revelation

history of their people. Of course, about this God he tells new things, amazing things, if you will. He rids this Old Testament image of God of misunderstandings that may exist among his listeners. He comes up against identifying God and law, God and letter.

But he does not simply equate himself with this God. He does not say: I am Yahweh. Yet he says: "I and the Father are one." Or: "Whoever sees me, Philip, sees the Father also."

It is obvious that he does not identify himself with God in all respects. But, of course, one must first of all say that he does not identify himself with the one whom he calls his Father. That is precisely why later theological reflection, which starts, of course, already in the New Testament, has distinguished between God the Father and the Word of God. It has also, of course, spoken of the Holy Spirit. That is why later theology has spoken of three persons in one God, three persons with the one and same divine nature. It has therefore only tried to put together in a clear formulation, in a more logical unity, that, on the one hand, Jesus puts himself really at the side of God, without for this reason leaving the side on which we stand, and that, on the other hand, he has nevertheless distinguished himself from God the Father—his and our Father.

May we come back once more to the formulation that you have used to start with: "Jesus is first true man" and thoroughly real man? It seems to me that our generation can believe this. When I say: Jesus is man, yes. But: Jesus is God?

There is no doubt that in both statements, Jesus is man and Jesus is God, the word *is* should not be taken in exactly the same sense. This, of course—completely overlooking for the time being all more abstruse problems—constitutes the difficulty of this statement. When one says that Jesus is God, one understands, almost involuntarily, because of the narrowness, the limitations and intricacies of human language, this *is* in the same sense as when one says that Jesus is man. And that, of course, is wrong.

Father Rahner, what allows us to interpret Jesus is God differently from Jesus is man?

The way Jesus understood himself commands us to do so, and also the doctrine of the Church. The doctrine of the Church does not say that if you want to be a solidly believing Christian you must understand this *is* in the same sense as the *is* in the statement Jesus is man. The doctrine of the Church says that when we clearly think it through we are not to understand this *is* in the statement Jesus is God as we do in the statement Jesus is man.

For me this is a theological subtlety. To me as a lay theologian the interpretation Jesus is man looks like one that is very simple, easy to believe, if you want. For, as we all know, it can be historically demonstrated. But that Jesus is God becomes infinitely complicated, for the is used here is not identical with the is in the statement Jesus is man. That is what you say, Father Rahner?

I must first explain precisely, insofar as we have time for it, in what sense each *is* is to be understood. In the case Jesus is a man I have an *is* that establishes an absolute identity between subject and predicate. In the other case *is* formulated an assertion that intends to affirm not an identity, but a unity of the human reality with God. It is certainly impossible to doubt seriously that the Christian faith believes in an incomparable, unique unity of this man Jesus with God and thence determines its own relation to Jesus.

Nevertheless, disagreement remains: the problem of many young people who do not want to accept so simply that Jesus is God. They say: Jesus as man, as defender of the little people, Jesus as the one who has radically chosen for the destitute, for the mistreated, this Jesus we accept. This man impresses us, we are willing to follow him, to believe what he says, because he is worthy of belief. Must they then, if they want to be considered Christians, still have to say unconditionally that Jesus is God? Or cannot faith in Jesus the Son of God be already contained in this veneration, better, in the of Jesus?

To this complex question I should have to answer very extensively. It goes without saying that people may, in a fully Christian sense, believe in Jesus the Son of God even if they do not use the statement Jesus is God—simply because they do not understand it, because they wrongly interpret it and as a result rightly consider it an absurdity. On the other hand, one should point out that simply to honor Jesus as a man committed to the service of his fellow human beings does not imply that understanding of Jesus that fully does him justice. A truly Christian understanding of Jesus is undoubtedly given only when one is convinced that one's own relationship to God, the Absolute, the Infinite, the Unfathomable, the Holy One, is based on this Jesus of Nazareth.

The Jesus movement in America does not say that Jesus is one beside Mohammed or Buddha. But for them Jesus is the one, the only one. "Jesus is the one whom we listen to, whose word we accept, whose direction and whose commandment and whose Sermon on the Mount . . ."

With what right can Jesus claim for himself the interpretation that Christianity ascribes to him and to his reality? I must point out that this question does not belong to our topic. For the time being we are only asking ourselves what we mean when we say Jesus is God? Whether he can rightly make this claim for himself and what reasons speak for this are quite different questions. As for these young people, I would say: They profess Jesus Christ. They do not only consider him, as you said, as any kind of man, albeit a most exemplary one. Now, if they add: With Jesus Christ, through him and his reality, the ultimate radical meaning of my own life is given to me, assured for me, promised to me, then I would say that such faith in Jesus is practically that which the previous formulas wished to express. But I would also say to one of these young people: Your formulations are quite meaningful and correct, they can express the proper nature of your relationship to Christ quite correctly. Yet do not consider your formulations so absolute that you are allowed to reject the traditional formulas of Christianity. Try to understand tradition, try to grasp its correct sense; then you notice that your experience of Jesus in this radical sense, of course, coincides with the traditional Christian formulas.

Father Rahner, you say Jesus is man. That is understandable and relatively easy to see. But Jesus is God. What does this mean for you, what does it mean in the tradition of the Church?

We have already said that this *is* means a unity of the human reality with God. When we ask how this unity should be formulated more precisely, be explained, be articulated, then we may fall back upon the normal Christian traditional formulas, including those that the Church has defined: "hypostatic union," "unity of two natures," "the divine and the human nature in the one subject" or "hypostasis of the eternal Logos." We might speak of a "substantial unity between divinity and humanity in the person of the Logos," and so on.

But is all of this not mere speculation? True, they are splendid theological constructions, which have at some time been of help, when certain questions arose. But do we need these "descriptions of a hypostatic union" and whatever belongs to it? Do we really need them to make clear to a person what it means to believe in Jesus as God or as the Son of God? Can we not simply put it this way, in order to express the simple human experience of the divinity of Christ, of the uniqueness of Jesus?

It is obvious that we must translate these traditional formulas. That is precisely our task and the purpose of these discussions. But at the same time we must, as carefully as we can, see to it that we really get the sense and the meaning of these traditional formulas. When I understand and affirm the absolute and ultimate meaning of Jesus for my salvation, when I feel that my life is based upon him and his reality, when I know that there does not exist anybody else of this kind, that there is no foundation beyond the one he supplies, because in him God promises himself radically to me as my absolute future, then I have—that is at least my conviction—really translated the traditional formulas. And I cannot help believing that one can to some extent really understand these formulas.

Now you have spoken in a language that is human and understandable. Yet I do not know what is meant by "God promises himself radically to me as my absolute future." Does this mean my death, my life, even my resurrection?

Ms. Peitz, do you grant that God exists?

I hope I do, Father Rahner.

Can you get the idea that you have something to do with this God, that he has created you, that you cannot live your existence in its whole length and breadth without somewhere and somehow encountering this God?

But I do not find my whole painful search for God in theological speculations.

That is not necessary either. You can find God by patiently accepting death, by really loving your neighbor, without gaining anything from it. Then you experience that there exists, so to speak, an ultimate ground and abyss that is called God. And with him you really have to do. Now when this God says precisely in Jesus: I am the ground, the origin, the end, the purpose, your absolute future, and so on, and this not simply at some infinite distance, as exists indeed between God and us, but in absolute proximity, by bestowing upon you my own life, my own splendor and reality—what the New Testament calls the Spirit of God, then, I believe, you can understand what is meant by God's self-promise, a promise made precisely in Jesus Christ. For I obviously experience, search, hope in a God of this self-communication and absolute nearness. But would I, a wretched creature, doomed to die like a fly that lives for a day, a pitiful sinner—this too is true—have the courage really to believe, to hope, to admit that this God wants this absolute nearness to me, if I did not look up to Jesus, he who was crucified, descended into death and rose from the grave? That is why I experience in my history, to which Jesus too belongs, that he is what I described as the "absolute unsurpassable self-promise of God." In this way, it seems to me, if I understand Jesus in himself and for me, I have come back to the traditional formulas of Christianity. Likewise, I also know that—precisely because I have understood and am allowed to understand them in this way—I cannot spurn these traditional formulas as mere cobwebs or Greek speculations.

But this Jesus does not expect speculations from me but—if I accept him as described by you—he asks that I follow him, by doing what he has done. When talking of the Last Judgment he desires from me not well-defined acts of faith, but what I can do for the least of my brothers. So this is the criterion by which I may judge whether I am a Christian and whether I believe in Jesus.

Right. You are speaking of this radical living faith that is indeed demanded from me, that takes over my whole being, that is demanded even more than what theological speculation would demand from me. But when you become aware of this faith that you have realized in your life, when you express it in a basically clear assertion—something which after all is very important for a human being—you will say precisely: Jesus of Nazareth is the absolute, unsurpassable self-promise of God in absolute proximity. Or you say: Jesus is the Son of God. Or: In Jesus God is absolutely, radically present for me. That means: Jesus is God. Theory belongs to praxis itself, and even for a Marxist there exists no praxis—even though praxis may be the ultimate end—that does not have a theoretical element. That is why one should say: Love your neighbor, and, if you do that radically, you have already loved a hidden Jesus Christ, as Jesus explicitly demands in Matthew 25. Yet this does not forbid me to know what I am doing. Nor does it forbid me to know that, by loving Jesus in my neighbor, I have really encountered him. So when you fully accept that in every human being I encounter Jesus, then you have understood an assertion about Jesus that is so radical, so deep and wide, that means something quite different from some cheap rationalistic chatter, something which everybody can quite simply know and understand.

But more important than the assertion would be what follows from it?

I do not claim that everyone in the concrete situation can make his or her own all that I have said, simply because I have talked to them for fifteen minutes. I can only say: I hope, even more, I am convinced that this is basically possible. The basic possibility of an insight into one's faith says nothing yet about the concrete possibility of the single individual. I must leave this to God, to providence, to the good will of each person. True, I may "preach" to them about it. Whether this preaching reaches them goes beyond my power and my responsibility.

So there would be many possibilities to express one's faith when I say that Jesus is God?

Yes, there are many. But I would like to express them in the faith and in the community of those who believe in Jesus. Now this community has necessarily a common formulation. And it is still possible to make this common formulation one's own nowadays, when it is correctly understood. Of course, it may also be translated into other formulations.

Translated by Joseph Donceel, S.J.
Fordham University

12 · What Do I Mean When I Say: Life after Death?

Interview with Marietta Peitz and Klaus Breuning on West Germany's Channel 2 (ZDF), Mainz (February 20, 1972)

Today I would like to ask the really decisive question: Can we say anything at all about life after death? There is that famous "wall" and from behind that "wall" nobody has ever returned.
Before answering this question some thought should be given to the meaning of the expression "after death." I believe that we imagine something here that has nothing to do with reality.

If I remember correctly, we were told in the catechism that the body dies at the moment of death, that the soul goes on living and, at some time, on the last day the body revives and both are somehow united again. However, I find it hard to see how we can speak of eternal life at all before having first spoken of death. What we are facing time and again is this: A person dies, a person whom we love. What happens at this moment? Is this not the first important question?
It is. Yet at the same time, you have no end of trouble with this mental picture. . . .

I have the mental picture offered by the catechism. But let us stick to the question: Somebody dies and nobody knows what happens now. Somebody has "passed away" from me. What remains of him or her?

Well, if I have to answer this question, do I necessarily have to use these mental pictures? They have a meaning, to be sure, but after all they are only there to help.

Am I forced to fall back on ideas that start by considering body and soul as distinct entities? Next they explain that the soul survives and survives forever, into eternity. Comes a time—at the end of world history—when the body is finally reunited to the soul. Or may I get rid of all these mental pictures and simply say that I am, I have a responsibility and a life in freedom that cannot simply perish? Does this not imply the firm hope that in death I do not simply perish, although I cannot imagine this "life after death"?

You have that conviction. But the people mentioned above, from whom the beloved person has "passed away" have nothing for the time being. They stand before a corpse, a dead body that no longer speaks. In other words, they see only the meaninglessness of death. Perhaps we should once more clearly inquire: Father Rahner, you said this is precisely the point where we must start our discussion. But, as I said already, I have only what the catechism told me. Do you perhaps know more, Father Rahner?

No, I know less. I mean that I refuse, in what I hold from my faith about human finality to introduce a time that starts after death, that continues in some way, and that only supposes that something should occur in this time. For then I would face the difficulty of explaining why in this new stage I might not start to do something quite different from what I did in my former life! In that case, the whole idea of a judgment happening at the moment of death, the idea of the definitiveness of my eternity would become meaningless! In other words, a really intelligent Christian conviction rejects right away the question: How do things go on after death? and says instead: Things do not go on! With death, history, understood as the flow of time, is truly over. What follows is the definitiveness of human existence as decided on earth and in time.

Perhaps I may ask one more question? You say that finality occurs only in death. But I would rather consider death as the definitive unavoidable fate that every human being has to face: I see nothing anymore, I hear nothing anymore, I see only a dead person, a corpse, a void.

I counter with another question. If you have a correct Christian idea of this "life after death," should it not be obvious that you can no longer perceive anything? If you say: I must perceive something; like the spiritualists I ought to be able to remain in contact with these people—for, if they are still alive, they should be able to let us hear from them—then you imagine eternal life in a way in which it cannot exist! Really to experience within history the finality of this freedom-decision would mean that it is not yet definitive. Therefore I would say that the hope of definitiveness also includes my surrender of any attempt to perceive this finality empirically here in my still ongoing history, in my life.

I protest in this context against the term freedom-decision. *Death is the opposite of a freedom-decision of man. Death is fatality.*

Can a freedom-decision with its responsibility, with its will to posit something definitive be reconciled with the idea that all this has been erased and totally obliterated by what we call death? This question decides between those who believe in eternal life and those who do not.

If I understand you correctly you say that after death everything cannot be over.

Right. But that statement "it cannot be" is a statement of my hope, an assertion of my free existence. Therefore, we have to do with a statement that is freely made.

How do you come to this statement? Is this not the decisive question?

Because I experience freedom, responsibility, love, fidelity, and because in this experience, if I interpret it correctly, I cannot help saying: Here something is occurring that is definitive.

That is what Father Rahner says. But another person, who does some thinking too, would say: I experience love, I experience confidence and fidelity, without being able to imagine that there is anything beyond all this.

Can you love and while actually loving think of the beloved person as somebody who vanishes in death?

I know from experience that this person is one who will die someday. And love also accepts the end of this love, precisely through the death of this beloved person. Yet this love and something of this person would survive?

That is, of course, the fundamental decision. Does my reflection succeed in putting into words, in expressing this hope of definitiveness that is included in such decisions of my freedom, or does it not? This question can be answered only through empirical checking. One person says: No, I cannot derive anything of the kind from reflecting on my freedom-decision. And the other will say: Yes, I can do it. Yet even to those who claim that they fail I would say: Where you love, where you carry responsibility that is absolute, from which you cannot run away, that you cannot shake off, there deep down you realize the statement: Here definitiveness occurs which death cannot take away, but only make really definitive.

Does this mean then, Father Rahner, that one must believe in order to admit that after death something may happen? Is this a question of faith, or is it only some kind of intimation, some kind of inkling that there must be something somehow there?

Let me come back to what I said. You add nothing to the reality of your responsible existence when you say explicitly: We are the ones who cannot push ourselves into nothingness. In the very act of your existing—whether you are aware of it or not—is implicitly, necessarily, and unavoidably contained the statement: Through our freedom we become everlasting. If you want to call this an intimation, all right, call it that. Call it faith, if you want to. In either case it is—insofar, of course, as it consciously steers our life—a free decision, without which this statement does not exist. You must, of course, hold on to this statement, as it were, with the utmost strength of your existence. You may say, to be sure: "Good grief, who knows anything about it? I really don't care!" By so doing you do not really give up the reality in question, but only your own awareness of it. But what is properly meant here happens to your life, when you make decisions, when you love, and when you face the absolute question whether all of this makes any sense or is nonsense. From that question you cannot run away.

I wonder whether we get any help from knowing or from believing that Jesus Christ has died and risen from the dead. For, as far as we know, Jesus is the only one who has come back. Let me put it even more sharply. Hitherto we have spoken of death only as philosophers. But we have really not mentioned what we mean, as Christians, when we say "eternal life."

That is not simple. It might well be the case that this ultimate decision for an absolute meaning, which does not vanish into nothingness, has itself occurred in virtue of that Christian grace, of which we may then speak explicitly in Christian terms. What I have said does not have to be a merely philosophical thing. What is at stake in this decision is concrete life, in which, let us say for instance, I assume some ultimate responsibility. And that, whether we are aware of it or not, ultimately involves Christianity and grace.

So you have put it this way only to get across, even for those who do not believe in Christ and in his promise of eternal life, what is meant when we speak of life eternal.

Yes. For there are many "anonymous Christians" who do not know that, deep down, they are living from God's grace and the power of eternity. Of course, to come back to what was said above—all of this becomes much stronger, clearer, and more certain when I meet Jesus than if I had to rely only on the awareness of my own personal experience.

The words of Jesus, "Whoever believes in me possesses eternal life," might back up your way of thinking, that we have to do with something that does not start only after we have passed the threshold of death, but . . .
. . . is something that happens here in our life and does not perish through death.

This means that what we need first is faith, if I may interpret you this way as a Christian and a theologian? And also hope, I suppose.
Right. Both are required. There is no need to separate hope and faith. Faith is hopeful faith, else it would not be faith. And hope is believing hope, else there would be no hope.

Does that which you mentioned at first, the fact that we know about the definitiveness of responsibility, the definitiveness of love, not point more in the direction of hope? I am not quite certain that all these things are forever.
I would say that you have no certitude except through hope. When I really let go, when I dive, as it were, full of hope, into the mysteriousness of my existence, that hope is filled with light, with confidence, with assurance. The question no longer comes up: Do I now possess a certitude that needs no more hope? Of course not, since without hope I no longer possess this certitude. But in the act of trusting in the meaningfulness of life, I hope. And in this act I discover the inner meaningfulness and wisdom of such an attitude and activity. Exactly as with love. When we look at love from outside, it is a rather strange thing that we do not really understand. Only those who love understand that loving makes sense. That is also what happens here. Hope is not blind hope in the sense that, without reason, one ideologically takes something for granted. No, the principle of hope in definitiveness is, insofar as I freely take hold of it, one that contains within itself its inner light, reliability, and credibility.

And when I meet someone who feels unable to hope in this way, who considers death only a dreadful reality, what can I tell such a person?
I would start by saying: According to your theory, death should be quite obvious. Why then do you experience it as something shocking, as the ultimate absurdity of existence?

Because a death that occurs, for instance, in a traffic accident is meaningless. It simply does not make sense that a human being has disappeared.

But for these people meaninglessness is obvious; it's to be expected; it's nothing to get excited about. Why then do they in such a sudden "traffic accident" discover something so shocking, something against which one should protest? They do it because deep down and without being aware of it they use a standard by which death may rightly be considered meaningless and dreadful.

That means that deep down in themselves they would have opted for definitiveness. They were so shocked by this accident because they were unaware of this option!

They would be horrified because they are unwilling to admit this principle for which they opt. Should they admit it, their own life would look frightfully scandalous to them. If they did not have this principle of hope, they could not experience this life as a scandal. Because they experience it as a scandal, they reveal that they do not trust this hope. And now there is, in a certain sense, only one question left: For what do I ultimately opt? For the principle of hope, for which these shocking events are only temporary and relative? Or do I opt for the shocking absurdity of death, however and whenever it occurs, and say that the principle of hope is undoubtedly a false ideology of humankind?

If this is true, would it mean that deep down all human beings somehow harbor hope without having to know it?

Yes, without a doubt. But the question comes up then how they freely opt in the face of this unavoidable hope. For they might declare in an ultimate decision of their freedom: This hope that I cannot uproot from my heart is the greatest absurdity.

Considering everything provisional makes it impossible for me to attach great importance to my life. It is the fog, the opium that prevents me from attaching importance to this world's tasks. Might we not agree here too with Marx? I am not sure of it. I remember discussions between Garaudy and you, in which Garaudy was quite willing to attribute a meaning to life, as long as it lasts. But then, with death, the meaning vanishes. So that would not imply that, as long as it lasts, life is made meaningless on account of death! But Father Rahner says: No, I disagree.

Right, for I would say: I may at first conceive of a provisional meaningfulness. I may even live with it. But when I consider it absolutely and explicitly as merely provisional, that meaningfulness simply vanishes. This is, of course, a question that requires further reflection. At any rate, wherever one is "provisionally'' satisfied with a meaning that is unconsciously considered provisional, everything works well. But when such temporary meaningfulness is considered definitive, then nonsense and contradiction emerge. And everyone faces the question whether they are willing to be satisfied with this ultimate contradiction.

But have some Marxists—Garaudy, for instance—not accepted to live in this contradiction?

If one probes deeper down, a man like Garaudy, whom I esteem very highly, will, in his absolute commitment for an improvement of society and a more human future, do something different from what he consciously claims. He believes that life makes sense, deep down he believes that this sense is definitive. That is why he can commit himself absolutely, without having explicitly interpreted himself as Christian.

That is where, in Garaudy's name, I would demur and say: You trick me by attributing to me a Christianity or a principle of hope that I do not have.

Well, why can I not say that a man like Garaudy, whom you have mentioned, really hopes? Garaudy would certainly not deny this. A man like Garaudy will say that he must have that absolute hope, that he is not even allowed to give up that hope. In other words, he posits something absolute and definitive that is previous and superior to the admitted and perceived relativity of the partial ends.

Father Rahner, you are a Christian and a theologian, who hopes, who dies. How do you picture to yourself what may lie "beyond" for you? Or let us not speak of what you picture, but of what Father Rahner hopes?

I picture nothing for myself. What kind of picture would do? What I affirm as the definitive is at once affirmed as the absolutely incommensurable, which can in no way be compared with the present temporal existence. When I say that time ceases, when I say this whole space-and-time structure ceases . . .

That means, of their very nature, these realities cannot be pictured, because pictures cease to exist with my death.

I can wholly accept and endorse this statement, provided you do not imply that what I cannot picture does not exist.

I did not say that.

But people often understand this statement that way. When you say: I cannot imagine anything, I say yes to this statement. If then you conclude that the unimaginable is not real, I would contradict you. To put it another way: We say that the history of concrete people in their freedom and responsibility posits a definitiveness that does not stop with death. This is an abstract statement. I think this statement and, in doing so, I imagine nothing. Yet it means something that is true, it refers to a reality. Moreover, what I mean with this statement forbids me even to try to picture anything in my mind! Hence, this is not a case of being unable to put things more clearly. The topic itself excludes all possible images of the beyond. I can imagine an ongoing time; I cannot imagine an existence that is no longer ongoing; but I can undoubtedly think it.

But do I not need something that I may grasp, something to hold on to?
Sure. As soon as you are aware of the inexactness and the difficulties of your imagining, you may once more use it. In other words, I know and must keep in mind that I speak in images, in comparisons.

But I must ever anew destroy these images.
I must in some way use these images, always formulate them anew, modify them also, always in the awareness that they are inadequate and, ultimately, again and again shunt me over to sidetracks that lead nowhere.

So it is quite possible to construct acceptable images, provided one does not give them—whether they come from the catechism or from dogma—any absolute value.
Sure. Every theology must necessarily . . .

be left behind . . .
. . . work with images, and within these images we grasp in faith and hope reality itself, that is the freely wrought definitiveness of my existence, which was given to me in time but does not continue in time, but turns before and with God into the definitiveness of my history.

Translated by Joseph Donceel, S.J.
Fordham University

13 · Hans Küng and the Dispute over Papal Infallibility

Interview with the *Spiegel* editors Werner Harenberg and Peter Stähle, Hamburg (February 21, 1972)

Professor Rahner, in your opinion, the central thesis of Hans Küng's book on infallibility, that popes and councils are unable to pronounce infallible statements, is not Catholic. The Congregation for the Doctrine of the Faith, formerly the Holy Office, earlier still the Roman Inquisition, is directing a case against Küng. What judgment should they make, if they come to the same opinion?

First, let me explain that I have nothing to do with what is taking place between Rome and Küng. I know nothing about it.

But in Germany you have been active against Küng in two instances. You edited a book in which fifteen theologians sought to refute Küng. And is it not true that the position paper of the German bishops' conference regarding Küng's book was essentially authored by you?

The questions are distinct and require more precise wording. Regarding your first question, I am not ashamed to have written that Küng's central thesis is not Catholic. Küng maintains that even *ex cathedra* definitions of a pope can be in error. In doing so, he leaves the circle of inner-Catholic theological discussion. To my understanding of Catholic faith, there are certain opinions which cannot be surrendered; one of these is that there are teachings of popes and councils that are guaranteed free from error.

One often reads in papers like the Vatican's Observatore della Domenica: *If theologians like Rahner are against Küng, then he must have written something really dangerous and terrible.*

I strongly deplore such statements, even when made in a Vatican paper. It is most unfair, first to paint me as some kind of progressivist left-wing theologian and then to play me off against Küng. The Roman authorities will have to take seriously the other things I say with which they do not agree.

Many wonder how you could cooperate in any way with these proceedings, when you yourself had to suffer Roman censorship in 1951 when you were not allowed to publish a book about Mary's Assumption.

I am a member of the doctrinal commission of the German bishops' conference, and in this capacity I took part in drawing up the position paper which was approved and published by the bishops.

Doesn't it disturb you to be part of a theological debate and then sit on the bishops' doctrinal commission to judge Küng?
First, my cooperation up to this time has not harmed Küng. . . . Second, something like this is practically unavoidable. You cannot a priori forbid a theologian who serves as an adviser on an offical church commission from expressing his personal theological position in such a matter. Third, there is a difference between my serving on such a commission and my participating strictly speaking in a possible condemnation. In such a situation I would declare myself prejudiced.

How would the Roman proceedings conclude if the head of the doctrinal congregation was named Karl Rahner instead of Franjo Seper?
I cannot imagine that Rome would in any way excommunicate Küng. There is an exchange of views going on among theologians which Rome should not interrupt too quickly or abruptly.

But that is the Roman tradition.
It gives me grounds for hope that Rome has waited a year and a half in this case and not done anything. If Rome believes it has to do anything at all, I hope that it proceeds slowly, carefully, and in a way that is objective and fair in this matter.

And if the doctrinal congregation condemns Küng or his book?
Such measures are most improbable. Rome would have difficulty pronouncing a global condemnation in light of the pluralism in theology, which did not exist earlier, and also in light of the terrible but unavoidable differences in theological language.

There you seem quite close to Küng.
And with many others. But even if Rome would take a position in this case, the pope would not be teaching *ex cathedra.* Such a condemnation would not constitute a definition. Given the nature of the case, even an official condemnation of the book these days would have a provisional and not a definitive character, and would not essentially change the theological discussion in this question.

And so such a condemnation these days would mean almost nothing?
That is poorly worded. It would have the weight that it assigns itself: a declaration of the Roman teaching office that commands serious consideration and respect from theologians but does not close the discussion.

When would you regard an administrative action by the magisterium against a theologian as justified? In other words, where for you is the line that a Catholic theologian may not cross?
Where a theologian directly and simply denies and rejects a definitive declaration of the Church's magisterium, a pope or council. The question in this case is whether Küng has done so. Theologians disagree. And I do not think that my opinion should be the decisive one for Rome.

But you still believe that Küng denies such definitive declarations, such dogmas.
Yes, for the time being, I would say that, but with the various provisions made in my articles, to which I can only allude here. But other theologians, Walter Kasper at Tübingen, for example, have a view different from mine. Here the views of various Catholic theologians are divided.

Father Rahner, are there dogmas that you question? . . . in the sense that certain dogmas are quite meaningless to you? . . .
Dogmas have very differing degrees of importance. Of course, my faith in Jesus Christ means much more to me than the teaching of the First Vatican Council about the pope. The first is very important to me; the other is secondary, which is not to say it does not bind.

Küng has written critically regarding the last four dogmas, those about papal infallibility and primacy and those about Mary's Immaculate Conception and the Assumption. Would a Catholic theologian be free to say that these four dogmas are not necessary, that they are basically superfluous?
I am not ready to say that any of these dogmas is simply so mistaken as to merit being thrown on the rubbish heap of history. But under circumstances which would have to be spelled out in detail, I would be ready to admit that such explicit, official, papal definitions about them could have been omitted.

And why has no other theologian of note besides you and Küng said that?
Perhaps because no one has sufficiently thought it through. Before these dogmas were defined, there was discussion not only whether they were objectively correct but also whether it was opportune to define them. I am not bound by the decision regarding their opportuneness. If Pius XII had asked my opinion in 1950, I would have advised him against defining the dogma of the Assumption.

Is the fact that the Church existed nineteen hundred years without this dogma an indication that its place is on the lower rungs of the so-called hierarchy of truths?

You could say that. But that would not necessarily make it superfluous. To say that would be to have a basically unhistorical conception of Christian truth. Christian truth today cannot be what it was fifteen hundred years ago.

What are the practical consequences for a simple Catholic, when a dogma is low on the hierarchy of truths?
The fact that a particular statement is a dogma of the Catholic Church does not require every Catholic Christian to take a position regarding it in any positive way. . . . If Catholics come to me and say they cannot understand this or that or make any sense of it, I advise them not to reject it completely out of hand, for there are things in the world and in the realm of truth that are inaccessible to one personally. If you want to believe the basic truth of Christianity, you have the right not to worry about secondary matters in the hierarchy of truths and just let them be.

Would that mean that a religion teacher could remain silent about such secondary truths of faith?
Religion teachers today have the sacred responsibility and obligation to bring the basic and central teachings of Christianity to people as best they can. It does not matter if many secondary things elude them.

Why then all the commotion about Küng's book, since it deals with secondary matters? Is the dogma of infallibility secondary for theology but primary for church politics?
Here I share a concern of Küng's. In the praxis of the Catholic Church over the last hundred years, infallibility has been broadened to such an extent that it is no longer identical with the real meaning of the dogma. There has also developed in many ways an absolutist style of governing that is not identical with the nature of the Church. I have nothing against Küng when he fights on this front. On the contrary. But one could fight more effectively with better tactics, proceed more shrewdly, and have a better outlook for success.

Küng's statement, "If the pope wishes, he can do anything without the Church," has been regarded as scandalous, even un-Catholic. We believe Küng is right. You regard the statement as false.
There are Catholic theologians extremely close to Küng who also regard that statement as false. Moreover, the pope has never done such a thing.

And the encyclical Humanae Vitae, *in which Paul VI forbade the pill as a means of birth control?*

He did not make use of the supreme power accorded him by the First Vatican Council in this encyclical.

Certainly, he did not explicitly declare his prohibition of the pill was infallible. But he did make the declaration without the Church, even against the Church. The majority probably of the bishops, certainly of the priests, and most certainly of the laity think differently from the pope.

Much could be said about this, but we do not wish to repeat our *Spiegel* interview of 1968 (see pages 34–45 of this volume). According to Catholic understanding, it is not possible for a pope to make an *ex cathedra* definition without the Church.

A difficult area. On the one hand there is a dogma that says such definitions do not require the consent of the Church. On the other, you are saying now that the pope cannot make ex cathedra *decisions without the Church. Who can stop him?*

There are no clear juridical restraints.

Not only are there no clear juridical restraints, there are no restraints at all.

If the pope would come out and declare that there is no Holy Trinity, it would be clear that the pope is a heretic and is no longer pope.

Your example makes it too easy. Imagine instead that the pope would declare a definition that, at first glance, seems Catholic but is regarded as heretical by the majority of theologians and bishops. Who would declare that officially?

My God, we have nothing in the Catholic Church like the supreme court of the Federal Republic of Germany. We would have to see how it would be done, if something like that would occur. Essentially, it is the same situation as when someone determines that the pope is dead. The factual situation must be ascertained by someone other than the pope, and this factual situation also has considerable legal significance.

Physical death is easier to ascertain than. . .

It is also thoroughly conceivable that a pope would be insane.

That would be a spiritual death. But if the pope declared something heretical . . . who would determine that? According to the teaching of your Church, not even a council of all twenty-five hundred Catholic bishops would be in a position to do so.

I agree. These other bishops would not depose the pope but only determine that he is no longer pope. Just as they determine that a pope is dead, so they could determine that he is insane or heretical. There is no set procedure for such a thing, because it would have to be decided as a question of fact and not of formal law.

Why could it not be at least institutionalized that the pope would have to seek the consent of all the bishops before he defined a dogma? Pius XII did that before he defined Mary's Assumption.
That is not out of the question. . . . It is not only possible but desirable, I would say.

It's to be hoped that you won't get into the same trouble as Küng with such a statement. Isn't that conciliarism, making the pope dependent upon the consent of the bishops?
I am not making the pope legally dependent and thereby contradicting the teaching of Vatican I, but I am calling for a legal regulation of the cooperation between pope and bishops.

Catholic theologians defend infallibility by appealing to the supernatural help of the Holy Spirit, as if Pius XII's declaration of the Assumption in 1950 was the result of a higher protection by the Holy Spirit than his other decisions. Isn't this an appeal to miracles?
You don't need to imagine a special miraculous intervention. . . . Naturally, there are some pious Catholics who imagine the pope is inspired in a special way, but you don't need to equate the protection of the Holy Spirit with a psychological inspiration. The pope knows what the Church believes, he asks the other bishops, consults with theologians . . . and comes to a decision that a dogma can be proclaimed.

Let's imagine that the pope would announce on Wednesday that in the future a council will take place every two years and on Thursday would define a new dogma, that Mary is the Mother of the Church. Wouldn't you have to believe as a Catholic that the Holy Spirit was more present on Thursday, even though the Wednesday decision is much more important for the Church?
As a Catholic I need only to have greater certainty . . . that a completely wrong decision was not made. Nothing more.

You wrote in your book against Küng: "It is obvious that only someone convinced by faith that such a teaching office enjoys the assistance of the Holy Spirit can see it as something other than as an authoritarian-totalitarian system." Turning that around, does that mean that anyone who does not have this faith is free to consider the Church as authoritarian and totalitarian because of its claim to papal infallibility?

. . . Someone looking at this system and teaching office without believing in the assistance of the Holy Spirit could come to the conclusion that it is a totalitarian system, I admit. But one could come to the opposite opinion too. I would go so far as to say that an absolutely totalitarian system is not feasible in the Church or anywhere else.

Regarding the historicity of the dogma of infallibility, did it go back to the beginnings of the Church? Did Jesus know during his lifetime that after his death Peter would be infallible?

Obviously he did not know about it in such terms. Hypothetically, if I imagine reading the 1870 definition of the First Vatican Council to Jesus in his lifetime, he would probably have been amazed and not understood a thing about it in his empirical human consciousness.

Does that mean nothing for you, or a great deal? Certainly you must be able to trace the dogma of infallibility back to Jesus.

It is a difficult question, which cannot be answered in two sentences, how a Catholic theologian today must regard the origins of the Church and its truths as coming from Jesus. But the connection cannot simply be denied.

May a Catholic theologian today admit that that famous quotation "You are Peter and on this rock I will build my Church," was not spoken by the Jesus of history but was ascribed to him first after his death?

To be sure, but one must not immediately conclude that this quotation has nothing to do with Jesus. Regarding infallibility, Jesus considered his message about the reign of God pressing near as being invincible. I believe you can grant him that. And following from that, it can also be granted that he thought of the indefectibility and indestructibility of the Church and somehow of church office.

Many exegetes these days agree that Jesus was mistaken regarding the nearness of the reign of God. Like the Jehovah's Witnesses, he seems to have believed that it would begin in his lifetime or at least in his era.

That is the view of some, but naturally not all exegetes.

It is the view of many, if not most. Doesn't it disturb you that you want to establish infallibility on the basis of what could be called an error on Jesus' part?

You are oversimplifying. It is not so easy to say where there is an "error" in such things and where there is not. In any case, the real basic conviction of Jesus is true: With him the reign of God is pressing near, challenging and invincible. It is secondary for him and for us how he formulated that concretely in his lifetime.

Thank you, Professor Rahner, for this interview.

Translated by Ronald Modras
St. Louis University

14·Ten Years after the Beginning of the Second Vatican Council

Interview with Karl Wagner, editor of the *Münchener Katholischen Kirchenzeitung* (MKKZ), Munich (January 2 and 9, 1972)

   . . . In looking back at the Church these last ten years, one sees liturgical reform but hardly any progress in the renewal of religious devotion.

The whole liturgical reform will have the effect of really better prayer, compared to the old liturgy, when personal faith and love in community are given priority over liturgical rubrics. But we are not there yet. It's fine that there are several eucharistic prayers . . . in the Mass and that we have eliminated a lot of old accretions. I don't want to belittle or deny the importance of the liturgical reforms that we have had so far. I also don't believe that every theologian should compose new eucharistic prayers. . . . The basic problem, it seems to me, is still how can I carry out the liturgy from the center of my God-directed existence without a gap between liturgy and interior attitude. . . . That problem has still not been overcome.

You say not much can be done with liturgical rules (rubrics). What still needs to be done?
I don't believe that every priest in every situation and in every parish should be allowed complete freedom in liturgy. That would be worse than anything we had before or have now. But under certain circumstances couldn't creative liturgies be promoted for smaller groups? Rubrics and formulas exist for people, not the other way around. And nowhere is it written that the only liturgies that are theologically deep and beautifully expressed are those composed by Rome or bishops' conferences.

You speak about a gap between liturgy and everyday life. What do you think of the attempt many are making to bring everyday life into the liturgy?
The distance between liturgy and people's concrete life is simply too great. That does not mean that a primitive everyday mentality should dominate the liturgy. But it's quite clear that liturgical reform is still not ended and must continue, if you have to change into another person as soon as you enter a church, or if you can expect this only from people who are used to the schizophrenia and don't feel it.

Does this require a greater independence of local churches? Has anything in this regard changed since the Council?
The autonomy of local churches is still not a reality, apart from the secondary authority of bishops to grant dispensations and the use of the vernacular in the liturgy. This is too little independence for local churches to be fully responsible. . . .

. . . How do you see the situation in Germany?
We are at the beginning of the synod and do not know yet what trends are really alive. . . .

Will modern developments make the position of individual Christians more difficult?
Individual Christians used to expect the Church to provide them with general norms which would relieve them from making their own conscience decisions. The mainstream of Christians were morally regulated in an undifferentiated fashion. Now it is difficult, naturally, to refer people to their own consciences

and not offer concrete norms for behavior. What should you do with your possessions? How should you live your marriage? A Christian may no longer experience the radical challenge of Christianity or erroneously feel free of any moral obligations. Only after the present transition period will Catholics no longer expect church leaders to provide them with norms in every detail or believe that anything not expressly forbidden by the Church is therefore allowed. Even if factory owners are not asked in the confessional what they are doing with all their money, this must still be a worrisome question for them.

Christians are criticized today for their lack of social and political involvement. Isn't that ultimately due to a corresponding lack of spirituality?

Though there is a false privatizing of morality in the Church, there is also a false socializing of morality today as well. There are many young people for whom practically all morality is concentrated on or confined to social-critical involvement. But how they treat their parents, their girl friends or boy friends, whether they should learn to pray—these are far from their interest. But the two poles of human existence, God and neighbor, come together precisely at the point where involvement for society and one's neighbor disturbs our inner existence and drives us to God. . . . The two poles cannot be separated from one another or absorbed in one another. . . .

Liturgical reform has not yet reached its goal. But precisely today Christians want these necessary supports.

Every historical epoch in the Church has had its own onesidedness. There is even such a thing as a good onesidedness. There is a danger when everything is "on the one hand . . . but on the other hand" that everything is there but nothing works or goes right. Onesidedness . . . has never been so possible as today. We still have to get used to the pluralism that is resulting. But why shouldn't there be different forms of parish life and a pluralism in theology?

You once compared the efforts of the Council to uranium. You need many tons of it to get one ounce of radium, that is, faith, hope, and love. How do you see that relationship today?

When you look at all the meetings and discussions in the Church today, you get the frightening impression of a Church taken up with so many secondary matters. You wonder . . . if that is all necessary to achieve a little faith and hope in God, and love for God and neighbor. . . . This is what matters, nothing else. What an immense apparatus has been built up, self-propagating institutions and authorities, which forget in the end why they are there at all. . . .

Do you see the apparatus, the institutional Church, as still necessary?
. . . The apparatus is needed. But you sometimes get the impression that, in its efforts to maintain itself, the apparatus forgets its purpose. Its capacity to speak of ultimate things diminishes. . . . Maybe Christians don't need such a complicated ecclesiastical apparatus. . . . Maybe we should not be experiencing our Christian life merely as cult and indoctrination. Life itself must be liberated.

But the Church cannot be seen as an exclusive monopoly on salvation.
People can achieve the ultimate purpose of their existence outside the Church. The Church explicitly teaches that you can find salvation, without the Church as an intermediary, by following your conscience. That does not mean that you can win heaven with just good will and without that which is essential to Christian existence. The Council does not say people who do not know anything about Christ are saved because the "poor devils" couldn't help it. Rather, it presumes that they know God in a way that includes a genuine faith and a corresponding hope and love. If faith, hope, and love are something real and bring about an existential and religious experience, then Christians have to be able to talk about it with more excitement and enthusiasm than we clerics usually do. In this connection there is too much uranium and too little radium. There is no shortage of externals, but there is too little of that spirituality that the wonder of God's grace awakens in the innermost center of our concrete lives.

Is this where Christians today must "climb on board"?
Spirituality should not be seen as being alongside other obligations, separated from social involvement, or outside the rest of life. Then it would appear as a luxury for people who have time for it or are paid for it.

Do you see a chance here for evangelization?
We may not presume that what is really essential is accomplished only by the pastor with a lot of catechetical book learning. That would imply that God's grace is preceded by the pastor. That would be heresy. We must first free up the clogged-up wellsprings, "underground" in every person. But the metaphor limps. We don't need to lay pipelines in an arid desert in order to bring in water that no one takes from a central pumping station called the Church. We need to bring people to themselves and thereby to the grace and God that are already in them. Then they will realize that they have a natural

need to be with others who have made the same fantastic, lifesaving discovery of their innerselves and thus, with an eye to Jesus of Nazareth, constitute the Church.

Translated by Ronald Modras
St. Louis University

15 · The Future of the Church in Germany

Interview with Karl Wagner, editor of the *Münchener Katholischen Kirchenzeitung* (MKKZ), Munich (November 5, 1972)

There are numerous interpretations about the present situation of the Church. What do you see as most decisive?
We are experiencing in secular history today the end of an era marked by homogeneous culture and commonly held public opinion.... Christianity was taken for granted as part of that cultural situation. There are still remnants of this traditional Christianity that enjoy public acceptance even today. But they are remnants, characterized by an earlier situation that served as a "grace" for the times, a help toward Christian existence. We cannot count on this grace for the present or foreseeable future.

One often hears people speak with a certain resignation these days about the "little flock." Is that where our development is headed?
Our development is in the direction of a Church of believers who understand themselves as Christians by their free personal decision, join together with others who share their faith, naturally wish their children to come to the

same decision, and are thereby able to distance themselves from the attitudes and opinions of the world that surrounds them. In this sense we are at the beginning of a "little flock." It does no good to hold on anxiously to the remnants of a homogeneous profane Christian society. But this is not to say that the Church on its own should withdraw into this kind of little flock or submit to erosion with patient despair. Wherever possible, if they can be shown to be genuine, such remnants should be preserved. But this will not account for the future of the Church. To put it bluntly: In such a situation, the Church must have courage and take necessary risks so that out of this profane society new Christians will arise who become Christians out of inner conviction and do not simply remain so because they happen to have been born of Christian parents and don't mind paying their Church dues.

The reforms of the Council have already shown that, when the Church takes steps into the future, it risks losing some of its own members.
Today more than ever before there exists a kind of "lack of contemporaneity" whereby different groups within our Church are characterized by different educations, different milieus. There exists a great danger of an un-Christian polarization, which must be avoided and resisted. Christians must really treat their enemies more considerately than their friends. But for us sinful Christians it is usually the other way around. Time and again we forget that we are shortsighted, narrow-minded, and marked by the mentality of a certain era, and it does not matter whether that era is yesterday's or today's. Under certain circumstances the Church simply must have the courage to give up positions that it staked out for itself. . . . The hard question has to be asked, whether everyone has the ability to make the march into the future. . . .

That sounds harsh. Can you be more specific?
First, an example from another field. If the Church has only limited means at its disposal for its missionary activity, it is certainly permissible for most of its efforts to be directed to those people who will have greater historical significance for the future of the world, and thereby leave the other people to the grace of God, which is after all more powerful than the Church. From this standpoint, it can be more urgent to expend our energies in Japan than to evangelize the Eskimos. Similarly, one may legitimately seek to keep those and win those who have an inner relationship to the future now beginning over those who do not. . . . It can be more important for the Church to win one believer for tomorrow than to hold on to two believers from yesterday. God will save these others, even though they are disturbed by a future-oriented preaching

of the faith. Obviously, we should use all our efforts to avoid threatening these traditional believers and seek, so far as possible, to bring them along with us into the future of our ancient faith.

Much is being said these days about a new orientation of church office. At least in externals the image of the Church has been stamped by its officeholders. What about their future position?

There will always be offices in the Church. But in the future the authority of these officeholders, their concrete effectiveness and not only their theoretical claims, will be based more on the free consent of those without office. If I may make a comparison, the Church is like a chess club. Those who really carry the club are the members who know how to play chess well. The officers of the club, the "hierarchy," are necessary and significant insofar as they serve the players. So too in the Church officers are necessary and important, significant and therefore deserving of respect. But Christians who love, who give of themselves, who speak out prophetically—they are the ones who really constitute the ultimate nature of the Church.

What must the Church of the future be as a whole? What must it be concerned about?

The Church must be concerned about people, all people, not about itself. That is often said but it's still not the practice of the Church.... A group beset by difficulties, if it refuses to give up, is necessarily tempted to think only of itself and its own self-preservation. But here the witness committed to the Church is at stake. The Church's mission to all peoples does not mean that outside its visible confines there is no salvation. The winning of new Christians is not a matter of saving people who would otherwise be lost. Rather, it is a matter of winning over witnesses, who can be a sign to all of the grace of God at work everywhere in the world.

Translated by Ronald Modras
St. Louis University

Part II

SPIRITUALITY IN A PERIOD OF TRANSITION

INTERVIEWS 1973–1978

16 · That the Spirit Might Blow More Freely

Interview with Walter Ludin of the *Neue Züricher Nachrichten*, Zurich (June 9, 1973)

. . . How should the magisterium exercise its function of issuing a "clarifying word" in today's complex situation?

More than earlier we must have the courage to admit that the magisterium simply doesn't have a "clarifying word" at its disposal for every special case. We must explain to Christians why this is so. It's because basic principles needed for a particular question should be offered to people in a living way. For example, if I merely say that according to Denziger (number so and so) marriage is indissoluble, and then draw consequences from that which are perhaps not absolutely binding, then I've done something wrong. For I haven't explained in a living and intelligible way the basic meaning of indissolubility as it could be done today . . . .

. . . You wrote that the Church must have the courage to issue concrete directives; indeed, directly on sociopolitical questions too. When, as with us in Switzerland, church circles themselves take up the issue of arms exports, they meet with strong resistance.

We aren't yet accustomed to the "concrete directives" I have in mind. The average Christian has the false impression that the Church must either offer absolutely binding norms in the name of a moral-dogmatic Christianity, or remain quiet . . . .

For example, in a consumer society a priest surely can't say that anyone owning a Mercedes 300 is no longer a Christian. But priests or bishops too must manage to issue an imperative or an initiative to a certain lifestyle. Otherwise, the Church finds itself in the situation in which its theoretical principles become always more abstract and their applicability to concrete lives always more modest. All this presupposes that, on the one hand, such a directive will be taken seriously and, on the other, not wrongly understood as if it were an absolute norm of moral theology.

You say that these directives should be taken seriously. But in fact we always end up with the rebuke that theologians or priests or bishops are incompetent in political matters, since such matters are very complex and even demand too much from the specialists.

For the most part, the competency of specialists can only develop different abstract and theoretical models for acting and deciding. But in the end this never involves making the final political decision regarding the use of a particular model. So-called specialists can't determine specific goals. Take your example of forbidding arms exports: There are good and obvious reasons for one or the other decision. We can't arrive at a perfect decision. We must decide and soberly say: We'll set this and that problem aside for now. In spite of this, we will act in accordance with our basic convictions.

In comparison with the specialists, does the theologian have worthwhile ideas to contribute to the decision-making process?

Yes, surely. A secular person of a more pragmatic bent will never introduce the basic Christian ideal into the decision-making process: that in certain cases what is foolish can be the correct thing to do; that even in actual living the Christian can have something to do with the Sermon on the Mount. . . . The nonviolence of the Christian, despite all the folly that appears in it, is something that the Christian messenger must add to the reflections of the specialist in certain cases.

Doesn't it happen that whoever makes this contribution to politically factual issues as a theologian or preacher runs into stiff resistance from many people?

Yes, today we have to live with conflicts! Perhaps someone who objects to a sermon proposing that we forbid arms exports overlooks the opportunity for serious reflection the sermon brings to bear upon the decision-making one must deal with when one votes. If one decides against the preacher's suggestion, one must neither write the preacher off as a mortal enemy nor, as a Christian, necessarily have a bad conscience one's self.

Translated by William M. Thompson
Duquesne University

17 · The Pope, the Voices of Opposition, and the Holy Year

Interview with Erika Ahlbrecht-Meditz of Radio Saarland
Saarbrücken (December 9, 1973)

Professor Rahner, the pope has voiced the hope that the Holy Year might lead to a reconciliation of different groups within the Church. I think he is touching upon something which is a cause of concern to many believers. For many, it is new and unfamiliar that opposition and difference of opinion be voiced sharply, and at times polemically. I do not think, however, that opposition as such contradicts the true reality of the Church. What do you think?

Perhaps there are lamentable instances of opposition and confrontation in the Church that do threaten the final, fundamental convictions of Christianity and the Church. There are also loveless confrontations and disunity that are really harmful to the mission of the Church in and for the world. . . . To the extent that this really is the case, one could, of course, announce the Holy Year as a year of reconciliation, understanding, love, mutual listening, and so forth. On the other hand, where there is Catholic faith and an acknowledged institutional Church, it is simply not true that everyone will necessarily live in self-evident harmony. No! There must be and should be different directions in the Church. This difference of directions belongs to the very life of the Church. It is a necessary element of the dynamism of the Church into the future. To expect everything to be peaceful and everyone to be of the same opinion is no beautiful dream. It is an utter impossibility that no one ought seriously to desire.

One need not expect to get any further with the help of simplistic principles: here confrontation, there reconciliation. Rather, we must seek together rationally, calmly, and lovingly, and, as the case may be, one will be able to see what both sides really mean. If they can agree, then they ought to, allowing for a difference in approach or formulation. Indeed, one can consider such diversity as a positive richness in the Church. Perhaps in another case, one must really say no; here we must agree by coming to a decision one way or the other. Something like a decision in the Church naturally varies in character with respect to the particular questions. An agreement or decision in a properly doctrinal matter is something quite different from a decision regarding a pastoral-theological approach in a given situation or some point of Canon Law, and so forth. We always have the task to live with each other in unity, peace, and love, but it is self-evident that conflicts and differences of opinion are nonetheless necessary and useful.

111

You have said that opposition is undesirable when it questions the foundations of the faith, when it argues without love and when it treats its opponents without love. I think that this is just where the problem lies. Some think that in a given case the foundations of the faith are not endangered at all but that a question has been raised that can be discussed. The other side, however, thinks that something nonnegotiable has already been attacked. And often, when a matter is hotly, even polemically argued, opponents might feel what they interpret to be lovelessness, but in reality is not lovelessness at all, but a language perhaps not yet heard, but nonetheless appropriate to the matter.

With respect to unity or disuinity in the ultimate fundamental attitudes of Christian faith, one must first say quite soberly that there are, of course, no principles that one could so formulate that they would clearly and as a matter of course, much like the mechanics of a computer, identify precisely what is to be held on to and what can be given up. There are no such a priori principles which could so regulate concrete history that the history of the Church would proceed with absolutely no friction. Naturally one can argue whether, from a particular perspective or in a given point, something belongs to the fundamental, irrevocable convictions of the faith of the Church. In such situations we must listen to one another, speak with one another, and if you like, fight with one another. Both sides must attempt to convince each other from the mutually acknowledged fundamental convictions of faith, what is and what is not an acceptable further articulation of Christian faith. As a typical Catholic Christian, of course, I am convinced that in such questions, and in situations where it is necessarily required, a decision by the magisterium may be called for. Such a decision is not authoritarian, but certainly authoritative. As such, it must be respected by Christians, particularly by Catholic Christians, in the inner conviction that wherever the Church makes a definite decision with and through her magisterium, God's Spirit is also truly at work.

Now I would like to address a very concrete matter. I remind you of the controversy surrounding Hans Küng, his theses concerning infallibility and the problem concerning the "ecclesial magisterium." To many it appears that in questions central to Catholic self-understanding a particular theologian or a certain group of theologians gets into trouble with the Congregation of Faith. This Vatican administrative authority, composed of a random collection of theologians and church officials, then decides for the Church what is right and what is wrong. For many, the reasons for such decisions are unintelligible. It is difficult for the typical Catholic Christian to see why this group can speak definitively for us in such fundamental matters.

Of course, in the two examples you have just given it is clearly not the case that an absolutely, finally binding decision has been made. The dialogue, the discussion, the argument, and the confrontation continue on according to principles that the Church herself recognizes. For example, according to the orthodox self-understanding of the Church, the Congregation of the Faith in Rome cannot make definitive decisions. This does not mean that it is irrelevant for the typical Christian or that it is to be ignored. But acccording to the principles by which the magisterium functions, it does mean that one must acknowledge an authentic but certainly not a definitive relevance to such decisions.

What then is the role of the faith-instinct of the entire People of God that is so often mentioned in such controversies?

The question concerning the faith-instinct of the entire People of God is especially difficult in relation to its practicability in the formation of a magisterial decision. This does not mean that it is without significance. Rather, magisterial instances must constantly return to the faith-instinct of the entire People of God and take it into account in their decisions. If you then say that they fail to do this, that their manual-theology has made them narrow-minded and in the end totally indifferent to all other suggestions, I would say the following. On the one hand, it must be admitted that it can happen that too little consideration is given the faith-instinct of the entire People of God by the Roman authorities. But I am convinced, and I say this just as openly, that wherever an absolute decision is made by the magisterium, and if one understands and interprets such a decision correctly, an absolute discrepancy between the institutionally formulated magisterial decision and the faith-instinct of the entire People of God will not occur. Of course, this is a hope that must be verified time and time again in the history of the Spirit in the Church.

Do you think that good communication in the Church between the magisterium and the People of God as a whole presupposes some sort of structural anchoring?

Both Vatican I and Vatican II, for example, indicate that when the pope makes a decision based on his teaching authority, he must also employ the necessary human means to ensure that the decision is made appropriately and according to the spirit of the gospel and the faith of the Church. Of course, I also think that the concrete, human means, which the magisterium, according to official church teaching and conviction must employ, ought to be made more transparent. In a certain sense, they ought to be more precisely institutionalized and more clearly tangible in the public forum of the Church.

Translated by John R. Sachs, S.J.
Fairfield University

18 · Those Who Hope Will Not Die

Interview with Erika Ahlbrecht-Meditz of Radio Saarland, Saarbrücken
(April 14, 1974)

Professor Rahner, even for simple believers the report of Jesus' resurrection isn't a literal sort of thing. People don't take it to be the reporting of an historical, observable event. Even simple believers know that these reports are the testimonies of the first community. They're more confessional statements than descriptions of external facts. It strikes me, on the other hand, that the risen Christ is less important for many Christians than the Jesus who lived among us as one of us. In other words, for many Christians, and especially for those who take their Christianity very seriously, it is enough to see in Jesus a model or a lifestyle that can give meaning to their lives here and now. What meaning does the resurrection still have today?

You have raised two very different issues. First, the correct way of interpreting the reports of the so-called Easter appearances and the conviction they mean to convey, namely, that Jesus has been saved by God, is alive, and is hidden in God's own life. That's the first question. The second, and very different question, is whether the resurrection, which we confess in the Christian creed as the expectation for ourselves of full salvation in God, can still have meaning for people today in the living out of their lives. In relation to the first question let me say right off that it's not possible to dispose of it in two sentences. It's obvious that the conviction that Jesus is alive, that conviction which occurs in the meeting with the concrete Jesus of Nazareth and his death in the power of that reality we call the "Spirit of God," is something different, something more fundamental and basic than the individual reports of the appearances of the risen one.

Obviously, the content of the reports and its credibility and correct interpretation live from this last fundamental conviction. Right now I don't want to say more about this first question. Let me only suggest that people can discuss this issue in a way that allows them to be true to both the faith and historical realism. The difficulties involved here are not insuperable, even for the modern Christian, even if no one can prove or demonstrate the conviction about Jesus' lasting validity and permanence before God. The Christian doesn't require this sort of thing from the Easter reports since they are, in a certain way, derivative vis-à-vis this final, basic conviction. This relationship between the reports in the New Testament and the basic faith-conviction isn't reversible, even if we cannot separate them from each other. But there is also a kind of mutual bond between them. That's putting the matter rather abstractly and generally, but I'm afraid that it will have to do for the moment especially since the second question seems to be the more basic one.

Some important distinctions are necessary to answer the second question. You see, if someone lives life in a final and fundamental attitude of fidelity, of love, of surrender, of unconditional obedience to conscience, whether it is "useful" or not, I would call that person someone saved, someone who lives in the grace of God, whether or not that fundamental orientation comes to explicit conceptualization in the individual. People can declare their lack of interest in the question of life after death. But they too can do something on the level of fundamental choice that includes and actualizes in an implicit way what we Christians call "the resurrection of the dead" and "salvation with God forever." But—and let me emphasize this—the resurrection of the dead, eternal life, final life with God, the fruit of our history of freedom, is an inalienable faith-conviction of Christianity. It cannot and must not be surrendered, no matter how much trouble the so-called contemporary person has in trying to make sense of it.

Why should I live my life with absolute seriousness if all of it is pointed toward nothingness, if it will dissolve into emptiness? What reason do I have for thinking that my life is a matter of radical, absolute decision when at the end it will fall into a final nothingness? The Church's proclamation needs to speak in such a way that, while nothing is lost of the substance of the faith, contemporary people who listen to it can discover that they are living out in their own existence what the Church proclaims. If I were to ask, how do you relate to the dead of Auschwitz and Majdanek, and so forth, do you have the right and the courage to view these people as the fertilizer, so to speak, for a later future, or must you give an account of yourself before them? If I put it this way, perhaps a contemporary individual can understand more easily that we can't get off the hook simply by saying that death is the end of everything. If I were so to portray eternal life that the statement seems to be simply added from outside to the actual living out of life and seems to picture eternal life as simply a blissful continuation of things as they are, then, of course, an individual can't grasp how the message of Christianity articulates and addresses the most interior and personal core of human existence that he or she is perhaps living out already.

Don't you think that it is anxiety about this so-called substance of faith that prevents the Church's proclamation from making sense beyond the circle of believers?

Every institution suffers the temptation of viewing its official statements, once they are expressed, as realities all by themselves, without bringing them back to the original sources from which the convictions arose. Party programs can be driven into the ground this way—the same formulas are simply repeated endlessly. No one takes the trouble to ask time and again where this formulation comes from, where I can discover its truth in my own existence, how such a truth would come to be formed from the innermost center of my life again and again, even if I didn't have the official formulas. By not going back to the original understanding of existence that God's Spirit makes possible, the Church's proclamation becomes something positivistic, doctrinaire, and static. You get the impression that the formulas have precious little to do with real life. It's like trying to communicate to people a profound doctrine of the metaphysical and anthropological nature of love. The upshot of such talk can be that they find it impossible to link their own personal life-experience as loving persons with this complicated, doctrinaire structure. Yet a synthesis of the two *is* possible. Thus if the official proclaimers of the Church's teaching had the courage to relax, to be independent, as it were, of the Church's doctrine, and to seek in themselves where what they say officially is part of them, they would be able to express the point of the formulas in a much more vital, original way. I suspect that then very many listeners would discover that what the Church teaches about humanity, eternal life, and the resurrection of the dead really touches them.

To return to our topic once again, resurrection and eternal life: How would you say, in a nondoctrinaire and succinct way, what resurrection means?

There are many ways of saying this in formulas that people can resonate with. Let me put it here this way: If I confess that I cannot shirk responsibility for my life as the task of my freedom, while I let myself disappear, so to speak, between the stage curtains of history into the emptiness and nothingness—if I admit this much, I have admitted what we mean by "the immortality of the soul" and what we're basically talking about when we speak of "the resurrection of the dead."

Translated by Brian O. McDermott, S.J.
Weston School of Theology

19 · What Makes a Marriage Christian?

Interview with Winfried Römel for Radio Free Berlin (SFB) and
Southwest-German Radio (SWF), Baden-Baden (July 28, 1974)

*Professor Rahner, people have reflected in every age about love between man and
woman, about marriage. Much has been written about the way to understand what
marriage is, much that is beautiful and much that is bitter and hard. So, it is really
nothing new when we pose today the old questions about marriage, for instance,
about the meaning of sexuality, of bringing up children, about living together in a
family. These questions are also asked in the Church. But perhaps the Second Vatican
Council represents a break in this respect. You were a theologian at the Council. How
at that time did the discussion about marriage really develop?*

Well, I was not involved immediately in the declarations of the Council on
marriage. I believe that one should take into consideration that within the
Catholic Church even before the Second Vatican Council there was already
underway a very comprehensive discussion about the meaning and essence of
marriage, of sexuality. Under Pius XII, these discussions in fact led to reactions of the Church's magisterium. But though these reactions were not
always fortunate, they did not pose definitive doctrine and so did not interrupt entirely or hinder the discussion. Thus, in the Second Vatican Council
there already existed a mood among the theologians and among the bishops
that, in some respects at least, led to a new formulation about marriage in the
Church. The differences were not as fundamental as one is sometimes led to
believe. Yet, in things like this, subtle shifts in formulation and accent display
a more positive attitude with respect to marriage and have a great significance.
So finally the Second Vatican Council arrived at a reiteration of the sacramentality of marriage and also—this is obvious—at a pronouncement about the
already given content in the doctrine and tradition of the New Testament,
such as the indissolubility of a genuine sacramental marriage, rightly contracted from the human point of view. And in the process, there came about,
of course, a subtle change of emphasis: The theme of partnership has led to a
positive appreciation of the sexual as such.

This positive emphasis on the sexual was really something new, wasn't it?

Up to a certain point you can certainly say that. As we know, there exists in
the history of the theological interpretation of sexuality some really note-
worthy changes. These start with the Fathers of the Church, beginning with

Augustine and continuing through the Middle Ages and the post-Tridentine theology, right up until today. One can, to be sure, say that the Church has displayed rather frequently a hesitant, even distrustful attitude toward sexuality, not in its definitions but in its practical directives and in its teachings as presented by theologians in the past.

Where does this distrust come from? So much is written, so much nonsense precisely about this particular question. For example, the accusation is made against bishops and clergy: How can they make declarations regarding marriage, when they themselves are not married? How does it happen that this silly accusation comes up again and again?

Well, I would concede that in the teaching of the Church in the past there was much that was mistrustful, negative, defensive, and fearful. Thus, the carnal act, with its "concupiscence" (as it was called), was frequently interpreted as if it received its justification solely as a means of procreating human life. Of course, you can certainly say that, especially since Augustine, a certain Manichaean trend has entered into the Church's teaching on marriage. But I think, too, that when one has admitted this honestly and without inhibition, still one has also to pose the counterquestion: How in the world does this Manichaean tendency get into people's heads and hearts? I must tell you that at an earlier time, when I heard confessions, I often had the impression that these people who had a curiously broken relationship with their own sexuality in marriage did not get it from the doctrine of the Church. Rather, there were at work in these people more basic defensive reactions than merely external indoctrination from the Church. One could often say to such married people: This or that is thoroughly human and therefore also thoroughly Christian; therefore this has nothing at all to do with sin and similar matters. And nevertheless, one was not able to relieve them of such inhibitions, even though one taught them matters in an official capacity in the Church. So, when one now cries out, and with justification complains, that there were at work in the Church Manichaean and Platonic tendencies inimical to the flesh, one still has to ask further where these tendencies actually come from. Precisely when one says that they are influences from outside of Chrstianity that have nothing to do with the New Testament and with belief in God who is also the Creator of sexuality, then for that reason, one has to ask again: Where do these other villains come from which have so distorted and perturbed the Church with their mentality? Exactly because these are things from outside of Christianity, one has to explain precisely where they come from. And there, I think, it becomes evident that sexuality is not such a harmless thing after all. Because it touches the ultimate, deepest human reality as a whole, one is dealing with the entire problematic of the finitude, of the corruptibility of humanity. This is the reality that affects human sexuality. Its history in humankind has never been paradisiacal, even outside Christianity, and has often given rise to great human tragedies. In other words, one ought courageously and clearly to move away from old ecclesiastical and even some theological positions concerning sexuality, and that is what the Second Vatican Council has done. But one ought not to do it in a way that implies that, in earlier times, only a few clerical villains were at work making sexuality into a devil just because they themselves were shut off from it.

It is, of course, very important that people today be clearly aware that the Church does not reject sexuality but rather fully affirms it. But as you yourself said, that brings up new problems.

This problematic becomes clear in the writings of the popular press. They show that a superficial understanding of sexuality does not liberate men and women but submits them to new coercions.

Here the Church is looking for a new way, the way of marriage as partnership. This is a fashionable word in our society, partnership, *particularly when one speaks of the "partnership dimension of marriage." What does a theologian really understand about this when it is said that we must try to make concrete a partnership form of marriage today?*

Well, first of all, the theologian has to begin with the fact that the Old and New Testaments do not deny but fundamentally affirm that man and woman are two absolutely and equally valuable manifestations of the one human reality even when their differences are acknowledged.

That is a great statement. I find that beautiful, because behind these words really lies a great appreciation of the value of the human as such, and in the form of man and woman.

Of course, in earlier times woman was often subordinated in specific ways. Even in Saint Thomas Aquinas one finds ideas that come from ancient biology to the effect that woman is a man who didn't quite come off, even though he considers woman necessary in order that children be brought into the world. From that kind of thinking, to be sure, the Second Vatican Council has completely distanced itself. Man and woman are of equal value. And, with that the Church emphasizes—and does this in the service of a magnificent interpretation of the sexual—that man and woman are different. A leveling of this difference cannot be in the interest of marriage and cannot be in the interest of the happiness, the self-fulfillment, and self-realization of the individual human being. But, what this actually, concretely means in a particular social order—that man and woman are of equal worth yet are different—is a very difficult question to answer. I believe that one ought to do justice to former times in this regard, to their practices and attitudes, in a very sober way. There exists no absolute standard that is equally valid for all times concerning the specific relationship between man and woman in general and with respect to marriage in particular. But today we would say that if and insofar as equality exists between man and woman, or if it does not exist but is being sought, then it is also absolutely desirable and demanded for a Christian marriage that it conform here and now to this general societal status of man and woman, namely, that it should as much as possible be lived as a partnership. As for specific questions, for example, whether in a difference of opinion between a man and wife in a marriage, the last word of decision should lie with the man or whether in such a situation the partners are absolutely bound to continue discussion of their differences until they reach a consensus—these have to be individually resolved.

Or in working life. That is a very specific situation for many marriages. The man and woman are both working. They have children and that, of course, brings up many problems. A partnership marriage is, therefore, in no way a loosening up of the old form of marriage, as may frequently be thought, but it brings with it really new problems.

About this subject a theologian cannot really say anything. Those are questions of society, of free decisions that are socially changeable, not only by the individual but also by the society. About such things one can say very little from a basically theological point of view.

You told me that a Christian marriage should orient itself by motifs which are valid in today's society. This brings up immediately the question: How does a Christian marriage differ from a marriage, let us say, not conducted in a Christian way? Or to put the question another away: What is specifically Christian about a marriage? The synod of bishops in the Federal Republic of Germany is about to tackle this problem, and when one reads there what marriage means within an understanding of Christian faith, it all sounds very theoretical, not at all concrete. For example, "Christian marriage is a marriage lived in faith, love, hope; it is lived in the Christian community as the specific locus of redemption and salvation, and is gifted with the healing power of the Church." I believe that these words, at least at first glance, are very difficult to understand. How can you translate these words? What is Christian marriage?

Yes, first of all, one has to be clear that one can understand the word *Christian* as a predicate referring to the totality of human reality, that reality as it is meant by God to be one, whole, and complete reality. Or, one can understand Christian as the specific difference in distinction from the human. In the first sense, the word *Christian* comprehends everything that is genuinely, fully, and purely human. In the second sense, Christian is something specific to the human who is Christian. In that second case, in addition, one can and must furthermore distinguish between the question whether such a Christian character is a reality that has been lived from out of what we Christians call grace, the "self communication of God," or whether this humanity is lived in a fashion from out of grace that also produces a reflective Christian awareness. You see, the Second Vatican Council teaches expressly that very many people (one might even perhaps say hopefully, all people) find grace-filled, supernatural salvation—even when they are not Christians, or even when they think that they must be atheists—as long as they are faithful and true to the voice of their ultimate conscience. According to the Council, such people, who on the surface are not at all Christians, possess an anonymous, unreflected upon, unthematic but ultimate and fundamental basic Christian reality that is given them—grace and the unity with God in hoped for eternal life. And so there naturally exists, too, anonymous Christian marriage, precisely where two people love each other, are true to each other, and help each other in good times and in bad, where finally they really leave behind their own egoism in a true love of each other, and thus surrender self to the other. In such a situation, one finds a grace-filled event in the power of the grace of God. In other words, even where those partners are not baptized, there is to be found an anonymous Christian marriage. . . .

You used a beautiful phrase just now, that a Christian marriage is a "leaving behind of their own egoism" and wherever this "leaving behind of their own egoism" takes place, wherever two people love each other truly, then one can say broadly, here is a Christian marriage. Apparently there are very many people who are not conscious of it, but who nevertheless live such a Christian marriage.

Naturally, I have to add something right away so that I am not misunderstood. You see in Catholic theology one distinguishes, in respect to all the sacraments, between the sacramental sign (for example, baptism) and that which happens in it. Or, if one thinks, for example, of receiving the eucharistic bread, the laying on of hands of the bishop, or the marriage vows of baptized people before the Church. All of these signs are something other than the reality of grace signified by them, namely, the inner, existential condition of man supported by God. Now, because of that, it can be the fact in respect to all of the sacraments that the grace-filled reality is given without the sacramental sign. And so, too, the sacramental sign can be realized, without what is signified being actually realized in the one receiving the sacrament. It can happen, therefore, that the existential and grace-filled reality of a Christian marriage exists in two married persons, but that they have not received the sacramental sign of marriage. For it may be they are not Christians or have not given their marital consent before the Church. Or it can be that the sacramental sign is there but not this innermost reality of a God-sanctioned, grace-filled love, as it were, opened to the infinite. Now, I can say, of course, that Christian marriage is only present in the fullest sense when to the love of two marriage partners there is added the reality of grace and when at the same time, there is also present the sacramental sign.

Christian marriage, therefore, is the presupposition, as it were, for sacramental marriage? Could I put it that way?

The grace-filled unifying of two human beings in love is that which the sacrament seeks to effect and yet at the same time presupposes. The sacramental sign is, according to Catholic teaching, an effective sign; nevertheless, it is a sign whose effectiveness depends absolutely on the inner disposition, the inner making-real of the one who receives the sacrament. Thus, when this making-real is there, grace is already there—the grace signified by and made effective by the sacrament. This is a complicated matter, and we cannot really go into it fully here. But you are right when you say that the sacramental sign presupposes that inner love of the marriage partners that is supported by the grace of God and that frees them unto freedom and final validity. And so it should not be celebrated unless the presupposition is present. If you wanted to formulate this according to the catechism, you would have to say that two Christians have to be actually in the state of grace to receive the sacrament of marriage in the Church; and they have to enact the sacramental sign in the Church. In other words, if they want to effect the sacrament of marriage in the Church, and if they do not want to profane and desecrate the sacrament, they must have a most inner love supported by the Holy Spirit of God, and also a love one for the other.

Translated by James F. Bresnahan, S.J.
Northwestern University Medical School
with assistance from Heinz Kuehn
American College of Surgery

20 · Approaches to Theological Thinking

Interview with Albert Raffelt in a seminar at the University
of Freiburg in Breisgau (1974)

*Father Rahner, we would like to deal in our final conversation in this seminar on
your theology with a number of points that have become the object of some controversy
among contemporary thinkers. This should give us a sense of the breadth and the state
of contemporary theology, a theology that has been quite substantially influenced by
you. One often mentions in relation to you people like Heidegger and Maréchal. These
are thinkers by whom in some way you are supposed to have been influenced. References
to Bernhard Welte, on the other hand, are more rare, although you did study with him
in Freiburg. Is there any dependency between the two of you, for example, in regard to
Welte's Christology? It is said that your Christology has undergone a real change.*

I believe, first of all, that I had absolutely no contact with Bernhard Welte,
during my years of study at Freiburg (1934–36). He was at the time, as I recall, the secretary of Archbishop Gröber and was concerned with questions
about the theology of confirmation. Welte's article on Christology appeared
later in a collective work on Chalcedon.

When you ask me now what kind of mutual or onesided dependency existed
then, I have to say that I no longer know. In regard to Christology, I would
myself be interested to know whether, in fact, a certain change has taken place
in my views, a change, for example, from a speculative Logos-theology of the
Incarnation on the one hand to a Christology of ascent on the other. In the
former, the Incarnation is seen as the self-expression of God who, when he
wants to utter himself, can in a certain sense do it in no other way than precisely in the "grammar" of what is called a human being (because if not it
would be impossible to understand, unless a miracle were invoked, how someone as a Christian could seriously say that God became man). The latter
begins with the man Jesus who as "expression" of us and as "address" of God
is the one who is accepted, the guarantor of the success of the supernatural
transcendentality of humanity. It is a problem for me whether these successive
positions really go together. It is not impossible that a Christology of ascent
which has, as it were, its final point in the phrase "and the Word was made
flesh" could in a certain, careful sense be turned into the Logos-Christology as
it was developed in my early articles. I myself am not able, as already suggested, to offer any simple answer to this question.

But if I were to look at myself critically, then I would perhaps say that spec-

123

ulative courage was greater in the earlier than in the second period, insofar as one can distinguish such periods at all. One could perhaps affirm that in the beginning there was present an almost pantheistic speculative sweep stressing the unity of God and the world—this was, naturally, only "almost" pantheistic. In the second period, the initial question was: In looking at Jesus the crucified and risen one, can I believe that I am not falling into the absolute abyss of meaninglessness?

From a human and speculative point of view those are quite different starting points. Although there is no necessity that they ultimately contradict one another, I would not be ashamed if someone were to prove to me that they represent entirely different, originally unmediated and unreconciled approaches. Then I would say that it is precisely characteristic of my philosophy and theology that one does not stand at some kind of zero point from which everything can be manipulated or seen through or from which, as from a final and unified systematic starting point, one can speculate. But you want to ask questions and I don't want to give an improvised lecture. . . .

Let us turn to another aspect of your theology, to a perspective that will give us a chance to hear at the same time another critical voice. Where is the place for suffering, for the cross, for the passion of Jesus and for a theologia crucis *in this theology? Hans Urs von Balthasar has been critical of Karl Rahner precisely on this point.*

Perhaps I may begin by referring to the dissertation of Anselm Grün, O.S.B., on my theology of the cross. He claims—and this is, I believe, the basic thesis of his work—that I really have such a theology. This shows that from this point of view at any rate critics such as Hans Urs von Balthasar and Bert van der Heijden have been unjustified in rejecting my theology. I think that it is true to say that some people believe that a transcendental philosophical starting point automatically eliminates a theology of the cross. I would say, on the contrary, that a properly understood philosophy of transcendentality is one in which the human person is precisely the subject who opens onto an incomprehensibility that cannot be systematized. Let this be said against German idealism, and I don't know if it is not ultimately the same thing in Heidegger and *mutatis mutandis* in Husserl as well, and so on. Building on this I would say that it is death, real *death*, naturally not speculation about it in a lecture hall, that is the only real fulfillment of this fundamental structure of the human person. And I would affirm this also over against Eastern mysticism. All Buddhist indifference, all that leaving of self with body and soul that the great masters of Zen teach, is beautiful and right and important. It can, however, in the last analysis, be nothing more than a preliminary exercise of that letting or not letting go that is given in real death.

If now from this point of view you regard the death of Jesus as the exemplary achievement of such a real leap into the indeterminability of God and that not only in itself but also inasfar as we are concerned, then the question arises whether the Christian dogma of redemption can be formulated adequately from this starting point. In regard to all that I have written many more questions could be asked besides this one.

Given this fundamental clarification, I would like now to formulate the question about my soteriology in the following way: How do you see (in a certain demythologizing sense) the fundamental starting point for an understanding of the Christian theology of redemption, a starting point that to some degree is natural, normal, almost profane, and that we can really make our own? There is no need to include in the soteriological starting point the whole of the Logos-Incarnation theology. This can be developed out of it. If I can point to a human being in whom the radical and total leap has succeeded and who has truly arrived at his or her goal, and if that is, in fact, for me spiritually and interiorly comprehensible—for that naturally belongs to what I am saying—then I would claim that I have in its beginnings both a soteriology and a Christology.

One could of course argue against me that if this is the case the Incarnation could happen more than once. But then I would answer: "Dear scholastic theologian, you who come out of the Middle Ages, you least of all are able to prove that the Incarnation *can* only take place once." For my part I would say that it is nonsense to imagine and to think that it could take place several times. Perhaps I have even offered better reasons against such an idea than are ordinarily given. The uniqueness of Jesus is, of course, an ontological uniqueness, but it is so because it is a soteriological one, because it makes sense that this answer of God in his taking up of a human being in a way that we can grasp can only happen once in history. And that is why there is only the one Christ. All that is not unique to him, however, takes place in all human beings . . . .

If you wanted, as it were, to give me some hints in regard to Christology, you would have to begin with my somewhat rationalistic and antimythological feeling. This is a feeling that I have when I see that in popular devotion and in average textbook theology people make the incarnate Word not the peak of the world of grace but a new level altogether, some kind of "higher closeness" between God and the world. I regard this view as mythological. I do not see why, moreover, one cannot affirm and maintain what is true and authentic in our dogmatically binding Christology without having recourse to such mythological notions.

Hugon, a scholastic theologian of the twenties in Rome, posed, if I recall correctly, the following question: "If you had to choose between Incarnation and grace or if you had to allow the human reality of Jesus to choose between the two, which would you favor?" The average Christian would certainly opt for the hypostatic union. Even the scholastic theologian, however, would answer: "No, no! Of what benefit would the hypostatic union be to the man Jesus if he were not in this way united to God as we are in the beatific vision and in grace?" To put it another way, the divinization of the world through the Spirit of God is humanly and speculatively the more fundamental basic conception for Christianity, out of which the Incarnation and soteriology arise as an inner moment. This is so because the divinization of the world must manifest itself in a historical way and must come in its history to an irreversible point. Clearly, once one has arrived at the Incarnation and soteriology in this manner, then the divinization of the world in the Spirit of God (if on whatever grounds I presuppose it as given) can be "deduced" from them or seen as their consequence. But in terms of the realities themselves, one must finally say: I hope because and insofar as I hope for the divinization of the world. And I would like to add: I can believe in an Incarnation as thinkable in my transcendental "arrogance" and as experienced in my hopes. Naturally, there has to be brought into this faith in the Incarnation all that is included in historical revelation. Only then do I think that faith in the Incarnation (1) has no mythological element in it and (2) implies or includes those elements of Catholic Christology that are truly binding.

But let us turn once again to the theology of the cross. If I were now to add anything over and above the reference already made to a basic conception of death, then I would have to know more precisely the nature of the inadequacy of my position. If I wanted to launch a counterattack, I would say that there is a modern tendency (I don't want to say a theory but at least a tendency) to develop a theology of the death of God that, in the last analysis, seems to me to be gnostic. One can find this in Hans Urs von Balthasar and in Adrienne von Speyr, although naturally much more marked in her than in him. It also appears in an independent form in Moltmann. To put it crudely, it does not help me to escape from my mess and mix-up and despair if God is in the same predicament. I know of course and I have emphasized that the classical teaching on the Incarnation and the theology of the hypostatic union include and must include, even while avoiding Patripassianism (a suffering and dying God the Father), a meaningful and serious statement to the effect that *God* died. I have no intention of denying or obfuscating this. But on the other hand, it is for me a source of consolation to realize that God, when and insofar as he entered into this history as into his own, did it in a different way than I did. From the beginning I am locked into its horribleness while God—if this word continues to have any meaning at all—is in a true and authentic and consoling sense the God who does not suffer, the immutable God, and so on. In Molt-mann and others I sense a theology of absolute paradox, of Patripassianism, perhaps even of a Schelling-like projection into God of division, conflict, god-lessness, and death. To this I would say first of all: What do we know then so precisely about God? And second, I would ask: What use would that be to me as consolation in the true sense of the word? Here one would have to take a closer look at that theology of the cross that, perhaps rightly, finds mine inade-quate, in order to see whether such a theology is correct and whether it is binding for Christians. (Perhaps it is possible to be an orthodox Nestorian or an orthodox Monophysite. If this were the case, then I would prefer to be an orthodox Nestorian.)

To what degree can one say that Jesus brought about redemption if what we mean by redemption was already present before him in the whole of human history?

When you examine the New Testament you discover two types of state-ments that seem almost to contradict one another. In John it says, "The [Ho-ly] Spirit had not yet come because Jesus was not yet glorified" (John 7:39b). On the other hand, we find the basic notion of a universal activity of the Spirit as the inner finalizing principle of the world. We have one teaching in regard to faith that is independent of the immediate message about Jesus and another that seems to say that salvation is only possible through faith in the crucified and risen one. In the tradition of the Church we also have the notion that pri-or moments in the history of salvation, for example and in a particular way, the case of Mary, happened by anticipating the merits of Christ.

You can conceive of the world and its history as if gracious and saving inter-ventions of God continually descend upon it from above, or you can think of it in such a way that the self-communicating God is its innermost heart. It is because God can first of all communicate himself to what is not-God that he is the one who can create at all what is other than himself. And if you were to say that the world is finalized and made dynamic by the intimate self-commu-nication of God to it, then you have from the very beginning a conception of history that involves a universal and supernatural revelation. God here is seen as the one who creates what is other than himself in order precisely to com-municate himself to it. In this view the history of revelation and the history of the world, while not simply identical, are always and everywhere co-existent. The history of revelation is naturally co-existent too with the history of salvation. That, of course, even if it is ordinarily not stated, is something every theologian must say.

You need only look at Vatican II's Dogmatic Constitution on Divine Revelation. The chapter on revelation begins by affirming that something revealed was communicated by God to our first parents. Then comes the leap of two million years to Abraham. What came in between is covered by divine providence. What precisely that means in this context is not made clear.

If you assume that history from the beginning is rendered dynamic through grace and finalized through the self-communication of God in the direction of glory and the beatific vision, then the question naturally arises in what sense in regard to any particular point, be it the Incarnation of Christ, the cross or whatever, can I say that everything, both what comes later and what came earlier, happens through, in, and on account of Christ. First, one has to realize, and scholastic theologians know this although they then forget it in the end, that the saving will of God in our regard is primarily not the result but the cause of the cross of Christ, preceding both the cross and the whole Christ event. He loved us and *therefore* sent his son to us (see John 3:16). The popular conception that presupposes a violently angry God who then in some strange way is reconciled through the cross of Christ, a God who would not himself therefore have been the free and unconditioned cause of redemption, is plain and simple nonsense. Of course, I must be able to say that I am redeemed through Christ, although Christ himself is the consequence, the effect and not the cause of the saving will that is (and insofar as it is) referred to me. One would have to develop here a category of causality that would perhaps be clearer than it is in our average soteriology. If and insofar as this history of salvation as supernaturally finalized and rendered dynamic necessarily tends to the Christ event as its historical and historically irreversible manifestation, then I can also understand such an event as the cause of the history of salvation. The notion of causality here is not the usual one and needs to be clarified more than I am able to do right now. This, however, is certainly the direction in which it is to be done. The manifestation in which what is being manifested comes to its own fulfillment and definitiveness can rightly be conceived as the cause of what is being manifested.

Here one might bring into consideration what I have said about the real symbol.[1] You perhaps remember a saying of Pascal to the effect that when you make a polite bow to someone and really mean it, then that is not simply a consequence and subsequent announcement of your respect for this person

---

1. "The Theology of the Symbol," *Theological Investigations IV*, tr. Kevin Smyth (Baltimore: Helicon, 1966), pp. 221–52.

but rather a physical, historical manifestation in and through which that respect is posited and realized. This is so even though the act remains distinct from respect itself.

The same problem that exists in soteriology also exists in sacramental theology. One cannot deny that unbaptized children are in heaven. What then is the meaning of baptism? If you say that it announces and makes manifest in the community what is already taking place, that is fine and right. You leave yourself open to the objection, however, that if it is just a proclamation then it is not important for the very existence of what is being proclaimed, in this case the saving action of God in regard to this child. But then you end up with an extrinsic concept of the symbolic character of the sacraments that fails to do justice to the Church teaching that sacraments are *efficient* signs.

In other words, you must have a concept according to which the effect, if one can put it this way, can be in a meaningful way at the same time a cause. In concrete and existential life we know the meaning of this, but we find it very difficult to apply it to the realities about which we are speaking. Your bow, a simple change in the spinal column, is in itself nothing existential. And yet it is possible that what is being symbolized only truly happens under this sign and through this symbolic action. Here, naturally, one would need to develop the incipient sacramentality of human existence itself. Then the sacraments of the Church could be understood as concrete ecclesial expressions of this fundamental sacramentality, and thus the universality of salvation could be reconciled with the particularity of the sacraments without at the same time denying their effectiveness. This of course presupposes that this effectiveness itself is not misunderstood. In a similar way, one would have to reconcile the universality of the saving will of God who in his Spirit is everywhere the inner dynamism of world history—everywhere, that is, where human existence is being realized—with the particularity of the historical event of Jesus. From this point one could perhaps develop a further theology of Christian consolation in the face of the massive particularity of Christianity in the world and in the history of the world as an answer to the question why, under certain circumstances, it can be not only allowed by God's providence but even willed by God that many, or even the majority of humankind, have no immediate verbalized and institutionalized relationship to Jesus Christ; and that in spite of this they cannot simply dispense themselves from it.

What is the fundamental affirmation of your theology and how would you formulate it in preaching to average people?

Let me begin by asking a preliminary question. How does it happen that I who don't understand how a television set really works am still able to use one? Here we have a contrast between an ability to deal with something that is important for me and a reality that I don't understand.

In theology today there is a trend to greater abstraction. I can no longer say that God is enthroned above in the *caelum empyreum* understanding this latter as a quite specific and final layer of the heavenly sphere that surrounds the world. There too sits Jesus Christ for he ascended above all the heavens. Suarez still struggled with the question whether Jesus must be in the *caelum empyreum* because outside of it there is no place, or whether he has to sit above it because he is *above* all heavens. This was all understood quite literally in terms of Aristotelian cosmology. It is no longer possible to think this way today.

When doubts are raised whether my conception of the resurrection of the flesh is sufficiently Christian because I say that it is nothing other than the absolute fulfillment and the salvation of the concrete human person, I cannot see what more my critic can imagine in regard to the resurrection. If he does, then he runs into all kinds of problems, as for example, whether in heaven people still eat, or what kind of hairstyle they have, or whether they are tall or short, fat or thin, or whether, as Origen is supposed to have thought, they are all transformed into round balls as the form in which extended bodies achieve their fulfillment. If you are not willing to deal with this kind of question, then theological language has to become more abstract than it was.

Are there then ways of speaking in a truly theological manner and yet of being immediately understood? Yes, such possibilities clearly exist. I can certainly make the resurrection comprehensible to the average person.

We will not be sitting on cold clouds and singing alleluia. That would become boring after a while, and cold feet are really not pleasant. I cannot therefore "imagine" heaven in this way. Let us think for a moment about "enlightened theologians" who probably have little interest in the Assumption of the Mother of God—although it is a very proper and good thing—and ask them what Jesus might have done with his body after the resurrection if there were no "address" in heaven, nothing corporeal to which it might be related. Thus, it is to be taken for granted that those who were saved before Jesus are now in heaven, in fulfillment, with body and soul. It is equally obvious that this fulfillment in our case takes place at death. Heaven is not a "salad" made up, on the one hand, of those who have already experienced the bodily resurrection and of "fluttering" souls on the other. To "imagine" this, however, is, of course, impossible.

If someone says: I will get there, I will be saved, and in doing so does not distinguish, or rather while distinguishing does not separate what are ordinarily called body and soul, then I would say that that person believes in the resurrection. This presupposes, of course, as Paul put it, that they truly hold in their heart what they confess with their lips. What this means is that one can still speak about the resurrection in preaching. The point of this example is to suggest that there are bridges and translation possibilities between theological statements that have necessarily become more abstract and the language of preaching.

But is there not also another relationship between these two elements that might be analogous to my use of a television set? There are popular writings today about the physics of all this, but I don't understand them either. And yet I can turn on the radio. Are not both these different approaches reflected in the relationship between theology and preaching, and is there not in addition a strange interference between the two?

At this point the theology of the sacraments comes in again, although in a quite different way. I say, for example, that I want to stand in a community of faith with Pope Paul VI and with the bishops. How does one determine that that is the case? We all pray the same *credo*, of course, but how do I know that with the same formula Paul VI and I both have the same thing in mind? When you say, "March! Out this door!" and the person spoken to goes out the door, then you have a verification that your words were understood. But how can one determine agreement at the level of consciousness? There is surely no simple answer to this question. Various components are involved, and they need to be analyzed for themselves and then synthesized. But I would say in regard to our issue that it is significant for me that both of us were baptized and that both of us take part in the same Eucharist no matter what in fact we might, at our own peril, think of it.

Things like these are part of this question about the tension between theology and preaching. When pious and orthodox Christians say on occasion that everything in theology used to be clear and that now it is all confused, they are not always wrong, although they are about 60 percent of the time. Why? Earlier they heard a formula; because they became accustomed to it they thought they understood it. Today one might hear three different formulations; because these don't seem at first hearing to agree with one another, people think they don't understand anything. Perhaps, however, they really understand more today than formerly.

I would like to ask you about the relationship of transcendental philosophy and theology to history and historicity.

Authentic transcendental knowledge includes a knowledge of the historicity of human existence and therefore also a knowledge of its own conditioned-ness. I have to confess, for example, that I would not have done philosophy in a transcendental manner had I not studied the philosophy of Maréchal and of Heidegger.

Historicity and transcendentality are the most difficult to understand of all the fundamental structures of human existence. They cannot be reduced to a single such structure, and they mutually condition one another. What comes into the foreground of consciousness is historically conditioned and implies a transcendental reflection. Added to that is the fact that all theology that works in a transcendental manner knows, of course, that it would not do what it does had it not previously lived the Christian religion in a concrete way. When, for example, I ask whether men and women have a transcendental will for resurrection rooted in the unity of their being, and when I answer this in the affirmative and attempt to demonstrate it, I am not thereby claiming that I would have come on this idea at all if I had never in my life heard about resurrection—and, indeed, from my kind, old parish priest.

It is exactly the same as the case of the peasant woman who says to me: "Here are two apples that cost so much, and since you have four they cost twice as much." In doing this she thinks logically although she has never heard of Aristotle's logic and would not have understood it if she had. So too can one realize something concrete and religious on hearing about Jesus' cross and resurrection without ever having done any transcendental theology. But when in a given historical situation certain problems arise, we have no choice but to take up Denzinger and to think philosophically and transcendentally. The peasant woman who thought that the smoke coming out of Vesuvius was from the fire of hell and who therefore had no doubt about its existence (After all, we can see it right in front of us . . .) was not in the last analysis so stupid. She was, in fact, more enlightened than many contemporaries because, in this way, she realized the absolute threat to her existence that hell represents. This realization is still valid today. When I say now that the smoke cannot come from hell, then I have to develop a number of theological thoughts in order to maintain and realize in a new way what I know the peasant woman realized in her way. Theologians are not more clever than pious people, or perhaps they are more clever, but not more religious.

How do you see prayer within the context of contemporary demythologizing?
I have already written a great deal on this topic.[2] In order to give it a new

---

2. See Karl Rahner, *The Practice of Faith*, ed. Karl Lehmann and Albert Raffelt, (New York: Crossroad, 1983) pp. 77–99

twist, I would say that it would be regrettable if an enthusiastic pentecostal movement were to come forward in the Church with the result that it was believed that all problems could be eliminated simply by prayer. In regard to this the strangest things are taking place. A week ago, an American professor of pharmaceutical chemistry came to me, a man of such intelligence and such scientific training that he could well become a Nobel prizewinner. He introduced himself as 100 percent pentecostalist. He spoke of baptism of the Spirit and of similar things. He spoke of breaking through into a final stage of Christian existence, breaking through into the freedom of God. . . . He was referring to an experience that is conceivable but which with most of us is spread out over an entire life. What drives one to despair about this is how naively such people absolutely identify their inspirations, their sense of peace, freedom, and being led by the Holy Spirit with the immediate and direct intervention of God. This is an example of the very great danger of such an all too naive theology of prayer. Such a theology can easily go awry when, for example, its ideas are immediately experienced as the pure gift of God, when in fact they come from somewhere much closer to home. These good people do not have the least idea what has been thought about these things in the history of Christianity, and perhaps under other labels, and how people have experimented with them. I wanted, however, with this only to say that a theology of prayer that is rational without being rationalistic in any stupid sense is certainly to be counted among contemporary requirements. The point of this is not to encourage people to talk cleverly about prayer instead of praying, but to ensure that such pneumatic-enthusiastic movements will not simply peter out in the near future.

Translated by Daniel Donovan
University of Saint Michael's College, Toronto

21 · Missionary Work—Liberation Theology— Protestant Theology

Interview with Hans Norbert Janowski and Eberhard Stammler, editors of *Evangelische Kommentare*, Stuttgart (1975)

... Are you saying that the Holy Spirit can be at work in other religions and even in ideologies?

Certainly. I am completely opposed to every form of atheism, and when the ideology of a state declares atheism as an inalienable element of its life, then I must say a resolute no to that ideology. But that doesn't keep me from developing the implications of my own Christian understanding of justice and love, of the state and the social nature of humanity in a new and more radical way than I would have without this ideology which I am rejecting as ultimately false.

Is such a meeting less a matter of missionary work than a kind of dialogue, a two-way street?

Every dialogue tends toward a consensus. It *is* a two-way street, but that doesn't mean that the same thing passes down each side of the street. On the side that leads from the Church to non-Christians there travels the message of the unsurpassable and normative role of Jesus and his saving meaning for all people. From the non-Christian side there travels something perhaps completely different, which can turn out to be very important for me.

But doesn't this call into question Christianity's claim to absolute validity?

No, Christianity's absolute claim only says that in Jesus Christ God gives God's grace away in an unsurpassable, unique, and irreversible way and that this grace is ultimately necessary even for the other people involved in the dialogue. I presuppose that this grace is at work in the others in our dialogue as well.

Then the dialogue does have a missionary element to it?

Even according to the mission decree of Vatican II there is nothing objectionable in the missionary beginning with universally human insights and activities. But as long as he or she wants to be a Christian and be in the service of the Christian message, this person ultimately has to have a missionary point of view.

134

How do you understand the role of the missionary, given what you've just said?

None of the existing non-Christian religions is an unadulterated expression of the right relationship between God and humanity; each is sinfully deficient also in profound ways. Thus they are not simply incomplete religions. (It's possible to ask whether something similar isn't true with us.) To this extent, these people are endangered in their salvation in decisive ways, and so I would see missionary work as always very important and necessary—although this would not be my final theological reason for missionary effort.

How do you assess in this context political theology and theology of liberation that enter into dialogue with other ideologies?

It's obvious that all of Christianity has a social, not to say political dimension, whereby the social dimension of humanity refers not to a particular aspect of men and women but to the whole of their humanity. To this extent theology, which wants to help people understand who they are, cannot leave this dimension out of the picture. Thus theology is political and socially critical —and indeed not only in this or that issue like Christian social teaching, but even the Trinity rightly understood is a sociopolitically relevant reality. This comes down to saying that a theology that wants to reach people, and a gospel that wants to be missionary, will enter into the concrete social and political situation of people.

That is one side of it. And what are your reflections on the other side?

On the other side, Christianity cannot of course let itself be reduced to a movement of social emancipation. Christianity rightly objects to that sort of thing, because individual persons cannot be reduced to their social roles and because human beings and their history are always transcending themselves into the absolute mystery that we call God, to God who has been revealed in Jesus Christ as the power over all in history and has been promised to us as our absolute future. Because of all this we have to view the theology of liberation with some reservation. If we conceive liberation in the New Testament sense of *eleutheria* we can subsume under this key word everything that Christianity has to say to humanity about itself and its God. But then this freedom, for which God's grace in Jesus Christ has freed us, is not to be simply identified with a social emancipation of humankind, for even if this fully occurred, people would not yet be fully free.

By way of conclusion, what would you expect from Protestant theology and what do you wish for it?

I would say that the so-called traditional controversial theology, and its issues, still exists among us, and it needs to continue to receive peaceful attention. It's possible to come to even clearer agreement than heretofore regarding issues such as ministry, the Petrine office, the sacraments, and the relationship between tradition and the New Testament. Yet, in the final analysis, I think that we theologians of all confessions need to pose to ourselves in a common and mutually influencing way the questions posed by our secularized world, more than those that Christians pose to each other. If we were to bring a greater consensus and strength and courage and enthusiasm to bear on those questions, then the controversial confessional issues with their lesser existential import would become clear to us and thus they would no doubt become much easier to resolve.

Translated by Brian O. McDermott, S.J.
Weston School of Theology

22 · The Archbishop Lefebvre Controversy

Interview with Paul C. Martin and Felix Schmidt, editors of
Welt am Sonntag, Munich (September 12, 1976)

Professor Rahner, a word has turned up that seems to have vanished from our language: schism, splitting the Church. It looks as if some Catholics want to break away from Rome and to follow the French Archbishop Lefebvre, who reproaches the pope and the church leadership that they have betrayed Catholicism and "destroyed the heart of the Church." What do you say of that?

When one brings up the word *schism*, one must also mention the other word that, in theology, acts as its counterpart: *heresy*. If Lefebvre calls the pope a heretic . . .

. . . He does . . .

. . . Then Lefebvre is, according to the Catholic understanding of the faith, not only schismatic but also himself a heretic.

Lefebvre believes that he has to defend the "genuine doctrine" against the "new conciliar Church." That means that the decrees of the Second Vatican Council—dialogue with people of another faith and reform of the liturgy—are too liberal for him.

If somebody, like Lefebvre, wishes to go on using the ancient Tridentine liturgy in the future, one may soberly and rationally discuss that point. This is not a heresy.

Why has the Vatican prohibited the Latin Mass, since the Mass has for many centuries been celebrated in Latin?

The Latin Mass as such is not prohibited. But it is absolutely false that ecclesiastical Latin is something that the Church cannot give up, that it is something that follows necessarily from the nature of the Church. In Rome the liturgy was first celebrated in Greek, up to the third century. At that time Lefebvre might also have objected to the introduction of Latin. I'll be a little malicious and ask: Why doesn't Lefebvre learn Aramaic so that he may celebrate the liturgy in the language of Jesus?

When one examines the new missal and compares it with the old one, many unintelligible words are still there. Who knows, for instance, what kyrie eleison *means?*

You should address that question to Mr. Lefebvre. For the High Mass which he celebrates contains many more rites, gestures, and words that one no longer understands. From your question one might at the most conclude that the liturgy should have been reformed even more radically.

Do you believe that there will soon be another Catholic Church?

No, Lefebvre claims that he accepts the Council of Trent and the First Vatican Council. Would he not then have to find another pope? Where will he get him? How will he legitimate him?

It looks as if Lefebvre wants to hold to the present pope?

How can he reconcile that with the declaration that the pope is a heretic? Here the good archbishop has run into a blind alley.

How do you explain that Lefebvre has such a great following? In France 30 percent of the Catholics are mentioned. In Switzerland, too, and in Germany he has already a considerable following.

We must distinguish. There are a number of pious, practicing Catholics who turn with a certain antipathy against today's Church. But they have nothing to do with those Catholics who would decide to found a new Church.

Yet they are training their own priests. The number of seminarians has gone down during your career. At Lefebvre's seminary there are crowds of them.

That is a false comparison. Just add together all the men who are preparing themselves for the priesthood in the seminaries of Germany. Then the number of those who have flocked together from all the world's countries to Lefebvre in the small Swiss city of Econe is still a comparatively small number.

In Econe there were about a hundred men who wanted to become priests, almost as many as there are seminarians in France.

One might wonder whether these Econe priests are those who can carry on the living and glorious history of France.

Why do you deliberately belittle the number and the resolve of Lefebvre's followers to establish a new Church?

I intend quietly to wait and see how many of the statistically ascertainable present followers of Lefebvre will really join this Church.

Is the pope's attitude in regard to Lefebvre not much too rigid? Why does a traditionalism that is based on four centuries not fit under the roof of the great Catholic Church?

The Church has certainly room for different mentalities. But unlike others who have a quarrel with Rome, Lefebvre contests the authority of the pope. And this is simply no longer Catholic. I repeat: This is not Catholic.

The liberals in the Church call the pope stubbornly reactionary, one who ignores the problems of the times. The conservatives, led by Lefebvre, brand him as a liberal progressive, who pays homage to the spirit of the times. How does one make sense of this?

The extremely contradictory judgments, which one may meet in all areas of human life, point in our case to the fact that, generally speaking, the pope seems to steer the correct course of an open conservatism. This, of course, suits neither the extreme liberals nor the extreme conservatives—if we may dub the extremes in this way. We have not mentioned particulars. Should the encyclical *Humanae Vitae* not have turned out differently from the way it did?

Could many reforms of the curia not have been more thorough? Could not the way in which the pope is elected have been modified? Rome would admit that these questions may be discussed.

It looks as if the pope has no clear line of conduct. The Vatican seems to have management problems.

He might perhaps have a clearer, a more persuasive, a more transparent line of conduct. That may be connected with the pope's personality. Give me the name of a person in an exalted position to whom you may not also address the reproach of a zigzagging course. In matters of discretion they have no other choice than to weigh the pros and the cons and then to decide. And a decision in such matters of discretion is then too conservative for some and too liberal for others.

We wanted only to point out the discrepancy that, on the one hand, in the liturgy the Church is needlessly progressive. These reforms were not as urgent for ordinary Catholic couples, not as frightfully pressing as, for instance, the solution of problems in the sexual domain, which the Church certainly does not for the time being answer in an up-to-date way.

Personally, as an unofficial theologian, I have, for instance, as many reservations about the encyclical *Humanae Vitae* as about the recently issued declaration on sexual morality. But do not forget that the Church's leadership has the right and the duty to take positions against the manifestations of decadence in the sexual domain. Whether she has done it very prudently, very exactly, very efficiently, may be another question. But simply to say that today people want to hear something new in the domain of sexual morality and that therefore the Church must give in—that I cannot admit.

The problems have become more urgent.

It stands to reason that problems in the field of sexual morality are existentially more important than whether the Church's language should be Latin or the vernacular. That is also why they are more difficult to handle and have to be solved with greater responsibility and greater caution.

Professor Rahner, may we return to Lefebvre? What would the German bishops do if a whole community with its spiritual leader would go over to Lefebvre?

If a community really secedes from Rome, the German bishops could only condemn this as a schism and a heresy. They should endeavor to explain to as many people as possible from such endangered communities that such a step is un-Catholic and also meaningless. Such a community could only turn into a sect, like so many in America.

Didn't Christianity start as a sect two thousand years ago?
Already at that time great thinkers, such as Origen and Clement of Alexandria, made strenuous efforts to make contact with the great cultural world of that epoch. The Church also adapted herself in a certain sense. Under Paul's influence she left, with immense difficulties, the Palestinian-Jewish milieu, in order to become a Church that entered into a dialogue with the times. That is what Lefebvre should do, and not merely "inveigh against Freemasons and Protestants."

Lefebvre claims that the pope no longer wishes to speak with him. Now, that is entirely un-Christian.
Indeed, he claims that the pope does not want to receive him. But if I am correctly informed, he has already been received once. However, the pope intends to treat with Lefebvre only on condition that the latter acknowledges his authority. That stands to reason. I cannot deal with the German chancellor if, at the same time, I deny that he legitimately occupies his office.

The pope has already forbidden Archbishop Lefebvre to teach and to carry out liturgical functions. That is next to the highest punishment that the pope can inflict.
That is not a punishment; that is a preventive measure.

The next one is excommunication. Should the pope consult you now and ask you whether he should excommunicate Lefebvre, what would you advise him?
I have no objection if the pope does not want to do this as yet. Neither would I be much surprised if he did it all the same.

What consequences does the conflict with Lefebvre have for the future of the Church?
I hope that it has none, or no important ones, and that it may remain a strange, unimportant episode in the Catholicism of Western Europe. In fact, I am convinced that history is not being changed by Lefebvre.

Translated by Joseph Donceel, S.J.
Fordham University

23 · How Is the Holy Spirit Experienced Today?

Interview with Gerhard Ruis of the Vienna *Presse,*
Salzburg (June 5–6, 1976)

In an age of technology, human planning, mass media, rational and depth psy-chology, it is no longer easy to find within our experience something we can truly call the work of the Holy Spirit. Is the Holy Spirit present within our secular world?

Right away, I would say that today also, even within everyday life, the Holy Spirit can be experienced. It is a transcendental experience by radical, elevating grace. Thus it is not an immediate experience that comes from the objective data of everyday reflections, which can be discovered and described by psychology. It is rather the experience of ultimate limits, the condition for any other experience.

Within our existence, which always thrusts us beyond particular data into the seeming emptiness of absolute mystery, we experience God through grace and God's Spirit. More often than not this experience is anonymous and is not reflected on or put into words. We usually suppress it in our preoccupation with the objects and tasks of everday life. But it is still there, and at certain times we become aware of it, even within everyday existence. It presses forward and offers itself to reflection and to human freedom. There is no lack of examples of such experience of the Spirit and of God in the Spirit.[1]

Is this experience of the Spirit something new? Wasn't it present in this form at earlier times?

Of course it was. For my theology or for any rational, Catholic theology it is understood that every spiritual-personal, human act has been elevated, or "divinized," by God's ever-present grace. In other words, this experience is given always and everywhere in the whole length and breadth of human existence throughout history. However, it is not generally reflected on and verbalized. Most often it is suppressed or left unnoticed as something that would disturb us. Nevertheless, those who are spiritual have the courage to place themselves before this experience. They nurture it and allow it to be without squelching it; rather, they welcome it.

If I understand you correctly, there is no want, as it were, of the Holy Spirit today. But it is up to those who are in partnership with God's Spirit, that is, people, to reflect

1. See Karl Rahner, *The Spirit in the Church* (New York: Seabury, 1979).

141

on the workings of the Spirit, despite a hectic lifestyle, superficial living, and the like, and to put into words, make known, and nurture the experience of the Spirit. What should we do to cause this to happen?

Naturally you can meditate. Following the counsels of asceticism, you can recollect yourself, become silent, and empty your consciousness of the multitude of earthly cares and tasks. However, the Spirit is also present in everyday life. Wherever there is selfless love, wherever duties are carried out without hope of reward, wherever the incomprehensibility of death is calmly accepted, wherever people are good with no hope of reward, in all these instances the Spirit is experienced, even though a person may not dare give this interpretation to the experience.

That would mean that in our world we cannot really talk about a lack or an absence of the Spirit. But what then is this "Spirit"? Is it something, as you once said, that need not always carry a church label?

Christians should of course intensify this experience within the course of everyday life. They should learn to receive it with freedom and sustain it, even suffer from it. If only this is what you mean by an experience of the Spirit, then we would have to conclude that it happens seldom today because of the clamor of everyday life, and that today, more than in previous times, this experience is hidden from us. But, on the other hand, it is also certain that the experience of the Spirit is offered by a sovereignly free God, who guides and divinizes the course of human life.

But doesn't this give rise to the reproach heard from non-Christians—for example —humanists—who claim they too intend the good of humankind? Or of social idealists (there are still a few around) who take responsibility for the weak and the suffering, are in solidarity with their need and fight for social reform, justice, and equality? They could tell a Christian who wants to credit these acts to the Holy Spirit, "Don't burden us by talking about souls. We want nothing to do with such language." Not only they but also many Christians wonder whether they should stop looking for the action of the Spirit only and especially in the Church. The Church shouldn't restrict its prayer, "Come Holy Spirit," to Pentecost. Yet where is the Spirit?

I would say wherever people live selfless lives, whenever they truly make the leap into mystery, into unearned love, into a final and radical truth, they are dealing with God and have received God's Spirit. The question whether they can define it as such or verbalize it may be important humanly speaking —for faith or theology—but in the end it is of secondary importance. Thousands of times people have authentic and basic experiences of the Spirit without recognizing them as such. They thus misinterpret their experience or even reject correct interpretations of it. Nevertheless, they have had the experience. A psychologist who holds that all human thoughts are merely sense perception, or associations, or behavioral patterns, and so on, will reject such a spiritual interpretation of experience. Still the experience is there. . . . Due to a lack of a correct theological explanation of faith the experience is not considered spiritual. Those who love totally and absolutely have already loved God and encountered the Spirit, whether they acknowledge it or not.

How does such an experience of the Spirit take place? There are certainly many who want to live by the Spirit and be true to the Spirit. Is this will enough? Is there something else necessary so that this mysterious partnership of the Holy Spirit with humans can occur?

I can't go into individual ascetical and spiritual norms and methods here. However, I would say very simply: In your whole life you should live, in absolute truth to your conscience, an attitude of love for others that tries to be selfless. At the same time, read Scripture to find a more exact interpretation of your experience, for Scripture unveils its meaning. These two suggestions give you both an experience of the Spirit and an understanding of it according to the teachings of Christianity.

Translated by James V. Zeitz, S.J.
Marquette University

24 · A Church of Jesus' Welcoming Presence and of Radical Hope

Interview with Erich Koch of Caritas in Nordrhein-Westfalen, Cologne (March, 1976)

. . . The text of the proposal of the German bishops' synod speaks of the welcoming presence of Jesus to the excluded and humiliated, the sinners and the lost. What would you say to the staff persons of Caritas in order to make this believable?

A difficult question by which I mean that I cannot answer it quickly and well. When Jesus says (Matt. 25:31ff) that we meet him in all truth in the excluded and humiliated, the sinners and lost ones, then reciprocally we have to say that the staff persons of Caritas must so relate themselves to those people that Jesus can be found in them: in their humility, their solidarity with the poor, in their selflessness, in their hope against all hope, in their trust that is defeated by no setbacks, in their respect for the human dignity that we must not forget even the most miserable possesses, in their joy, in an authentic compassion for the sorrowing. I know no other response than Paul's demand (Phil. 2:5) to have that mind in you that was in Christ Jesus.

In your view, what has to happen so that the Church, even as the "little flock," is able to be a sign for the world instead of a joyless sect?

In any case, the Church may not be a joyless sect. If she lives from the Spirit, to whom the bishops' declaration on hope gives witness, she is a Church of radical hope and cannot be joyless. She is not a Church that executes laws, but one who encounters the unspeakably dazzling promise of God byond all guilt and death. If she accepts and attests to this promise in hope, which is not only valid for her but for all, then she will be open to all humanity in a loving and trusting way. Only in a very guarded way is she to be understood as the "little flock": not as a closed society which views itself as existing exclusively for the salvation of the privileged, but as having a task to be (as the Second Vatican Council said) the sacrament, the sign of salvation for everyone. To be sure, much still needs to take place in the Church so that the Church, or more precisely the people in the Church, do not understand and experience themselves as strained and annoyed by detailed law, but as freed from death and empowered to a hope that has no limits.

Nothing seems so little in the future, so past, as the dead. What service could the Church take up which could give even them a future?

The bishops' declaration on hope rightly intercedes for the dead and sees here in Christian hope a characteristic of Christianity contrary to today's common philosophy of life. Naturally, the dead have their own eternal future with God, and this is through God and not through ourselves. However, through our hope they also have a future with us. For in God's totally far-reaching plan of salvation the salvation of each individual involves the salvation of everyone. Ultimately then, the salvation and future of the dead occur in our hope, despite the fact that we are saved at different times. This is thinkable because the Church's hope even hopes that it itself—this Church-sustaining hope— will never perish.

At its session of November 22, 1975, out of 266 votes cast, the German synod voted 225 yes and 26 no, with 15 abstentions, for the proposal "Our Hope—A Confession of Faith in Our Day." To what would you above all attribute the broad majority and the somewhat excited debates preceding the synod?

The voting at the synod, despite many objections during the discussion, produced a surprisingly large majority. Presumably, many factors worked together to bring this about. This proposal was certainly always that of a larger part of the synod, being the confession of the hope that they experience in their lives. Really very few felt they should reject either it or specific statements within it in the name of an orthodox Christianity. Much happened to this or that emphasis and, somewhat less, to the text's style. But the result of the voting seems to prove to me, contrary to a lot of pessimism spreading among us, that we still today can so express the good news of hope, the Church's faith, that a very large majority in the Church hears and confesses this declaration as its own.

Translated by William M. Thompson
Duquesne University

25 · After the Synod— Reflections on the Church's Future

Interview with Leo Waltermann of West-German Radio (WDR), Cologne (July 25, 1976)

. . . Father Rahner, in the past the Church was basically a "people's Church." Today we're experiencing its dismantling. We have to ask whether people need the Church's service any more. The issue of why many children are no longer baptized in the large cities is of less importance than the decisively recurring, problematic, and factual experience of whether people need the Church's demands, service, and information in this world in order to live properly, successfully, fairly, and in solidarity. Right now we have an experiential horizon that, subjectively speaking, can make the Church useless. Do you see the possibility of forcing open this horizon of the people's subjective experience? This would mean we can still tell people that they aren't yet finished with being a true neighbor, with shouldering responsibility for one another.

First of all, I do recognize the reality of the factual situation you've described. Naturally, this doesn't answer the theological question of how well such decent people, while claiming that they manage their own lives, actually do so from the long and complete point of view, in life's breadth and depth. Second, there would be a further theological question of the extent and manner in which a still demonstrable residue of historical Christianity underlies such a life and to what degree what we call the grace of God is hidden therein. Undoubtedly, it will also happen that many dimensions of human existence escape and will escape from the Church's immediate guidance and an institutionally structured Christianity. But I'm still persuaded that life's ultimate questions receive their explicit and, if you will, their institutionalized answer only through an ecclesial Christianity. The way this will occur, and the number of those who will accept the Church's answer as their own through God's grace in the midst of their lives, either now or in the future, I wouldn't dare to predict. But I am convinced—to be completely cautious for once—that there will always be a tangible number of people whose life-questions and the answers that emerge from their inner depths will express themselves in sacrament, word, and explicit ecclesial institution. In other respects, it's still not the case that today's Christianity must appear to be superfluous or outmoded in any way, not even to our actual, modern world. Why? Because I would like a final answer to the deepest mystery that I myself am. I would like to have something to do with God. I would like to have an ultimate hope for the validity and true reality of my existence. I wouldn't like to be consumed by the banality of the everyday. I would like to see myself in solidarity with the people of the past, who aren't simply the precondition of some kind of utopian future of success and consumerism. Where can we find an answer to these and hundreds of other similar questions outside of Christianity? For Christianity's unique message endures precisely in its answer to each of the questions we raised: that there is a final hope. Only on the basis of this experience can I initially understand in a basic way and somewhat meaningfully accept in a general way the whole detailed system of the Christian faith.

Translated by William M. Thompson
Duquesne University

26 · What Is Christianity?

Interview with Michael Albus of West Germany's Channel 2 (ZDF), Mainz (November 21, 1976)

. . . Could you briefly formulate the purpose and theme of your book, Foundations of Christian Faith *[New York: Seabury, 1978]?*
I really only want to tell the reader something very simple. Human persons in every age, always and everywhere, whether they realize it and reflect upon it or not, are in relationship with the unutterable mystery of human life that we call God. Looking at Jesus Christ the crucified and risen one, we can have the hope that now in our present lives, and finally after death, we will meet God as our own fulfillment.

Translated by John R. Sachs, S.J.
Fairfield University

27·Christmas—Fullness and Turning Point of Time?

Interview with Peter Pawlowsky on Radio Austria (FS 1), Vienna
(December 26, 1976)

Professor Rahner, yesterday Christians celebrated Christmas. They speak of God becoming man, and of the fullness and the turning point of time. If I try to describe the emotional background on which such words are being used, I believe that every year expectations are aroused that ultimately are always again disappointed.

One should ask oneself—everybody who celebrates Christmas—is this really the turning point of time? Is this for me the fullness of time? What has really happened and what do we celebrate here? And so we have every year again, I would say, this cycle of expectation, disappointment, and resignation. For what has changed for the Christian, as a result of what is being celebrated here?

It is true that Christians are living, in their own life, in the course of their own life history, in their own society and time, through an unceasing alternation of fulfilled and disappointed expectations. All this happens to belong to human life. It has to be borne with patience and also with hope.

Yet, in spite of it, Christians, I would say, have an absolute hope for the complete, unconditional fulfillment of their existence. It is not yet present, it lies still in the future. But on account of the event that we celebrate every year at Christmas it has become for us an absolute, solid, and palpable promise.

Yet when one considers this history from the time Jesus of Nazareth came into the world, one may be of the opinion that things have not changed much.

First, I would say that, judging from outside, one may undoubtedly say: A long time before Jesus, thousands of years, perhaps even millions of years earlier (who can put it exactly) world history was already under way. Even after the life of Jesus not much has changed in history. There are still wars, there is still poverty, there is still despair. There is still hunger. And death always lies in wait for every human being. To that extent, indeed, there really does not seem to have been very much change.

We should put it even more bluntly. Even in the history of the Church, which celebrates this Christmas event, there have been many things that do not look like the turning point of time. It is enough to remember the witchcraft trials, the inquisition, the way the Church has opposed many an effort to make people more free, the labor question during the last century. A long list might be made that would make it evident that salvation has by no means dawned even within the Church.

148

To be sure, the Church is not a paradisiacal oasis in which everything is quite different or much more lovely and more wonderful than outside, in the so-called secular domain. No, the Church is composed of people, she is therefore a Church of sinners. We profess that she is holy but obviously, she is even a sinful Church. With all human beings she has to carry the burden of being human, the history of wretchedness, the many disappointments. It is precisely amidst all this suffering, and not in an oasis of blessedness, that she has to safeguard, to realize, to carry faith forward in the eternal future.

We speak of the "turning point of history," of the "fullness of time." We Christians rightly profess a very radical break, because of God's Incarnation, because of the coming of the crucified and risen Jesus. But this does not mean that, previous to these events, the history of humanity was deprived of all grace, was not being carried by God's providence, by the power of his grace, by his concern for the world, by his love. In the creed we profess time and again our faith in the "Holy Spirit, who has spoken through the prophets." In other words: Even before Jesus, there existed already in fact a history that was essentially Christian, which was borne by grace and directed by God toward the final consummation.

So in the Incarnation of Jesus we may not see a break, therefore also no special turning point, but only a "milestone," as it were, in salvation history?

Yes, at first sight, if we consider the outer aspect of history before and after Jesus, this notable chiaroscuro of God's light and faithfulness on the one hand and of human finiteness, fleetingness, and wretchedness on the other seems to be exactly identical, because before Jesus history was basically already a Christian history. To what extent then has there, nonetheless, been a break? It has occurred simply because through Jesus and in him, the risen one, God has so adopted the world that he can no longer retract his powerful will of salvation and happiness, a will that in the long run overcomes all obstacles.

For faith and for world history the drama before Jesus consisted in the question whether history would terminate happily or unhappily. Because of Jesus, we are certain now that this history, which keeps going on, this drama of world history, which continues to look gruesome, dreadful, always heading for death, has nevertheless a happy ending for all those who, as Scripture says, believe, trust in God, and obey their conscience. Of course, this happy ending lies still in the future, is open, ambivalent, something that is presented to the freedom of humanity's history. Now all this is not a matter of course. It is rather, I would say, an unbelievable optimism that, despite their most disappointing experience with world history, Christians have and uphold. And this only on account of Jesus.

Has this not often led, in the Church's history, to the opinion that the kingdom of God has arrived, and that we realize it now, regardless of the way in which people live and die at the present time. Has this not often led to the conclusion that it is possible to make this utopia come true by means of violence and pressure? And this happy ending is not yet here.

This happy ending is not yet here. Let me distinguish two things: Neither the Church nor secular society may act as if, by their own efforts (which always end in failure, as people die), they were able to conquer and to bring about, here in the course of history, this realm of reconciliation, of the light and the splendor of God.

Does that mean that progress and the advent of a more humane society, for which people keep striving, are irrelevant for the coming of the kingdom of God?

No, not at all. To what I have just said I must add this: Wherever individuals or groups make reasonable efforts for greater decency, more love, greater justice, more humanity, one may say that all these efforts are concrete realizations of a real faith in the kingdom of God, which comes to us from God in history. When I ask what is meant by "Christian faith," I should not say that it means "keeping the bird in hand," and fostering, moreover, the so-called hope that, despite all the horrors of world history, everything will somehow have a happy ending. I must translate this faith in my actions. That means, in our context, that this realization is genuine, real and true only if, out of love for my neighbor, I let at times (in the words of the proverb) the bird go, so as to acknowledge that I expect the eternal consummation from the hands of God.

You see, to me the so-called conservatives often seem to be people who say: Let God's eternal kingdom come, we have no objection. But for the time being we hold on obstinately and anxiously to what we have now. The so-called progressives, on the other hand, look to me like people who think: Let the present time perish. Upon the soil of today's dying and sacrificed generations we ourselves will build the future paradise with our own hands.

It seems to me that Christians who have real faith stand between these two extremes. They are not rigid conservatives, who want to cling to the present, because they do not know what the future is bringing. And they do not sacrifice the present in behalf of a generation that does not yet exist. Christians are people who have faith. This means that, when the time for sacrifice has come, they always show their faith by working, step by step, for a more humane future. They do not believe, however, that they are able to realize God's kingdom already in such a way that, before we vanish in death, it would come to us or to a later generation as the kingdom of God.

What this means once more for individuals, for each one's life, is this: Even after Christ the Church does not dispense us from hearing troublesome texts. That is why during the year the passage of Luke will be read that describes the destruction of the world. Even today, the day after Christmas, she celebrates the feast of a martyr. Realistically that means: a person's murder. On the one hand, death has been vanquished. On the other, every human being faces it. Hence my question: Has death been overcome, or has it not?

I would say: Death has been overcome in faith, in hope, in the confidence and the readiness to accept it as the coming of God. It has not been overcome in the sense that we must not undergo it, that we must not suffer all that befalls an individual who faces death. This is also in a way the trademark of world history as a whole.

Do we have to understand literally the figurative apocalyptic descriptions of the New Testament, which speak of very hard and ominous times? Or is their purpose merely to portray graphically the existential attitude of readiness to accept one's own death? No attempt will be made to answer that question. At any rate, it is clear for Christians in their own individual existence that they must pass through the incomprehensibility of death. They are asked how they can cope with it. Do they accept it with total resignation, with faith in and hope for a fulfillment that does not come from themselves but that is named God? Or do they accept this death with total, perhaps unconscious, but real despair, with the idea that ultimately everything comes to an end in the absurdity of death? So the real question is this: Do we overcome death in faith, hope, and love for others? Or do we grimly and without any hope undergo death as the final end of an absurd existence?

Yet we are also told that death itself will die, that there will come an end to it, and that the Lord is coming. What is the meaning of the "coming of the Lord," if all is not over with Christmas, at the beginning, with Jesus of Nazareth? What is the sense of the promise that then Christ will come for good?

We know that in Christian language a distinction is frequently made between a first "coming of Christ" or of the eternal Word of God at Christmas, and a "final coming of God" as the Son of man at the end of time. I prefer to say that this coming of God into his own world history, a coming that saves this history and brings it to a blessed end, has itself a beginning and an end. In what we celebrate at Christmas God has already inserted himself into the world. At present things go on, presumably for endlessly long times, through disappointment and catastrophes. But ultimately they are, for individuals and for humanity, heading toward an irrevocably solid end: light, peace, and final reconciliation. We call this event the second coming of the eternal God into this world.

In other words: The last mentioned "Christmas" is the one that is still to come. How does a Christian live meanwhile? I am thinking not only of death but also of the events that remind us constantly, every day, of our finiteness. How does one cope with this? We experience again and again that reality makes sense. Yet time and again this meaning is shattered.

To my mind the experience of the meaning of innerwordly values, in love, in fidelity, in beauty, in truth, and so on, is finite. As such these values are a promise in their positive aspect, while in their finiteness they are an indication that we always must proceed beyond these partial experiences, in the hope of this infinite fulfillment. We do this, naturally, only if, in Christian resignation, we allow these innerwordly values, which we possess, grasp, enjoy, to be time and again taken away from us. In this way, Christians might be called those who enjoy nice things, without being pleasure seekers. They are not those who make the most of the present, as the New Testament puts it. Yet they are people who accept being led further on; in the hope of higher values, they allow whatever had been given to them to be taken away from them; through all this, they keep going ahead and in this way live their own lives patiently and full of hope. This they do until the whole fullness of their life that is called God is once and for all given to them across the dark portals of death—as they had hoped.

So we are allowed to believe in the meaning of individual experiences on account of this Jesus whose coming into this world is being celebrated at Christmas. May I ask you a personal question? As a theologian and a man of the Church you are one who has decided for this Jesus. Is it possible to say what it is in this Jesus that has seized you? I mean that has fascinated you so much that you have devoted your whole life to it?

This is indeed a very personal and very sweeping question that is very hard to answer. I would say that the whole life of Jesus, his work, his cross, his doctrine, and also what we Christians call his "resurrection," convinces me in its unique totality. My faith gives the impression that one can rely on that life. If I say yes to this life, it is—to the extent of my possibilities—taken into my life. If I make this life into the law of my life, if I have faith, hope, and love for God and for my neighbor—again, as richly, as poorly, as beautifully, as pitifully as one may be able to do it—then one (or rather, then I) hope that this life will reach a meaningful, an eternal fulfillment.

How do you envisage your future? Have you already asked yourself that question?

Well, I do not have much more to envisage in this respect. There are not many more possibilities left, but that does not matter. I have always known that I would have to die at some time, and I do not wish to repress that simple fact. I do not intend to banish it from my professional time, as if I had nothing to do with this fundamental fact of my life.

I do not know, of course, what I will do, how everything will turn out with me, what I will feel, and whether I will succeed in dying, so to speak, a personal-spiritual death, when this hour of all hours will be there. But I try, as well as I can, to live in such a way that, as soon as this hour comes, although I might have to say with Jesus and many a saint: "My God, my God, why have you forsaken me?" I can still add immediately with the same crucified Jesus: "Father, into your hands I commend my spirit." And then I hope that, when I have nothing more to say, God will say to me his full, his overflowing, his all-embracing word of life, of peace, of grace, and also of forgiveness of my sins, so that, despite everything, I may say: Now all is well.

Translated by Joseph Donceel, S.J.
Fordham University

28 · The Church in a Secularized Society

Interview with Hans Georg Koch and David A. Seeber, editors of *Herder-Korrespondenz*, Freiburg in Breisgau (1977)

Professor Rahner, one gets the impression that the Church in Germany finds itself facing a society that seems to move ever further away from it in a climate in which there are no answers. One sees this happening despite a new, perhaps deceptive, expectation on the part of the Church of a movement toward her on the basis of signs of a religious awakening and of ever more clearly defined social dilemmas. In what do you see the origins of this situation?

The relationship of the Church to the culture and society surrounding her was in history generally much more troublesome than we think as we look back. However, the features of this relationship were in general clearer than is the case today. There were times in which the Church was in the very forefront of societal and cultural development. There were times in which the Church set itself with decision and determination against this development. However, it was clear what was going on. If the Church appears to be confused today, it is because society is confused. Both go together. Sometimes I ask myself if, from the point of view of faith, this is all so bad. Why should we Christians and the Church in an age of confusion have answers for everything instead of putting up with the confusion along with our contemporaries? I believe that we must perhaps prepare ourselves for the fact that future history will appear grayer and more confused and will have less room for great and clear intellectual visions.

If that should as a matter of fact be the case, then must not the Church either be in a position to bring color into this boring painting, or else go astray as far as its own future is concerned?

I don't think that faith depends upon the ability to foresee the future of the Church. Consider the circumstances in which, for example, a Jew in the first century had to preserve his faith in the promises of God after the destruction of the temple. Judging from appearances alone, there was every reason to doubt. The holy place had been destroyed by pagans; the Jewish people had been dispersed to the four corners of the world and were, on all sides, surrounded or half-smothered by a hostile and foreign culture. What I am trying to say is that it is not the prospects for the future that create hope, but rather the fact that despite the unlikelihood (perhaps even increasing) as far as appearances are concerned, there are still human beings who wager everything by believing in God as the absolute mystery of their existence; human beings who do not avoid accepting unconditional responsibility for their lives; who pray; who accept death. And even if there were no other miserable and helpless person left to do these things, then I would give God the joy that there is still me.

But if one looks at our present situation, one can without a doubt see a swing from an optimism that characterized the conclusion of Vatican II to the troubled and disappointed discovery of an ongoing erosion of the Church...

The question is whether that has anything basically to do with the Council or if the Council has not rather, in what can be seen as the clear providence of God, built certain points of contact with a movement away from the Church, which would have occurred in any case, because the picture that the Church presents from the time of Pius IX to that of Pius XII would most certainly not have remained. The situation is there. One must intelligently give it a theological interpretation. One must clarify how one understands the existence and the function of the Church in this world. If we see the Church too much as the only ship upon the stormy sea of the world in which one can be saved, then we run into theological difficulties. If one, however, following the understanding of the Church that Vatican II offers, sees it as the sacrament of the salvation of the world, then perhaps an understanding of the movement of the world away from the Church is gained that is less likely to lead the Christian to pessimistic resignation and anxious expectation of the end of Christianity or of the Church.

The theological interpretation has no foundations, however, if there are no indications that the shrinking in numbers is something other than loss and that the Church is really alive and effective as "sacrament". . .

There are such indications. I would not lightly dismiss, for example, pentecostal movements with their charismatic enthusiasm, of which we have examples in the Church. I would also say: Thanks be to God that a few more candidates for the priesthood are again enrolling in the seminaries. But I would, at the same time, fear that one would put too much emphasis on such signs of hope and, as a result, be too easily consoled on official levels in regard to the struggles of the Church in our time and so not find the courage for really new paths of evangelization.

It is precisely this courage that seems to be lacking. Supposing we remain for a moment with the increase in the number of candidates for the priesthood that you have mentioned. Would one not thereby convert a small improvement to a great change, with the result that one would thereby shield oneself against fundamental questions, which present themselves in the area of priestly and pastoral service?

Without doubt there is some truth in what you say. I would consider it far from good if one would pretend that one need not pose any more questions in this area, and that there is no chance in the foreseeable future for changes in the structure of the priesthood or in regard to the conditions for admission to that office. What seems to me to be much more important is that through the small signs of hope, such as the increase in seminarians and the other things that we mentioned earlier, the difficulties that really challenge us are not removed—the inability to pray; the inability to find in the sacraments something religiously alive, which supports life and existence. The Church must realistically look at these areas and do far more than it actually is doing.

If one asks about new elements of religious living, one will often be referred to the development of small communities and groups. Here in Germany one does not see much of these; perhaps in the third world there are more. Aren't these groups a phenomenon that is too diverse and vague to counterbalance the death of parishes and the depopulation of religious congregations?

I don't know how large such groups are here in Germany. That is difficult to determine. I have the impression that there is everywhere a movement toward religious living in groups that are less institutionalized and less under the leadership of officeholders in the Church. That would not be all that bad. For where is it written that all religious initiative and activity must be officially blessed and channelled by Church officials from the beginning, as bishops normally seem to think is the case?

Can such communities achieve what is often expected of them? Or, don't these communities often become sects with ghetto mentalities?

There are certainly promising beginnings in building truly Christian communities from the ground up. But the official Church must more courageously and unhesitatingly than is customary support and permit such developments. One should not create any opposition in principle between base communities and officially constituted parishes. Why couldn't there be lively parish communities under the guidance of a lively charismatic pastor, who can break out of the normal patterns of pastoral care, and which are really base communities? I believe that there are already such parishes. Such base communities should not see themselves as envious or arrogant competitors as far as typical parishes are concerned.

Do you see in these grassroots activities an opportunity or a hindrance as far as the unity of the churches is concerned?

I advised those attending the Action 365 assembly in Frankfurt . . . not to develop in their action groups of Catholic and Protestant Christians a sort of third confession, as the result of which the ecumenical problem would not be solved, but only made more difficult. Such problems naturally come along with grassroots groups. But we must also ask whether such communities can somehow attract or incorporate interested non-Christians, or whether that doesn't work.

Don't such communities have more opportunities the more they not only live in a Christian manner themselves but also see their primary task as bearing witness for those "outside"?

If they live in a genuine Christian manner, then quite obviously they give witness. I would like to refer the question of "opportunity" not only to the base groups but also to those pitifully small developments that one can call signs of hope. In regard to these "opportunities" I would soberly and critically ask for what they are supposed to be opportunities. Should it be an opportunity for the Church to win back again to a certain extent in the larger society the dominant position that it perhaps once had? Is it a question of the opportunity of preventing the number of baptized Christians or of people attending Mass or of couples who are married in Church from dropping too low? Or are we rather speaking about an opportunity for the genuinely religious life of prayer, of hope in God, of the ability to face life and a period of history that is gray, offering little hope, and culturally not very inspiring?

One cannot completely separate the second and the third understandings of opportunity . . .

Naturally, one would wish that the groups we have spoken of would become more numerous and larger, that the living parishes would involve not only 5 percent, but at least 10 percent of baptized Christians. I am asking very soberly what hopes we can realistically entertain for the Church. Are there theological or historical reasons why I must have as a goal a Christianity that holds a majority position in society? Why I must measure the success of the Church in terms of reaching that position? Perhaps that is simply no longer a possibility, and perhaps this majority status in earlier, post-Constantinian times and in the Middle Ages was less a religious than a cultural phenomenon. In any case, I cannot from the point of view of theology and faith measure the success of the Church by measuring the degree to which the Church has attracted a majority of the population.

But don't the leaders of the Church themselves still think more in terms of the organizational Church and its resultant societal influence than in terms of spiritual and religious influence?

May I first of all make a simple observation? It is still today a fact that the higher ranking church officials are drawn from a homogeneous, certainly Christian milieu. No one will challenge that fact. I ask myself if it would not be a fine thing if in the future, say one third of the German bishops would be people who through God's grace had personally to struggle to Christianity, as

Saint Augustine did. They would perhaps have a much greater sensibility for the question of how one could Christianize the secularized heathen of today. As it is, that question should torture our bishops during their sleepless nights. I obviously don't know what they struggle with during their sleepless nights. Perhaps it is precisely this question. However if it is, I pick up too few evidences of the fact.

Still, more than their origins it is apparently their societal position which leaves its mark on the bishops' style of exercising their office. Because of their social position they have still more opportunities for external—even material—influence than would correspond to the de facto *interior influence that the Church has on society . . .*

Although the picture has changed somewhat since 1945, we Christians, priests and bishops, should not deceive ourselves regarding the fact that the Church today still has a stronger social and political position than would be the case if it had to win this position anew by virtue of the spiritual influence of its representatives. But naturally even high-ranking church officials cannot somehow demonstrate what charismatic and spiritual influence they possess independently of the sociopolitical weight of their positions. To be quick to criticize or even condemn one single bishop would certainly be very perverse. It was only about a year ago that I experienced a situation where a group in Germany that was up to 80 or more percent non-Christian was very deeply influenced by the simple honesty and humility of a bishop and his courage in bearing Christian witness. Such things take place, and one should not overlook or disparage them.

Nonetheless one ought not to underestimate this discrepancy between societal influence and actual spiritual influence . . .

The potential for such a spiritual influence is already present. Naturally, the light of the truth of God and of Jesus Christ still burns in the lamp of the Church. But the question is: How does the Church present this light of Christ? To what extent have the windows through which it must shine become opaque or insufficiently transparent? How could and must the teaching and living of the Church, of ecclesial authorities, be such that they are convincing? Without doubt there are missed opportunities, anxieties, cautious concerns merely to move along in the manner in which things have been done up to now, which diminishes the spiritual influence of the Church.

Aren't members of the Church far too little aware that already in our generation, but especially among the young, there is a completely different manner of relating to

Church and of being religious? Or even a fully new manner of abstinence from these things? This seems to me to be a major problem.

There is certainly much discussion of the new sense of religion. But has it moved sufficiently from the area of hunches and feelings to a realm of sufficiently existential seriousness and responsibility, so that the question of the relationship of this sense of religion to the Church can be seriously posed? There is value in the fact that many modern men and women are no longer content with a simple rationalism, as were many so-called educated people of the nineteenth and of the first half of the twentieth century; that they have become more questioning in regard to the wisdom and the power even of the human and societal; and that thereby the question of religion arises from a new source.

But this questioning as such is not yet of a religious nature. . . .

There I would also have my doubts. As long as these religious developments have not achieved sufficient depth that people are aware that they touch upon fundamental values from a Christian point of view—namely, upon eternal life, which one can fail to achieve—so long as this has not been realized, these movements have not yet become a really new possibility for the Church. Until that happens, the Church appears at the most as one shop among many that offer to satisfy certain religious sentiments, perhaps even as a specialist in giving meaning to life, as a dentist is a specialist for handling toothaches. But it still does not appear as the plank of salvation on the stormy sea of the world.

One side of the question is whether the Church will again become a question for the human being who is religious in a new fashion or even who is not religious. The other side is whether the Church takes the difficulties of these human beings seriously enough. Don't we know what we should say to them?

Naturally, it has become more difficult to speak even among Christians of the necessity of the Church for salvation. If you read an apologist of the nineteenth or early twentieth century, you will find him saying that whoever is not baptized will be lost; whoever does not have sanctifying grace is not cleansed of original sin. At that time, then, the question of the necessity of baptism, of what concretely pertained to church membership, was more immediately pressing than today, when even the average Christian says, "Yes obviously I will have my children baptized . . ."

. . . Even that is no longer so immediately evident . . .

" . . . but even if they are not baptized, they will still get to heaven, if there is a heaven." The problem is as a matter of fact theologically more difficult than it appeared to be to Catholic or Protestant biblical scholars fifty years ago. I myself cannot simply and without further qualification describe an un-baptized child as suitable only for limbo and not for heaven, as we used to do. It's clear that even within the Church we have more difficulty than earlier ages had in speaking as Christians of the ecclesial aspect of religion and of the relationship of the human being to God. It is certainly still a difficult task to convince someone that his or her personally experienced sense of religion, which is perhaps also only vaguely articulated, has its correct and appropriate place in the Church.

But not only a relationship to the Church, but even a sense of religion and faith itself threaten today to disappear from awareness, because people are no longer able to achieve them. Elders are uncertain about religious education, the religion class is often vague, work with the young people in the parish is to a great extent only spoken of on paper...

Yes, these are difficult matters. Take the example of a mother, who in an earlier age had grown up in a Christian milieu. Because it seemed so clear to her what Christianity was all about, she had no hesitation in training, in a thoroughly good sense of the term, her child in her own devotional practices. Today such a mother, even if she has an interest in things religious, has difficulties in praying with her children, which previously did not exist. One cannot remove such difficulties with an order or with the proclamation of the obligation of parents to educate their children religiously. Religion class is in the same situation. Even the smallest child sees today that many foreign workers are Moslems, and that Yugoslavians because of their nationality must be atheists, and that daddy never goes to church on Sunday. These are simply facts of life.

But are these facts of life sufficiently taken account of in pastoral practice?

I'm afraid not. Everything depends upon coming to the sober insight that one must, to use the words of Jesus, spread the seed over all possible fertile and rocky fields and ways; that only in a small area of the field the sowing really comes to a good harvest as far as the Church is concerned; but that nonetheless the sowing is extraordinarily important for broader areas of human society, which are officially or expressly not Christian. What we have called influence must also mean that the seed has effects in the lives of the most diverse people without their becoming "churched" in the strict sense. There is the known fact that, if I am correctly informed, twice as many people in Japan consider themselves to be Christians as there are Christians formally registered in the Japanese churches. We have to take account of a similar phenomenon here in Germany, namely, that the work of the Church does have an influence, but that it does not automatically increase the ranks of the churched.

You speak of Christianity or of the Church as something that was previously obvious and is today not obvious. Abstractly expressed, that means nothing other than that the relationship between freedom and religion, between freedom and faith, between freedom and Church is seen in a radically new way. Naturally, there was always a theoretical bond between faith and freedom, but today that has become a very practical fact. Neither the parish communities nor the pastors and the holders of high office would have been able to take sufficient account of this fact.

The Second Vatican Council has without doubt made a very respectable and important advance with its theory of freedom of conscience. However, in a sort of reverse logic, this now makes more difficult for the Christian the insight that, concretely, in his or her own individual existence one can be bound and summoned to a fundamental decision in faith, although other people make this decision in another way or not at all. The Christian is surrounded by a crowd of other people who are non-Christians or, for all practical purposes, not Christians. Nonetheless, the Christian does not deny their good faith or their loyalty to their own conscience or their real opportunity for salvation.

Nonetheless, to acknowledge that a faith decision has absolute importance as far as salvation is concerned is, as a matter of fact, much more a difficulty in the existential and practical than in the theological and theoretical sphere.

Both obviously go together and the official teaching, preaching, and pronouncements of the official Church have not yet given sufficient cognizance to that fact. From the pope down to the associate pastor in the pulpit the fundamental-theological grounding of the faith, both in theory and practice, is not sufficiently presented along with the truths of the faith. Generally, only a call to the formal authority of the Church is made, as if the formal authority of the Church were more convincing than the contents of what is said. Mostly the reverse is true.

Doesn't this error also come to expression through the fact that conflicts within the Church on various questions are changed very frequently into conflicts over authority?

Honestly, I do not want to call into question the formal authority of the Church, teaching office, pope, bishops, and so on. But it is surely clear that if this formal authority is accepted with greater difficulty in faith than many other items of belief regarding God, the final meaning of existence, and so on, then I cannot base the possibility for assimilation of statements of faith on the formal authority of the Church first and foremost. Alban Stolz, the influential pastoral theologian and popular spiritual writer of the last century, said that as a doubting youth everything was unclear to him even in regard to the existence of God and the immortality of the soul. But at the same time, he declared in a sort of supreme effort that he believed what the Roman Catholic Church believed. Later he certainly joined an interior bond of a very deep, almost mystical sort to these articles of the faith. But this is not the sequence according to which faith develops today.

Isn't theology also guilty in regard to the deficiency in evangelization in that when church officials emphasize their authority, theology falls back upon its status as a purely objective science?

There is much theology that disregards the question of faith decisions and concerns itself only with what can be scientifically studied in the area of faith statements. It is not interested in their relationship to human existence. There is no point in such a pure theology today. A pious and believing theology professor once said to me that one could not really prove the divinity of Christ from the New Testament; as far as the evidence there is concerned, one could just as readily argue to an Arian position; what is to be said regarding the divinity of Christ is said by the teaching office of the Church. Such a schizophrenia, at once fideistic and rationalistic—scientific, simply doesn't work out in the long run any more.

Whether the Church can avoid isolation and open itself forcefully to society or not depends upon a workable theology and upon the ability of ecclesiastical officials to make use of it. What is important if one wants to find the correct language?

Theoretical considerations about the correct language in theology help as little as recipes for effective lyrics. One must look at the subject at hand and attempt so to express it that one grasps it and is grasped by it. The teaching office of the Church should make every effort to express the old truth in a new manner, so that the statement does not strike one's ear immediately as old. It must approach making such statements with the greatest trust and tolerance. For if one says the old truth in a new manner, it sounds only too readily, for ears accustomed to the old statement, as if it were a change in the content of the statement itself, although in reality it is not that. In such new statements one should without anxiety avoid old expressions. The one who cannot do without them is shown to be not yet speaking to the person of today.

Aren't there also obstacles within the Church itself that don't let theology unfold its positive potential? Isn't there a fear of theological insights at large in parishes and, in another way, also in the teaching office of the Church, which expects confirmation from theology rather than new initiatives?

Theology exists because it is, ought to be, and wants to be the science of faith, not a haven for stupidity and narrowness and laziness in thinking. Theology does not dispense one from critical questioning of the most radical sort. Parishioners must be educated to take into account all the problems of contemporary theology—to know that pastors do not know everything; to know that even important and fundamental statements of faith are almost unavoidably stated with a certain mixture of time-conditioned concepts, and so on, which will later prove themselves to be false. The people must be acquainted with the fact that, indeed, the pope has the right and the duty to publish encyclicals about concrete questions of faith and morals; that these are seriously to be respected; but that nevertheless the guarantee is not given that everything contained in them is an eternal truth. If Christians in such a situation collapse into total uncertainty and think that one has no idea any more what should be believed, then they have been poorly instructed.

But that is still to a great extent the case, and now as earlier even official statements lend their weight to the confirmation rather than to the change of this situation.

The German bishops have said in their public statements, along with the particular message of the faith being taught, important and correct things about the sense and the limits of teaching authority in the Church. However, they don't seem to apply this expressly when they take a position in regard to concrete questions. There they suddenly act again as though there could be no doubt at all as to what the correct answer is in this or that concrete question. If the bishops defend their very legitimate point of view in a particular instance, then they could nevertheless make Christians aware of the finality or lack of finality with which they speak and argue.

Behind these difficulties of teaching is the unresolved task of reconciling the identity or gospel of the Church and pluralism in the teaching and life of the Church. Doesn't that become repeatedly clear not only in the theological area but also in the ethical or social-ethical and also the political arena?

The model of uniformity undeniably holds far too prominent a place on the side of the teaching office. Moreover, when one must as a matter of fact allow pluralism, one does it with a bad conscience. Both of these actions are connected with an uncertainty regarding fundamentals. If we would have greater success in bringing about the Christian's assimilation of the substance of Christianity to real life, so that he understands what is the basis of my trust and that without which I cannot live and die, then one could, if not allow every opinion to be taught within the Church, at least be patient with much that oneself judges to be false. Let me say this another way. If someone is convinced that the living God even as incomprehensible mystery is near to us and communicates with us; and second, if one abandons oneself to the divinizing nearness of this merciful and forgiving God with an eye on Jesus, the crucified and risen one; and third, if one takes it to be self-evident that this faith is to be lived with others in what one calls the Church, which I know, without elaborate historical investigations, to have been in at least unbroken continuity with Jesus since its earliest days—then, I believe, such a person is a Roman Catholic Christian.

The difficulties arise in the attempt to understand particulars of this fundamental content of the faith . . .

Certainly. But then one should not get upon one's high horse and decide that specific theological questions have been settled for another or for oneself, without allowing for further discussion. One should really not be so stupid, especially today in our skeptical and relativistic age. If someone has a conviction of the substantials of Christianity reached in the manner we have described, even though this conception may have leaks here and there that let in the winter cold; and if one keeps oneself open in principle to the unfolding of these substantials through the Church's preaching, then one need not fumble about with all sorts of individual catechism questions or with all the individual statements of Pope Paul VI's "Credo of the People of God."

But isn't the opinion fairly common that one must counter a skeptical attitude by presenting as fully and detailed as possible the entire teaching down to its individual practical consequences?

That is impossible, I might say, because from the almost physical grounds of the finitude of human intellectual energy, it is impossible today to make a positive synthesis and integration between everything that I as a Christian and I as a profane human being know. Our intellectual hide is unavoidably much more speckled than used to be the case. A Suarez could still integrate in a positive synthesis the whole of profane knowledge on one side, insofar as it had existential and religious relevance, and his theology on the other. One cannot do that today; indeed, not only in regard to subtleties of an intellectual or religious sort but also in important things. Let's take a concrete example. I am not at all convinced of the transmigration of souls. But when I see the extent to which this concept is spread about the Eastern world and the self-evident manner in which one accepts it there, then I would as a Christian, who personally has no inclination for it, still say that I don't know exactly what truth, which escapes me, stands behind this belief, and I don't know exactly with what sort of arguments I could reach someone who is committed to such a teaching.

Isn't that a somewhat extreme example that touches the substance of revelation?
Because it is an extreme example, I can use it to show what I mean. Naturally, I am as a Christian convinced that I will stand at death before God's judgment over my death and life—which is also "only" a picture. But this Christian conviction, which is also my own solidly personal conviction, is not a simple denial of the teaching of reincarnation in the sense that it reduces it to a stupidity. Now exactly how a respect for this belief and my Christian conviction fit together, I'm not too sure. Although I had much time to do theology, I have not yet come to a historically researched explanation of the genesis of this belief, or to a clear synthesis or rejection of it from the point of view of faith. There are many similar questions.

Is it true that the more one succeeds in achieving an existential grasp of the fundamentals of faith, the freer one can be in regard to individual teachings?
I would say, at least, that the contemporary Christian would be helped if supplied both with Christianity's basic convictions that I have summarized earlier and with the courage for a questioning and relativizing of one's own opinions. The same is true in regard to respectable Church officials and theologians who are often so very convinced of their views. In many difficult cases one can calmly surrender to the development of ongoing individual and collective intellectual and theological history to find a clearer and more obvious way of stating the matter.

The Council spoke of the hierarchy of truths. In the Church's teaching, however, one statement continues to be placed alongside another—the divinity of Christ next to the primacy of Peter, eternal life next to the priesthood of women. The same is true in moral teaching, where in the area of sexuality—as in the report of Archbishop Degenhardt to the synod of bishops—abortion is spoken of right next to premarital sex. However, if one admits that one has not the ability for making such distinctions, then it is hardly convincing when one calls another to the discernment of spirits . . .
In most cases the correct, profound, beautiful, and important statement about the hierarchy of truths has remained more or less a statement. One would

have to say, however, that there are not only to a certain extent different "hierarchical levels" of objective truth, there is also an existential hierarchy of truths, in the sense of a justifiable difference of degrees to which truths can be existentially assimilated by the individual or even beyond the individual by particular social and collective groups. I sometimes ask myself whether we don't have more to learn than we think from the experiences that Protestants have had with their inner-church pluralism over their four-hundred-year history. Of course, their multiplicity has also been excessive. The elderly Bultmann once wrote to me in a letter in which he expressed his reservations in regard to this question that he could at times almost envy me the pope. But we ourselves must first learn that there can and should be a greater legitimate pluralism within the one faith and the one Church than we generally assume. In the really official teaching nothing should be allowed to stand as permissible that certainly and clearly is contrary to defined teaching, and certainly not what is against the basic truths of Christianity. However, that does not simply mean that one can and must attribute to everyone a positive ability to assimilate every indisputable truth, and must therefore so act, as if every Catholic with a little good will must have and manifest a positive relationship to every truth of the Church.

Isn't such a distinction between the basic validity of a truth of the faith and the de facto obligation of the individual believer in its regard ultimately without any consequences?

Why should it be impossible in the Church that certain truths, while not being denied, be offered for the existential assimilation of Christians, without their being practiced and realized always and everywhere and by all? Suppose someone comes and says: "Say, I can't understand what the Immaculate Conception of the Mother of God means. I can't make head or tail out of it." I would say: "My friend, you really have no ground to deny this truth. If for the time being you can't make head or tail out of it, and have enough to do to believe in God and eternal life, then you still have the right to live in the Church as the Christian you are. You need not learn the entire catechism by heart and pretend that you understand it all." Such an approach is perhaps also conceivable for larger groups in the Church.

Are you thereby formulating an ecumenical principle?

If you want, yes. Supposing we were to bring about a unity with Protestant Christians. We must not then demand from these Christians that they have the same reverence for the papacy as we were legitimately accustomed to between Trent and Pius XII. No one would be allowed to say that the pope is the Antichrist or to deny the correctly understood dogmas of the First Vatican Council in regard to the papacy. But one could surely have another relationship to the pope than Catholics. Perhaps it would only be something like that of a thirteenth-century Christian like Saint Thomas, who indeed knew that there was a bishop of Rome who had a special importance, without that fact playing all too large a role in his religious thinking and daily church life.

As far as the task of accurately distinguishing between the identity of the gospel and the plurality of forms of expression is concerned, is it not more important and at the same time more difficult, to draw boundaries there, where the substance of the faith as such is ideologically falsified? Does the Church have the intellectual instruments to do that?

In the Catholic Church we must take into account much more that there are hidden but deeply rooted falsifications of genuine Christianity that have not reached the level of consciousness, but that are much worse and more important than certain officially designated heresies that emerged in theological disputes and were then officially condemned by the magisterium. It could well be that, for example, a certain large-city or small-town bourgeois mentality of conservative bent is fundamentally a much greater heresy, even though it is so seldom singled out as such, than if someone were to say that there are no angels, or that one could not imagine what original sin could be. Such is certainly possible. That one does not critically bring such diffuse contemporary mentalities to consciousness and condemn them in the name of Christianity as horrible heresies might be the result of the fact that the official representatives of the Church along with their theologians live somewhere in an area in which such heresies emerge only in an acceptable form. The other sort is found in the evil world, in which these bishops and theologians are not involved, and whose opposition they don't find it worth the effort to face and denounce.

With such a mentality one obviously hinders the possibility of speaking to the addressees of evangelization where they really are. If one wants to achieve that, where must one begin in order to meet the contemporary situation and the people living in it?

I am not at all for a "horizontal" Christianity. God, his honor, the responsibility of living before the judgment of God, the hope of eternal life, Jesus Christ, the crucified and resurrected one, remain the eternally central themes of the life and the preaching of the Church. However, could it not be in our country that if the official representatives of the Church were to stand up much more clearly and radically in teaching and practice for justice in the world, even against our widespread bourgeois egoism, if they would in this sense do more "political theology," they would also find a hearing for their ultimate truths among those upon whom tomorrow depends, especially because the command to love one's neighbor is, according to Jesus, one with the command to love God? It is also worthy of note that the Church says that it expects "the world" to take its gospel as foolish and old-fashioned. Mustn't the Church, then, critically check out its evangelization, asking if its teaching regarding justice and love is not delivered in a manner that is too neutral and abstract, if this teaching encounters no contradiction?

Translated by Donald W. Reck, S.J.
St. Louis University

29 · The Church Must Have the Courage to Experiment

Interview with Ignaz Kessler and Joachim Widera, editors of
Saarbrücken Zeitung, Saarbrücken (July 14, 1978)

We recall a lecture which you gave during the Second Vatican Council after the completion of the decree on the Church. You spoke especially of the definition of the Church as the sacrament of salvation for the world and projected at the time something like a futuristic picture of the Church. You said that the Church would be increasingly in the situation of the diaspora, yet simultaneously an avant-garde of humanity. Do you still maintain that picture or have there been developments in the meanwhile that would cause you to modify it?

The prognosis of a relatively small Church, the "little flock," extended throughout the world, but everywhere in diaspora, is today unfortunately almost more valid than it was ten or twelve years ago. Of course, in what detail my statement must be distinguished is a different question. What is the picture of the future of the Church in South America? What is the picture of the Church in Africa? How will Christianity exist in the communist world or in China? These are naturally individual questions that must be individually answered, questions that one can reply to in detail only with great difficulty. There are certainly regions in the world where one can be more optimistic.

Nevertheless, it is still true that this concretely so hard-pressed and percentwise small Church is the avant-garde, the sacrament of the salvation of the world, not existing for itself. This is a theological statement that really cannot be disowned on the basis of any experience in a relatively short period of history. For example—even if the example employed is somewhat crazy—when you baptize a human being, you do not need to immerse the individual entirely under the water; a relatively small gesture suffices, which is applied to the entire person and promises salvation to the entire person.

I would then say, with certain reservations, of course, that the Church is that small, modest sign that may only maintain itself with difficulty, a sign that God establishes for witnessing his salvific will for the entire world. And for that purpose the Church is a small, quasi-sacramental sign.

Professor Rahner, a scoffer is supposed to have once said, "The mills of God grind slowly, but the mills of the Vatican's curia grind terribly fine." To put that into other words, one could naturally allow oneself to look mainly to the future to trust to later temporal periods or even aeons. But that surely cannot be the correct view of the Church's life in which one is involved today. What can the Church do to come more out of her ghetto, her sanctuary, her diaspora, here today and not perhaps in some distant future?

I think that the Church must be a missionary Church, that she, if I may say so, should not rely on God's promises so as to do nothing, simply to petrify in a boring conservatism. One could apply here also the paradoxically formulated expression of Saint Ignatius of Loyola that one should so trust in God as if all depended upon oneself and, inversely, when one then does anything, one should so do it as if all depended upon God. It goes without saying that the Church—be it laity, priests, or bishops, the same applies to all—should not say that even the small flock is a good sacramental sign for the salvation of the world and that God will manage. No, the Church must do everything to advance on its own. And I think that there were very many impulses and potentialities given in the Second Vatican Council that are far from realized and not yet exhausted.

My personal feeling—here I speak not of South America nor of Africa nor of the Philippines nor of Japan—is that our central European Christianity more or less maintains the tendency to rein itself in conservatively, to preserve itself as much as possible, to value caution more than audacious experiments. In this way, in my opinion, the spirit of the Second Vatican Council is violated, even if one cannot show that definite sentences of a juridical type have been infringed. There are already, in my feel for the situation, regressive, reactionary tendencies.

I am not of the opinion that changes are correct merely because they are changes. Heaven help us! That would be simple nonsense. I have complete understanding for it when certain experiments, individual experiments that have shown themselves to be false or have not accomplished a breakthrough (if such a judgment is possible in ten years), have been put off to the side. When, for example, someone comes and says that many things that pertained to an older formation in a seminary were better, more intelligent, or more useful for education than many things that were carried on in a seminary during the last ten years, I would say: Good, we can discuss that intelligently and see what is proper there and, for my part, terminate certain experiments. Yet these are all particular questions that we cannot discuss in detail at the present time.

When I ask myself what must be the basic tendency, the basic mentality, then I am still of the opinion that today the Church must have courage for experiments, courage for a new type of proclamation, courage for new pastoral practices. And I think that the Church should not make a full or half turn toward a restoration of the old on the ground that everything has not been successful or that everything has not prevailed.

We often have the impression that the Church is no longer courageous, but has become timorous. The window opened to the world by the Second Vatican Council has been blown shut or, at least, has been opened so narrowly that drafts are no longer allowed in the Church. Or?

Yes, I think the same thing. But of course one must be careful in individual cases. We cannot throw everything into the same pot, and it stands to reason that sooner or later the Second Vatican Council will more or less prevail. There has never been any medicine in the Catholic Church that can destroy a true council.

There are, moreover, without doubt many things that have become old and obsolete and can be put aside without raising a ruckus or special reflection. As a result, after another twenty years, the Church will certainly be very much more different from the Church of the "epoch of the Piuses" between Pius IX and Pius XII. One cannot do anything against that. One can only ask, of course, whether in individual cases the brakes were wrongly applied or resistance was wrongly offered or false tendencies to return to the old were implanted or introduced where it was not intelligent to do so.

In this connection how do you judge the movement centered around Archbishop Lefebvre that recently consecrated a church and established a school in Saarbrücken?

As far as I have heard, Lefebvre does not intend to consecrate any bishops. If he consecrates no bishops, we can quietly wish him a blessed old age. But in ten years Bishop Lefebvre will be dead. According to Catholic principles, who then will ordain the priests of his reactionary movement? I believe that these things will simply die out.

According to Canon Law could he not really consecrate a bishop?

Yes, he could do so, just as the Old Catholics have validly consecrated bishops. From a dogmatic viewpoint he could validly consecrate a bishop. But you can find on another page that this bishop has no legitimate governing power in the Church, though he would be a bishop consecrated according to Catholic norms, who has the sacramental power to ordain other priests.

Nonetheless, as far as I know, Lefebvre has made known that he will consecrate no bishop, but will rely on divine providence so that despite everything—I do not know from where—priests of his orientation will come. But I can only imagine that this will be a wretched form of what is Catholic, which has no prospect for longevity.

Nevertheless, as we note in the mass media, just such occurrences like that concerning Archbishop Lefebvre or the case of the exorcism in Klingenberg arouse great interest. These occurrences create the picture of an odious Church and impossible Catholics. Yet the real Church does not dwell on exorcisms or live, if we may put it so, in a paraschismatic condition—does it?

No. There is no spiritual and at the same time socially institutionalized movement that does not have its dissidents, that does not have its battles for giving the proper orientation, that is not threatened by smaller or larger splinter groups. Rather, one has to ask what power or dynamism such a group possesses.

Do you consider the overall situation of the Church to be healthy on the whole?

From the viewpoint of Canon Law or the institutional Church I do not consider the Lefebvre movement a significant concern. Naturally, it is an entirely different question whether I believe the Church to be in a satisfying condition overall. To this one has to apply diverse standards of measurement.

Do you mean the condition of the Church with respect to an exceptional piety and spirituality which rises even into mysticism?

Do you mean a Church of an intensive life of religious orders or of a radical following of Jesus?

Do you mean the Church with respect to the clarity and straightforwardness of orthodoxy, of her faith?

Do you mean the Church with respect to her radical confession of the true, really Christian norms of society?

Do you mean the Church with respect to her intervention for the pariahs and the poor in contrast to a more bourgeois, comfortable, traditional Church?

There is a prodigious number of viewpoints according to which the actual condition of the Church, as measured by her proper task, can be judged. But such a judgment is very difficult, especially because conditions are so diverse in individual countries.

In my opinion, nowhere in the world is there such—if I may use these words —an established, organizationally fortified Church as here in Germany. Does that fact bring joy? Does that fact disqualify any opposition, even though one may be permitted a doubt with regard to the question about the inner vitality of this Church? All that is too difficult to judge, and I really do not dare to do so.

Let us remain then on one point, spirituality. Let us observe therefore the German Church, German Catholics. There are indeed new movements, for example, overwhelmingly of young people, who are searching for a new spirituality. How do you judge this?

Here the question would be: Do you mean spiritualities that are consciously and self-obviously ecclesiastical, or do you mean those spiritualities of charismatic, mystical, and other tendencies that develop independently of the Church? With regard to spiritualities within the Church, I would say that there are such, thanks be to God, but they could be considerably stronger.

We know that our bishop in Trier places great hope in these groups. That is frequently expressed in his sermons. He encourages these people under all circumstances, and he even goes so far as to propagate them. How do you look upon this?

These basic groups with a truly authentic spirituality are good, if there are such—and insofar as they exist, it is therefore very good. The question, of course, is to what degree they have already developed a persuasive missionary profile. On this point surely there would be a great deal to do.

Finally, the simple question remains: Can you measure such things by the spectacular impression that such groups make on wider public opinion? If you read a German tabloid newspaper for a year and discover that such basic groups are mentioned once in a ten-line story, but not otherwise, must you not then say that the Church cannot effect anything, that she has no offensive power? Also, how much time do you allow such movements until you declare them ineffective or dead, or attribute to them a manifest historical success?

Perhaps we can return again to the Church as institution. With that we come again to the picture of the papacy in our time. Professor Rahner, you have over the years taught that discipline which is named the queen of the theological sciences, dogmatics. We know certainly that such a man as Hans Küng has considerable difficulties with the dogma of infallibility. Now a question for you: Is it just individual people in the Church or outside the Church who have difficulties with this dogma and with the papacy, or is the image of the papacy actually changing?

On the one hand, in a properly understood sense, I confess without reservation the teaching of the First Vatican Council with regard to the authority of the pope in teaching and ruling the Church. On the other hand, I would not excessively play up such differences of opinion as Hans Küng announced.

It is obvious that today the question about God and his existence, our proximity to God, the forgiving God, God the Father of our Lord Jesus Christ, and so on, are very much more important and basic than the question of the papacy. It seems to me to be obvious in itself that a persuasive, attractive, missionary proclamation of these fundamental truths of faith is a more important, more decisive task, which perhaps Hans Küng also is attempting to attend to in his own way.

The concrete manner in which a Roman pope exercises the task assigned to him in the Church is a pastoral-theological question, a canonical question, which is to be distinguished clearly from the proper dogma of the First Vatican Council. There is a Roman centralism that I consider superfluous.

If, for example, Freiburg needed nine months until Rome finally decided which of the three candidates for bishop should be named—this is just an arbitrary example to which I attribute no great significance—then I would say: Here a Roman central bureaucracy dominates, which in itself has nothing to do with the essence of the Church and where the Romans act contrary to the spirit of the Second Vatican Council. That they also have their reasons in this matter and that they do nothing out of ill will, I easily believe—I do not want to ascribe to them any immoral motive or desire for Roman domination. In that respect let everything be proper and correct and allowed. Nevertheless, such things should not happen.

Or, for example—I say this with respect to the directive of the German bishops—whether we let our children go first to First Communion and then to confession or send them in reverse order should really be left up to a large regional Church. Such things need not be prescribed from Rome in such a way that the bishops must suddenly turn completely around against the synod and proclaim loudly that they suddenly all see clearly that in this matter Rome is right.

Cases like this have, of course, fundamentally nothing to do with the dogma of the First Vatican Council. And in such matters I expect and hope for very tangible and obvious changes in relations with respect to Rome's manner of ruling.

Translated by John M. McDermott, S.J.
Fordham University

30·The Immediate Experience of God in the Spiritual Exercises of Saint Ignatius of Loyola

Interview with Wolfgang Feneberg for *Entschluss*, Munich (1978)

Father Rahner, the readers of this interview are engaged laypeople and priests, not experts in the Ignatian Exercises. They would like to understand the Exercises anew and at the same time be stimulated to make the Exercises themselves, to distinguish what is correct and what is false in the retreat offerings, and to find help in their search for God. Since you are an expert in the field of the Ignatian Exercises, what counsels can you give them? How do you understand the various types of retreats which are offered today under the rubric "Exercises"?

I would first like to distinguish from the Exercises themselves two practices, which, although they are not the Ignatian Exercises, nevertheless are perhaps meaningful and even necessary; yet they are not to be described as Ignatian Exercises.

The first type and event would be a course of theological instruction. I readily admit to you that perhaps all the books that I wrote about the Ignatian Exercises are, on the whole, not Ignatian Exercises in the proper sense of the word, but theological treatises.[1] These can be profound or pious or modern; they communicate a verbalized theological thought. So something can be meaningful and necessary, can positively contribute help for one's personal life, but a course of theological lectures, even with the intent of edification and the goal of a concrete practice in life or of a change in one's way of life, is not what Ignatius meant in the strict sense with his Exercises.

The second type, which today is quite popular and in certain circumstances can positively be a help, consists of practices of a meditative type, particularly in the style of Eastern meditation and perhaps mysticism—if that which is here offered and intended can be so named. It is a matter of becoming tranquil, of a certain silencing of purposeful thoughts, of quiet, perhaps also of a certain openness to deeper levels of one's humanity. But even these various courses, which I have not characterized exactly, are not yet Exercises in Ignatius's meaning or at most can be considered as a preliminary step, which in certain circumstances is even necessary or can be undertaken with profit in order to attain the psychological-technical and existential possibilites of making the Exercises.

In contrast to letting oneself become present to oneself, insofar as this is possible, and in contrast to a verbal, theological indoctrination, however important these things are, the Exercises are concerned with something else, something more fundamental. It is a matter here of letting the Creator and the creature, as Ignatius says, deal directly with each other. Ignatius presupposes as both possible and actual an experience of God which, however many objectivized, verbalized moments or preparations or instrumental helps are included, is not identical with a verbalized, conceptual knowledge of God. In the Exercises Ignatius wants to lead one to nothing else besides this experience. Why and how something like this is bound to an immediate encounter with Jesus, why these two things mutually condition each other—namely, experience of God and immediate encounter with Jesus, which is something other than taking a mere historical interest in Jesus—that I cannot explain in greater detail here.

1. Karl Rahner, *Spiritual Exercises*, tr. Kenneth Baker, S.J. (New York: Herder and Herder, 1965).

How and where can one find a director of the Exercises, who is, in your words, neither a modern, transcendental, or yoga psychologist nor a theological indoctrinator?

To a certain degree one can assure oneself in advance whether an offered course tries only to present one of these two mentioned possibilites or really is a preparation for the Ignatian God-encounter with Jesus. Therefore, when it is clear from the kind of offering that only the first two types are offered, one can always consider whether this would, nonetheless, be good and useful. One can take this course, yet not expect thereby to receive or to make Ignatius's Exercises.

It is, of course, in principle and in practice possible that, where theological lectures are given and theological indoctrination is carried on with a certain existential engagement, an individual who listens to these lectures will be stimulated to something deeper, more radical, indeed, to the immediate encounter with God himself. In such a way, in such a course of existentially moving theological lectures something similar to the Ignatian Exercises happens.

Father Rahner, how and in what way does this immediate encounter of Creator and creature in Ignatius's sense have a special significance in our time, and what particular element of the encounter of Creator and creature—insofar as this is possible—is emphasized and made available to the person who makes the Exercises?

I am convinced that such an immediacy between God and the human person (we need not say Creator and creature) is of greater significance today than ever before. All the societal supports of religion are collapsing and dying out in this secularized and pluralistic society. If, nonetheless, there is to be real Christian spirituality, it cannot be kept alive and healthy by external helps, not even those which the Church offers, even of a sacramental kind—considering the sacraments directly and in themselves alone—but only through an ultimate, immediate encounter of the individual with God.

It has already been said that the Christian of the future will be a mystic or will not exist. I believe that this perhaps somewhat sharply formulated sentence is on the whole correct. Fundamentally, it means only that an immediate, personal experience of God must be found, which naturally is always formed by the characteristics of our time. But it is a matter of an experience of God which finally, to a certain degree, makes the person independent of the social milieu and refers him or her in its highest form to a church way of life, but does not derive from the traditional church way of life. This is perhaps expressed in an exaggerated way.

Father Rahner, another question: In what manner do you believe the Exercises help one to come to this immediacy of the experience of God so necessary today? This is, I think an existential question of all those who make such Exercises or wish to make them today.

I am trying to answer this question very simply insofar as I say that one should do it according to the quite normal, sober instructions of Ignatius, to be alone, to pray, to keep silence, and, of course, to make one's own the contents offered in the Exercises during the first, second, third, and fourth weeks.

If that is done, then it has to be seen if one notices that one has penetrated to a certain degree beyond a merely verbal conceptuality about God to God himself.

If that does not happen or if no movement of the spirits occurs even after sufficient time, as Ignatius presupposes, then either the Exercises were not made as Ignatius wants them made, or the necessary help of the retreat director was not received, or the *kairos* of such an encounter promised by God's grace has not yet been given. Indeed, Ignatius gives instructions about all of these things. I could, of course, hold a theoretical lecture about the theological-metaphysical nature of such an encounter with God, but in this context it makes no sense. Someone hearing it would still ask whether once again a theory of mysticism had become confused with true mysticism, whether a subtle discourse about God had become confused with an immediate experience of God.

In conjunction with that an interesting question would be what you believe might be Ignatius's instructions today, if he could make additions to his Exercises.

The great problem is whether and how we can still make the Ignatian Exercises today as Ignatius prescribes them or if elements of group-dynamics and similar things must be introduced into the Exercises. Even though I do not understand much about it, I am not of the opinion that all group-dynamic events, even if taken in a religiously sublimated sense, could not be something meaningful in themselves. Just as I said that there can be tremendous courses in theological reflection and meditative practices in the manner of Zen, so in principle I am not of the opinion that such common religious experiential practices would be a priori absurd or would have no real, authentic religious meaning. Nevertheless, I do not think that such things should be called Ignatian Exercises, because they are something else. One can and should not label with a magnificent name from the tradition everything that may be useful and offered today. Ignatian Exercises in the old style of individual solitudes, into which certainly the person is brought as a social being with all his or her tasks and demands, possess today a greater meaning than ever. If persons cannot put up with themselves in loneliness and perhaps in abandonment, therefore in silence, then they may not yet be suited for the Exercises. What these persons can do, what they can understand, and what one can offer them should not then be called Ignatian Exercises. Ignatius had not thought that the Exercises were the only possible way, the only sensible way that there is or can be in the world or in the Church, but he thought that in the form of the Exercises he could help a person to find God and not just talk about him.

How far one can and must now make the Exercises differently in many respects than previously, even where one wants to make them according to their original meaning—this is an entirely different question.

What do you mean by "make them differently"? Does that mean, for example, to introduce elements of witnessing, of dialogue, of reflection, or slide-meditations?
I do not know. A slide-meditation could certainly be introduced into the Exercises. Ignatius uses the application of the senses; why should not this be assisted or facilitated with slides? Questions of fasting and similar things, which Ignatius presupposed more or less naturally from his spiritual tradition, have to be thoroughly rethought. There is also the question whether the sequence of the Exercises, as Ignatius structured them in four weeks, is the only possible structure. Many things about meditative practices, recollection, quiet, and openness to the experience of God could perhaps be anticipated in a "zero week" before the first week begins.

Father Rahner, do you believe that in a time of extensive loss of faith, that is, in a time when the mass media are characterized by at least nominal atheism, the Ignatian Exercises present a special opportunity for the motivation to concern oneself with the question of the search for God?
Of course, Ignatius does not answer in his Exercises how one could bring today's skeptics or atheists to make the Exercises. Neither did Ignatius answer the question how I could win these persons over to "make the Exercises" for a couple of weeks in a situation where they would be completely thrown back upon themselves. One does not find anything in the Exercises about how I would have to make a start with such persons before they had an experience of God and perceived it as such. Even though Ignatius intended as the goal of the Exercises the modern, radically individual, irreplaceable experience of God, in contrast to today's world, he could presuppose an entire environment of self-obvious faith. Here is a task for a director of the Exercises: to reflect on how today's atheist could be led to an experience of God and be converted.

For Ignatius the moral conversion was simply the first thing that had to be accomplished—the first week demonstrates that. Today, previous to moral conversion, though this need not occur in an external, temporal sequence, a theological conversion would be the first thing.

This theological conversion, could it be related to or at least be seen in conjunction with today's very serious problem of resignation and depression, which is considered the specific sickness of our century?

I certainly believe that both these things are related to each other. A director of the Exercises, who wishes to lead people to an encounter with God, must of course begin with people as they are today, the resigned, depressed, skeptical persons who are tired and to whom all pathos seems but empty talk.

Perhaps a radicalization unto its final conclusion of the attitude of today's person would be the way to allow someone to break through it or to attempt such a breakthrough.

When mysticism speaks about the dark nights of the senses and of the spirit, these are not simply to be identified with any psychologically or sociologically induced depression that people today suffer. Yet these things are related to each other. The final conquest of humanity's present difficulties is basically capable of being attained only by the final, loving and hoping capitulation of the person into the incomprehensible mystery that we call God. To such an extent, present mentalities can certainly provide a starting point for the Exercises, as they should be given today. They cannot be given in the dry, simple words of Ignatius. That is impossible, for four hundred years separate us from him. We and our world are different from Ignatius and his world. Nevertheless, what Ignatius ultimately and properly intends is still relevant—even in the manner and form of individual Exercises in which the person goes off into solitude.

Father Rahner, you said that solitude and quiet are the goal of Ignatius. The common choral prayer of the monastic orders and other forms of spiritual contemplation, of quiet, of pilgrimages, of the entire liturgy actually intend nothing else than to render possible and attain the encounter of God and the person. What then is the specific assistance offered by Ignatius that people of today receive through this form of spiritual exercises?

It is hard to answer that question. Ignatius was a man of the Church; the common liturgy was self-evident for him, something that he accepted not only with patience but also with joy. All these forms of communal piety should always be supported by the greatest possible immediacy of one's relation to

God. Such a communal piety can also provide the stimulus for this immediate encounter with God. Yet normally, that immediacy to God, which Ignatius directly intends in his Exercises, will only be a subliminal, accompanying symptom in other religious practices and liturgies. It cannot be anything more than that in such practices.

If I were now to say to you: Come, let us pray the Our Father together, that would be a very meaningful thing. One could presuppose that each of us intends to pray seriously and does pray with full dedication, seriousness, love, and hope. One could easily suppose that in such an event are realized that faith, hope, and charity which imply absolute immediacy to God. Nevertheless, no one will maintain in all seriousness that when we pray this Our Father, however piously and seriously we do so, that immediacy to God of which Ignatius speaks in the Exercises is attained and realized as Ignatius wants to attain it and as he seeks to distinguish it from other religious or pseudo-religious happenings among people in the rules for the discernment of spirits.

Without doubt there are stages with respect to the immediacy to God and, parallel to this, also with respect to the existential radicality of freedom's execution. In the usual case, for example, the liturgy, however much it possesses its own meaning and significance and is irreplaceable, cannot of itself attain the final radicality of the meeting with God immediately in himself, which Ignatius sets as his goal.

I willingly allow for exceptions, yet if one is upright and intelligent, one must see that a Benedictine, who has to pay attention in choir to sing properly the chant which is tied to a definite sequence of words, cannot possess the final, radical, naked immediacy to God, which once again surpasses every mediation and which Ignatius sets as his goal. With this statement I do not wish to say that such a common liturgy would not contain anything meaningful or correct or is not indispensible. The liturgy can be the preparation for and the final notes of a mystical experience of God such as usually cannot be accomplished in the liturgy, and which Ignatius sets as a goal in the Exercises.

If someone perceives this as a depreciation of the liturgy, I cannot be of assistance to him. Generally speaking, it is especially the ultimate personal decisions and the ultimate mystical proximity to God that do not happen in the normal accomplishment of the liturgy as such.

Does not the modern person, impregnated by individualism, have a special chance under such circumstances to discover an opening to the liturgy and church life?

Of course, when such a person has vitally achieved his final proximity to God, which to a certain extent has consequences, and when (if we might say it in the words of Ignatius from the "Contemplation to Obtain Love") this person also experiences the descent of God into his world and experiences a simultaneously mystical synthesis not only between Jesus and himself or herself but also between what Ignatius names the concrete will of God and God himself—when that has been experienced, such a person is naturally capable of church life and the liturgy.

Translated by John M. McDermott, S.J.
Fordham University

31 · Following Christ Today

Interview with Slavko Kessler for *Entschluss*, Munich (1978)

It seems that belief in God is practiced less and less in our prosperous society. Discipleship, in day-to-day living, has become a problem—an occasion to reflect upon this subject. So-called political theology, in particular, has thought through how Christianity can be lived under altered societal conditions. Could you shed some light on this concept for us?

In the Catholic realm, Johannes Metz, my student, colleague in Münster, and friend, is trying to develop a so-called political theology. Now this does not mean that the theologian defends specific sociopolitical teachings or tendencies, or develops day-to-day politics, but only (putting it simply) that in theology, dogmatic theology and fundamental theology, the sociopolitical backdrop of human life must be taken into account. Furthermore, this means that one also receives stimulation for doing theology out of social needs, and so must ask oneself, in turn, what social consequences arise out of the Christian gospel and Catholic dogmatic theology.

Professor Metz maintains that following Jesus has a mystical and a social component. What does this mean, concretely, for the life of a Christian?

Although the statement that the following of Jesus has a mystical and a social component sounds unusual and surprising at first, it really is obvious. Ultimately, it simply means that the following of Jesus must fulfill the great commandment to love neighbor and God through the power from Jesus' Spirit. One could ask why Metz reformulates the obvious commandment that people, in order to be Christians, must love God with all their heart and their neighbor as themselves into this statement about a mystical and a social component.

First, let us look at the phrase "mystical component." In the days when the conviction about the existence of God was absolutely evident in society, the individual person could simply be convinced of the existence of God, because everyone spoke about God, and society in its explanations and indoctrinations clearly taught and emphasized the existence of God. And so this conviction had an almost insurmountable power in the consciousness of the individual. "God exists" was as obvious as "two and two make four," or as obvious as "no one may take his neighbor's life without sufficient cause." In our day, however, there is no society in which the conviction about the existence of God is publicly taken for granted. Today, the conviction about the existence of God must not, and cannot any longer, simply come into being only through indoctrination from outside, through the ideological power of society.

Then this is clearly the point at which the mystical component in following Jesus gets its meaning for the individual Christian?

Deeper sources for the conviction about the existence of God must be unearthed in individuals. This most personal and most intimate kind of conviction has the power to make the individual person, at least to a certain degree, independent of the theistic or atheistic ideology which is dominant in society. Of course, at this time I cannot give a lecture about such an inner, existential, personal experience of God. One would have to do so in another context. But the question does arise: Is there such a thing as an immediate experience of God? If Ignatius of Loyola is convinced that, at least during the Spiritual Exercises, the Creator deals directly with his creature, then there is such a thing as a mystical component to Christianity. If, in other words, we do not only have objectivized and verbalized concepts of God in our consciousness—while he himself nonetheless remains at an infinite distance and our thoughts only point in this direction—but if we do have an immediate, preconceptual experience of God through the experience of the limitless breadth of our consciousness, then there is such a thing as a mystical component to Christianity.

What are the tasks, then, for the uniquely Christian proclamation?

The mystical component must be much better developed. The individual priest and pastoral person would have to pay more attention to it; he would not only proclaim a message which comes only from outside the person, he would have to appeal to the innermost, personal experience of the individual person in his or her loneliness and absolute responsibility. Today a lively Christianity can exist even in an atheistic society only when the exterior message of Christianity knows that it is not powerful in itself alone, but is willing to encounter the innermost experience of the person, which is the mystical component of Christianity, and actualize it, making it come alive, digging it out from under the rubbish of everyday awareness. It has already been said that the Christian of the future must be a mystic or no longer exist, precisely because he or she no longer has any protection against the general societal ideology. This is a bit of an overstatement, perhaps, but basically it is correct.

Father Rahner, up to this point you have explained the meaning of the mystical component. What is its connection with what is meant by the "societal component"?

Let us look at the other component, then, which Metz has labeled "the societal component." Up to this point we have spoken as if there were a mystical experience of God, which occurs only in the deepest interior of a person, where the person is precisely not just a part, an instance of society, but where the person is a unique individual, answerable to himself or herself alone. That does not really have to be taken back. There is a lonely human mysticism in which, as Ignatius says, the creature and the Creator interact directly. What kind of person is capable of this? If you want to answer this question more precisely, you would have to say: Only the person with love of neighbor is really capable of such a mystical experience of God. In the New Testament love of God and love of neighbor already form a unity. The experience of the absolute worth of another human person and absolute respect for another human person's unique worth are basically presuppositions for and consequences of our relationship with God. They are not only consequences—this is obvious in Christian awareness, because it is convinced that whoever loves God must also love neighbor, and that the love of neighbor is a duty, a consequence of our relationship with God. But we must also say that this love of neighbor is, at the same time, a precondition for our relationship with God.

If love of neighbor is a precondition for our relationship with God, then every person who practices love of neighbor is already on the way toward God. Correct?

Vatican II declares that a person (even if one thinks oneself an atheist) can be incorporated into the paschal mystery of Christ and be saved if the voice of conscience is followed with inexorable fidelity and selflessness. This means nothing less than that so-called atheists have found God, even if anonymously, when they selflessly follow their conscience—practically this means loving one's neighbor—essentially overcoming their own selfishness. In other words, this selflessness found in love of neighbor, which is a breaking out of the prison of egoism, indicates not only a breakthrough to one's neighbor but is already a breakthrough to God, even if it is as yet unspoken and unreflected upon.

One breaks out of the narrowness of one's own existence in some way. One comes into a wide-open space, which no longer has boundaries and which moves one well on the way toward God, whether one reflects on the fact or not. These are only very primitve hints at the meaning of the statement that love of neighbor is the precondition and the result of love of God. In other words, one can only transcend one's self when a movement gets underway that does not stop, but arrives not only at one's neighbor but finally and ultimately arrives at God.

What then is the uniquely sociopolitical dimension of Christian love of neighbor?
Now, if love of neighbor is the precondition and the result of the love of God—precondition, if you will, of an anonymous love of God and the consequence of an expressed recognition and love of God—then one should not assume that this means it is only a private, purely subjective relationship of one person with another. Love, in a Christian sense, has, of course, an absolutely personal dimension, a dimension of intimacy, of heart, and of feeling. But love of neighbor in the Christian sense has a thoroughly unique social and sociopolitical dimension. If a person truly wants to love his or her neighbor, that person must, to some extent, not only offer the intimacy of his or her heart up to a certain point, but that person is bound out of love of this neighbor to do all that can be done, so that the sociopolitical structures of society are such that they serve the neighbor's freedom and development, that they do not enslave or exploit the neighbor, and do not lead to injustice toward the neighbor.

So then, when we say that the love of neighbor is the precondition and the result of love of God, we intend to say that this love of neighbor brings with it its sociopolitical task.

Could we now summarize, briefly, what following Jesus means in our day and what it demands of us Christians?
If Christianity is love of God and love of neighbor, if in our day love of God

can only be realized in a mystical experience of the nearness of God, and if love of neighbor can only be realized in the maintaining of a sociopolitical task, which every human being has, then I think that what Metz says is clear: Precisely in our day, Christianity has a mystical component and a social component. And precisely in our day, because without the mystical component a mere external indoctrination of the existence of God and of Christianity and its content does not suffice. And precisely in our day, a sociopolitical or social component is of special significance, because the modern person cannot find believable true love of neighbor, which comes from God and witnesses to God, if it were to limit itself to a merely intimate realm between persons, and not take into account the actual social, sociopolitical and sociocritical task.

Translated by Robert Braunreuther, S.J.
Boston College

Karl Rahner's parents, Luise (1875–1976) and Karl (1868–1934).
Photo: Karl-Rahner-Archiv, Innsbruck.

As a two-year-old (*center*) on Shrove Tuesday, 1906, with (*left to right*) sister Anna, brothers Georg and Hugo, and a cousin. Photo: Karl-Rahner-Archiv, Innsbruck.

Toasting his mother on her hundredth birthday with Theophil Herder-Dorneich, publisher of Herder Verlag. Photo: (Alber-) Bildverlag, Freiburg.

As a novice in the Society of Jesus (1922).
Photo: Karl-Rahner-Archiv, Innsbruck.

With Karl Barth (*left*) and Eduard Dhanis, S.J., at the International Congress on the Theology of Vatican Council II, Rome, 1966. Photo: Karl-Rahner-Archiv, Innsbruck.

With William Monihan, S.J. (*left*) and William V. Dych, S.J., in San Francisco during U.S. lecture tour (1967). Photo: Karl-Rahner-Archiv, Innsbruck.

With Roland E. Murphy, O. Carm. (*left*) and Hans Küng at an annual meeting of the editorial board of *Concilium*. Photo: CIRIC, Geneva.

With Johann B. Metz and Julius Cardinal Döpfner. Photo: Karl-Rahner-Archiv, Innsbruck.

At the Joint Synod of West German Dioceses in Würzburg (1971–1975).
Photo: KNA-Bild, Frankfurt.

Advocate of structural change in the church at the Würzburg synod (1974).
Photo: KNA.

Conferral of the Cardinal Innitzer Prize by Franz Cardinal König of Vienna (1976). Photo: Karl-Rahner-Archiv, Innsbruck.

With President Walter Scheel of the Federal Republic of Germany at an annual meeting of the West German Order of Merit for Arts and Sciences. Photo: Karl-Rahner-Archiv, Innsbruck.

At the World Congress of Jesuits, Frankfurt, 1977.
Photo: KNA-Bild, Frankfurt.

With young members of the staff of the journal *Entschluss* in Vienna.
Photo: Karl-Rahner-Archiv, Innsbruck.

Photo: Adolf Waschel, Vienna

Photo: Adolf Waschel, Vienna

Photo: Adolf Waschel, Vienna

Part III

THEOLOGY IN A
PERIOD OF TRANSITION

INTERVIEWS 1979–1980

32 · Karl Rahner at 75 Years of Age

Interview with Leo J. O'Donovan, S.J., for *America* magazine,
Munich (March 10, 1979)

*Father Rahner, you've had seventy-five years of human experience now. Would
you be able to tell us what the major turning points in your life have been?*

I don't know whether I've had major turning points in my life, or whether
the brook or river of my life has always gone more or less in the same direction, so that now the time has gradually come for this river of time to flow
into the sea of eternity. You know, I grew up in a Catholic family. It was a
family with seven children, middle class, and on my mother's side, but also on
my father's Catholic as a matter of course, without being at all sanctimonious.
After the *Abitur* which comes at the end of German secondary education, I
entered the Society of Jesus at eighteen. There I did my studies and have had
my life's work.

So there weren't really occasions to experience major, radical changes or
upheavals. In fact, I'd probably say just the opposite. The remarkable, unusual,
but obvious thing about my spiritual life was that every new situation somehow revealed and brought home the one same ancient and genuine future—by
pointing ever and again toward God and his life. Naturally, there's an outer
course of life: youth and age, studying and teaching, writing and lecturing and
preaching, meeting all sorts of people. Think of the Weimar Republic, the
Nazi period, the thirty years after the Second World War, and so forth. But
all these different times, that you naturally do experience in a certain way intensely and alertly, still didn't cause any upheavals in my own life, even though
they were all so different. Basically, they made clear ever and again the one
same reference to the incomprehensible mystery that we call God.

Now, I admit that other people, authentic Christians, too, can experience
life differently. In other words, a person's life can include historical turning
points, demands, new ventures and hopes for the future, disappointments,
and so forth. And, according to God's providence, they can experience and
have experienced these things more intensely and radically than I have. But
my own life, even with all its natural share in the cultural life of the last sixty
or seventy years, has run in a certain sense monotonously. I don't mean it in
the sense that every life should be that way. But that's the way it was with me.
Even with all the changes of our time, the external circumstances of my own
life were to a certain extent quite regular.

I've been a Jesuit since 1922. So I've been a Jesuit for fifty-six years. As far as the external style and conditions of that lifestyle go, the life of a Jesuit, at least for myself, was really relatively homogeneous. The work of a theologian probably has its own natural development, its new realizations and so on. But I would say that my life was characterized rather by a certain monotony, a regularity, a homogeneity that comes from a person's turning toward the final theme of theology, of religious life, and also of human life in general—which comes from the one, silent, absolute but always present reality of God.

In your life you've met people both inside and outside the Church. Who, for example, influenced or impressed you especially? You've already mentioned your family.

That's another hard question. If you ask me only about people I've met outside the Church, then first of all I would have to make some reservations— that I can't activate my memory so quickly for such a question.

Naturally, there are interesting people outside my order and the Church whom I've met and who have indeed made a certain impression on me. Martin Heidegger should, of course, be mentioned first of all. And then there are naturally other people whom I've met and who are relatively well-known figures. I have come to know Heinrich Böll personally, and Golo Mann and Erich Fromm. I knew Ernst Bloch and was at least once in Karl Barth's company. Among theologians, I also knew Friedrich Gogarten. If I could test my memory now more closely and exactly and longer, I would certainly want to name others. And if I did look more closely, then I would not want to be ungrateful and underrate the influence and the significance of all these people, nor the influence of poets and philosophers one knows only through books.

But if, in fact, I ask myself, for example, whether Heidegger exercised a great influence on me, then I would say that I am not exactly sure. Naturally, I am grateful that I was able to sit in his seminar with a few others for two years. Certainly, I learned a variety of things from him, even if I have to say that I owe my most basic, decisive, philosophical direction, insofar as it comes from someone else, more, in fact, to the Belgian philosopher and Jesuit, Joseph Maréchal. His philosophy already moved beyond the traditional neoscholasticism. I brought that direction from Maréchal to my studies with Heidegger and it was not superseded by him.

Perhaps it depends on the monotony of my life or on a somewhat monotonous self-interpretation when I say that I have not actually met major figures who have turned my life around or changed it radically. I don't consider this an advantage, but just recognize it as a fact, and maybe even a regrettable one. Even the teachers I had in my order, for example, teachers who were certainly industrious, learned, well-read and educated, seemed to me at least to be relatively second-rate people for whom I was not so enthusiastic as a disciple would be for his master. I cannot say that in my Jesuit philosophy and theology I met a master who, so to speak, overwhelmed or deeply stirred or inspired me. That could be my own fault, and perhaps unfortunate. But there again, I would say: That is how it has been.

Naturally, I know that people like Heidegger or Ernst Bloch, or a Nobel Prize winner like Heinrich Böll, and even Erich Fromm, were men of greater ability, greater teachers, and more creative thinkers than my teachers in the order. But even among such people, I would not really say that I have met the great master to whom alone, in one way or another, I was bound in a blazing discipleship. So I am, if you want to put it that way, like every other human being, the product of my environment, but really more the product of a diverse, a perhaps anonymous and symmetrical environment that worked on me from different sides.

With respect to the Society of Jesus, would you say that Ignatius of Loyola has molded your own religious experience?

Naturally, I don't want to say too much about that, because it isn't really anybody else's business. But I do think that in comparison with other philosophy and theology that influenced me, Ignatian spirituality was indeed more significant and important. There, too, to be honest, I cannot say that individual Jesuits, spiritual directors, retreat masters, and so forth made an overpowering impression on me. In fact, I would honestly admit, if one may be allowed such a confession, that I made eight-day retreats, for example, with the late Father Augustin Bea, who later became a cardinal, and with Franz Hürth, who was an important moral theologian in Rome, but that I found both these men, who really were important in the Church, disappointingly traditional. But I think that the spirituality of Ignatius himself, which one learned through the practice of prayer and religious formation, was more significant for me than all learned philosophy and theology inside and outside the order.

Of course, there were also some men in the generation of Jesuits just before me whom one should mention and who were already, in fact, forerunners or initiators of a breakthrough from the philosophy and theology of neoscholasticism. I'm thinking now of men like Peter Lippert, or even more of Erich Przywara, perhaps also Dunin Borkowsky. In this connection, I should perhaps say also that without ever having had the intention of becoming a researcher in the field of spiritual theology and its history, I did read a relatively large amount of major spiritual literature. Then later, just before the Second World

War, I edited an expanded translation of Marcel Viller's book, *Asceticism and Mysticism in the Time of the Fathers*; this was a translation of Viller, but I did write half of it myself. In addition, you know, I also wrote an essay on the mysticism of Bonaventure. And so, I grounded myself fairly well in the original sources of Jesuit spirituality. Also, for that matter, in Teresa of Avila and John of the Cross, and so forth.

In short, even though I remain a poor sinner, I think that the great spirituality of the Church in general and especially of the Jesuits had a larger and broader influence on me than did my immediate teachers both inside and outside the order.

Do you think that your pastoral concern in theology also grew out of this reading and research?

I have already said quite often, and I think that it's correct, that however abstract and schoolmasterly my theology may have been, it still has had in the end a pastoral, ministerial inspiration. I mean, I have never or at least very seldom done theology for theology's sake, like "art for art's sake."

It's not so much because I was able to be very active pastorally. Naturally, especially when I was younger, I did preach relatively often. In Innsbruck, for example, I preached every Sunday for ten years. When I was younger, I gave retreats relatively often—not for everyone, for example, not for students in secondary schools, but still, in fact, for a variety of people of very different sorts: priests, members of religious orders, religious women, educated groups, and so on.

I also did pastoral work, though I didn't do a great deal of it. In Lower Bavaria during the war, I helped out in the ordinary parish ministry. From 1939 to 1944, during the war, I was a member of the Pastoral Institute in Vienna, where Monsignor Karl Rudolf, who has long since died, had developed and built up a type of diocesan pastoral institute that was scarcely heard of before, I think, at least in central Europe. In earlier times, the chanceries were really more or less bureaucratic administrative centers. By founding and developing and organizing the Pastoral Institute, Rudolf shifted the diocesan administration's center of gravity from the bureaucracy to central institutions of living pastoral care. And in that year, I was also one of his modest co-workers who went through this.

In short, both from a personal, existential concern, but also from such an understanding of pastoral needs, I hope and I think that my theology was never really "art for art's sake" in the way that was usual in scholarly theology, at least in dogmatic theology, before my time. You see, I certainly don't want to take anything away from Martin Grabmann. He was a devout priest who also thoroughly understood pastoral tasks and worked to meet them as well as he could. But a Martin Grabmann, an Arthur Landgraf, and so forth were, in fact, theological scholars who lived more or less in the conviction that systematic theology in its proper sense could not make great progress any more. Landgraf said this directly, that all scholarship, properly speaking, at least in dogmatic theology, concentrates on its earlier history, so that research into this history is important, attractive, and interesting but, in fact, has no very great significance for preaching the gospel today, or for today's spiritual life, and so forth.

In other words, in those days, at least in systematic theology—I'm not talking now about moral theology or pastoral theology or catechetics, and so forth —in properly dogmatic theology, one pursued, in fact, a retrospective theology out of historical curiosity. Of course, I don't want to say that I never did anything like that myself. The eleventh German volume of my *Theological Investigations*, with my essays on the history of penance, certainly shows that. But this type of learned, restrospective theology for its own sake was really always foreign to me. And as a result of a certain spirituality, of what compelled me in a present and existential way, and of pastoral or ministerial work, I did see, I believe, new and important tasks that were also posed for a systematic, speculative theology.

You have also treated the theme of hope and the future fairly intensively and have expressed yourself rather optimistically on that score. Would you characterize your theology on the whole as optimistic, or perhaps rather as realistic?

Under certain circumstances, you can naturally find veins or levels in my actual theology that have a philosophical or, better, an optimistic vein. For example, when I spoke earlier about the hominization of the world and so forth, or when I said that nature on its own terms is no longer simply the environment for humanity but a construction site for a world which humanity itself builds. In statements like these, it could naturally happen that other points of view of a more pessimistic sort, if you will, were not sufficiently noticed. But I would say that being conditioned by time in that way, and perhaps also by temperament, and so forth, is not so important. It's not so important for this reason: In contrast to a modern, liberal, Marxist futurology, I have always emphasized, first, that the final and absolute future is God as God himself, and second, that this absolute future can only be reached through the medium of death. And so, over against a liberalistic, futurological optimism of an enlightenment sort, there was always the Christian conception of a pessimistic world that is in a certain sense given over to death and permanently ensnared in guilt.

I would think myself that "realistic" would be a better word—better than optimisitc or pessimistic.

If you place each and every thing, every knowledge and every reality, at least basically and intentionally under the sign and seal of God as the mystery which is never set aside, then, naturally, optimism, pessimism, realism are all very indeterminate and imprecise criteria. What does it mean to be realistic? To be realistic means only to accept reality unconditionally just as it is. Now, if in the first place this same incomprehensible God belongs to this reality as its ground and encompassing power, and second, if this incomprehensible God is really accepted in faith, hope, and love as giving and sustaining the meaning of our lives, and if, third, this acceptance of the absolute mystery fundamentally always occurs in an unconditioned surrender to God through death, and only in that way, then what really should we mean, then, by realism or optimism or pessimism? I never wanted to be a pessimist of despair. I never wanted to be an optimist who overlooks the mystery of death for the individual and for the world. If someone then wants to call this other view realism, all right. But this realism is certainly not the realism of a narrow-minded banality and a superficial life. On the contrary, a person is realistic in my view only if that person believes in God and lets himself or herself fall into that tremendous, unfathomable abyss. So what does realism really mean!

Are there themes, or perhaps a theme, Father Rahner, that concern you especially today, something that you would still like to work out?

That's hard to say. One or two years ago, perhaps, I really had the intention of writing something about a possible orthodox teaching on apocatastasis [the doctrine that all free beings will eventually share in the grace of salvation]. To be sure, previous theology has considered the existence of eternal damnation and hell an already given fact or one that was absolutely certain to occur, in the same sense that it considered heaven and eternal beatitude certain. Today, I think, not only I myself but other theologians, as well, would speak differently, without wanting to represent a heretical teaching on apocatastasis. Within my own historical time, I must indeed reckon absolutely and unconditionally with the possibility of being eternally lost. But despite certain texts in the New Testament, I do not know with absolute certainty that this eternal loss occurs for any particular people. And I can say: I hope, without being able to know this now for sure, that God has in fact created a world in which all questions indeed find a positive solution.

So I would still really like to have written something about such a teaching on apocatastasis that would be orthodox and acceptable. But it is a very difficult matter. You would probably have to study and answer once again new questions in the history of dogma and especially also in exegesis; you would also have to consider questions of exegetical and philosophical interpretation. For all that, my time and strength may not be sufficient anymore. And so, I don't know how it will work out.

In any case, the thirteenth German volume of my *Theological Investigations* appeared in the fall of 1978, and so did a small book written together with Father Karl-Heinz Weger.[1] This year, also, since it is already more or less ready, the fourteenth German volume of *Theological Investigations* will appear. And so, for the time being, even without this question of apocatastasis, I have enough to do.

Among your own writings, is there any text or work that is particularly impor-tant for you yourself?

First of all, I think, one should distinguish this question with respect to my so-called more devotional, spiritual writings and then my more systematic theology—although in my own case, in fact, perhaps more so than with other theologians, there is no exact boundary between these two.

Let us just take the difficult problem of the prayer of petition. I think I prob-ably handled that in my own case for the first time in my small devotional book *On Prayer*.[2] And there, in fact, I probably put things theologically in a way not really very different from those texts which are more systematic. The little book, *On Prayer*, is therefore for me at least just as important as those more scholarly matters—even though it is "only" a devotional book.

Then you might also say that, from another point of view, it is not a certain book but certain ideas that are very important to me. And here I am certainly not thinking only of what people commonly call Rahner's "transcendental theology," but also of other questions that basically seem important to me. Take, for example, what I have called "the logic of concrete individual knowl-edge in Ignatius Loyola," about which Father Harvey Egan in America has also written, I think.[3] Such matters are important, I believe; they are new to a certain extent and really could still have consequences for other questions and groups of problems, even where people do not yet see this so clearly.

Once, for example, I wrote an essay in which I tried to show that this same

---

1. See Karl Rahner and Karl-Heinz Weger, *Our Christian Faith*, tr. Francis McDonaugh (New York: Crossroad, 1981).

2. See Karl Rahner, *On Prayer* (Ramsey, N.J.: Paulist, 1968).

3. See Harvey D. Egan, S.J., *The Spiritual Exercises and the Ignatian Mystical Horizon* (St. Louis: The Institute of Jesuit Sources, 1976).

logic of concrete individual knowledge is basically and typically Jesuit, but that it had no place whatsoever in the traditional type of fundamental theology written by Jesuits.[4] But it could have played an important role there. And so, the scholastic Jesuit theologians did not use the greatest and most important riches from the *Spiritual Exercises* to fertilize their own theology. Instead, they presupposed some sort of essential and rational theory of knowledge as the only possible one and didn't realize that Ignatius had taught them something entirely different.

And so, there are questions like that in my work. But if you ask me whether I have a sort of favorite book, then I really don't know. You could say, the earliest books are the best, you know. Or you could say, no, that's not true, a late work like *Foundations of Christian Faith* is the most important. But then, I don't know that either.

Would it be too much to ask at the end, Father Rahner, how you yourself would identify the center of your theology?

That's hard to say. The center of my theology? Good Lord, that can't be anything else but God as mystery and Jesus Christ, the crucified and risen one, as the historical event in which this God turns irreversibly toward us in self-communication. So in principle, you can't name just *one* center.

Naturally, all geometrical means of representation are inadequate. But even apart from that, we have to remember that humanity is unconditionally directed toward God, a God which we ourselves are not. And yet, with this God, who in every respect infinitely surpasses us, with this God himself, we do have something to do; God is indeed not only the absolutely distant one, but also the absolutely near one, absolutely near, also, in his history. It is precisely because of this that God as this center at the same time makes Jesus Christ the center. I don't know what you should call that. Why should I decide, so to speak, for one center that I can characterize with one word? I don't think you can do that.

So you look on theology, in fact as "systematic" but not as a final system?

No, no, no! One should never stop thinking too early. The true system of thought really is the knowledge that humanity is finally directed precisely not toward what it can control in knowledge but toward the absolute mystery as such; that mystery is not just an unfortunate remainder of what is not yet known but rather the blessed goal of knowledge which comes to itself when it

---

4. See Karl Rahner, "The Logic of Concrete Individual Knowledge in Ignatius Loyola," in *The Dynamic Element in the Church* (New York: Herder and Herder, 1964), pp. 84–170.

is with the incomprehensible one, and not in any other way. In other words, then, the system is the system of what cannot be systematized.

And now, let's stop there.

Thank you, Father Rahner.

Translated by Leo J. O'Donovan, S.J.
Weston School of Theology

33 · For an Open Church

Interview with Christian Modehn for West-German Radio (WDR) Cologne (February 21, 1979)

Father Rahner, in your book The Shape of the Church to Come *[New York: Seabury, 1974] you come out decidedly in favor of further reform in the Catholic Church, especially here in Germany. One of the central chapters in your book is entitled: "A Declericalized Church." In that chapter you plead for the need within the Church of greater responsibility for laypersons and for the further need of not only encouraging small basic Christian communities but also of giving them further rights. Is your conviction on these matters still the same today?*

Yes. I still have the same opinion. To talk about a declericalization of the Church is not to deny that Christ entrusted a proper mission and task to ordained priests, bishops, and so on. My comments were concerned rather with the relationship between clergy and laity that exists nowadays that has been affected by religious and cultural factors. Precisely because the Church in today's world is no longer supported by visible social structures or factors, the Church needs, for the possibility of its very survival, a much more personal and authentic participation by all the laity. That means, of course, by the very nature of things, that laypersons need greater rights, greater influence. Nobody can be expected to collaborate if one is still treated as a simple servant by a Church which sees itself constituted essentially by hierarchy and priests for whom the so-called laity are only objects of pastoral care.

Now in Germany there are some areas, especially in small town communities, where the laity already are conducting Sunday worship services and frequently are regarded by the faithful as a kind of pastor. Do you think that this practice will lead to the introduction of something new in the Church?

I think it's quite understandable for a community to want a specific leader to serve as its coordinator and who bears responsibility for this community. Naturally, this community might, on a short- or long-term basis, want to arrange for the possibility of a eucharistic liturgical celebration even if the presence of an ordained priest is not possible. In that case, the coordinator would not have to be ordained in the usual way. This would mean that equivalently such a layperson could be ordained a "priest" even if married.

What you are suggesting then is acceptance of more than one kind of ordained priest. Are you saying that there should be not only celibate priests but also married priests?

I presume that over the long term one could not rule out a development along those lines.

Another important chapter in your book contains a plea for stronger ecumenical praxis. A key notion in your exposition is the unity in practice of the churches from different confessions.

I am convinced as a theologian that the classical doctrinal differences that separated the churches do not exist as much today as they once did. Let us presuppose that perhaps apart from the question of the papacy, the differences in teaching are no longer confessionally dividing or that those that do exist could be rather easily overcome. If that is the case, then, in my opinion, a question needs to be addressed to the hierarchy and the appropriately, ecclesiastically designated leaders of the Church whether they really have the courage to recognize this fact and thus to provide some kind of real organizational and social unification of the various churches (as for instance, the churches in Europe). That doesn't have to mean, and about this I am thoroughly convinced, that all the churches thus united into a real and authentic unity would have to disavow their own historical origins in effecting the emergence of a

Roman Catholic unity along the lines of existing Canon Law. That is not necessary. Neither faith nor theology require that. I mean, once and for all, we need finally to draw practical consequences from the situation that exists in modern theology.

Are you suggesting that small groups, ecumenical groups within Germany such as Action 365 could act as a sort of catalyst encouraging the advancement of ecumenism in Germany.

Yes. Of course, I don't think that groups such as Action 365 can simply prescind from ecclesiastical regulations or that they should introduce ecumenical liturgies in the strict sense independently of the hierarchy. That would surely not serve the ecumenical movement but would only produce a third confessional group alongside the two other confessions. In other words, that would be the very opposite of true unity. But those involved at the level of basic communities should speak up and repeatedly question church officials: How are preparations continuing? What are you doing, not just through pious words but through concrete action, to achieve this unity?

Do you feel that in fact the faith which Christians of different confessions profess is for the most part already identical?

I believe you can honestly say that. Of course, I don't mean to imply that the mere fact something exists in the consciousness of nominal Christians ought to be interpreted as the absolute, unqualified norm for what the Church must believe. But the fact that the faith whereby practicing Christians today live their Christianity draws its inspiration not from what separates the confessions but from what unites the confessions should provide material for reflection to theology and church leaders on the basis of which we can and must draw conclusions.

You repeatedly describe Christian community as being a place where each person, each thinking, present-day individual must have a place, where even those who do not identify totally with the teachings of the Church can likewise be accommodated. In short, an open community. What are your views on that today?

Well, I wouldn't want to say that every atheist who emphatically and explicitly states his or her atheism can or should also have an equal place within the Church. That's quite impossible. The Church needs a common creed, a common doctrine, even a common practice. But I do believe that if you look at this from a strictly theological point of view and you don't consider as binding matters that ultimately are not binding, that the Church could accommodate contemporary men and women more than it presently thinks. In addition to that the Church must be open toward others; it needs to show understanding for others and to engage in conversation with others who are not yet strictly speaking Christian members of the Church so that they can express themselves, be listened to and be understood. And of course in many other things such as sociopolitical concerns the Church can collaborate with others. These are matters where a real unity exists or could exist, even when there is not yet unity on more subtle theological doctrines (which still have importance).

As a theologian dedicated to reform, as a theologian involved in Vatican II, when you look back over the reforms that have already in fact been achieved, where would you like to see a stronger commitment to reform especially in the German Church?
Both as far as the letter and the spirit of Vatican II are concerned, I'm convinced that there are many more possibilities for improvement and development, even in the German Church, that could and should be realized than has happened up to now. I've already mentioned a broader participation of the laity. At the German pastoral synod there were many hopes, proposals, desires expressed to Rome, which in fact were partly either rejected by Rome or which partly failed to receive much subsequent attention. In all these and many other matters, I think, the German Church should not be simply dominated by conservative, anxious worries, as to a great extent it has been up to now.

Professor Rahner, when one looks at the Catholic churches in neighboring European countries such as the Netherlands or France, one has the impression that Catholic life is able to develop there in a much more lively fashion at all levels, even, for example, in regard to political pluralism. In Germany, on the other hand, one has the impression that the Church still carries the burden of bourgeois attitudes which results in the fact that here Church reform can be achieved only with much more difficulty. How would you explain this phenomenon?
We should make several important distinctions. I don't think that everything that happens in France, the Netherlands, or perhaps even Spain should automatically and unquestionably become a model or, even less, a requirement for us too. But I do feel that we in our situation could draw from all these other churches a bit more courage and trust in the possibility of living Christianity in a way more in touch with the times. And you are quite right. I have the same impression that the German Church is somehow a Church that reflects bourgeois society and which accordingly feels most comfortable when it neglects, all too frequently, other groups (against its own theory). It's a

Church that has little courage to try for once to preach the gospel to others in such a way that it could be understood by them. In this connection I feel as though the German Church is really a Church characterized by excessive passivity, anxiety, and petty bourgeois outlooks.

When a person looks at your publications and sees over and over again the effort you've made to introduce reforms into the Church, and when one takes into account that you are now almost seventy-five years old, one wonders: Do you look back with a certain degree of discouragement knowing that quite a bit of what you tried to achieve has not been realized, or do you say, well, my whole life's work in which I have invested so much energy was in the last analysis all worth it?

I would have to say I have accomplished a little bit, and more creative and fruitful results will follow from what I have endeavored to say. In the life of every ordinary Christian and theologian there has to be an element of frustration. Is it different anywhere else?

You have resigned from many committees including international commissions. Was your decision motivated by discouragement?

Don't forget—I will soon be seventy-five years old. And so, of course I have the right and even the duty to tread lightly and not to wish to be present everywhere. That does not imply that I have become discouraged, but rather that I have begun to draw conclusions from my age. That too is part of Christian living.

Professor Rahner, the Church in Latin America appears to be in a very lively situation. They have had the courage to become involved socially in basic Christian communities, and a new theology has emerged there, the theology of liberation. How do you assess this breakthrough, this new breakthrough in Latin American Christianity?

If one shares the dogmatic and theological conviction that every large Church must offer its own unique contribution to the life of the worldwide Church, then one can in principle, I think, only rejoice at seeing in Latin America a large lively Church which doesn't receive its Christian and theological goods only as exports from Europe, but has its own individuality in theology, in church practice, in building communities, and so on. And so I am completely delighted about the efforts that have been made in Latin America.

But not every theology of liberation, no matter how it is conceived and thought out, is necessarily a true Catholic theology of liberation. But I am convinced that a true Catholic theology of liberation can and must exist. (I gladly confess to having been a theologian of late European individualism.) I can only rejoice when a theology develops in Latin America which is built up on the experience of community, on the grassroots experience of the Church, on the sociopolitical task of the Church.

As a theologian and as a European theologian you have in part drawn upon themes of Latin American theology or at least you have supported and defended this theology against attacks that originated even here in West Germany.

Well, that would be a source of satisfaction to me if it were indeed the case. There is a certain amount of exchange here and there. A Latin American theologian will pay some attention to my theology, and I, even given my age, am quite ready to learn from Latin America and its theology.

Since even the Latin American Bishops' Conference (CELAM) in Puebla (1979) cannot turn back the clock on this movement for liberation theology, do you believe that it is a movement strong enough to survive?

You ask me a question that I am not qualified to answer. I don't know what the pope will say, and I don't know who in the Latin American Bishops' Conference will have the most say. There will certainly be efforts at compromise, perhaps that is a good thing; but, in general, I hope that Puebla will continue and will be allowed to continue to foster the goals of Medellín (1969). I hope that it does not lose the courage of its own convictions, but meets the new challenges which face it at this time and which as such have never existed before in the Church's history. Church history is not a mere repetition of what has been done before. These challenges must now be faced courageously and must be overcome. Of course, that is a process that will continue for years to come because Latin American society includes persons of very different backgrounds and tendencies, and yet all are and ought to be Christian in their own way. All must find a place in the Church.

When you once again look back at the list of your publications (and you have in fact written on practically all the issues of Christian theology), where would you today, if you were to start over again as a theologian, put greater emphasis? What would you consider today as the major issue for the Christian in modern society?

That's a very difficult question. Those "what if" kinds of questions can never be answered. I would, on the one hand, say that the unity of love of God and love of neighbor needs to be worked out in a more radical way, that Christianity, the Church has a task toward society that is political in the strictest sense of the word. On the other hand, I would perhaps emphasize more that when humans are truly open to the absolute mystery of God, and entrust themselves to God in a worshiping, loving, forward-looking, hopeful way, that Christianity is only present when it looks at the crucified and risen Jesus Christ. This Christianity which stresses the adoration of the living God can not be replaced by a sociopolitical humanism, however respectable that humanism might be.

In any case you would say, as you said in the beginning, that there is a close connection between the experience of God and the experience of humankind. That implies therefore that all theology at the same time must be rooted in human experience.

Yes, of course. Then Christianity is not a simple form of external indoctrination such as conveying to someone the fact that there is a place called Australia, but it really is a very explicit form of mystagogy into one's personal experience of grace, which every person really possesses. One needs, therefore, in some way or other to challenge, interpret, clarify the Christian fact within human beings, and one should not attempt to drum into somebody an authoritative doctrine that is external.

Professor Rahner, human experiences have a central place in your theology. You attempt to show, it seems, that it is precisely as a human being with experiences, with experiences of life, that one is already tending toward Christian faith.

Yes, that is not only a characteristic feature of my theology, but it is something that I consider to be extraordinarily important and decisive in my theology. I am convinced that Christianity is, in fact, not a doctrine that comes from the outside, something that is drummed into us, but that, since it is God's grace and God's grace offered to all is also a revelation, Christianity is and essentially must be something that is rooted in one's interior life, in one's inner, human, personal experience of God. External indoctrination and internal experience must meet and mutually influence and assist one another. This is something that exists and this is something that is extremely important especially today.

Is every person who hopes, loves, believes, by that very orientation already a Christian? Are you saying that being Christian is not so much something restricted to narrow confessional boundaries?

I would say with Vatican II, that where someone is true to his or her own conscience, even if one were to claim to be an atheist, or that where one loves and reaches beyond self in hope and love, that such a person already is part of the Easter mystery of Jesus Christ and that such a one is most inwardly already a Christian. Of course if that is to develop, to become conscious, to be visibly expressed, then it must do so in Christian teaching and in a life within the Christian community called Church.

If one accepts such a view and applies it to the concrete Church, which often complains about how, according to religious statistics, it is becoming smaller, then your way of looking at things is fundamentally much more optimistic since it holds that even apart from confessional allegiance Christian life can be lived quite a bit.

Of course! But that should not be a excuse for doing nothing by way of preaching and church involvement, and for simply saying that God in his kindness will save everybody. I can say that only when I have come to the end of my possibilities. Then I can speak like that. But when I can still do something myself, where I do theology, preach, share in church life, practice service and charity, there I must act and give witness both to the love of God for humankind and to the gospel of Jesus Christ.

Translated by Michael A. Fahey, S.J.
University of St. Michael's College, Toronto

34 · A Theology of the Church That Seeks to Serve

Interview with Meinold Krauss for South-German Radio (SDR), Stuttgart (April 14, 1979)

When I published my *Foundations of Christian Faith* two and a half years ago, I received this drawing anonymously.

I am supposed to be there at the top, the "theological atomic physicist," that is, someone who speaks about theology in such a way that no one can

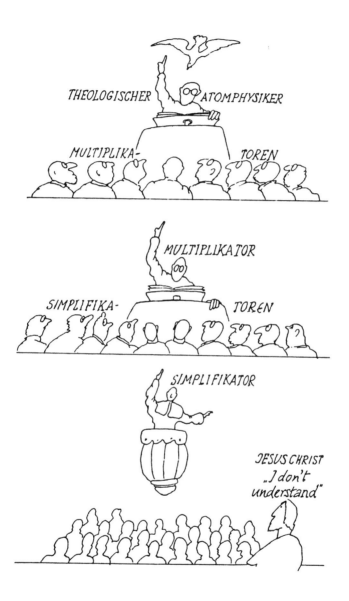

understand him. Then come the so-called multipliers, those who somehow are supposed to hand on the nonsense I spoke to the so-called simplifiers, that is, those who popularize this unintelligible stuff in a better and more understandable fashion and communicate it to the people. And there is the individual simplifier who preaches this to average people, while off to the side sits Jesus Christ who says, "I don't understand." This cartoon captures to a large extent the lot of a theologian.

How many books have you written?
Oh, I don't know the answer to that. There is a bibliography that lists thirty-five hundred articles, books, translations . . . there are enough.

How is your last book doing?
The last major book is called *Foundations of Christian Faith*. More than thirty thousand copies have appeared in German, and it has been translated into Spanish, English, and Dutch.

Professor Rahner, you are a theologian who has never shied away from conflict with church authority. Bluntly put, one could say: You have often stepped on the toes of church authority. Why?
A theologian certainly has, according to the teaching of the Catholic Church, the right to distinguish the various degrees of binding force that there are in official statements of the Church. To that extent a Catholic theologian has a certain scope of freedom even for criticism of the official statements of the Church where they have no absolutely binding character. And even in *that* case the question would still be open as to what such a definitive church decision means. Consequently, a Catholic theologian can make use of such freedom; that this has not perhaps been sufficiently done in the last two centuries in no way changes the right to do so. And if one does so, there is, of course, a certain possibility or danger of coming into conflict with certain expressions of this magisterium of the Church. But that doesn't hurt anything and won't be held against one in the long run.

How should or how must the Church appear today so that she can reach persons with her message?
That is a question that is practically unanswerable for me as an individual. I suppose that she must be a Church that does not seek herself, but seeks to serve people, that has and witnesses to a really living, concrete faith in the liv-

ing God; that receives this faith not merely as a theoretical doctrine, but bears witness to a genuine personal experience of God. This Church must at the same time seek to serve people in an absolute unity of love of God and love of neighbor. She must raise her voice even where she is likely to suffer for doing so, and she must, if I may say so, be a Church not so much of clerics who remain necessary, but a Church that grows up out of the basis of a living Christian experience.

Such claims are of course very general, but there is no history that can be sketched a priori. Rather, it must be concretely lived and suffered, as it comes to one, and insofar, I think, as one is supposed to love God and to serve the neighbor and leave the rest to God and his providence.

Can one be Christian even outside the Church? Is there something like an "anonymous Christian"?

According to my average Catholic conviction, one ought, of course, to belong explicitly to the Roman Catholic Church. But there are obviously baptized Christians outside the Roman Catholic Church as well, and they—if they follow their own convictions, are true to their consciences—also have a genuine, immediate relation to Jesus Christ and his redemption and, therefore, obviously attain salvation. On that point there can be no reasonable doubt. Catholic teaching says only: If and insofar as you recognize the Roman Catholic Church as the most concrete, most clear, historically most continuous manifestation of the Church of Jesus Christ—I emphasize, *if and insofar as*—you must become Catholic. One who does not have this recognition, who has decided to reject it in good conscience, obviously may not and should not become Catholic.

Is there for you an "anonymous Christianity"?

Obviously. "Anonymous Christianity" means that a person lives in the grace of God and attains salvation outside explicitly constituted Christianity. A Protestant Christian is, of course, "no anonymous Christian"; that is perfectly clear. But, let us say, a Buddhist monk (or anyone else I might suppose) who, because he follows his conscience, attains salvation and lives in the grace of God; of him I must say that he is an anonymous Christian; if not, I would have to presuppose that there is a genuine path to salvation that really attains that goal, but that simply has nothing to do with Jesus Christ. But I cannot do that. And so if I hold that everyone depends upon Jesus Christ for salvation, and if at the same time I hold that many live in the world who have not expressly recognized Jesus Christ, then there remains in my opinion nothing else but to take up this postulate of an anonymous Christianity.

What does being a Christian mean to you personally?

I believe that the human person is embraced by the absolute mystery that we call God; that this mystery draws close to us in love; that it penetrates our whole existence, wants to communicate itself to us and that the certitude and the definitive historical reality of this self-bestowal of God to humanity is given in Jesus Christ. If these two moments, more or less explicit but really, are present in a person's existence, then he or she is a Christian (as I hope that I am), either anonymously or explicitly. Of course, one cannot say any more, for ultimately one knows nothing absolutely certain about one's own existence with reflexive certitude. One can only say: I hope I am a Christian, that is, that I am open to the absolute mystery of the self-communication of the infinite God and that I am open in hope and trust to Jesus Christ, crucified and resurrected.

What significance do you ascribe to the papacy?

For my Catholic faith according to the teaching of the First and Second Vatican Councils on the office and function of the Chair of Peter the papacy is an essential institution in the Church, an institution that has a final, clear responsibility for the Catholic teaching of the faith. That does not, of course, mean that the concrete form that the papacy has attained in the course of history and even in the course of the last two centuries will and must necessarily always remain such. I can imagine the concrete function of the pope as considerably different in a Church of the future, in a Church of ecumenical unity. And to that extent it would certainly be an important, perhaps even decisive task of the ecumenical dialogue to ask how the concrete form of the papacy should appear today and in the future. Thus non-Catholic Christians might come to feel that they could live with such a pope in unity and peace.

Where should the pope in your opinion speak out today unconditionally, and where should he be unconditionally silent?

I would not want to pose the question in that way, but would say first of all: The teaching office of the pope must not enter so much into theological details and provide clarifications on them, but seek to preach the ultimate contents and foundations of the Christian faith in as lively and convincing a manner as possible. Second, I think that where he goes beyond these ultimate, obvious foundations of the Christian faith in his preaching, a pope today ought to make clear even more explicitly than before the relative degree of binding force that this teaching has even according to his own conviction. Today an encyclical, such as *Humani Generis*, must in my opinion, if it is supposed to succeed, explicitly mention what binding power such a document has or does not have in the conviction of the pope.

Do you regard the pope as the highest representative of Christianity?

That is a difficult question, for I consider the unknown person who is, none-theless, most radically bound to Jesus Christ in faith, hope, and love to be the highest representative. If you ask me who is the highest representative of the office of the external constitution of the Church, I of course answer: the pope. But someone completely different, an unknown will occupy the highest position in the *spiritual* hierarchy of humanity, presumably not the pope; that is not to be expected of him and for that reason need not be made into a reproach against him.

Professor Rahner, you are now seventy-five years old and were in recent months occasionally ill. In this connection you have also spoken of death. What does death mean for you? Are you afraid of death?

That is a question that is almost impossible to answer. I know that I am facing death. This nearness of death is in my case by human standards very great, greater than with very many other people who are much younger. In meeting death, we know, a person's destiny is determined in a final fashion, and I hope that I can accept this determination, which I cannot control, in a final hope, even if to a certain extent I otherwise know nothing. I allow myself, if I may so speak, hoping with trust, confident, believing and loving, to be taken into the incomprehensibility of God beyond all my decisions, and I hope to die so. Whether the beginning of one's own existence as one that is absolutely completed occurs in the moment of medical death or in a moment much earlier is once again a question that is basically of no importance. If I die in this physiological or medical sense, then nothing more will take place in me at the conscious level. But that is also not necessary, for I go to meet this mystery of death now while I still have some understanding and free will, and I hope that I accept it willingly.

You speak of the mystery of death; does that mean that you are not afraid of death?

I think that fear of death belongs to the nature of death, and I am not of the opinion that a Christian must necessarily die as a Stoic or as a Socrates. If a Christian can do so, there is no objection against it. But he or she need not; a Christian can also imitate Jesus in the Garden of Olives or pray as he did on the cross, "God, my God, why have you abandoned me?" and then add, "Into your hands I commend my spirit, into your hands, O absolutely incomprehensible God." That too is possible. In other words, I can confidently meet death and also accept the fear of death in a final confidence and surrender.

Translated by Roland J. Teske, S.J.
Marquette University

35 · A Theologian's Lot

Interview with Karl-Heinz Weger for Radio Austria (FS 2),
Vienna (March 2, 1979)

Father Rahner, you have received numerous honorary doctorates and scientific prizes. How do you see yourself? As a scholar; or as a Jesuit and a theologian, as someone more concerned with the preaching of the gospel; or do you try to combine these two?

Well you know it's not that these things present a real alternative which one must choose. Yet, if it really came to choosing, I would say that scholarship is not so important to me, and that the real, immediate preaching of the good news of the gospel is what, at least, should be specific and proper in my life.

I understand your theology as an ongoing attempt to mediate the traditional truths of faith to people today in such a way that they touch life, so that they mean something in daily life. God plays an important role in your theology.

A theologian deals with God: To stop doing that is to stop being a theologian; nor should the theologian try to replace God with something else.

You often represent in a reasonable way the view that the old proofs for the existence of God—in the way in which they are presented—are of a very strange nature.

On the one hand, they wish to present themselves as if they intend to prove something about which people have never heard; on the other, such proofs are presented by people who do not have the slightest doubt about the existence of God. It seems you want to say, I think, that doesn't work any more today. God cannot be dragged in from the outside, he can't be learned; someone can't live a long time and then unexpectedly hear someone say that there might happen to be a God. In your recent book about Ignatius of Loyola you assert that every person experiences God.[1] Isn't that rather daring? I have never had an experience of God.

I don't believe you; I just don't accept that. You have had, perhaps, no experience of God under this precise code-word *God* but you have had or have now an experience of God—and I am convinced that this is true of every person. If I could go back to something you said. Naturally, the proofs for the existence of God, as they were previously presented, are not false, but they don't get very far today . . . apart from whether I reach by such a proof to this inner experience of God that everyone has (if by other names).

This inner experience of God is naturally (and necessarily) very difficult to describe. What love is, what fidelity is, what longing is, what immediate responsibility is—are all things that are difficult to express and to think about. We start stuttering, and what we say sounds odd, provisional, difficult. But that doesn't prove that a person has not had experiences of fidelity, responsibility, joy, truth, love, and so on. And so it is with experiencing God.

A story from your friend Albert Görres comes to mind. The Jewish atheist Salomon visited the synagogue every Sabbath; the rabbi addressed him: "Salomon, why do you go every Sabbath to the synagogue since you're an atheist?" Salomon answered him: "Naturally I am an atheist but how do I know if I am right?" So, I ask you: Are you certain you are right?

I am, if you want, also challenged by atheism; I am one who can understand how today there can be people who are skeptical, resigned to such an emptiness that they let God fall away. But on the other hand, I must say that I cannot imagine there is an experience in my life which could keep me away from being convinced of the existence of God. Every experience to date and every imaginable experience—of joy and of terror—point beyond itself into the future, into the nameless inexpressible, into the land of unlimited hope; and from that point I must say: There is nothing more obvious for me than that there is a God.

---

1. Karl Rahner and Paul Imhof, *Ignatius of Loyola*, tr. Rosaleen Ockenden (Cleveland: Collins, 1979).

Nevertheless, imagine that the unthinkable would happen—you would lose your faith in God, would that have consequences in your life, would your life change?

You know, I must consider, when I think about it, that I would live, as do many people today who call themselves atheists, in the consciousness of an absolute responsibility; they are people of fidelity, of love, and so forth. Some kind of faith in God is basically there, whether they know it or not, reflect upon it or not, call it that or not. Their reflection upon it is not unimportant, but it is still a secondary question. If once I were to be really convinced in an absolute way that all we live, do, and think is circumscribed by an absolute, meaningless nothingness, then and there, I think, it would be better to cease to live.

Years ago we talked for a long time about the existence of God and at the end of this discussion you said: I believe because I pray. Do you pray?

I would be careful and say: I hope I pray. You see, when I take note of the great and small hours of my life, how I border on that ineffable, holy, and loving mystery that we call God, and when I allow myself at the same time to trust, hope, and love this mystery, when I receive this mystery, then I pray—and I hope I am praying.

You are thankful that you are in grace, that you are redeemed. What does that mean for you?

Redemption, being redeemed, means nothing other than that God does not want to be the distant, withdrawn Creator of a world different from him but wishes to give himself to me, the infinitely small creature, me the sinner, the one who failed. Redemption and grace mean that I am received by God in such a way that he wants to make himself be my eternal life.

You once said in an interview, "There is that which I call 'anonymous Christianity' because, as far as I can see, there is no religion in which the grace of God, if only in a repressed way, is not present." You must know what I am getting at. For you every person who lives honorably according to his or her conscience is an anonymous Christian. But you certainly have known that there are people who reject this incorporation, or even call it an insult.

First, I am convinced—and this coincides with at least today's teaching of Christianity and the Catholic Church—that God offers every person his grace and this grace of God in the Holy Spirit also comes to fruition outside of Christianity, where someone is true to conscience and at the same time moves into God as the absolute future. And to this extent there is something like an anonymous Christianity.

You speak of an anonymous Christianity and of an explicit Christianity. In one of your books you wrote that you could picture the Buddha as a prophet or a saint. I presume you would view all the founders of religions in that way—except for Christ.

Without going into dogmatic formulations of Christology, I would say that Christ or Jesus is more than this or that prophet because he is the last, irrevocable word of God's address to us.

You would explain to someone who has little exposure to the New Testament or the teaching of the Church that Jesus is more than a man, more than a prophet, more than a saint.

Now I would naturally have to say: If you never really take the time and effort to look into the Gospels with an open heart and spirit, then not much can come of that. But if you meet Jesus in the Gospels as he was, as he spoke and acted, as he loved and acted for others; if you experience that he persevered in his trust in God even in his greatest need on the cross, and how he carried through his solidarity with people even into death; and then if you really comprehend that he is the resurrected one, in the way in which he has already tried to say it, then, I think, you can really grasp as well that God has spoken an unsurpassable word to you in Jesus.

The ultimate reason for your faith and my faith in Jesus Christ is the resurrection. You were not there, I was not there. Have you ever thought that the disciples may have imagined it, without wanting to be malicious? After all, there are legends in every religion.

Well, first we must be clear about what the resurrection actually means. If I begin with the fact that the human person cannot be divided into body and soul but is always a unity, and if I presume that this one true human being can be saved by and into God in a way I cannot imagine, then I have basically the idea of what is meant by the resurrection. It does not mean a return into this biological, temporal, and spatial life but the definitive being-saved of one man in God. And if I hope that for myself—because I would give myself up to an empty meaninglessness otherwise—then what I see in the life of Jesus, what I confess is not so terribly unthinkable or unbelievable: This man with this life is really a totality saved by God.

May I ask you directly: What do you find in Christian faith that you do not find in other religions or world views? What attracts you to Christianity?

Naturally, fascination or enthusiasm need not mean something emotional and superficial. I don't need to walk around the entire day, radiating with enthusiasm. But, when I say that in Christianity the God of absolute freedom, of mystery, of blessedness, and of truth is near to me and that he himself affirms me, then that is for me ultimately and trustworthily found only in Jesus. Then Christianity for me—so understood—is more or less something obvious even when it always touches upon the act of faith and a hope needing new fulfillment.

You have given a new tonality to Catholic theology. Do you think that the hierarchy, the bishops have understood this? Do you have the impression that the directions of your thinking have changed the Church somewhat?

In such a large community, society, and organization as the worldwide Church with millions of Christians, with thousands of priests and religious, one can hardly expect that what one person thinks and writes will be accepted at once even if it is good and useful. Certain ideas and approaches have certainly been accepted: I took part in the Council.

I believe that through your theology you have sustained many theologians and apparently very many Christians in their faith. Despite this you would have to say: I have not attained everything I wanted. Is there something you definitely wanted to attain?

Well no one attains everything one would want to achieve or reach for. I think that this or that in my theology has already been actually accepted by the Church, particularly through Vatican II. Naturally, I would have to admit that my theology within the Church is being viewed more critically than before (there are signs that this is so), and reservations and suspicions against it are being formulated anew. That is the lot of every theologian and so nothing odd. Much of my thought is not yet grasped; if I may say so, my theology makes a certain contribution towards demythologization here and there, although that is not my theology's ultimate purpose. I would like to help my fellow Christians to relinquish the understanding of the Holy Trinity as a presentation of three persons in the modern sense of the word *person*. I would like grace not to be understood in such a way that one can isolate it clearly in individual places and yet view other dimensions of human life as existing totally without grace.

It struck me as I read your writings that for a long time, decades even, you have been concerned with death. Does this topic interest you particularly?

First, death is a topic which belongs in a Christian theology (we have only to think of the death of Jesus). When I say that I am redeemed by the death of

Jesus on the cross, then a Christian theologian cannot avoid the theme of death. But recently I have not worked much on it. Earlier I talked about it a great deal; slowly, however, the time arrives when you have to let happen what previously you spoke of.

You are convinced that after death, something continues—differently, better? Do you have thoughts or fantasies about what and how?

The word *continues* is not too happy a choice because beyond death there is not a time where something continues in ever new temporal periods, without any cessation. I would say that I do not know *how* it continues but I am convinced in faith that I will be confirmed in my life by God and that I will be with God, the eternal, definitively.

Father Rahner, along with your scholarly writings you have composed many prayers. Can you think of what prayer you would pray as you were dying.

At the time of death—in some way, if one can do anything at all in freedom —I would hope that I will say: "I believe and hope and love. Into your hands I commend my spirit"—even if I would also have to pray with Jesus, "My God, My God, why have you forsaken me?" Looking toward Jesus I hope to be able to say, "Father, into your hands I commend my spirit" . . . I also hope to be able to do it.

Translated by Thomas F. O'Meara, O.P.
University of Notre Dame

36 · Why Doing Theology Is So Difficult

Interview with Karl-Heinz Weger and Hildegard Lüning for
South-German Radio (SDR), Stuttgart (March 19, 1979)

The basic reason why I asked Father Rahner to collaborate on this little book[1] was that I was convinced that Christians of all confessions have many, many questions and doubts about their faith, ones that are not at all being addressed and answered. I wanted to formulate these questions and who was better skilled to work out answers than Father Rahner, who fortunately agreed to take on this challenging task.

You know, Father Weger, when you give that explanation I must add that I do, in fact, answer questions which you posed and worked out, and that I try to give answers in a very intelligible and lively manner, in language accessible to the nonspecialist of today. But my answers were only as good or as bad as was possible for me to formulate within the limitations of the project. Often I had the impression that it's easier to ask more questions than it is to provide a hundred answers.

What I mean is that the difficulty one has in answering a question belongs fundamentally to the nature of Christianity and theology. If God is truly the incomprehensible God, whose incomprehensibility perdures for all eternity, even there where we see God "face to face," as Christians are wont to say, then it is completely obvious that a theology that wishes to answer all questions clearly and thoroughly is guaranteed to miss its proper "object." But still I can console myself when I experience this feeling of powerlessness, a feeling of total helplessness faced with questions addressed to me, because it cannot be otherwise.

I do not completely share your view because in fact you have answered many questions even if you are sometimes forced in your answers to bracket certain aspects. But you were speaking just now of a certain sense of helplessness that is part and parcel of Christian theology or faith in God. Could you explain more precisely what you mean? You have a specific idea of how a human being arrives at faith in God. Already implied in that way of looking at God (as far as I can see) is that sense of helplessness in comprehending one's experiences of God as you describe them.

In my theology I wish to proceed from the fact of an essential and absolute, ultimately insuperable sense of helplessness. When I approach God to the extent I understand him, I only reach him when I perceive him as the absolute mystery that surpasses me. And when I do not perceive him as the absolute

1. *Our Christian Faith: Answers for the Future*, tr. Francis McDonaugh (New York: Crossroad, 1981).

mystery, then I have to say: Stop! You're on the wrong track, this path certainly does not lead to the true God of Christianity, the God of eternal life. If you intend to "explain" God with a certain rationalistic clarity, as is done sometimes even in Catholic theology, then you have certainly failed in your task. For me, God is precisely that mystery of the incomprehensible, the inexpressible, toward which at every moment of my life I am always tending. If a human being in thought or in existential living could avoid this experience of being related to the incomprehensibility of God, then one might say: Let's forget about every form of atheism and about faith in God. But in my life and in my thought I cannot avoid these questions that, at the same time, touch upon the incomprehensible. Since I cannot, I cannot therefore avoid theology and Christianity.

Why can you not avoid theology? There are many persons, contemporaries of ours, who manage to avoid it very well!

I would say that very many of our contemporaries suppress it; they don't want to accept as true that they are forced to deal with something like that. But I would say to these people: Take an honest and close look at your life. Isn't there still an unanswered question that keeps popping up even if it is pushed aside, expressed in an absolute love, a radical responsibility, an ultimately fundamental, unavoidable hope? If such experiences and similar ones exist, and they will be present in every life, then one is undergoing the experience of relatedness, the unavoidability of absolute mystery that we call God.

If I understand you correctly, you are saying that if I don't reckon with God in my life and if I don't include God, then ultimately I cannot explain why I love; I cannot explain or understand why in fact I am faithful. I have no foundation for values that others recommend except egotistical self-assertion and material self-indulgence.

Yes. That's one way of putting it. Only we would have to look at it from the opposite point of view too. There are very many people who profess an atheistic theory and interpretation of life, who in their concrete living are expressing something completely other. There are quite a few atheists who are just as faithful, just as honest, just as upright as many Christians, although in fact it does not "benefit" them. But I would like to say to them: You are unknowingly doing something which is ultimately believing in God. You presuppose unreflectively an absolute foundation and meaning for your activity; and that is what I am reflecting about; the end result of this reflection is precisely the incomprehensible mystery that is called God.

May I perhaps jump in at this point. You are always using the expression, "the mystery," the "incomprehensible mystery that we call God." Surely that implies that you presuppose a certain experience which subsequently receives a name. One could then, if I understand you rightly, substitute, let's say, the term XY for God. As far as the reality we are dealing with is concerned, the name is somewhat arbitrary.

Precisely. If I frequently prefer to use the expression, the mystery that we are accustomed to call God, my purpose in using this phrase is only to underline the fact that in speaking the word *God* we should not imagine the ridiculous: an old man with a beard, a moral tyrant who spies on our conduct, or the like. In order to avoid this misunderstanding that is nevertheless common among very many naive, everyday atheists, I consistently use that rather cumbersome expression: "the mystery that we call God." Of course, I am thoroughly convinced that very many people have a positive relationship to this mystery although they, in theoretical reflection on themselves and in their lives, claim to be atheists.

Yes. Then I gather that we, or rather you, commonly use the expression "anonymous Christians." Could you perhaps at this time touch on that theme. You created the expression "anonymous Christian," which is used rather widely and is well known. Please clarify for us what you understand by that term. What is an anonymous Christian?

First of all, I must state that I don't attach all that much importance to the expression as such, but only to the reality to which it points. This reality consists in this, that, according to the teaching of Vatican II, persons who are true to their consciences in a final and absolute way—something of course that is, when you come right down to it, not all that easy, and which many people basically only imagine they are doing—that such persons *de facto* have a positive relationship to God, meaning that they implicitly affirm the existence of God.

Of course, connected with this theory is the further claim we probably can't go into at this moment, namely, that such persons also have a positive relationship with Jesus Christ. The Bible suggests this, for example, in chapter 25 of Matthew's Gospel, when Jesus says that whatever you have done to the least of my brethren, you have done to me. Unless such an assertion is meant to be taken as a joke, then it implies that when you visit someone in prison, or struggle for freedom, or give money to the poor, or act kindly toward your neighbor, then you have a relationship to Jesus Christ and you will be judged on that. One's relationship to God and to Jesus Christ and one's relationship to neighbors, even though they are not one and the same thing, are nonetheless inseparably connected. This is, more or less, what I mean by anonymous Christians.

We have been using the word Christian. *In your book,* Our Christian Faith, *you have a chapter at the end entitled, "I Believe in Jesus Christ." There you say something that struck me quite a bit. You describe yourself as a person who hopes to be a Christian to the extent that you persevere. This is the assertion of a person who has done theology for fifty-five years, a man whose theology quite clearly bears the imprint of a reality difficult to describe (we hope to come back to this later), namely, the experience of God. May I ask what you mean by being a Christian? Do you mean that one must always become a Christian and that one is never definitively a Christian?*

I have two things in mind. First of all, the simple fact that a Christian, in fact, every person, is permanently in a state of becoming, and has new experiences which must be integrated into the total experience of one's life up to that present moment. Through them, one learns to become more mature, one becomes perhaps more generous, and so on. So of course, there exists quite obviously and objectively a Christian who is becoming and who can say: I hope I become a Christian, a person who asymptotically approaches more closely the ideal of a Christian.

Does that relate to one's practice of faith then?

Behind the statement that I hope that I am a Christian lies also something else. You see, when I remove from myself all that is not the decision rooted in the inner core of my existence, but is my background, milieu, education, psychological demands of a profession, and so on, when I remove all that, when I think how easy, in fact, it is for one to deceive one's self, how one is perhaps a terrible egoist and yet claims to be abounding in charity and selflessness, when I reflect on all that, then I must turn not to others but to myself and say: Dear God, help me not only to claim to be a Christian but at least gradually to become one who is partly successful, so that somehow or other I may make some kind of breakthrough out of this inward-looking existence, out of this egotistical prison, by finding the freedom of love, fidelity, hope, selflessness. All persons are ultimately in danger of remaining turned in upon themselves and of considering that choice the right choice and not recognizing how they would feel if they were to break out of their egotistical prison and reach for the freedom of love and selflessness, to reach ultimately to the freedom of God. Therefore that is what I mean when I say that a Christian who bears an office in the Church: a cleric, a bishop, even a pope, has to say: Dear God, help me so that I may not only claim to be a Christian but may also really be one.

Father Rahner, throughout your life as a Christian and your theology, (this I conclude from many of your writings), you also had some personal experience with the efforts of the ecclesiastical magisterium to restrict the freedom of theologians. But on the whole I have the impression that you perceived, and perhaps even still perceive, your life, as a Christian and as a theologian, as being a history of freedom. When you speak of Christianity you speak also of a history of freedom.

Yes. Correct. My view is that ultimately in a normal, true interpretation of Christianity, a human being must slowly break out of being egotistically turned in upon one's self. A person must arrive at what is called faith, hope, and especially charity. One must achieve a position or attitude in which one freely loves one's neighbor and through one's neighbor loves God. By doing that and only by doing that is a person ultimately free. And therefore, I can conceive of Christianity as a whole and every experience of becoming a Christian as a history of freedom. Now just how this theologically and theocentrically understood idea of "history of freedom" is connected with the "history of freedom" in sociopolitical anthropology—well, that of course is another question.

Translated by Michael A. Fahey, S.J.
University of St. Michael's College, Toronto

37·Concrete Questions about Life and Psychological-Theological Answers

Interview with Karl-Heinz Weger and Hildegard Lüning for South-German Radio (SDR), Stuttgart (March 19, 1979)

Father Rahner, in the last analysis you see faith as the movement of becoming increasingly free from self and of growing into something which does not limit itself to me. However, we live in a historical context in which people want nothing more than to become themselves, to realize themselves. Self-realization is one of the great slogans of our age, also one of its legitimate aspirations. Those of us who have grown up as Christians have learned that self-denial—especially as wives—is a primary goal. For me, it was actually a liberation when I—within the context of my professional training and experience—was introduced to psychology. It taught me: To become yourself is entirely splendid and essential; know yourself, accept yourself, and realize yourself. Today I see a contradiction between self-denial and self-realization.

I think that contradictions do not really exist here. Conflicts, contrasts between distinct norms, do occur from time to time in the course of life, so that one situation calls especially for one norm and another situation requires a different one. Yet fundamentally I would like to make two points. Of course a person should realize herself and, in this sense, become herself. Nevertheless, I also think that such an ideal—I am intentionally speaking somewhat provokingly—is to a certain degree a chimera. I am still bound by a thousand influences which I can never shake, no matter how much I legitimately strive for self-realization and political changes. In other words, the authentic person and the authentic Christian possesses the courage to accept patiently and with hope in God one's historical, cultural, and genetic limitations. For example, I must accept my old age. I could not choose my deceased parents. I did not select my era in history. I cannot live as though Auschwitz never occurred. In thousands of ways I am a human being who is shaped by influences that I cannot overcome by my own efforts, and therefore to experience human limits belongs even to Christianity. When Christianity says "deny yourself," and the modern world utters, "become yourself and realize yourself," then I have to say that Christianity's utterance is established in the New Testament.

Does the New Testament mean "deny" or "empty yourself"?
All right, fine; they mean the same.

221

No, I do not think so.

Well, if you interpret the denial in the sense of "self-emptying," we can quickly agree.

I think that this self-denial means the acceptance of the incomprehensible arrangements of life and the acceptance of duty to one's neighbor—a duty which a person need not happily assume. "Deny yourself" simply means: Become selflessly loving; serve the other in the hope of God's eternal freedom. It is self-evident, I think, that the political goals of liberation are not to be denied.

Could psychology, psychotherapy, and our other contemporary ways of finding ourselves answer the very question which these disciplines pose to theology: How should I ever know who I am? Strictly speaking, only Jungian psychology has acknowledged in some way that a person does not create herself and is not created by herself. To this extent we indeed need theology which however—as I see it—has concerned itself very little until today with being human.

Of course, this is an historical issue. Did Augustine know as much, even if perhaps in other ways, as we do today about the human person?

However, leave the historical question aside, for I would like to say this: Modern psychology in all its special subdisciplines fundamentally has the tendency to define me as a product not of myself but of genetics, history, environment, and so on. This means that psychology has the tendency to unburden me of myself, so that I do not need to face myself in a radical way. I would say that modern psychology knows a great deal about being human but it cannot define the human person, for the human person herself—to return to a favorite theme of mine—cannot be reduced to concepts, not even refined psychological concepts. We cannot adequately explain the essence of the human person. That is, we cannot rationally reduce this essence to one element whose composition then defines the whole person. A human person necessarily always remains a mystery, and in the act of her freedom—a freedom that psychology must not deny—a person must entrust herself, a mystery, to the absolute mystery of God who is loving, trustworthy, and forgiving.

To defend psychology a bit more, let me say this: There are of course psychological orientations, for example, the school of C. G. Jung, that do not deny guilt and do not set a person free from guilt. Rather, these schools help a person finally to learn to see guilt more profoundly, and to take another approach to guilt. While we are on the topic, I would like to add this: A difficulty for many people and also for me is actually the question of guilt and sin, and also of the judgment of God at the end of life

or at the end of time, however one wishes to see this judgment. It is increasingly dif-
ficult to believe that men and women can be entirely and consciously opposed to them-
selves, opposed to their own salvation, opposed to their own happiness—a happiness
which, in any case according to our image of God, God wants for all people, which
God offers all people, which God holds available, so to speak, to all people and with
Jesus Christ has proclaimed for every single person. In part, I think, the crisis of faith
is bound up with this so that we have a hard time recognizing what guilt is, where we
actually have become guilty and where we must turn over a new leaf. In our social
relationships we know full well what guilt is. But concerning our relationship to God
this is another matter: Men and women are seeking to explain their sins away.

I think that previously in the good, old, if somewhat naive days we thought
we knew clearly—even theoretically and objectively—what was morally good
and evil. Today this matter is extraordinarily complex and dark in the theoretical sphere, especially when one becomes somewhat more concrete. But formerly, people presupposed too simply and too easily that they knew exactly, all the
more in the specifics of their actions, that something would be morally good
or bad, and that this could be established in an unequivocal manner—unless,
of course, juridically speaking, they were incapable of this. Therefore, you
fundamentally had the impression that you could know God's judgment ahead
of time.

Today psychology with its distinct subdisciplines and different lines of inquiry enables us to see how difficult it is to determine the degree of freedom,
guilt, or blamelessness in a particular situation. Moreover, I am a Christian
who may not pass judgment. With Saint Paul I must say that whether I am
justified or not, I do not know; the one who justifies me is God and only God.
Having said this, a Christian can honestly say that, on the one hand, I may
not shirk my own responsibilities and seek to excuse myself morally with the
help of modern psychology or sociology from the outset. I must remain a person of responsibility who can own up to something. On the other hand, a person cannot really know reflexively how things stand, but must surrender his
or her whole life to God and to God alone. What do I ultimately know about
myself? Am I, therefore, this committed Christian and paragon of virtue, as I
view myself according to external norms? Or, is this in the last analysis a fa-
cade, behind which lies something different, perhaps disbelief or atheism, or
lack of love and egoism, and so on? Therefore, to put it briefly, I think Christians today must see both sides, the thousand possibilities for the exoneration
of a human person, which the person should directly apply vis-à-vis others,
and yet the impossibility of dissolving human responsibility and the freedom
of the person in a determinism which basically is not workable in life. How

well both sides come together in a concrete situation one does not fundamentally know.

I wish to pose my question again. I have understood everything you have said; it is not totally new to me. And to that extent I agree with you. Where I am not able to agree concerns guilt before God. I can agree somehow with the Church's moral teaching when it concerns guilt in my interpersonal relations, but what is guilt before God? I no longer live out of my childhood catechism. There the Sunday obligation was prescribed, and if I did not fulfill it, then I sinned gravely. There were, for example, the external commands regarding Mass and prayer which said to me: You can become guilty before God, even insult him; you give new wounds to Jesus in his passion. There was no mention of giving these wounds to your neighbor—which, without doubt, are recognizable, experiential, and have a direct effect. But how can I become guilty in relation to God?

First of all, we should recall that the implications of an earnest and radical no to God—this belongs to the essence of that which in Christianity one calls a serious sin—are often not demonstrable. It will often not be obvious, and in a specific case not demonstrable with absolute certitude. However, as a Christian, drawing on the New and Old Testaments, I cannot say a priori that inhumane behavior in this world is indeed undesirable but that it has nothing to do with God. At issue here is the question of how negative behavior toward the world, myself, and my neighbor is to be understood and interpreted in relation to God. To my mind, this is a problem which theology has not taken up with sufficient thought.

One simply says: God has established this and that as moral norms; and if you do not obey these, then the one who established these norms will regard you as evil. Here an anthropomorphic view of God is presupposed. Nevertheless, I cannot accept the idea that my inner, final, really free moral or immoral conduct has nothing to do with God. Just how we clarify this complex issue further is another question.

I would, for example, offer this as my personal, theological opinion: If I did not have the relationship, based solely on grace, of immediate, personal love with God, who gives himself to me in this love, then the breaking of the so-called Natural Law or—to express this differently—doing injury to human nature and to the world would not so "offend" God, as the Christian—correctly, I think—presupposes. Of course, this applies only where it can be genuinely said: At this moment this human person is saying no to God, even though in a way that is implicit, not explicated, yet genuine. How often this actually occurs I do not know.

We can calmly hope—hope, I say—that God has so designed the world that hideous denials of God have occurred either through amoral or nonmoral ignorance or through primitiveness, and that world history, by and large, unfolds well for all or at least most people. Whether this is so, we do not know. I would say that here we come before God's incomprehensible decree, and we need to wait peacefully. For we do not know how world history will finally turn out. Perhaps we preoccupy ourselves too much with the shameful acts of other men and women, and we do not attend to our own guilt-laden egos. It can be otherwise, namely, that through God's grace to a peson it is perhaps made ultimately easier to love God and to turn away from self. What has in fact occurred in a specific instance, God knows, but we do not. I would not doubt that the Church has often appeared somewhat primitive and anthropomorphic as the representative of God's moral authority.

Father Rahner, one of your famous colleagues[1] has uniquely presented the view that God only affirms us, that God does not ultimately demand anything of us but rather is the one answer implicit in all that we think, wish, need, want, and would like. Perhaps I have done the book an injustice, though, after a long radio broadcast with him, I have become no more insightful. In any case, I wish to know whether you would venture to characterize God as one who is indeed a challenging God? In asking this, I realize that you speak of God as the unsurpassable mystery.

I do not wish to offer an interpretation of Hans Küng's book. This would take us too far afield. On the issue you raise I would say this. The God of Christianity is no longer really being spoken of when someone perceives God no longer as the incomprehensible mystery and no longer as the one who in the last analysis must be prayed to and loved, as it were, beyond our own powers; when God is no longer the God of freedom and judgment; when God is self-evidently simply an item in the calculation of our lives that guarantees our books will balance. I am not saying this is the case with Küng's view; his task is to preserve God. I am saying, once more, that God is no longer being spoken of when God is only the name or the token for that which concerns our self-absolutizing egoism.

However, the negation is always easier to present than to say it positively: When God is . . .

At the moment of course when I, to a degree unconditionally, petition God in hope, faith, and love—at this moment, and with this presupposition, I may

---

1. Hans Küng, *Does God Exist?*, tr. Edward Quinn (Garden City, New York: Doubleday, 1980).

and must of course say: God is the God of love, the God of forgiveness, the God of the final meaning of my own existence. However, to a certain extent I can only say this presupposing that I surrender myself without conditions to God, and when I have made this surrender, then this view of God follows.

And then does God always bring me where I do not want to be?

May I once again give an example? It is exactly similar to true, interpersonal love. When I seek my happiness, then I have already mismanaged love. However, when I lovingly accept another person, then immediately my happiness also begins, at least it can begin. Similarly, this is our situation before God. I have already named this the unmanipulatable transcendence of God; this means: Our relationship to this absolute God cannot be manipulated for our happiness, our freedom, and so on.

Jesus said, "Seek first the kingdom of God and all else will be given you." One could also say: Seek God in his absolute sovereignty, freedom, greatness, unconditionalness—upon which you depend, though God is not dependent upon you—and then you will be given peace, love, grace, forgiveness, and so on.

How can a person seek God, this God? There are indeed still many people who think that they could come closer to God through the study of theological texts. Does such study lead to God?

Theological studies are entirely good and meaningful, but they are reflections on an existential life-process, which is something different. Someone could write a five-hundred page book about love, as Max Scheler has, and still not have actually loved. And conversely, someone would understand such a book only if she had indeed had the experience of love. So too there is a Christianity of faith, hope, and love which precedes these theoretical, theological reflections, so that, conversely, all speaking and writing about God is only understandable if a person has arrived at this out of the experience of God, which one then calls grace.

How can a person come to this? and how has a man like Karl Rahner come to this?

A person should not think that she must pursue something outside of herself. Rather, she should reflectively, willingly, and clearly aim at discovering that which she already is in the circle of experience and reflection.

A few years ago we had a discussion about the existence of God in which you said in conclusion, *"I believe because I pray."* In hindsight I can speak about this circle and say this. If you presuppose this circle, then I can only believe if I pray; and conversely I can only pray, if I already believe. The question is therefore: Where is the possible entry point for belief in the existence of God?

A human person does not climb, as it were, from the outside into such a conviction, rather one discovers—of course through free choice—that she is basically already standing in this condition. When someone notices, I love, I am faithful, I bear responsibility where I am actually only a failure, even where others benefit at my expense and I receive nothing for this—such experiences are already experiences of God. Everyone has these kinds of experiences, unless she is some kind of demon, and she need only reflect on these and be astonished and to say: "I actually believe. . . ."

We must then find what is already there.

Of course it must be there. However, take another example that may make this clear: I, who until this moment am an egoist, love so and so. This other person is so important to me and in a certain sense so interesting that I can really forget myself for her. I need this person not as the means to my own self-preservation or as the goal of the liberation of my feelings, and so on; rather, she is the one with whom, so to speak, I come out of myself, with whom I am most concerned without turning back to myself; and then she says: This is what normal people call love. Something similar occurs, I think, in our relationship with God.

Just how far this kind of reflection succeeds and how far conventional Christian theoretical formulations of these human relationships enlighten a person is another question. Also, it is another question whether this interpretation, which I as a Christian offer of the personal experience of a human individual, is under the circumstances primitive, whether it displays deficiencies, and whether it makes it difficult for someone else to recognize herself in this description. Even a pope can speak in very pious, very Catholic, and very orthodox terms, and still a modern listener may think: What do all these words—this, please excuse me, "word-salad"—mean? It is not as though these words were the reality in itself, and I, the Catholic, could not grasp and fully comprehend the reality itself. Rather, through no fault of one's own this way of speaking may not really be successful.

Translated by Robert A. Krieg, C.S.C.
University of Notre Dame

38 · Interpreting and Experiencing the Words and Deeds of Jesus Today

Interview with Karl-Heinz Weger and Hildegard Lüning
for South-German Radio (SDR), Stuttgart (March 19, 1979)

We are talking about faith and life, and we come now to a topic which is worth discussing for many Christians, today. Father Rahner, we are learning more and more from biblical researchers that a great deal of what we supposed were actual sayings of Jesus are not. Now this is my question: Does this exegesis actually weaken the faith, or how can one deal with this intelligently?

Today's exegesis will certainly cause difficulties, at first, for those Christians and persons who up until now have understood individual expressions of the New Testament in a way that they interpret to be literal and binding. If, let us say, taking a random sample, someone used to be convinced that in Matthew, chapter 28, the words, "in the name of the Father, and of the Son, and of the Holy Spirit," which should be pronounced over the person to be baptized, came directly from the mouth of the historical Jesus, then that person will, of course, be shocked at first, if a modern exegete would explain that this is unlikely and that this is something that comes out of a later reflection on the Trinitarian God, and has only been placed on Jesus' lips.

But I would answer, basically, as follows: Does modern exegesis actually threaten the truly genuine Christian faith in its binding substance? In no way! The New Testament must, of course, be understood as an expression in writing of an already reflective early Christianity, which is directly anchored to the historical Jesus, to be sure. If it is understood in this way—and I think it should be understood in this way—then, of course, there stands behind the actual, literal wording of the text a deeper more genuine faith-conviction about Jesus, who is the absolute self-promise of the grace-giving and forgiving God. Only that which stands so savingly behind the text, and that which expresses itself so authentically and engagingly in the text, is what we really can attain in its essence, so that there is a correspondence and convergence between the word of the text—correctly read and understood—and the faith-conviction of the early community expressed in the text and in one's own faith-conviction. In this way Scripture can truly be read as an expression of that which a Christian who is related to Jesus in his or her own existence can also personally experience today. I am not sure whether I have expressed myself clearly in this matter.

Perhaps I could pursue the question a bit more. You said that the new exegesis does not threaten faith. I would agree. But is not faith made more difficult, in as much as today we can no longer know automatically or obviously what Jesus thought of himself, whom he thought himself to be? For we can no longer say that these are the words that Jesus spoke. Perhaps we must first say that these are what the early Church put into his mouth. The danger which I would like to address here is simply the following: How can I prove, then—in as much as such a thing is provable, at all—that Jesus is more than a man? This is a question that has plagued me for a long time now. I could grant everything, and I believe that many people think the same, namely, that Jesus was a holy man, a great prophet. He was a living human being. He was faithful unto death. Granting all this, how can one really prove that he was supposed to be God? Would not his own personal witness be necessary to prove this?

Now, of course, you are raising a subject that is so vast, that it is difficult to give a short answer to it. Jesus did not, of course, say: I am God. Although this statement, correctly understood, belongs to Christian faith, it can still be misunderstood, and understood in such a way that a modern person can say in all fairness: That is unbelievable; Jesus was not God. But one must determine exactly what this means in Christian, magisterial teaching, as it was already formulated in antiquity. If this is certain, on the one hand, then an intelligible connection can be made between this magisterial Christology and the self-interpretation of the historical Jesus.

A quick question thrown in: Why could not Jesus have said: I am God, or, I am God-man?
Because that would have been absolutely misunderstood.

Why?
You can see that even today it could be misunderstood. If someone imagines that the eternal Word of God, wrapped up in a sort of servant's uniform, looks after what takes place in this world (which he has actually created), and is trying to bring into line the world that has gone off track—if someone were to imagine Christian Christology to be like this, then that person is really off-base, and cannot bring this into harmony with the historically provable self-understanding of Jesus.

Now, I do not know how far I should explain correctly and in detail magisterial Christology to such a person—or even begin to explain. After all, this Christology is based on the fact that two thoroughly and absolutely different, though not separate, realities exist in Jesus Christ. I do not know whether I should develop such a Christology or point out how it is connected with the self-understanding of Jesus, and that out of this self-understanding . . .

To me personally the other question is actually of more interest. You like to speak of Jesus as the last prophet, as the absolute redeemer. I propose this question: Could not the last prophet, the absolute redeemer, just be an especially graced human being?

No. I would say that you could not any longer maintain that, although Jesus was truly the last prophet, he was only a human being, once you presuppose and really understand that through and in Jesus, the absolute and last prophet, history has entered into its unsurpassable phase, even though history in itself can continue and all sorts of things are thinkable in the limitless possibilities of God. For this last unsurpassable and irrevocable self-promise of God in the man Jesus is precisely that which the Church's official Christology intends to say about the unity of God and man in the God-man.

I believe that this is really quite difficult. It is quite a theological question, and also quite a theological answer.

True. But look. I think we must deal impartially with history, and the history of the Spirit, and the history of the Spirit in Christianity, the history of the theological expression of Christianity. And in such a history events always occur, which are surprising in a certain sense, which could make one think that things could have happened differently, although the final and basic reality would have remained the same. And if we, for example, with this supposition were to say: Whenever a human being encounters Jesus, the crucified and resurrected one, in his destiny, in his word, in his final permanent state as the ultimate, unsurpassable self-promise of God (and I think that such a thought is still possible for a person to have today), then this person has already essentially accepted, even though the words and perspectives are different, the dogmatic Christology which the Church teaches and upholds in its formulations, at least for the present.

Christology in its true sense will always remain the same. But it would be thoroughly thinkable that one could formulate what is actually intended in another way, which would create new difficulties in understanding, of course, but which avoids some difficulties in understanding which were present up until now.

As long as we are on the subject of "crucified one," "resurrected one." . . . In our world there is not much difficulty in understanding the idea of the crucified Jesus. This became very clear to me during my Latin American stay in connection with the

Latin American Conference of Bishops, in those countries where entire nations have such a natural access to the suffering one, to the man of pain, to the crucified one, the beaten and thorn-crowned Christ. But belief in the resurrection is so much more difficult there, because it presupposes that one have in one's own life, in one's own environment, something like a taste of the resurrection. That means that the liberation theologians in Latin America, with whom you have also occupied yourself a bit, are very busy at the moment reflecting on this: What can we, or must we, do here, today, to arrive gradually at an intelligible Christology after we have strongly emphasized for so long the history of liberation which the God of the Old Testament lived and effected for his ancient people, Israel. For the nations which recognize suffering, repression, pain, and injustice, but which have not experienced up to this time in their entire history as a nation something like a transformation, must be lifted up to the resurrected one. Here is a linguistic connection between resurrection, rising up, and rebellion—I have put it crudely. But I think we really have difficulties with this resurrected one.

Let me say this, first of all. To turn toward the crucified one who is not at the same time the victor over the cross and defeat would be only to turn toward the picture of an absolutely deadly and all-devouring absurdity. Clearly this cannot be the intention of these people in South America. They turn themselves toward the suffering Christ—and they recognize in him their own existence, of course—but they also hope that this crucified one will not just repeat their own question, go through it himself, but that he will actually answer it. Where someone believes, hopes, and builds on the conviction that this fate of death, of ruin, is fulfilled by a final promise, that it enjoys a final victory, there one believes in what is called Christian resurrection.

You are right, of course, when you say that today's liberation theologians would like a bit of the anticipation of this last, victorious freedom and deliverance to appear now, and, furthermore, not only in the intimacy of the private realm but in the history of the people. In this you are correct. Someone who has only had the experience of the absurdity of death, of the cross, of senselessness, and of nothing else could never imagine that all this is only the beginning, and shall be overcome through a victory by life and glory. To this extent the Latin American liberation theologians are thoroughly correct when they say: We Christians have the absolute duty and task so to structure our societal situation that one can read in it a positive hope for eternal joy, eternal freedom. In this they are correct; that ought to happen, of course. But to what extent that can come about, to what extent actual human life is a strange mixture of the experience of life and the experience of death, that is another question entirely.

I cannot say that I can only become a Christian when the Latin American nations have achieved the degree of political freedom toward which they rightly strive; for when will that actually happen? And does not every positive advance in such things bring negative realities to birth. Despite all the ordered, committed work—work to which we are bound at the same time under penalty of eternal damnation—work for freedom, justice, love, and selflessness, do we not move, again and again, from one prison to another in this earthly life? So in this area I am, of course, a bit skeptical, and more than that. But, as has been said, wherever such Christian skepticism leads to political inertia, laziness, and to the stabilizing of unjust relationships, there it is not Christian but a nasty trick, truly the opium of the people, a mean trick, which the powerful use to hold the poor people in their power.

I have one more question, for which we have just enough time left, perhaps: our difficulties with the afterlife. Father Weger, you touched on this in your book, and added to the discussion. It says that even we Christians who are believers are very worldly. We really do not have a deep need for the afterlife here and now. I am expressing this for myself, but I know that I am expressing the sentiments and thoughts of others. The more I learn to grasp God and God's presence and God's history with humankind, which fulfills itself in the here and now, the more liberated I am from that which the generation of my parents and grandparents stressed so very much, that is, that true reality and all that we can experience is first fulfilled in the afterlife. And the more we notice how much things fulfill themselves here, when we take the here and now seriously and try to structure it, the more we lose a sort of yearning for the afterlife, or heaven, or whatever we want to call it. A hope for salvation which says: Then, after your death, with your death, everything really is fulfilled, is really disappearing. Does this hope belong inextricably to the Christian faith?

I think a Christianity that simply absolutizes the present moment into a horizontalism, an actualism, or into an eschatology of the present moment—or whatever you want to call it—and supposes that one already enjoys and experiences in this present moment that which makes up the ultimate sense of human life—such a Christianity would no longer be Christianity.

One must ask, again and again, in a self-critical way: Does the determination that many people today are uninterested make that lack of interest legitimate? If I explain that actually I am very content in this world, and I think that the good fortune of the moment should be so grasped that other questions do not even arise, then I would ask quite simply: How do you know that such a stance is legitimate? The fact that something is not in vogue today is hardly an argument for saying that it is all over with, definitively. A completely different mentality could return very quickly.

Furthermore, of course, one must say that current experiences of good luck, of life, of joy—from a Christian point of view—will not utterly vanish. What Christianity really preaches does not arrive only after these experiences have seemingly passed away. Rather our current history is that which achieves its own final reality in what we call eternity. Nothing completely different is coming hereafter; rather, time, history, my life come to their own full completeness and form without losing anything.

I do not see how one could actually enjoy this life if one were clearly and honestly convinced that it is to be simply, utterly destroyed. Then I could say with at least as much right: Let us not even begin anything at all. Then the achievement of this destruction is the reality toward which we are striving, and the so-called grandeur of human life with its tasks, its love, its friends, and so on, also with its pain overcome, would actually be that which demonstrates its own senselessness precisely through its own final destruction.

If someone says: In this moment of time I am experiencing the absolute meaning of just this moment, then I would say: Then you have just experienced, in truth, that which—understood correctly—is precisely Christian eternity, or will be Christian eternity, or carries in it Christian eternity—or however you want to express it.

Translated by Robert Braunreuther, S.J.
Boston College

39 · Is Political Theology Dangerous?

Interview with Franz Alt for Southwest German Radio (SWF)
Baden-Baden (November 23, 1979)

What is your evaluation of the political theology of Johann Baptist Metz?
I am not a representative of political theology, but I believe that the kind of political theology which Metz represents is thoroughly orthodox.... If I were a bishop, I also ought to let those theologians speak out whose theology does not appeal to me, even if I believe that I have pertinent objections, provided, of course, that one could not claim that such a theology was no longer Catholic.

Father Rahner, do you see in Cardinal Ratzinger's rejection of Metz as a theology professor in Munich a symptom of a backward movement in the Catholic Chuch?
I am afraid that one can come to such an interpretation.

Translated by John R. Sachs, S.J.
Fairfield University

40 · A Plea for Pluralism in the World-Church

Interview with the Catholic News Agency, Munich (1980)

Bishops from the Third World frequently complain about Rome's centralized authority. Indeed, they must often have the impression that people are not adequately informed about the Church's situation in Third World countries, or that their urgent

234

pastoral concerns and desires for reform are falling victim to some "universal directive." We're thinking here, for example, about a reform of the Church's law regarding marriage, or about the demand to allow women or married men in the priesthood, or about the introduction of new liturgical forms. How much diversity does or should the world-Church tolerate?

I think it's self-evident that only in recent decades has the Church moved from being a European Church (which had, of course, the potential for universality) to becoming genuine world-Church. God intended Christianity to be for *all* people, but until recently it was in fact a European religion which was, of course, massively exported to the rest of the world. What was exported was objective truth, valid for all people, but that truth was spread throughout the world with the help of European colonialism. This is not to condemn past practices, but rather to point out the need for the Church gradually and confidently to become less a European Church exported to the world, and more truly a world-Church.

This means, however, that this world-Church has to promote a greater pluralism among its local churches than was formerly the case. There will be greater differentiation among the theologies of the individual regions of the Church. The Latin American Church, with its theology of liberation, has already begun to develop a theology rooted in its own unique situation and to speak effectively to that situation. Eventually, there will be something like an Asiatic theology, and certainly also an African theology, though this latter will emerge slowly.

Besides theology and liturgy, there are other areas in which a necessary and legitimate pluralism must be developed—within, of course, a Church that always is one and that is under the guidance of the pope. It isn't at all necessary that Canon Law be so uniform throughout the whole Church. Rome is presently preparing a new code of church law, and one hopes it will leave room for a legitimately independent development of large regional churches.

Clearly, in spite of all the differences in theologies and in ways of preaching, ultimately there is and must be one and the same revelation of God in the Church. Accordingly, extremely difficult questions on various matters must be thoroughly investigated before such differentiation in the universal Church be admissible. Basically, though, I would say that the Church of the future, as a world-Church that has to live with various cultures, demands a greater pluralism than in fact is practiced in the Church today.

For example, one could ask if a secular priest's celibacy is still valuable, meaningful, and appealing within a genuinely African culture with its totally different mentality; we could ask if this notion of celibacy, for all its actual and potential meaningfulness, did not in fact arise in a Western culture; and whenever that cultural basis is no longer present, then an institution like celibacy can no longer survive. In these and similar issues such as the Church's laws about marriage, Rome tends rather to hold things in check than to push for further developments. Part of the reason for this, of course, is that the episcopate in Third World countries has not yet been granted that measure of trust in its own autonomy which is necessary for it to achieve its own needs and ideas and pastoral plans in each country.

As a theologian you've always sought and nourished close contact with those who form the basis of the Church. Also, you've always been concerned to read the "signs of the times." Today, however, there are completely new signs, thanks to Church developments in Asia, Africa, and Latin America. What influence has this had on you? Or have you concluded that there's really nothing new in these developments?

I think that the question of a vigorous development of the so-called basic churches or basic communities poses an important task for the Church of the future. A clergy that is more or less self-enclosed, that exists, lives, thinks, reacts in almost total independence from the people of the Church, is hardly conceivable in the future. Those who form the basis of the Church must be allowed to experience Church, Christianity, grace, and revelation; they have to exercise their legitimate influence on the Church's hierarchy. This by no means implies changing the dogmatic structure of the Church; however, even dogmatically permanent and divinely ordained structures in the Church have always had a historically conditioned concrete form. And in the future these structures will be different from those we have now or that we've had in the past and are used to.

There are basic communities in Latin America because all the sociological relationships there are different from those here in Europe. There must be basic communities here, too, but in a completely different sense and perhaps in a completely different manner: The sociological structure of our society is different than it used to be. A Church in our pluralistic, secularized society is necessarily a different Church than before; it has a different basis, and there's a different relationship between that basis and the clergy or episcopate.

We will be unable to adopt several functions carried out by the basic churches of the poor, of those directly oppressed socially, of the persecuted. But we in Europe shall be able to learn a great deal from those churches, and many of the things they have newly developed, experienced, and suffered can speak to us, too. Because the social structures of today's society are different than before, and because the structures in other areas of the Church are different from our own here in Europe, basic communities here must develop "from below" in their own unique ways, and they must have an enormous influence on the entire Church's leadership and on the episcopate.

In comparing poor and rich nations, one often hears about the North-South differential. This differential exists, too, between poor and rich churches: between, for example, the Church in Upper Volta and the Church in the Federal Republic of Germany. For the most part, Europe's Christians donate only what is left over to their brothers and sisters in the Third World. Efforts by the Church in the Federal Republic of Germany to economize and save on behalf of the poor are rare, even today. How do you evaluate this deeply deplorable phenomenon?

We shouldn't deceive ourselves by thinking that European Christianity is suddenly going to start living like Francis of Assisi by donating thirty percent of its gross national product to the poor churches. We have to be realistic. Realistically speaking, it's impossible for everyone to be poor; there are sociological and psychological barriers to poverty that the Church has to live with now and in the future. Nevertheless, I think we can and should demand far more from our European churches than is presently being done. We should of course, be careful. The Church in France, for example, is much poorer than the German Church; in France, the clergy themselves (with some exceptions, of course) are part of that group of decidedly poor devils who strenuously must earn their own living.

In this whole matter there is one thing I'd like to highlight. What sacrifices on behalf of poor churches can the German episcopate demand of the average German Catholic without a radical reversal in the former's way of thinking? The episcopate should, if I may say so, be a step ahead of the average believer's attitude, and this should be reflected in the episcopate's directives for pastors, for the faithful, and for the disposition of the tax monies collected for the Church. On the other side of the coin, where in Germany are the faithful who are urging the episcopacy to live closer to poverty, or who want the episcopacy to demand more from the faithful on behalf of the poor than is presently being done? I frankly don't know of many faithful who are urging pastors and bishops to dig even deeper into the pocketbooks of the faithful for various Church aid programs. These works are fairly well supported and they have nothing to be ashamed of; think, for example, of Miserior, Adveniat, and so on. But one could certainly wish that those who form the basis of the Church would take their own initiative, and not simply wait to be pushed by the episcopacy.

Translated by Michael C. O'Callaghan
Marist College, Poughkeepsie, New York

41 · Death as Fulfillment

Interview with Gerhard Ruis for *Die Furche*, Salzburg (April 2, 1980)

Death has troubled persons in every age and has kept open the question about the origin, cause, and meaning of human dying. Every person at some time in his or her life is concerned about an answer to the old question: What is death? How should and how can one speak appropriately about death?

First of all, with death it's all over. Life is past, and it won't come again. It won't be given one for a second time. Death for the Christian is the event in which his or her one and only life is completed.

Now I believe that all serious and reasonable persons—even Far Eastern adherents of a belief in the transmigration of souls—will hold that one's task is to escape the cycle of birth and death and to complete one's own history of freedom in an ultimate and eternal fulfillment.

I find no problem in thinking that every person can in the life that has been given him or her manage to achieve this. Wherever in a human life freedom, that is, decision of a radical sort, is thinkable, there fulfillment is also possible.

As a theologian you surely believe that serious talk about death takes place only in the horizon of serious talk about God. Therefore, to be able to speak appropriately about death there is need of a word that we cannot speak to ourselves. Is it the gospel, and the gospel as "word about the cross" (1 Cor. 1:18), that first makes our talk about death appropriate?

Ultimately I would say yes to this question. Only one has to start from the fact that there are innumerable people who are not confronted with an explicit interpretation of death through the biblical revelation. We Christians are, nonetheless, convinced that in meeting death all humans are given the ultimate possibility of deciding for or against God.

Where people decide concerning themselves in an ultimate and definitive fashion, and indeed for their definitive state, they either accept the ultimate ground that bears their existence, namely, God, or they commit themselves to the ultimate absurdity and nothingness of human life.

Since death is the event of an ultimate, total self-interpretation of the human person one way or the other, it has to do with God. God is the word that means the embracing, upholding, all-conditioning ground of human existence in its unlimitedness and unboundedness.

Death appears in the biblical understanding in a specific relationship with the sin with which persons burden themselves in the course of their lives. You yourself said once: "Death is the visibility of sin. . . ."

Here you are touching upon an extraordinarily difficult theme of the Christian revelation. The Bible certainly teaches that there is a connection between sin and death. However, for us today this doctrine is not immediately intelligible, since, on the one hand, we have recognized biological death as a phenomenon that existed long before the history of human sin and since, on the other, we cannot imagine that the person was supposed to have lived continuously and forever without sin.

I suppose that we can simply say: Death precisely as the coming to an end of the history of freedom is an event that has always existed even prior to sin. Wherever there is history, it will have an end. Freedom and fulfillment belong together. A fulfillment that in coming to an end does not possess itself and cannot control itself, but occurs as a coming to an end in the incomprehensibility of a divine judgment, such a death has something to do with sin. The darkness is a sign of the person's sinful condition.

It is still another question whether this sinful condition has come to be through personal sin or is a consequence of a sin in the beginning of human history or whether it is both.

Death appears also to have a dimension of reconciliation. Schelling [and] . . . Bloch . . . have developed an understanding of death that grasps it precisely as the ultimate and genuine act of human self-realization. They have even described death as the act of the person fulfilling his or her own life, even as "the act of willing itself."

The magnificence of this sort of interpretation of human existence can only be defended under the presupposition that all this is seen as action and disposition of the Creator.

Where one supposes in an idealism like Schelling's or an optimism like Bloch's that death must automatically be the beginning of a blessed final state of the person, the Christian will say: Yes, I hope for that myself, but it is God who judges me. The Christian will hope for death as the eternal fulfillment but, at the same time, humbly fear the possibility that his or her end could really be one of loss. The Christian is thus torn between anxiety over and hope for salvation, and this tornness is the ultimate driving force of his or her history.

Christian faith stands and falls with the confession that in the death of Jesus something happened to death itself. The Christian faith proclaims a new beginning from the destructive nothing of death as the resurrection from the dead. Father Rahner, what is the genuine content of what the Bible wants to proclaim to people as their hope by the symbol of resurrection from the dead.

First of all, we must as a matter of fact admit that the interpretation of the word *resurrection* has not been 100 percent uniform in all the Christian centuries and in all the schools of theology. Up to the Enlightenment, the notion of a fundamental distinction between body and soul presented no intrinsic problem in conceiving the destiny of the so-called immortal soul independently of the destiny of the body: the result is a concept of resurrection that is related exclusively to human bodiliness.

If, on the contrary, one were to envision the relationship between the body and soul in a more modern and somewhat less platonically conceived anthropology, then, of course, as a Christian one would not deny that there is a difference between what we call the body and the soul. In addition, one would not deny that something can be affirmed relative to the ultimate state of this human reality called soul which is not exactly the same as the ultimate state of the human body. However, the expression "resurrection of the flesh" in its Old Testament tradition is more a shorthand expression for the final salvation of the one and total human being. What is being presupposed is that this ultimate state of the one and total human being which we call one's survival after death should not be misunderstood as a sort of pure blessedness and perfection of a soul freed from a body.

Today, as Christians, we can, without getting into dogmatic difficulties, see both that the human person as one, concrete, and bodily can ultimately have only one destiny and one fulfillment and that this one total fulfillment of the one—and bodily—person can be called "resurrection of the dead."

Translated by Roland J. Teske, S.J.
Marquette University

42 · Old Age and Death

Interview with Erika Ahlbrecht-Meditz of Radio Saarland
Saarbrücken (October 21, 1980)

The philosopher Karl Popper says that life, far from becoming meaningless because it is finite, derives its real meaning and value from its finiteness. The Viennese neurologist Viktor Frankl agrees, and in your own writings I have also found similar ideas, namely, that to live on forever would basically be the hell of meaninglessness. I wonder now whether one should be as old and as successful as Popper, Frankl, and Rahner to share this view.

First, this view defended by Frankl, Popper, or me and others is one that is based on the nature of freedom. For all of us freedom does not mean that we can keep on adding to and changing our activity forever. It is rather the positing of something definitive—over a period of time, of course, but in such a way that, of its very nature, this period of time should lead up to the definitive. That is why I believe it to be quite true that freedom and human life must reach an end in order to make sense. The Christian doctrine of eternity, of responsibility before God, of the last and definitive judgment about a life presupposes that hereafter things do not go on as they do now, but that—as we put it—a life is being lived in the definitive intuition of God, a life that stands far above this mere going on and on. Of course, such a doctrine of the meaning of freedom, of freedom leading up to the definitive, does not solve the following problem: What about a life that in our human eyes looks too short, what about children who die in infancy? About those things I would in all sincerity say that we know nothing, not even from our Christian faith. The Christian message is addressed to human beings that are endowed with freedom, who must answer for their life and are also capable of doing so. To them the message says: You must reckon with a definitiveness and everlastingness that are the product of your own free decision; they stand before you as the unending fulfillment of your life and as the ground of an absolute and radical responsibility. But what happens with the children and the human beings that do not possess or do not seem to possess what is presupposed for such an outcome—namely, the real, true, concrete possibility of a free decision—we really do not know. Nor should we worry about this. We have to save ourselves, to work out our own salvation. We do not have to worry to the same extent about hypothetical boundary cases of a possible biological ending, not preceded by any personal free development.

241

I would like to come back once more to these dying children, because I have a hunch that it is probably a meager consolation, say for a mother whose five year old child dies from a brain tumor, to be told, "A boundary case. Something good must somewhere be foreseen in God's will for that child." Such a catastrophic ending looks so casual, is felt as so arbitrary by the mother, that your explanation falls flat.

But right now I would first like to say something more about old age. You have written a paper about old age which starts by saying that old age is a grace, a special task, but also a danger. And you note that formerly—probably in part because only a few people reached it—old age enjoyed special privileges and consideration and had also a clear social function, which no longer exists today. So I wonder how older people, who may be herded into nursing homes may still experience old age as a task, since society no longer admits that they have any task?

First, are you sure that every task—supposing that it is accepted consciously and willingly—should also be offered and guaranteed by society? When I am old and unable to do anything else but—excuse me for putting it this way—say my Rosary, I may experience this as a thoroughly important and quite noble task. If I say this is not for me, all right then, I cannot come up with any encouraging answer. We Jesuits have a catalogue that comes out every year and which tells what we do, how old we are, and so on. It also contains, of course, the elderly and the sick, each one in the house where he lives. It never says: "He used to be a preacher," or anything of the kind. It says, "He prays for the Church and for the Society of Jesus." That is very realistic yet also very meaningful. Of course, society should provide opportunities for the elderly as well as for the sick, and not shut them up in nursing homes where they vegetate in a dreary humdrum. That stands to reason. But we are not discussing this here.

The theologian is asked what he has to say, when all these other things that would be good, meaningful, necessary, obligatory—when they no longer work. And then he will say, "As long as these people possess their inner personal freedom, they are still able to turn meaningfully toward God, to accept their life, which grows, of course, more and more restricted, with Christian patience, in hope of eternity." And, as a theologian, I can only say that for those, who out of pride or as a protest against life do not accept this, I have no other consolation.

And where do you see the danger of this stage of life? We are speaking not only of tasks or opportunities, but also of dangers.

Of course this stage contains quite a number of dangers. Every stage of life has its own opportunities, all of which also have a negative side that is troublesome, dangerous, disagreeable, and that has simply to be accepted without complaint. The same applies to old age. When I am tired, when I grow old, when I vanish, as it were, from the stage of world history, when I have the feeling that my environment is making out as well as before without me, when, at the same time, I also grow physiologically weaker and notice that I am failing, that I no longer hear well, that I no longer see well, when I tire easily, and so on—these are facts that I must simply live with. Not with the help of beautiful ideas that charm all this away, or serve as tranquilizers against such bitter old-age experiences, but by simply saying that this must be borne with patience and in the hope of life eternal.

As long as one can find solace in other things, there is nothing wrong with that. When somebody is old and thoroughly enjoys a walk, or a friendly get together or an interesting book or jotting down one's own life reminiscences or taking pictures or—you name it—there is nothing wrong with that. And those who live with old people should look out for such entertainment more than they usually do. But once more when all these things no longer work, are perfectly useless, and I nevertheless keep my wits, there really remains nothing else than to say that I can and must somehow manage in the hope of eternal life. Should one find some other solace, all right, nobody takes it away. If some people succeed somehow in bearing their failures and their pain in stoic heroism—like, for instance, Freud with his cancer and dreadful operations—I can only take off my hat to such people with great respect. Yet I wonder whether deep down they have not despaired. And there is also the question whether, looked at from the theological and metaphysical point of view, this heroism is not deep down the ultimate achievement of a person who believes anonymously. Finally, I might add: If I can manage in some other way than Freud, in my own way, who can blame me for it?

And, of course, we must also remember this: Occasionally pain, unbearable physiological pain, may grow to such an extent that, in the personal theological sense, it takes away all responsibility. When you undergo a Chinese or some other kind of brainwashing that shatters you physiologically, the theological question of responsibility before God stops automatically. The same applies to old age. If I suffer such pain from cancer that it becomes basically impossible for me to steer my life responsibly, then theologically speaking there is no more problem. I may then be nothing more than a human entity that still has to go through a final physiological stage. But I am saved and at peace with God through my former actions. From the religious and human point of view this last stage is unimportant. That is, by the way, why it makes no sense needlessly to prolong it through medical intervention.

Twenty-three years ago you wrote a theology of death.[1] *I have reread it to prepare for this conversation. I had read it then, twenty years ago, and after consulting the book again after such a long interval I was amazed how much one can say, how much one can explain by using the Church's Christian doctrine about death and the life hereafter. And I cannot get rid of the question whether today you still accept these answers as answers.*

First I must say—excuse me for admitting this—that I really no longer know exactly what I wrote twenty-five years ago. Who knows whether I might not say with the Swabians about many points that are my own theological speculations and not the obligatory doctrine of faith, "What do I care about my stupid opinions of yesterday?" I am not quite sure. But from my whole way of doing theology I would guess that my theological development would rather lean more to admitting that we do not know this and that, hence more to a legitimate Christian skepticism. Not to any kind of skepticism, but to one that is acceptable for a Christian; we do not have answers for everything, but we entrust ourselves in hope and love to the incomprehensibility of God, knowing that precisely this act of ultimate capitulation to God's incomprehensibility is precisely the last thing that is asked from us.

In your theology of death you start from the fact that death is something that concerns the whole person and you ask what remains, and what happens to what remains? I remember that you reached the conclusion that the soul, that which remains of the person passes into the foundation of reality, that it becomes pancosmic. I do not know whether this is a very cheerful idea for us. Do you still think that way today?

I am not quite sure whether I still think that way. This idea derived simply from the fact that there was a problem in my traditional Thomistic metaphysics. On the one hand, Thomas—unlike the Augustinian tradition—holds with Aristotle that there is a very radical unity of spirit and matter. On the other, as a Christian, he speaks quite naturally, as seems unavoidable, of a "separated soul," of a soul that death has totally stripped of its body. It seems to me that this presents us with a problem that Thomas has not solved thoroughly enough.

Hence it occurred to me that, when one thinks the Thomistic idea of matter through to the end—I cannot explain this here in detail—a relation of matter to the soul after death would be quite conceivable. Moreover, it seems clear to me that this conception takes into account—perhaps better than used to be done—a legitimate claim of the modern mind. The modern philosophy of

---

1. *On the Theology of Death*, tr. C. H. Henkey (New York: Herder and Herder, 1961).

nature wishes to understand the materiality of spiritual realities, if I may say so, and does not want to think of the spirit as the foe of matter, as something that is totally alien from matter and the cosmos.

While we are speculating about theology, I keep constantly in mind that the funda-mental presupposition of our conversation, namely, the belief in a loving God offers the greatest difficulties for most people. Amidst so much senseless unhappiness and casual destruction of life, they hardly succeed in making rhyme or reason of their life, not to speak of their death.

Sure. But I think that one also sees that such a middle position, which simply notes that life is a mixture of stupidity and beauty, of sense and nonsense, that there is nothing one can do against it, that one has simply to swallow the indigestible mixture—such a position is basically and in the long run untenable. Ultimately, there must be an absolute either/or. Of course, one *can* reach the conclusion—and I even believe that my theology has paid special attention to this—that even when one protests, when one is miserable, when one is drowning in skepticism, there still may subsist an absolute yes to life. Such is our life and such the nature of the spirit that, even in what seems to be provisional, conditional, a hodgepodge, there lives, deep down, even when people are hardly aware of it in their humdrum lives, either an absolute yes or an absolute no, an absolute untrammeled hope or a dreadful ultimate despair.

A mother who continues faithfully to love her child whatever may happen; those who, although they reap no profit from it, cling to the truth of their convictions, even when they are not popular or fashionable; such people—whether or not they are aware of it, whether or not they interpret their position in this way—profess an absolute yes to the meaningfulness of existence, even if they correctly experience many things in their life as failures, as meaningless and bitter. That is why, it seems to me, one may, despite their wretchedness, their cowardice, their seemingly endless compromises, have a high opinion of human beings. In the whole shabby concoction blended of darkness and light there subsists an ultimate absolute to which a person consciously or unconsciously pays fealty.

I do not share the opinion you mention and others have defended that, at the moment of biological death there occurs something very special, grandiose, decisive, when people once more turn their whole life upside down and reverse its direction. I do not believe that this is true. Despite all the theories of Kübler-Ross and of others who studied the dying, death may occur very uneventfully and unconsciously. But somewhere within our lives there happens —or there may at least happen—an absolute letting-go, an absolute yielding-all.

This may constitute death in the theological sense, which may ultimately consist in the unconditional, quiet, yet trustful capitulation before the incomprehensibility of one's own existence, and thus also before the incomprehensibility of God. I believe therefore that people may be very pessimistic, very skeptical, and very relativistic in their life. They do not have to deceive themselves, to act as if one had only to exert oneself a bit to have life turn out as an unmixed blessing. With me, at least, such romantic American recipes for running one's life meet with massive skepticism. And I do not believe that one must find everyday life in one's job and in one's relations with others quite so grandiose. But I believe that in life taken as a whole and at some particular specially blessed moments a decision is reached about one's own life. Let me describe it as follows: One gives up everything, one lets everything go. And precisely in this seemingly dumb, dreadful and frightening emptiness there dawns the arrival of the infinite God and his eternal life.

Nowadays there are theologians who have more or less taken over the way in which biologists understand death. They do not consider death as a misfortune, as a catastrophe, but as needed for evolution, as something positive. Should most theologians accept this conception of death, would this not do away with a very essential theological doctrine, namely, the idea that death is a punishment for sin?

The Christian doctrine that sees in death a sequel of sin is a dialectical theological statement that cannot be understood and interpreted correctly, unless it be combined with the other statement that the death of a person who really believes is a dying-with Christ, as the absolute triumph of life, because his and our death is a dying into resurrection. Therefore, in what sense death should be experienced as negative is a difficult question.

To put it briefly and simply, and reserving the right of further explanations, I would say: Death would have to be interpreted negatively if we did *not* die with Jesus, he who was crucified and rose from the dead. So the previous negative statement is true only under a certain condition. And Christian faith tells us that this condition has long ago been eliminated by Jesus Christ. One may say that a paradisiacal immortality would certainly have been worse than death in Christ. For there can be no doubt that for theologians and their doctrine, and for Christian faith, the Christ event is not an arduous restitution of the person's paradisiacal destiny, but something far superior. Hence we may safely say that—forgetting all evolutionary theories and speculations—death may certainly be conceived as a positive event of life, as the triumph of absolute life in the dimension of the finiteness of the human person, a triumph which demonstrates that once more, even in the seeming absurdity of the person's death, God and his eternal life are victorious.

Of course, most people die in a very sad manner. At least, that is the way it looks. They are unconscious, they rattle, one waits almost impatiently for everything to be over. They are pushed somewhere into an intensive care unit, and their relatives are perhaps forbidden to be present. And they may even, if they are sincere, be happy that they do not have to be there. All this is sad, all this is perhaps dismal, and maybe should be different. But in the final analysis, that is not the main point.

All human beings die in such a way that everything is taken away from them, and Christians are convinced, while they live and when they die, that the ensuing emptiness is filled to the brim by what we call God. And basically we have understood God—as the incomprehensible, of course—only when we say: He is the one who belongs in this ultimate existential void created by our death, as the fulfillment; as the fulfillment that is definitive; as the fulfillment that is incomprehensible; as the fulfillment that, as incomprehensible, we hope is our blessed salvation. We know very little about the beyond. We have in this respect become more discreet than former times, which painted grandiose pictures of the beyond. The possibly ensuing demythologization is quite legitimate, and we, as Christians, should not oppose it. On the contrary, for it reveals more clearly, more radically, more uncloudedly than in former times the ultimate core of the Christian belief in the beyond that has always existed. To face death skeptically is not yet a denial of Christianity. Rather, human life has to pass through this apparent nullity, if it is to be fulfilled not by this or that, but by God.

Translated by Joseph Donceel, S.J.
Fordham University

43 · The Hans Küng Controversy

Interview on "Night Studio" of Radio Salzburg (January, 1980)

Professor Küng is accused of doubting papal infallibility.[1] What do you have to say about that?

Of course, it is up to every theologian to make clear, even to the point of rigorously proving that the opposite is not true, which certainly has not been demonstrated here, that the theologian is interested in the truth and nothing else. This praiseworthy and basically obvious intention does not prove, of course, that the theologian in question is right. It is always a question of truth in the thousands of disputes within the fields of theology and philosophy. Everyone who voices an opinion in such matters seeks to tell the truth—as well as represent it. Even with the best of intentions, it is not possible that everyone is always right. Therefore, it has to be asked who in this case is right. Even granting high intelligence and the noblest striving for truth, a theologian may not only err but may also promote his or her error in good conscience.

The Catholic teaching, self-evident to me, is that the Church's faith awareness has to decide. However, this faith awareness of the Church also manifests itself in the official documents of the Roman Catholic magisterium, even though in varying degrees of obligation. Küng probably does not hold this opinion in such an absolute and binding manner. He will probably say that even though the ecclesiastical authorities declare that the First Vatican Council is absolutely binding, this declaration itself is questionable and, therefore, nonbinding. Who then actually decides what can and cannot be taught as Catholic teaching in the Church? Küng would probably say that this matter will be decided by means of disputation in the constantly ongoing history of the Church's faith awareness.

With regard to the Catholic teaching—let us speak with great caution—of recent centuries, I am, on the contrary, absolutely convinced that there is a competent position in the magisterium (the pope and bishops) for drawing such a line, to which I as a Catholic theologian feel bound. If I came into a serious conflict with this line that has been drawn and my sense of truth demanded that I make a decisive protest, then I would have to draw the conclusion that I am no longer a Catholic. I would approve the conviction of

1. On December 18, 1979, Hans Küng lost his right to teach. The questions on this matter are dealt with in *A Documentation of the Efforts of the Congregation for the Doctrine of Faith and of the Conference of German Bishops to Achieve an Appropriate Clarification of the Controversial View of Dr. Hans Küng* (Washington, D.C.: U.S. Catholic Conference, 1980).

the countless people in the world, especially in the rest of the non-Catholic Christian world, that they are not able to be Catholic in good conscience.

All Christians in the world who do not live in unity with the pope say, of course, that the claim of the pope as defined in Vatican I and repeated in Vatican II is not acceptable to their sense of truth. Understandably, one is able to come to such an opinion; otherwise, these countless people would be stupid or of bad will, neither of which can I obviously maintain. However, I stand by my opinion that the magisterium has the right to determine what can and cannot be taught as Catholic doctrine. The Catholic theologian only remains, strictly speaking, a Catholic theologian when he or she respects the line drawn by Rome.

What do you say to the accusation of an unclear circumscription of the essential identity of God with Jesus Christ?

With regard to the question of whether Jesus was one in essence with the Son of God, I see no absolute defiance on Küng's part. I have read Küng's book *On Being a Christian* from cover to cover—perhaps, there are not so terribly many people who have done that—and I have to confess that I could not discover any absolute defiance against a defined dogma in his Christology. Whether Küng's Christology completely "includes" all the official teachings of the Church is, of course, another question. The matter is, you see, as follows: Since the Councils of Ephesus and Chalcedon, we have dogmatically binding Christological pronouncements. It is, of course, self-evident that these pronouncements, which in the last analysis represent an inexpressible mystery of God in his relationship to the world, must be constantly thought out anew in terms of their understandability and assimilability.

The "nonorthodoxy" of Küng is not as clear to me in this Christological question as it is in the question regarding official papal teaching. I wonder why Küng did not simply state the following: Of course, I affirm my obligation to the Christological dogmas of Ephesus and Chalcedon; I am just reflecting to the best of my knowledge and in good conscience how to make Christology understandable and express it in a modern perspective. Then the magisterium could not find fault with him in the Christological question. I do not understand why Küng did not simply—if I may say it this way—"parry the thrust" of the Roman congregation.

One should not be too quick simply to throw together the different pronouncements of Küng criticized by Rome. Otherwise, under the circumstances, one could really accuse Rome of doing Küng an injustice. For me, the Chalcedon dogma is of an absolutely binding dimension. This fact, however, does not prevent me in any way from thinking through this dogma anew from different viewpoints. It does not prevent me from offering my contemporaries —as far as it is possible—reflections, formulations, and aids to understanding, which would not have been offered through the pure repetition of the old dogma. As a Catholic theologian, I must search for these aids today for my fellow believers.

I may boldly say today that I once protested openly at the Würzburg synod against statements made by Cardinal Höffner in this matter. Cardinal Höffner said: Jesus of Nazareth is God. I replied: Of course, that is a Christian, irreversible, finally binding truth, but one can misunderstand this sentence too. While other sentences with the verb *to be* express an identity of a simple type with the content of the predicate, such an identity between the humanity of Jesus and God's eternal Logos just does not exist. A unity exists here, not an identity. I only say that to make clear the fact that there are questions remaining and even differences of opinion regarding Christological dogma within the Church and its orthodoxy. Also, concerning Christology, the question of how far Küng can go can simply not be answered by me.

There are presently dangers of a sterile, reactionary, backwoods mentality in the Church, which could become realized to a certain degree. The integralism that reigned in the last years of Pius X is an example of how such reactionary trends can become powerful in the Church. However, that in no way means that such a reactionary atmosphere will be victorious in the end. The history of the Church continues and it always moves in a certain up and down motion, under the direction of him who preserves the Church in the way of truth—and so I agree with Küng on this point.

Translated by Eugene P. Finnegan, S.J.
Canisius College

44 · Dogmas—Their Importance and Their Limits

Interview with Karl Wagner, editor of *Münchener*
Katholischen Kirchenzeitung (MKKZ), Munich (May 25, 1980)

The German bishops have engaged themselves in the Küng case at great expense,
not least of all, because the propositions that were at issue in the debate are of great
importance for the faith of believers. How is this connection between dogmatic propo-
sitions and lived faith to be assessed?

Christian life and piety on the one hand and precise theological dogmas on
the other are certainly two different things. There are those who perhaps understand very little of what their catechism taught, but who are nevertheless
authentic and active Christians, people who love God and neighbor, and trust
in Jesus and his cross.

And there are certainly learned theologians who know precisely what the
textbooks hold, and in spite of it, their hearts are empty of God, his grace, and
the love of Jesus. This is an experience we have in life again and again. But,
and with this we come to the main point, there is also quite certainly an important relation between precise theological propositions and actually living as
a Christian in God's grace and love. Of course, in certain cases someone can
live a good life, and in spite of this affirm theoretically false propositions. The
Second Vatican Council thus said that a person can be in God's grace, even if
the person believes in good conscience that he or she must deny God's existence.

But for that very reason one cannot say that it doesn't make any difference
concretely whether someone affirms or denies theoretically the existence of
God. Accurate and clear propositions concerning humanity, its destiny, its
relation to God, and so on, are finally and quite certainly of significant importance for humanity. For example, those who deny God's existence, and actually live their lives culpably in accordance with this false proposition, would
also quite certainly make mistakes in their concrete lives, become unhappy
and miss their final goal. . . .

One of the essential propositions of faith says that Jesus is the Son of God. How can
and should a Christian today understand such a proposition?

A Catholic Christian will adhere absolutely to what is affirmed in this proposition and if I may say so, permanently. Nor will he or she say that such a
formulation, and the linguistic usage it implies, may no longer be useful today.

But a Catholic Christian will obviously also acknowledge, without for that reason in the least becoming liberal or unorthodox, that all words in such a formulation have in themselves a certain indefiniteness, and despite this can be understood.

When I say, "Jesus is the Son of God," therefore, it is self-evident that in this proposition concerning the relation of the eternal Word to the Father the concept of begetting and also of sonship is an analogous one that can be misunderstood. I can understand the proposition Jesus is the Son of God even in the sense, though this is not the only way, that we say of ourselves that we are children of God.

The sanctifying grace which makes us children of God was also given to the human reality of Jesus. Consequently, it must be pointed out that, on the one hand, a proposition such as Jesus is the Son of God must be steadfastly acknowledged in the Church's faith consciousness but that, on the other hand, it contains inevitable misunderstandings and obscurities.

Since eternal truths must and will be stated in finite words, are these words with all their limitations valid and unrelinquishable? Could you clarify this?

This brings us back once again to the fundamental question: Why and how clearly are dogmas, which are ecclesiastically determined and supported, significant for the concrete piety of the normal Christian's life? Let us answer this question once again with an example. I say briefly and concisely, perhaps, alas, without thinking much about it: Jesus is the Son of God.

But if I say that in this Jesus, his life, his word, his death, and his resurrection, I, wretched and otherwise perishing without hope, am promised the last, the comprehensive, the unsurpassable pledge: God so loves me that he will make his divine life itself my own in eternity—then I think since it intends to sum up exactly what has just been said, the proposition Jesus is the Son of God has an unsurpassable significance for my concrete Christian life.

Jesus is the Son of God, that is to say in yet another way: The incomprehensible God loves me in a love which mediates God's self to me. And that has been revealed in an irreversible and unsurpassable way in Jesus of Nazareth, the crucified and the risen one.

I think then that it is really self-evident that such a proposition has fundamental significance for concrete Christian living.

Perhaps one could substitute for this proposition one formulated in an entirely different way. The Church has then the duty and the right to hear and to test this other proposition, which perhaps wants to say the same thing, and thereupon to examine whether it does say what the Church wants to say permanently with its proposition, and under certain conditions say: No, I (the Church) cannot be satisfied with this other proposition. As I (the Church) hear and understand it, this new proposition does not say with perfect clarity what I say in my theological propositions, and for that very reason your propositions may not become the only valid ones in the Church.

Translated by Robert Masson
Marquette University

45 · On Becoming a Theologian

Interview with Peter Pawlowsky for Radio Austria (FS 1), Vienna (July 11, 1980)

Professor Rahner, you first saw the light of day in Freiburg in Breisgau, located in the southwest corner of Germany. To the east lies the Black Forest, to the west the borders of Switzerland and France. Would you describe the atmosphere of your childhood as "wholesome" even though the word nowadays sometimes has negative connotations?

Perhaps one could use that word. But why should one be ashamed to have to admit that one first saw the light of day in a normal, yes, pious, hardworking Christian family in which everything was, in fact, pretty much in order? Perhaps sometimes the children were lazy or quarreled among themselves; perhaps sometimes our parents complained, but my mother had a lot of work to do and my father, besides his regular job as a high school teacher, had to take on additional tutoring in order to support his seven children properly. Sundays we would be served cake and we would go into the hills near Freiburg to visit my grandmother. In short, family life was quite ordinary. The children all grew up normally, they all went to school and took their final exam (*Abitur*), even though at least fourteen years separated the oldest child from the youngest. On the other hand, life was not especially exciting; I can't relate any big, unusual incidents from my childhood.

Well then, if I understand you correctly, you went on directly to continue the rest of your education. Had you already decided even before you took your matriculation exam to enter the Jesuit order?

My brother Hugo, who was four years older than I, had already reached that decision. After presenting himself briefly for military service, he entered the German Jesuit novitiate located in Feldkirch, Austria, in January, 1919. You could say that everything, at least looked at externally, went by normally, uneventfully, without incident. Still, don't misunderstand me. All young people have problems, at least interior ones, that maybe they just learn to live with. In my own case, I had to live with my Black Forest temperament, I mean, my skeptical melancholia; of course, I have never been the sort of person who by temperament saw life as simple or joyous. But, as I say, when you ask whether I grew up in a wholesome atmosphere, then I'd have to say, yes, that's right and thank God!

What motivated you at that time, as a young man, to become a priest and a religious? You entered the Jesuits in 1922.

First of all, I would have to say that theoretical questions whether to become just a priest or also a religious, whether to become a Franciscan or a Jesuit were never big issues for me. I always wanted to become a priest; likewise, I always wanted to become a Jesuit. Exactly why, I am not too sure any longer. One time I stated, I think it was in a Spanish periodical, in reply to questions about my motives that obviously they must have been reasonable motives. To be sure, they were religious motives, colored by a certain view of theology which could be enumerated. Still, such motives in a young man fade; in later life they are not so retrievable. And it is not all that necessary anyway.

When you ask me whether I would again choose to become a Jesuit, I'd have to say that if I were now as I was then, surely I would. I don't regret any of the present consequences which follow from that decision. As I see it, you make a decision in a wholesome environment responding to a genuine call. Such a call makes certain claims interiorly on a person and you persevere in such a choice. Before you know it, you're a senior citizen, happy about your past life.

You just mentioned for the first time the word theology. *What then in fact caused your fascination right from the start with theology, with scholarly theology?*

First of all, my family. My father was a high school teacher, my other brothers and sisters also attended university. Many young people with their philosophical problems had ties with our family. In the family there was a predisposition or a certain penchant for religious, perhaps even apologetic matters. That was not something remote from my family's interests. Among the books my father read was [Houston Stewart] Chamberlain's *Foundations of the Nineteenth Century*. I'm sure the book is no longer known. In those days we used to discuss works such as *The Decline of the West* by Spengler. Then there was the youth movement, groups such as "Fountain of Youth" (to which I belonged) and "Highlands" (in which my eldest sister was a member). All that created an atmosphere of religious interest, which at the same time automatically raised strictly philosophical and theological questions.

You studied philosophy first of all as part of your regular formation as a Jesuit. Then I understand, you were originally assigned by your religious superiors to pursue further studies in philosophy. How would you characterize yourself? Are you more a philosopher or a theologian, or do you consider that you combine the two?

I would never bestow on myself the honorary title of professional philosopher. Really, I have not read widely enough in philosophy to make that claim. In Pullach, where we did our Jesuit training in philosophy, first I studied with some insight and success the standard, neoscholastic philosophy in its various subdivisions. At that time also, I became acquainted with the writings of the Belgian Jesuit philosopher Joseph Maréchal, who perhaps was one of the first to effect a fruitful encounter between scholastic philosophy and Kant. Discovering Maréchal was a major breakthrough for me; it expanded my horizons somewhat beyond the scholastic philosophy of the manuals. But as I was saying, my original assignment was supposed to have been to teach the history of philosophy at Pullach. This plan remained unchanged through my Jesuit studies in theology. After I finished my regular course of theology, I then, together with Father Johann Baptist Lotz, studied philosophy for two more years in the University of Freiburg and there I wrote a doctoral thesis in philosophy.

That thesis was turned down, was it not?

Yes, my dissertation was not accepted. Today I am still proud that I have an honorary doctorate in philosophy from Innsbruck. But my philosophy thesis written at Freiburg under the direction of Martin Honecker (and not Martin

Heidegger) was turned down. Still, the work was eventually published[1] and went through several German editions and was translated into French, English, and other languages!

But, your doctoral dissertation which in fact did earn you a doctorate was, if I'm not mistaken, never published?

Correct. It was never published.[2] Since I suddenly received a new assignment to teach theology at Innsbruck, I became a bit indifferent about my philosophical past. I plunged right into theology and I have remained in this field my whole life, although I should hasten to add, and I have consistently stated this, I have never been a theological scholar and in fact never intended to be one.

This is quite an astonishing assertion from a person who has written such a vast collection of scholarly theological treatises.

No. Strictly speaking I have not produced scholarly works of theology; more exactly, I have produced only very few scholarly works of theology. Compare my work with that of my Jesuit colleague, Father Alois Grillmeier, who is almost my age. Throughout his whole life he has been investigating the history of Christology from the New Testament to the Fathers of the Church and he has written terribly learned tomes on the history of dogma. As regards my own work, if one prescinds from my book *Foundations of Christian Faith: An Introduction to the Idea of Christianity*, published very late in my life (1976), in fact my publications address individual questions. I only attempt to clarify those individual questions that modern readers are interested in understanding better. I would say that I have always done theology with a view to kerygma, preaching, pastoral care. For that reason, I have written relatively many books on devotion in the standard sense, such as the book *On Prayer*, and *Watch and Pray with Me* [tr. William V. Dych, S.J.; New York: Herder and Herder, 1966], and similar works. I also had published by my friend Herbert Vorgrimler a short book on *Mary, Mother of the Lord* [tr. W. J. O'Hara; Wheathampstead: Anthony Clarke, 1963], which contains biblical sermons. In short, I am not a scholar and don't intend to be one . . . I want to be a Christian who takes Christianity seriously. I want to be a person who unabashedly lives in modern times and from the perspective of modernity addresses this problem or that, a third problem, a twentieth problem, about which one then reflects. If you want to call that theology, well, fine!

1. *Spirit in the World*, tr. William Dych (New York: Herder and Herder, 1968).
2. "E Latere Christi. Eine Untersuchung über den typologischen Sinn von Jo 19,34." Th.D. diss., Innsbruck, 1936.

But precisely to accomplish that, precisely to address so many different individual problems you needed, I feel, a foundation, and surely that has been philosophy for you. May I return to that topic once again? To what extent did Martin Heidegger influence you? His seminars were already famous in those days and you certainly participated in them at Freiburg, did you not?

I did participate in Martin Heidegger's seminars for two years. I worked in them like every other graduate student. Now and then I had to give a sort of resumé ("protocol" as we called it in Heidegger's seminar) of the previous seminar session. I had to read this out loud which caused me some fear and trepidation and I was happy if the great master praised my summary. On this topic I would like to make a few distinctions. First of all, the subject matter of my own research has really been theological: purgatory, the nature of the sacraments, the Trinity, and so on. I have delved into topics about which Heidegger does not provide material as far as the content of the research goes. A second point to note. Heidegger's philosophy that was characteristic of the years 1934 to 1936 was quite distinct from his later philosophy. The Heidegger that I learned was the Heidegger of *Being and Time*, the Heidegger of the battlecry, perhaps even the Heidegger of metaphysics. That was the Heidegger with whom I learned to think a little bit, and for that I am grateful to him. Insofar as it is philosophical, my theology does not really show the systematic and thematic influence of Heidegger. What he communicated was the desire to think, the ability to think. Then, of course, up to a certain point, influenced by my early interest in Maréchal, I studied what is called, in a very vague and general sense, existential philosophy or existential theology but which, strictly speaking, was not necessarily linked with Heidegger. I would say that Martin Heidegger was the only teacher for whom I developed the respect that a disciple has for a great master. That had little to do with individual questions or individual formulations of my theology. I would say that Heidegger had little influence on my philosophy or even my theology, although I am really extremely grateful to him. Later in life I had several subsequent contacts with him. I met him once in Innsbruck and we had coffee together. Otherwise, I had less contact with him in his later period than did my colleagues Johann Baptist Lotz and Gerd Haeffner who Heidegger claimed was one of the few persons who really understood him.

Professor, can you describe the ecclesiastical and theological scene that existed before World War II? As far as theology is concerned you wrote a few years after the outbreak of the war that we lacked a comprehensive biblical theology, a history of scholastic theology, a major Catholic history of religion, a history of moral theology, and in

Germany major scholarly Old Testament and New Testament commentaries that would make us less dependent on Protestant exegesis. We lacked, you noted, a New Testament theology, a theological dictionary of the New Testament, a manual concordance of the Bible. When a person reads such remarks one would have to wonder what was the state of theology in those days.

Here we need to be extremely precise. And I wouldn't necessarily still go to the stake for those statements that you just cited from my writings, which go back some thirty or forty years. To be sure, many of the lacunae noted before have now been eliminated. We now have major, theological, Catholic biblical commentaries such as those written in Germany by Schlier, Pesch, Schnackenburg, and so on. Even in the Old Testament our exegesis is gradually approaching a level comparable to that of Protestants. Quite a bit has also been accomplished in the history of dogma.

But in those days weren't there still unanswered questions with which the young generation of theologians began to wrestle?

Remember this. Between the two world wars there was perhaps no major breakthrough toward a truly new and modern theology. But there was a very fundamental breakthrough to a more open Catholic, and thoroughly Catholic way of thinking, which departed from traditional neoscholasticism but still was part of the Church's patrimony. In the years before World War I we passed through a period of what is called integralism and a still somewhat rigid neoscholasticsm. But if you look at the period after World War I during which Guardini, Przywara, and others like them were writing, then you see already a completely different atmosphere in thought. No longer were people afraid to be censored by Rome at any moment. This then developed into a particular, new theology. Of course, in France there were theologians such as de Lubac, Bouillard, even Daniélou who later became a cardinal, and especially Congar, theologians who had certain conflicts with Rome but who, by and large, in very different ways conceived and nurtured a theology that outdid traditional neoscholasticism. A similar development took place, of course, in Germany and I would have to admit that I also belong to this group of theologians.

Translated by Michael A. Fahey, S.J.
University of St. Michael's College, Toronto

46 · New Theological Impulses Since the Second World War

Interview with Peter Pawlowsky for Radio Austria (FS 1)
Vienna (July 11, 1980)

What was the intellectual framework of theology just before the Second World War? Looking back after the fact, one has the impression that it was relatively non-political, although at the time great political changes were certainly taking place. So to my question: How did you encounter National Socialism, which you must have experienced at the latest when it dissolved the Innsbruck faculty? How did National Socialism impinge on your perceptions, life, experience?

To be honest, I would make a distinction. For people like me, already priests, grown up in a German Church with a Central Party, National Socialism, insofar as it pursued an absolutely un-Christian and clearly anti-Church tendency, was an impossible thing, right from the start, as we have already mentioned. I believe that there were really no Nazis among those who were church-going Catholics and interested in the Church and its freedom. But it is a different question whether we, at that time, already perceived the undemocratic elements so well that we would have rejected National Socialism on those grounds too.

Take a bishop like Gröber, and in a sense Faulhaber and Galen—they were courageous fighters against National Socialism insofar as it was anti-Christian and anti-Church. It had practically forbidden all church organizations. But even these bishops, in the general human, democratic area did not have sufficient vision and decisiveness to oppose National Socialism. Of course one could say that we pastors of that time had enough to do to protect our own skins, but we should also have been much more out to protect the skins of others, Jews, non-Christians, and others, than in fact we were.

One man, a friend of yours, the Jesuit Alfred Delp, was effective in this resistance, and was hanged in Berlin in 1945. Do you have memories of Alfred Delp?

Of course! After my philosophy years I was a prefect in Stella Matutina for two years, and taught Latin and Greek in the novitiate, where I met Alfred Delp for the first time. We were also together in theology at Valkenburg (though not in the same year) and remained friends from that time on. I visited him even during the war after the confiscation of our houses, when he was a chaplain in Bogenhausen. I must say honestly that I knew nothing of his work with the Kreisauer Circle, but then when he was arrested and imprisoned in Berlin,

I knew of his lot. There were priests like Alfred Delp, but one could not say they were typical of the ordinary priest of the time.

Let's go one step farther. At that time you went to Vienna; what kind of work did you expect there? And especially which people do you remember best?

First of all, the faculty at Innsbruck was removed right at the beginning of the Third Reich in Austria, and then also the Jesuit college, our own house, was confiscated. That's why I went to Vienna. So at the beginning of the war, insofar as our young people were not drafted, we lectured in theology, partly at the Scottish monastery and partly at Lainz. As that came to an end, if I may put it this way, I slid more and more into the work of the Vienna Pastoral Institute, then under the leadership of (the later Monsignor) Rudolf. Also with us were the Benedictine Leopold von Suchow, Mauer, and such people, with whom I enjoyed intimate friendship and the exchange of ideas. Archbishop Gröber made an elaborate investigation against modern tendencies in piety.

The archbishop of Freiburg?

Yes. So I had to compose an opposition paper in the Pastoral Institute; I preached and gave lectures. At that time there was a good, solid "new-start" mood in the Church.

Was it possible to book up with that after the war?

I couldn't really say that.

One important direction of your activity seems to me to have been in the area of entering into dialogue, with science perhaps, or with the Paulus Society, with Marxism. Is that, or does it seem to you to be something important for those days? Especially, does it seem possible to you to continue the dialogue with Marxism begun in those days?

Again, things were such that one would get an invitation, or a particular need arose where one would jump in, and so pretty much muddled around from job to job. Here's the way it went: Kellner, for example, who founded the Paulus Society, had been our student in Brieg during the war, and approached Jesuits whom he knew. So he came to me and the Paulus Society was formed. At first, there was dialogue with natural scientists, and then Kellner switched to dialogue with the Marxists. That went well for a while and was very interesting. People came, like Garaudy, the leader of the Communist party in France at the time. Then Furtwängler and I founded the *Dialogzeitschrift* (Dialogue Magazine); I believe that was after the Council when they were asking for dialogue with the Marxists. But that fell apart because party-bound communists couldn't really talk to each other. If you invited such a party-bound communist to contribute to the magazine, you would get the old formulas rehashed; if, on the other hand, you invited a freer, somewhat thinking communist to write something in the magazine, then the "real" communists would cry, "He is no communist."

Do you think that dialogue between Christians and communists is needed and important today?

Since Marxism, even in widely different forms, has a great and broad importance in the history of thought all over the world, one that is not at all sufficiently imagined, it is really obvious that Christianity, one way or another has to remain in dialogue with such an intellectual force. If the others do not want to listen, one must nevertheless continue to try. Naturally, the whole confrontation with atheism, including Marxist atheism, is altogether one of the most fundamental tasks of the Church and Christianity today. How any one individual gets into this and helps out is, of course, quite another question.

Professor Rahner, it just dawned on me as you speak of the party communists that you yourself have had difficulties with officials, church officials. As far as I know, you wrote something in 1950 on the doctrine of Mary that fell under the censure of your order, and so on. You got into some trouble with your speech at the Austrian Catholic Congress in 1962, "Extinguish Not the Spirit." Right at the beginning of the Council there were those who made trouble for you. How did that look to you, and how did you deal with it?

First of all, one has to say that such difficulties are basically nothing to get excited about, but are more or less to be expected. That I usually thought I was right is again another question. When Father so and so from the Gregorian did not let my book on the Asssumption get through censorship, I was nevertheless still of the opinion, and I can be even more sure of it today, that I was right and not he. I had a few more difficulties too. I had to be admonished to hold my lectures at Innsbruck in Latin. I was once forbidden to speak, which was probably dumped on me by the late Cardinal Bea. Shortly before the council I received an order from the Holy Office that I not publish anything theological until it had passed Roman censorship. At that, I said that I would then write no more. But nothing came of the whole affair, because then the Council came, and during the Council I got along very well with Cardinal Ottaviani, head of the Holy Office. And as things go in Rome, such matters are not solemnly revoked, but simply disregarded. So, in fact, I have kept on writing, and have never had to endure a Roman censorship.

That brings us to the Council. You were brought to the Council by Cardinal König as an adviser. Did this make a great impression in your life? What have you brought with you from the whole time of the Council? Wasn't that also a certain breakthrough for you personally, since much of what you had thought all along now found official recognition?

I would be careful there. Grillmeier, Semmelroth, and similar people had a certain common theological mentality, which came through in such constitutions as *Lumen Gentium*. But that I had any importance right at that point, that I do not remember. Right at the beginning it was perhaps a bit different.

Right at the beginning Ratzinger and I prepared a theological draft of the constitution under the aegis of Cardinal Frings, which was then duplicated and sent by the German bishops to all the bishops' conferences. That was soon dropped, but it had not a little to do with the fact that practically all the preconciliar schemata were dropped, and the Council began anew with all the decrees and constitutions. The schemata of the preconciliar type, put together by the Roman theologians before the Council and for the Council, were full of neoscholasticism, so that in many areas one can really thank God they were dropped. Apart from this thrust, which was actually brought about by John XXIII under the influence of Cardinal Döpfner, Frings, and so on, apart from the abandoning of the preconciliar schemata and the admitting of new ones which contained a quite different theology, I would not say that I performed anything special that one could pin down. I did work very hard; it was frightfully tiring work—I can't even picture how such a decree, in some cases after hundreds of suggestions for corrections from bishops and others, finally found a formulation which was then accepted by the Council.

The Council has been over for fifteen years, and one often gets the impression that we are on the road moving backwards. Is that your impression too?

There I would be a little careful—not only because I am in Vienna and I respect the statement on this matter from Cardinal König. I think that the ultimate, basic drives of the Council definitely remain, if only for the reason that they are not problems in the collective consciousness of the Church, not even in the minds of the conservatives. Take, for example, the formulation of freedom of belief and freedom of conscience as put through by John Courtney Murray and other Americans: Today this formulation is so taken for granted that even the most conservative see no more problem with it. Even in the conservative wing of the Church there have been extraordinary changes. Naturally, there are reactionary movements in this or that area; that can be. If the bishop of Augsburg, for example, makes a rule that once a month a Latin High Mass is to be celebrated in the Church, one could call this a reactionary move, but one could still ask whether it is not quite reasonable.

I would like to tell a little story here that fits in well. I once had a private audience with Pope Paul VI and said to him at the time, "See, Holy Father, ten years ago the Holy Office forbade me to write another word about concelebration, and today you concelebrate yourself." These things, which were then problems for the Holy Office, no longer are, even in the heads of the conservatives. One could count up a number of similar things, where the Council, without people noticing it, marks a definite cut-off point. One can presume that there are many reactionary things around. I was with the new Holy Father, John Paul II, and wore a dark suit and tie; he said nothing. But I don't know, it could be that there will again be some decree or other coming from Rome on clerical dress. Such reactionary things are possible, and some do exist.

Something else: In a remarkable way, the Council took place in a kind of atmosphere of great expectations, which was noticeable politically and in the world of thought generally. How did that affect you as a long-time university professor? You were some years in Munich, and finally in Münster. How did students' questions change over this long period, and especially how did you experience the late sixties?

To begin right at that point, I was in Münster in 1968, so I got a little something from the student business. One time some students, not members of my class, came into the classroom and made a lot of racket and wanted a discussion on, I don't know, a kindergarten of the bishop's or something like that. But otherwise, apart from the juridical changes and university laws, we did not notice all that much in the theology faculty.

Of course there are things today that are quite different among the student population from, for example, Innsbruck twenty years ago. Twenty years ago we did not have the question of political theology, or liberation theology and similar things, and a present-day theology teacher must handle these things.

One of the present day writers on political theology, Professor Johann Baptist Metz, is a student of yours. Do you have the impression that his theology stands upon yours? Is it a child or grandchild of your thought?

You would have to ask Metz that one yourself, I don't know exactly. In any case, Metz himself is convinced that real political theology is his own invention and does not come from me, so political theology strictly speaking could not have been inherited from me, though I have nothing against that. Whether, and in what sense, Metz does his theology with a certain heritage from me rather than from neoscholasticism would be worth discussing, and he would probably gladly concede that point.

Professor, in conclusion, a few personal questions. You were born in Freiburg, you taught for years in Austria and then in Germany. What do you feel yourself to be?

My great-great-great-grandfather came from Kössen in Tyrol, and I grew up in what you might call outer-Austria. I was in the novitiate in Austria, and then, when the Nazis drove us out, I was again in Austria; during the war I was in Vienna, and then from 1948 to 1964 professor in Innsbruck. That all of that rubbed off on me I would expect, and I would be happy if that were the case.

Looking back on your life, could you say what in particular fulfilled you and made you happy, and what was especially repugnant?

That is a question that one can answer only with great difficulty. Very little was so terribly repugnant, as one would say in Austria. The great experiences of two world wars, the Third Reich, and so on—that's something else.

It occurs to me that you accepted the restrictions, which you now and then suffered, with much greater tranquility than present-day theologians do, as we know from recent events. But you have also, in recent years, entered into the fray much more energetically than formerly when the question is of internal, ecclesiastical disagreement, if I see this correctly.

Ah, yes. There was the argument with Bishop Hengsbach; I defended Metz against Cardinal Ratzinger, and such matters. I was present for the formation of the *Public-Forum* and when it was "done in" by the German bishops. I have had many disputes in the Würzburg synod, even with Cardinal Höffner. But for my seventy-fifth birthday the German bishops congratulated me very ceremoniously and heartily.

I would like to be an "old-fashioned" Jesuit, to whom it can make no basic difference whether he is now teaching theology, or perhaps in Brazil worrying about a bunch of kids, or working away in India. I have put myself in the service of the Church and the gospel, not that I might become a famous professor, but that I might do my duty, and be somehow there for others—granting any egoism, which of course is always there too.

Translated by Thomas A. Caldwell, S.J.
Marquette University

Part IV

THE CHURCH IN A PERIOD OF TRANSITION

INTERVIEWS 1980–1982

47·Christianity on the Threshold
of the Third Millennium

Interview with Hans Schöpfer for the Swiss magazine, *Civitas*,
Fribourg (January, 1981)

*We are almost into the third Christian millennium, which will be like the past in
one respect, that it will bring with it problems. This prospect should induce contemporary Christians more than ever to take stock of errors committed in the past and challenges facing us in the future. What problems do you consider especially serious for
Christianity at this time, and, in view of them, what is required of us by way of
response?*

There are so many problems, ranging from the oil crisis to politics proper
and beyond that to problems of what people think about reality and life—
hence all the problems of philosophy and theology. Given this, I hesitate to
say that one problem is the most important. Even if I now go on to declare
certain problems important, it could be that on reconsideration I might consider
other problems weightier and more urgent on the scale of priorities. For the
present let me say this: The most serious problems are perhaps the ones that
people today think are not so serious.

Take, for example, the fundamental theological problem, God. For one
thing, most people would not take that as an important question today, at
least on the surface of their everyday consciousness. To the extent that it becomes a question, at most it would concern how and why God could be important *for human beings*. In my view, this anthropocentric question about
God is, in the last analysis, turned around, preposterous. Perhaps, therefore,
the most fundamental problem area of our culture is this remarkable oblivion
to which we have consigned God. I am not saying that people do not talk
enough about God or that not enough books are printed about God. But I
think that there are too few people who remember that, in the last analysis,
God is not there for them but rather they are there for God.

Now in the jargon of theologians I belong to the "anthropocentric" theologians. In any ultimate sense that is nonsense. My aim is to be a theologian
who says that *God* is the most important reality there is, that we exist to love
him in a self-forgetting way, to adore him, to exist for *him*, to leap out of our
own domain of existence into the abyss of the incomprehensibility of God. It
is obvious that a theologian has to say that it is the *human being* who, related
ultimately to God, must forget self for God. In this sense one can never do

theology anthropocentrically enough. A basic reason for this is that God clearly does not figure as some individual object *in* our world, not even as the most sublime thing in the universe. Rather, God is the absolute, the unconditioned, on which we depend, but who does not depend on us in anything like the same way; the one to be worshiped, the one to whom we must unreservedly surrender ourselves with Jesus, the crucified. That is really the most fundamentally human problem. And the most fundamental problem today is that most people ordinarily do not see things that way.

Of course, there is more to it than that. This vanishing of the world into God does not occur primarily where theologians go on about it, nor even where pastors and popes preach about it. This most basic act can take place in a quite unannounced, almost anonymous way. Wherever a person does manage to be selfless, to love selflessly, to maintain one's integrity where integrity does not pay, to accept death beyond rancor or anxiety in the sterile anonymity of a modern hospital, wherever a person does break out of the incarceration of egoism by hook or by crook, there something takes place that I regard as the most fundamental thing a person can do. It is certainly good to talk and preach about it, too, and for some people to endeavor in one way or another to make this kind of ultimate life-task into their worldly profession (so to speak).

But one may hope that what really matters ultimately takes place in our humdrum daily lives. Perhaps where Vietnamese children died or where people continue to die on both sides of the barricades we erect, that counter to all expectations, counter to all human appearances, by the grace of God and, if I may use the phrase, with unimaginable adroitness, the last word is—who knows?—overwhelming bliss, beatitude, perhaps forever. One could say: The ultimate and most authentic problem, one that is not even regarded as such, is this absolute sovereignty of the infinitely incomprehensible God *along with* the hope for ultimate happiness, despite the evidence humanity provides of cruelty and of preoccupation with everything but God. It is in this line that my theory of the anonymous Christian—a theory that Hans Urs von Balthasar and Hans Küng reject with haughty disdain (for all I care), must be understood and evaluated.

Now, of course, the fact is that besides this one and only basic human problem there are myriads of concrete problems weighing on people's minds. What has to be realized is that only when and if we exert ourselves to cope with these problems can we find the one great absolute problem solved. To say it more simply and theologically: Only when we love each other can we love God. Love of neighbor is not just one among various commandments of God; it is the actual way in which human beings can encounter God. That too sounds pretty abstract, I grant, but what I am getting at is this: As soon as anyone realizes that what we call Christian love of neighbor as the way God saves us is not only the norm of the family circle or of private life, but today has a social or political dimension, this old commandment speaks to us also of political responsibility.

I never developed any political theology. I suppose I do not quite understand what it is that my friend and former student Metz is developing and championing under that label. But I am thoroughly convinced that the true Christian of the present should not only be a respectable person in the realm of sexuality and in money matters, but also must deal with horrendous societal and political issues, even or especially if one is accustomed to pay them no mind or retreat from them into a private sphere, and even if many a preacher never thinks of pouring out any moral indignation over them. In this connection, I am also thoroughly convinced that church teaching and formation would have to be structured very differently than it is, from bottom to top. There is no question in my mind that the German bishops are in the right in their campaign against abortion legislation, but I admit that I would like to see the bishops and the whole official Church put the same energy into many other issues.

Today we live in a very much manipulated and manipulable world. Modern technology is applied successfully to more and more problems that a little while ago were considered an unavoidable part of life. That can lead to a certain feeling of having things all taken care of. In your opinion, how does this development affect Christian faith?

I think that moderns, in a certain respect, do have it a lot harder being Christians than our forebears did. First of all, consider the fact that every active person simply has so much more to do today than our predecessors did, with the consequence that it is in fact much more difficult just to find the time that earlier generations had at their disposal and could devote to religious purposes. Take the case of the Dutch Calvinists two-hundred years ago: they looked forward to three-hour sermons on Sunday and thought a pastor who did not use the whole time was a shirker. By contrast, we can see that there is a difficulty for the life of faith in our own times that did not exist then. It is just an extrinsic factor, perhaps, but it is something the official Church should take into account more than they do.

Add to that all the difficulties that unavoidably play a role. A modern person does not have the simple, straightforward relationship to the past that was the case for many earlier Christians. Decisions taken two centuries ago (for example, by one's own city fathers) are alien to most of us and leave us quite indifferent. There are reasons for that, again, but we do not have to go into them now. All the same, can one be particularly surprised if such a person finds it difficult even to imagine that he or she was redeemed in Jerusalem in the year 33? Besides the difficulty of the relationship to history, there are difficulties in principle, not to mention the matter of a world that has become enormously differentiated: a universe whose temporal and spatial boundaries are beyond our horizons, a world that has developed. Therefore, this world, which a contemporary, even a not very well informed one, more or less takes for granted and experiments with, is a world in which a relationship to God has to be articulated in a quite new way, completely different from what used to be and had to be the case formerly.

It seems to me that the Church (including its highest representatives) is not yet trying, in the radical way that is necessary, to develop that mystical experience of God in the individual person and make it accessible to broad masses of ordinary modern people. It will not do, if I may be candid, to present the doctrine of the Incarnation in a way completely insensitive to the difficulties that contemporaries may have, as is the case with the first encyclical of the present Holy Father. I am as firmly convinced of this doctrine's truth as the pope is, but all the problems with it that a Hans Küng has expressed need to be . . . at least in the back of the writer's mind. You would have to render the old, abiding, basically Christian truth in such a way that a person can tell you are addressing not only those who believe anyway but also people of today.

The fact is (and we should look it in the face) that the truth, the fundamental, saving, necessary truth of the Incarnation of the Word of God strikes a person who does not come out of a thoroughly Catholic environment pretty much as if he or she would hear that the Dalai Lama was the incarnation of God. Hearing something like that, a person does not spend much time reflecting whether that could be true or not, but rather considers it so improbable as simply to go on to his or her daily business. We have to preach with the awareness that we have such "unbelievers" in front of us. Failing that, we practice a theology that is very true, but makes no impression on people such as they are today. Of course I do not want to load all this on a single encyclical —it cannot say everything at once, either. But even in Rome one has to have breathed more deeply of the air of unbelief in order really to preach the gospel for today, with courage and a sense of identity, but also in a way suited for contemporary culture.

You are already being called a "Father of the Church." There is no question you deserve this honor, given the signal contributions you have made to church thinking in this century. As a professor of theology you are inside the same Church that today holds you in high regard, but in the past occasionally held you in suspicion. From some of your utterances of recent years one could surmise that you are disquieted by certain developments in church affairs. What do you deplore in the official Catholic Church, perhaps also in contemporary theology, and what would you like to see improved in the church life of the present?

As a matter of fact, there is much in the Church that gives me a great deal of distress, for instance, the centralizing tendencies of the Vatican, what we call "Roman centralism." With the Second Vatican Council, our Church has become in fact as well as in principle a world-Church. It can no longer expect to live exclusively off European and Latin export goods. Let the new churches in Africa, Asia, Australia, and South America recognize their historical roots in the Mediterranean and North Atlantic churches, let them also keep various European features in their further history, even if they are not "of divine right," but—let them also reject or modify such features, without Rome issuing prohibitions.

In the aftermath of Vatican II, I thought it was my duty, given my convictions, to defend clerical celibacy—ironically, Cardinal Ottaviani even sent me a letter of praise for that! Nevertheless, I must ask, in the special cultural situation of Africa, why the African bishops' conference could not examine the question and decide, with Rome's blessing, whether the celibacy of the diocesan clergy has to remain an obligatory feature there or not. Given the existence of churches, holy Catholic churches that are not Latin but Eastern, which do not have obligatory celibacy, then I do not see why the issue of an African Catholic celibacy law or its absence is not a proper question for the African episcopate itself. Of course, this church still stands under Rome's superintendence. But the Church of Rome does not need to insist on reproducing itself in uniform manner everywhere, which unfortunately it still does to too great a degree. You do not have to be Latin to be Catholic.

With that you have answered a question I had in mind to put to you, about the mandatory celibacy of priests. There are other questions of a similar nature that are creating quite a stir among Catholics. What is your view, for example, of the demand for a better integration of women in the service and leadership functions of the Church?

Well, you put me in an uncomfortable position with that question. When the Vatican declaration against the ordination of women (even in the future) came out a few years back, I published an article ["Women and the Priesthood," *Theological Investigations* XX:35–47], saying that it failed to convince me (of course, it was not an infallible definition). Rome is digging in its heels, it seems to me, against a development that one ought to admit calmly might not be a bad thing. To be sure, there are many regions in the Church where the ordination of women is not a live option, simply because of the concrete societal situation and because of mentalities that the Church could not change if it wanted to. But it may be an altogether different situation in other regions (say, North America), making the question one to be taken seriously. Perhaps the relationship between male and female (which is malleable and not altogether predictable over time) would be so constituted in North American society (and I do not know whether this is a fact or not) that women's ordination would seem advisable in the circumstances and actually would not give rise to grave difficulties at all. Then I would conclude from my principle—namely, the Church is not meant to be a centralized, homogeneous, holy state—that one should leave the matter up to the Americans. After all, the Eastern churches in union with Rome differ from the Latin-Western churches. This fact shows that there may be circumstances in which the laws may differ, while working well together wherever that is required or possible. If there were no celibacy in Africa, it would not follow that there could be none here in Europe either.

Many things that we do not need in Europe may all the same be good and useful in South America, and the other way around too. At the time, I also said explicitly that the obligation of the Church to provide sufficient clergy is of divine right and takes precedence over the ecclesiastically desirable law of celibacy. If in practice you cannot obtain a sufficient number of priests in a given cultural setting without relinquishing celibacy, then the Church must suspend the law of celibacy, at least there. I would be the first to concede that this kind of trend is perhaps not desirable, perhaps not absolutely necessary, but I do not concede that it is impossible a priori on theological grounds. This development or this cultural situation has existed in the Eastern churches. How can we be so sure that an analogous situation will not develop in some part of the Church in the future? There cannot be any theological arguments proving the absolute impossibility of such a thing; we may wish or hope, but we cannot *know* that it will never be the case.

Similarly, I hope that the pope can reside in Rome until the end of time; but we have no divine revelation that this will happen. Therefore, I can speculate about what the Church is to do if the pope has to live in, say, the Philippines, in order to carry out his duties, if the communists should drive him from Rome. Things like this are possible; likewise, changes in the matter of celibacy for the secular priesthood are conceivable.

Amid our present turmoil, exemplary Christians continue to emerge, trying new paths for living up to their obligations as Christians and members of society. They are pioneers, exposed to discrimination, persecution, and sometimes even death, if that is what comes in their efforts to realize the ideals the gospel inspires in them. From the Christian point of view, what would you most urgently recommend to such brave people?

That is a question that is absolutely beyond my capacity to answer, because the concrete situations of individuals are so different that one can hardly address them very precisely. I did once say in regard to certain theologians of political theology and of liberation theology: All well and good, but my mother was an authentic Christian and she never took a political stand in her life.

On the other hand, it seems to me that today's younger Christians should display a greater will for societal change than they in fact do and that you can also find—although sometimes in the strangest and also most deplorable forms —among non-Christian youth. Basically, I do not see why the young people attached to the Church in Germany should coincide with the conservative wing of society. It may be that a Catholic should have an understanding and acceptance of tradition, of history, of what is tried and true, and therefore has an easier time of it in this regard than a completely secularized contemporary. But why is it taken for granted that the bulk of Christians in our country, insofar as they are really involved in the Church, will be in the conservative camp? . . . If the only actual alternatives really were the stark choice between being *either* a conservative Christian and Catholic *or* espousing a non-Christian social policy, then I would remain a Catholic and hope that God's judgment on my life would be merciful. But in that case, I still would try and come up with a third alternative that would allow me to be Catholic and yet not conservative in this sense that stifles social consciousness.

In the latter part of the nineteenth century, among people I grew up with, if you wanted to be thoroughly Catholic and devout, then you had to prize certain minor "Catholic" authors and regard Goethe as inferior. Of course, there were devout Catholics who did not conform to that pattern, but it was typical. All the same, it was not healthy. Similarly, it seems to me the equation I see being made in contemporary Catholicism between solid Christianity and the kind of conservatism that only wishes to preserve the status quo is a very peculiar phenomenon—to my way of looking at things, absurd. Of course, I know what one can say on the other side. One can affirm that the authentic conservatives are the ones who are far more open to a worthwhile future than those usually branded as leftists. But let us leave Germany aside for a moment.

If I were in South America, I would certainly not be for the capitalists there, but rather, in the name of my Christian convictions—so as to find a merciful God judging me—I would probably be on the left. There is no question in my mind about that!

Would it be appropriate to put a question mark after certain Roman statements that suggest a wholesale "retreat of priests into the sacristy?"

I would characterize the question, whether priests must themselves be political officeholders, as one that also could be answered in the negative. But when Oscar Romero speaks out in such a way that he gets murdered, then one might honor his witness somewhat more than has actually been done. Imagine what kind of praises he would have received, if he had been killed for a sermon against abortion! But preaching against social injustices which may drive more children into misery and hunger than are aborted—in his country, at least— then the best he can hope for, unwelcome troublemaker that he was, is to be passed over in silence.

With or without human successes and theological expertise, a Christian must find some time for the inner life. May I ask you about special experiences in regard to prayer?

I do not wish to speak of my experience; but there is no question that the whole apparatus of the Church from the pope and Vatican congregations with all the bishops and dioceses, from the sacraments to collections, and so on, are there only so that a tiny bit of faith, hope, and love may be fostered in the human heart.

In a talk I gave at the end of the Council, I compared this whole apparatus of the Church . . . to a huge quantity of uranium ore. If you can get a few grams of uranium out of it all, then it has been worthwhile: otherwise it is worthless. In the last analysis, a human being has to give back his or her life to God in responsibility and love of neighbor; everything else is only a means to this end.

Allow me to close this conversation with a personal question. If you had to draw a kind of balance of your life as a member of the Church, priest, and theologian, what would you say? Might you have a word to tell your fellow pilgrims out of your wholly personal experience of life?

No, I would prefer to turn the question around and say that my life has been, at bottom, a very prosaic affair. Nothing very exciting happened; in general, one just tried to do (at least) one's duty as well as possible; there weren't any spectacular peaks. That is how it should be. As with a woman who takes in laundry and brings up her children and has to wait and see if they turn out well or not, until it is over for her. Something like this seems to me to be the normal life for most of us and this too is what my life has been like.

I never had terrible diseases; I came through two world wars in an almost indecently untroubled fashion; I never came close to starvation. No particularly dramatic things happened in my life as a Jesuit and priest, either. I never had the slightest inclination to write memoirs, an autobiography, or Confessions in the manner of Augustine.

A year ago in March I had a private audience with Pope John Paul II. I knew him already from Cracow. He started out by inquiring how things were going. I said in German: "I am retired, living in Munich, and waiting to die." Perhaps it took him back a bit. But what I said was accurate. I have managed to live the life of a schoolmaster, without either heroic high points or terrible trials. That is something I cannot do anything about; it simply happened that way and I have accepted it. How does Goethe put it, "dreary weeks, cheerful feasts"? I have, of course, had my share of that too.

One's personal life is nobody else's business. What I have to say, therefore, is only: Accept the moment. See to it that you do what one can call, without any folderol, your duty. All the same, be ready again and again to realize once more, that the ineffable mystery we call God not only lives and reigns, but had the unlikely idea to approach you personally in love; turn your eyes to Jesus, the crucified one; come what may, you will be able to accept your life from him when all is said and done. I cannot really say more than these well-worn Christian platitudes. I wonder how much longer it will last before night falls forever. I do not know. You go on as long as daylight lasts. In the end you leave with empty hands, that I know; and it is well. At that moment you look at the crucified one and go. What comes is the everlasting mystery of God.

Translated by Paul Misner
Marquette University

48 · The Church in Unity and Diversity

Interview with Gwendoline Jarczy for
France Catholique Ecclesia, Paris (June 5, 1981)

Both Pope Paul VI and Pope John Paul II worked toward a realization of Vatican II: The whole Council, but not more than the Council. What do you think about the implementation of the Council, and the twenty years that have passed since its conclusion?

I have no doubt that Paul VI had, and John Paul II still has, the desire to implement fully the decrees of Vatican II. But that's not to say the implementation is very far along. The point is that many things depend on an accurate interpretation of the Council's texts, and it's only normal that there are differing opinions on how they should be interpreted. Many people are convinced that their interpretation is theoretically and practically in accord with the Council's texts. Others regret that this or that text is not adequately taken into account.

There is no question but that Rome itself—I'm not speaking of the papacy here—has the upper hand and operates in a generally very conservative atmosphere; ultimately, this leads to apprehension within the Church's administrative structure to take actions and initiatives that are not in accord with the Council's original spirit and letter. Still, one should not fail to recognize that there is an attitude of caution in Rome, a braking system, which could result in a sudden jerk backwards. Even what the pope himself does varies between being clearly responsive or more restrained. Consequently, no common denominator can be found. I, for my part, am convinced of the possibility of obtaining a hearing in Rome for a specific request. And making such a request corresponds both to the Council's spirit and letter.

Can you please give an example?

The Council has found very beautiful words for those themes that affect local churches. It grants them a certain autonomy. They are not seen as purely administrative clones of a universal church government whose only concern is homogeneity. Stress has been placed on the fact that the churches of different regions not only can but should have their own unique imprint and, consequently, their own distinctiveness. I don't believe enough attention has been paid to this aspect of the Council's decrees. In many concrete questions of Canon Law that deal with the liturgy or the form of the Mass, it's my impression that Rome beats its drum more for church unity than the legitimate plurality this unity allows; a plurality already justified by the existence of the large number of local churches.

Furthermore, Vatican II rediscovered a collegiality where the entire episcopacy is united around the pope. For Paul VI this led to the synod of bishops. Similarly, at the beginning of his pontificate John Paul II underscored his intention to deepen and actualize the meaning of this institution. It's my impression that things have not progressed here to the point they were promised. I regret that the synod of bishops to this very day has not taken any really creative initiative.

About the local churches you referred to before...

They have their distinctiveness and a relative autonomy which emerges from it; and they must have it. Now, we know about the efforts being made in Rome with respect to the publication of a new code of Canon Law. The *Codex Iuris Canonici* has been in force since Pope Benedict XV. This code of law must certainly be modified and adjusted on the basis of later developments in the Church. Still, I'm afraid that the new code will be drafted in the same style that has been employed until now: a code that must be applied uniformly in the Church, otherwise local churches in various parts of the world would take the opportunity to express their own mind.

This is also significant in another way. That is, one should not hope for progress in the direction of a unity of the various Christian churches if one is not prepared to acknowledge their legitimate uniqueness—a uniqueness which belongs to them and which must also be respected.

How is one able to effect a concrete, practical unity between the Roman Catholic Church and the churches which have proceeded from the Reformation on the basis of a plain and simple "reversion" that goes counter to everything one finds in law, liturgy, and spirituality?

What concrete ecumenical possibilities do you see?

Take the nomination of bishops. Nominations are made through Rome. But isn't this one of the areas where the Roman Catholic Church could demonstrate that it is not only content to tolerate the practices of particular churches that have established history on their side (e.g., in the Catholic Church of the East), but that it realizes that plurality is completely normal and compatible with its own unity and dogmas and that it also practices it? Without this, one shouldn't hope to achieve a unity of other Christian churches with Rome.

Why is it so difficult for the Roman Catholic Church to favor plurality?

A number of things converge: First, it's certain that the Western Church's homogeneity is the result of an historical process. After the Eastern churches separated from the Roman Catholic Church, the Church's temporal and natural sphere of existence was centered in the European West. Part of the Church's homogeneity, then, is due to cultural uniformity. A number of other things should be added to these historical factors: the Latin language, which became the Church's language, and the Roman liturgy, which ultimately became the liturgy for all. Particular liturgies, the Milanese [Ambrosian] rite to give but one example, became so entirely second-rate as not even to be counted.

The Church has been constituted this way since the Enlightenment. It had to express itself vehemently against the tide of the times and defend itself against secularizing tendencies.

There is also the matter of papal primacy. Once and only once in the course of the centuries has such a conception of unity been formed and it can only be understood as developing slowly out of its Roman center. On the purely theoretical level, for example, it is well known that the Canon Law of the churches of the Middle East in communion with Rome differs from Roman Canon Law. And the same is true for the liturgy and governance of these churches and their dioceses. All these differences, however, remain peripheral. They don't impinge on global attitudes, much less call them into question.

Unity and homogeneity are unique to the Roman Church. Had it known that there were various liturgies, analogous forms of Canon Law, and so forth (I'm thinking here especially of the differences which exist, though relatively insignificant, in the churches of Ireland, North America, and western Spain), it would not have perceived such variety as being in its own best interest and would even have minimized it in favor of greater concentration on Rome and the pope as representative and symbol of unity.

The truth is that our reverence for the papacy goes back to the time of Pius IX; in earlier times, reverence did not manifest itself quite this way. An emotional attachment to Rome is entirely legitimate and understandable, provided it is seen in its historically conditioned context. Still, it should not be equated with timeless dogma. Ambrose of Milan, for example, was certainly inspired by the desire for unity with the Chair of Peter. But, unlike *our* custom, he didn't think of Rome as a focal point from which and upon which all church life should be concentrated.

Indeed, one can say just the opposite: The past is the past and does not in any way determine the present or the future. That's correct. But why shouldn't this also hold true for the nineteenth-century Church? Legitimately and in its entirety, the nineteenth-century Church concretized what is commonly called the essence of the Church. But this is not sufficient basis for deriving a model of the Church which perdures for all time.

An overly defensive and self-perpetuating Church is inclined to identify its concrete image of itself with its essence. What else can be concluded? In the final analysis, though, this can't be an absolute yardstick for the truth.

What, finally, are the genuine reasons for looking toward Rome?

I am thoroughly convinced that the Church's tendency toward introversion is closely allied with its neglect of world sociopolitical problems. Since the French Revolution the Church has had to defend itself against political forces and the currents of the time. Obviously, this defensive posture can't be isolated from the way in which these problems presented themselves.

For example, take the liberal, anticlerical bourgeoisie of the nineteenth and twentieth centuries. As you probably know, the Church had to fight them, restrict their bounds of freedom. It's not astonishing, then—in fact it was almost inevitable—that the Church lost much of its energy in its efforts at self-preservation.

Here again, to the extent that the Church's experience of the world is not continually engaged in having to deal with anticlericalism, that is, an anticlerical mentality, it will have an easier time addressing the problems which exist today, for example, in the Third World, the environment, and so on.

This doesn't mean that mistakes might not be made or that there won't be delayed reactions to historical circumstances.

Some examples: One of our last popes said that the Church had lost the working class. What this indicates is the Church's tardiness in responding to sociopolitical issues which had been coming to the fore since the middle of the nineteenth century. Pope Leo XIII addressed himself to "modern industrial society" long after Marx and *Das Kapital*, and the people of Bishop Ketteler's time [1811–1877] received no response from the Church. These examples show some of the difficulties the Church faced. Difficulties for which it was not really responsible.

What can be done to justify and establish pluralism in the Church?

Not all pluralism is good. We know cases of false pluralism in theology, Canon Law, the liturgy, and so on. But this doesn't change the fact that the Church hasn't adequately encouraged a legitimate pluralism.

There are untold possibilities for an authentic pluralism. But these possibilities can't be realized until—and it's totally understandable—we can name every suspicious theological venture or "legitimate" attempt which is nationalistically inspired and clothes itself with the mantle of pluralism.

What comments do you have on the need many Christians feel for dialogue, confrontation, and interchange in the Church?

To a greater or lesser degree every confrontation and even every dialogue involves difficulties. After the Revolution the French Church was constantly confronted with a variety of trends. An external unity existed in much the same way it did in the German Church (before and after the Council); but it was certainly not an ideal unity. In France, differences, even opposition itself —including opposition within the episcopacy—are much easier to ferret out. It's not that easy for us.

I'm not afraid to say it: It might be good if our German bishops didn't always act as though they were of one and the same opinion. It's clear that such an attitude is not in line with the truth. Thus, difficulties are dealt with behind the scenes and, as far as I'm concerned, that doesn't do me a bit of good. It would be better if one could be present at free and open discussions with the Church's administrative structure and the episcopacy.

In France differences are articulated in the Catholic press. Our publications, on the other hand, generally disseminate the same views. The *Rheinische Merkur*, for example, claims to represent true Catholicism; so does the Central Committee of German Catholicism. The only place where substantial criticism is expressed is *Public-Forum*. This is not an enviable situation.

Can this situation be explained on the basis of the threat many fear from the socialistic East? Is it similar to the situation in Poland?

It's possible that official German Catholicism understands the socialistic East as a fundamental threat to Western culture and thus also to the Church. But think back fifty years: While French Catholicism lived with its differences— *Action française* on the one side, totally opposite groups on the other—we were dominated by an official kind of homogeneity and party-machine discipline long before fear of Russia justified it.

There are reasons for this. After 1870 German Catholicism was at a distinct disadvantage. Protestantism, influenced by the spirit of the Enlightenment, presented real difficulties and the Church had to struggle to succeed. Given these circumstances it was only natural that an *esprit de corps*, discipline, and a harmonious attitude developed similar to what we see nowadays in Polish Catholicism as it faces the threat from the socialistic East. It seems certain in such a situation that the Church's administrative structure cannot allow differences of opinion. To this new development we can add those reasons I've mentioned, which for a long time now have urged this particular expression of unity among us in the German Church.

The vigor of the German Church was apparent when John Paul II made his visit in November, 1980. However, some problems also surfaced. We'd appreciate your thoughts on the ecumenical issues that emerged from that visit.

It's difficult to give an accurate assessment. The old scholastic axiom applies here: What is known is known according to the way and mode of the knower (*Quidquid recipitur, ad modum recipientis recipitur*). The German Catholic population is stratified. There are a variety of societal and spiritual levels and each level reacted very differently to the visit.

Still, one can say that everyone responded very sympathetically to the pope himself—and not only Catholics. Most significantly, with respect to specific political and moral issues in German society the pope demonstrated prudence and discretion. John Paul II avoided all questions which might have been considered invidious or caused offense—especially the question of contraception, but others as well. The impression he left with intellectuals as well as non-Catholic Christians was, on the whole, very positive.

Oh, some thoughtless accusations were made, especially concerning the cost of the trip, but that was inevitable and really nothing more than background music. Even before his arrival there was some disharmony between the Evangelical churches and the Catholic episcopate. . . .

I believe today everything is in order.

Possibilities for ecumenical encounter between the pope and representatives of the Evangelical churches were temporarily curtailed, but given the circumstances it was hardly possible to exchange more than friendly gestures. Subsequently, an agreement was reached to form a commission whose task is to deal with ecumenical questions. I certainly don't want to throw a wet blanket on this commission. After all, there's enough skepticism around. Even less, I wouldn't want to justify the standstill that presently has the edge in ecumenism. What I really mean to say is that we shouldn't expect too much from this commission.

Germany already has all kinds of commissions. Joint meetings, colloquia, and ecumenical discussions go on constantly. Over the last thirty or forty years these meetings have produced considerable results. There are theologians, Catholics as well as Protestants, who are of the opinion that the controversial pre-Reformation issues, including papal primacy, no longer represent any insuperable difficulties. But where meetings between bishops of both confessions are concerned little has changed or improved. Look. When Bishop Lohse, the president of the German Evangelical Church, says that the jurisdictional primacy of the Holy See is out of the question for the German Evangelical Church and, on the other side, Rome says it is an inalienable right, it becomes difficult for both churches to arrive at some common ground on the question of office.

For that reason, the Evangelical churches have said they prefer discussions of practical, concrete issues: joint Holy Communion, and so on. They have shown very little interest in discussing dogmatic and fundamental ecclesiological issues. Rome, on the other hand, is dead-set against changing its present position regarding these issues.

What's your personal opinion here?
The apparent insurmountable dogmatic differences must be dealt with successively on a theological level, one after the other, as well as on the basis of office in the strict sense. Can't both churches—with honest ecumenical and Christian hope—choose a specific issue and gradually solve it without one side or the other getting the impression that it has to abandon its faith?

Take something I've already mentioned: the way in which bishops are appointed in the Roman Catholic Church. According to Catholic dogma it is not the only possible way. And, occasionally, Rome has made concessions here; taken into account local matters and political pressures. Thus, it's not impossible to imagine that the nomination of a bishop in the Evangelical Church that might be united with Rome would be done in a different way than it is presently.

This and other issues can be discussed, provided there are concrete proposals from one side or the other; obviously, such proposals would not lead to church unity today or tomorrow, but they can still be helpful for achieving a real reconciliation which is based on something besides mere words.

If, 'til now, Rome hasn't made any significant concessions, the same holds true for Protestants. We in Germany often have the impression that Protestant churches are merely expecting concessions from Rome without wanting to give up something themselves. A leading Protestant theologian told me that the Evangelical churches, theologically and religiously, underestimate the value of the Holy Eucharist. Perhaps this can be explained historically on the basis of the strong influence of the Enlightenment in the Evangelical churches; but the Eucharist belongs to the essence of Christianity and has deep doctrinal roots. It cannot be compromised.

I simply don't have the time to explore all the possible avenues of discussion that exist on both sides and which are far from being dealt with adequately. I dislike talk about the Catholic Church's eventual "reacknowledgment" of office as it is understood and practiced in the Evangelical Church. I can't help but think that neither Rome nor the German bishops have examined this problem in all its dimensions. If the outward relationship between the churches remains as it is now, there is little hope for achieving unity in the short run. The quest, however, should not be abandoned, but pursued. All churches and bishops, on both sides, acknowledge that the quest for unity is a mission; but declaration of intent has brought few practical results.

Certainly, one can hope for rapid progress toward unity with the Orthodox churches, but with each passing day optimism wanes. And if the difficulties of achieving unity with the Orthodox churches are more than one can anticipate, they're much greater still with respect to Protestantism.

Recently you said in Rome that it was necessary to draft an encyclical on the modern problem of atheism. Can you give us your reflections on how to proceed in developing this theme?

The following thoughts come to mind: It appears to me that the Church, East and West, shows too little concern for the fundamental and global problem of atheism. And isn't one of the concrete signs for this lack of concern— let's rather call it a practical minimization of the problem—simply that there is no specific encyclical on atheism? Indeed, the Church did show its concern here, especially during Vatican II. "The Pastoral Constitution on the Church in the Modern World," for example, contains some good and important things. But the entire matter needs to be carried deeper and further. A lot of questions still hang in the balance. I'm not only thinking here of a statement about God, his essence, existence, and so on, but about a specifically theological exposition which relates precisely to the phenomenon of atheism.

If God exists, if he desires the salvation of all, and supports and permeates all things, then it is certainly astonishing that such global atheism is possible; at no time in humanity's history (until today, that is) did anyone imagine the magnitude of this phenomenon.

Today we see and experience an atheism which is becoming the official doctrine of many states. Consequently, thousands of questions pop up. What about the salvation of the atheist? Vatican II made some very profound declarations on this. But the believer's daily conscience is far removed from pondering what the Council said. And so, the Church must be more attentive to this phenomenon; we must preach about it; and where the preaching speaks of God, the preacher must have this problem, its difficulties and obscurities in the back of his or her mind so that the necessary consequences can be drawn from what the preacher says. The essential question is something like this: How do I share with a person today what I mean by the experience of God?

I've said it elsewhere another way: One needs a "mystagogy" in order to enter into this God experience. God doesn't simply come to a person externally through "indoctrination." It's not the same as teaching someone about life in Australia. A doctrine about God must be united with a particular, irrefutable experience. Obviously, a catechism isn't absolutely necessary. In fact, it might even present further difficulties. In any event, the Church must carefully consider the issue in a way that conforms more to the public conscience.

These are some very difficult questions and they fall chiefly within the competency of theologians. . . .
The curious thing is that really great theology has addressed itself to such questions better than pastoral theology actually realizes. This must change. The theological critiques of a Feuerbach, a Marx, a Nietzsche, or a Camus have, unfortunately, not yet penetrated the Church's everyday consciousness —I should say the consciousnesses of pastors as well as the faithful. And one of the reasons for this lies in the fact that the official church has said relatively little about the issue. It would be interesting to know what the last four or five popes have said about atheism.

How come so little has happened in this area?
Well, surely there has to be deeper reflection on and consideration of the theoretical, historical, and sociocultural reasons for denying God; then it would become clear to every Christian where, on the basis of the gospel proclamation, pastoral responsibility lies.

You also say one of the reasons that atheists have become so numerous is because the Church has not made concerted efforts to deal with the problem.
Certainly, one can't label the actual causes of atheism, insofar as they fall within the purview of pure theory or the domain of the history of ideas, as theological. But neither can those causes which are strictly linked to sociopolitical conditions be identified with an incompetency on the Church's part and its proclamation of the living God. Still, I'm convinced that in the wake of a theoretical and practical atheism of global proportions more decisive efforts must be made here.

Do you see a possible answer to the phenomenon of atheism in the more simple claim of the faithful in the Latin American Church: We cannot really proclaim Jesus Christ without partiality for the poor?
We must finally come to the realization that the bulk of atheism is not found among the poor. It has, however, always been a fact among the well-to-do,

landed European classes. The rich, the fed-up bourgeoisie, that's where you first find atheists.

There's no doubt that the Church's proclamation of belief in God hits a snag when the suspicion arises that the Church is not concerned about the plight of the poor. Then one day people say: We don't want to have anything to do with a Church that cooperates in supporting unjust social structures. From there it's only a short jump to concluding that God himself is an accomplice of injustice. After all, the realities of God and the Church are fundamentally related to each other.

It's possible that because the Latin American Church is concerned for social justice the poor won't throw their faith away, as has been the case with us in Europe. It may be, as it were, a predetermined and wonderful plan for the Latin American Church that the poor will carry on the proclamation of God's existence in a manner that *actually* reverences this living and eternal God.

Translated by Bernhard A. Asen
St. Louis University

49 · The Pope Can Still Learn a Thing or Two

Interview with Siegfried von Kortzfleisch of the
Lutherischen Monatsheften, Hanover (April, 1981)

Once more a new Protestant-Catholic commission will shortly convene. Only more bishops belong to this one than to the former ones. Is the formation of a new commission not merely a self-deception, a vain promise for those who complain about the stagnation of the ecumenical dialogue?

I would not accuse anyone of willful self-deception. But unfortunately, one does not see objectively how this may lead to any worthwhile results. Of course, one's Christian conscience feels responsible for some action and progress in ecumenism. And so one sets up a commission that goes on talking, although there are already enough commissions of the kind. One gets the impression that this is a dead end. Can the Church make ecumenical progress without either of the "parties" having to give up its traditional basic convictions? This might be possible.

But on all points where it should be translated into practice the Catholic bishops say no: intercommunion, pastoral care of mixed marriages, ecumenical religious instruction. What can still feed ecumenical optimism?

We should examine whether we can accomplish much more on *these* issues on the basis of the Catholic Church's actual self-understanding. That is certainly open to question. At any rate, about intercommunion it seems to me that, according to the traditional Catholic conception, we might advance a bit more. But special attention should be paid to whether the Catholic Church might not undertake a courageous ecumenical offensive in a much larger framework of ecumenical deliberations. Concretely: Might the Catholic Church not declare in a somewhat binding way from Rome that certain things no longer should constitute obstacles on the road to church unity. Moreover, all ecumenists of all confessions consider as obvious that the unity for which we work cannot consist in the absorption of the Protestant churches by a Roman Catholic Church that, on her side, would have undergone no changes. Thus, why could Rome, without losing face and without having to give up any dogmatic position, not declare that the union of the churches does not do away with a plurality (to be described more precisely) of the united churches.

In what respect might they remain different, for instance?

It is evident, for instance, that the way in which, according to Canon Law and actual practice, the Roman Catholic Church appoints bishops, is not a dogma of the Church. Electing and appointing bishops might be done with other juridical procedures. So when a Protestant Christian or bishop or ecumenist says that appointing bishops as practiced by you is absolutely excluded for us, why then can Rome not clearly and unequivocally declare that this way of appointing bishops or other regulations of Roman Catholic Canon Law are not things that should stand in the way of ecumenical unification?

But is the pope, who has been molded mainly by his native Poland, where one does not care a bit about other churches, does not even notice them, ready at all for such aggressive ecumenical thinking?

If the pope, because of his Polish descent, is not used to take other churches into account because he had never, as it were, laid eyes on them, then, for goodness' sake, he can learn to! Why would he be unable to do so? Everyone knows that, when he goes to the Philippine Islands, he must first carefully inquire whether he has to be cautious in that country, so as not to upset more than to edify. In the same way, there are also things that he might learn about ecumenical problems, should he not know about them yet.

But experience shows him to be a pope who shows himself more and more opposed to all compromises.
I do not know whether what may be true for questions of moral theology applies also to ecumenical questions. Has he not declared that, before the end of the century, union with the Eastern Orthodox Church can and must be achieved? So he must have given some thought to the ways in which that is possible. It seems to me that—despite the fact that we Catholics have so much in common with the Eastern Church—the basic and essential difficulties between Rome and the Eastern Orthodox Church are not easier to overcome than between Rome and the Protestant churches.

Can the churches draw nearer to each other before having first changed? Or will the churches change when they draw nearer to each other?
It seems to me that this is not really a question of either/or. If the churches really have a genuine desire to draw nearer, they must ask themselves what this requires. Therefore, they should also find out how they may eventually transform themselves, in order to draw near to the others in the right way.

But it looks as if the Catholic Church is afraid of too much change in the post-conciliar time. Is she right to be?
It is impossible to give a general solution to the problems which your question brings up. There are so many things about which Catholic Christians, even in the postconciliar Church, even if they have the courage to be progressive, can have their misgivings, whereby they will not wish to see any progress in this or that direction. What in this or that domain is really desirable, wise, truly Christian, what really brings us mutually nearer to each other? That must be asked for *each single* instance.

In practice, we have noticed for several years now that in some domains where cooperation had already existed between Protestant groups and organizations and Catholic groups and organizations the German Catholic bishops have recanted. It looks like a segregation policy. One might almost compare it with developments at the time of the Counter-Reformation. Are these strategical moves or the way in which a widespread conservative mentality goes about it in the Church?

At the time of the Council there existed, naturally, a certain euphoria, a feeling that things might change, perhaps also that things should change. A euphoria to which the episcopacies reacted with a mixture of uneasiness and compliance. Next came a stage where one got the impression that here and there a Catholic bishop had to have the courage to say no, even if some groups or circles among the faithful were of another mind. This, of course, is more evident in our time, in which an anxious reactionary conservative mentality is widespread, even socially. And so the bishops naturally give the impression that they use the brakes more than is justified. Fifteen years ago, for instance, the German bishops would not have interfered as a matter of course in the appointment policy of the Catholic faculties as they do today. It slowly begins to look as if the Catholic theology professors were in fact appointed by the bishops. And there are more instances of the kind.

Is there not a danger that parts of Vatican II might very quietly be made "harmless"?

On the one hand, we must say that the present pope, at least in his official pronouncements and encyclicals, does not put the light of Vatican II under a bushel. To what extent there is not, here and there, in practical matters, some movement against the spirit of Vatican II is, it is true, another question. One should first inquire: Are there many instances in which *it can be shown* that things have been done against the letter of the Council? I am thinking not so much of single instances but of measures of a wider scope. That will not be so easy to show, because in a Catholic Church, where Canon Law and the written letter matter more than with the Protestants, this is rather difficult. When the letter has not been violated, many people may cry that the spirit is being violated, but that is difficult to prove. That is why such "crying" does not achieve much. Nevertheless, and the pope himself admits this, Vatican II has ushered in a new stage for the self-understanding of the Catholic Church, and in the long run this prevails sooner or later.

For many years theologians have examined the points where they can agree. The remaining hard points of conflict have, as it were, been bracketed. Would it not clear the air if in the future all possible theological acumen was used for a while to define in what the disagreement consists?

Theoretically that would be great. Only the disagreement is not so easy to locate. Suppose that you or another Protestant theologian were to formulate a thesis about the teaching function of the pope in the Catholic Church and to add that such a thing is unacceptable to Protestant theologians. Right away, we Catholic theologians perhaps might reply emphatically: In fact, you have basically misunderstood us. I do not say that I would be right, but formally speaking, this theoretically meaningful and useful method which you propose for making progress in the ecumenical dialogue would lead to something of the kind.

But does this apply to all points where we disagree?

There are also other points of disagreement. I do not wish to deny that. Thus, we might discover some disagreement about the pope's primatial power. And I might also perhaps grant that you have understood the Catholic position, and you reject it as such. Another example: In 1950, when the Assumption of the Blessed Virgin was defined, Protestant theologians unanimously—I say this now with some malice—uttered a frightfully indignant cry: How unchristian and unbiblical this was. If today, as a Protestant theologian, you were to think this over and to say that, of course, with death every Christian, every person who is saved, reaches this total fulfillment implied by the so-called bodily assumption, no Protestant theologian, therefore none of your colleagues, the theology professors, would claim that this is unchristian and deserved an anathema.

But you are now simplifying Mariology.

No, it merely looks that way. The Catholic Church has with Mary—quite legitimately, on account of her special function in the history of salvation—a reason for asserting, in her maturer understanding of the faith, something like the Assumption, while she cannot yet assert it about others.

Without venturing into an apologetic dialogue about Mary, it is certainly true that it is not more difficult to discover disagreement than agreement.

At first blush you might naturally say this. But I can imagine that, for example, Moltmann or Jüngel agree with me that the definition of Chalcedon is correct and states an undeniable truth. Nevertheless, if we take a closer look, we may, in this agreement that is real and suffices for church purposes, discover theological differences that are very far ranging. I would consider as false several statements of Moltmann's doctrine of the Trinity and of his Christology—even granting that Moltmann and I sincerely accept certain official church doctrines. To that extent, it is difficult to decide whether it is easier to discover an agreement or a disagreement.

In what way should the unity of Christians be organized?

I am inclined to say that this is a problem which the church leadership should examine.

Is it enough to agree about faith?

How do I find out that I share the same faith as, for example, my colleague Heinrich Fries? First, I do not have the slightest difficulty saying that I do. He has been baptized a Catholic. He wishes to be a Catholic in whatever he does and says. He accepts the magisterium of the Church. So do I. But when I take a closer look, I might perhaps discover in many opinions differences that I am not allowed to consider as against church unity, since we are in the same Church and of the same faith. How does one distinguish such differences of opinion that do not break up the unity of the Church's faith from those that do break it up? My Protestant colleague Steck in Münster, for instance, held the opinion, if I understood him correctly, that the difference between Protestant and Catholic Christians is so deep and radical that we do not have one and the same God. I would not speak that way. But this shows how difficult it is to see and to accept differences of opinion on the one hand and not to consider them as splitting the Church on the other.

The Catholic Church has considerable experience not only of events that broke up unity but also of others that did not.

There have always been in the Catholic Church—among you too, of course—differences of opinion that did not split the Church. During the sixteenth and seventeenth centuries the Jesuits and the Dominicans bitterly quarreled about the relation between God's sovereign power and human freedom. They disputed throughout as if this difference of opinion were rending the faith. The Dominicans said that the Jesuits were basically semi-Pelagians. And the Jesuits said that the Dominicans were basically Calvinists. But the Church's leadership spoke: Hush now and stop demolishing each other. The Holy See rejected neither doctrine. Nowadays too I could think of very serious differences of opinion among Catholic theologians, which might be brought into the open, to which the Church should react in the same way, although both parties speak as if a difference of faith were involved. But this is not being done, because the rationale that would justify such a reaction has not yet been theologically worked out at all.

If you discover so many differences within the one Church, might one imagine some way of unifying the churches even before there is doctrinal agreement?

I would be unable to imagine anything of the kind where either "party" declares and feels that a solemn official declaration of the other "party" is absolutely unchristian and in conflict with God.

But if one excludes such cases, does this make possible communion without full agreement?

Yes, evidently. To mention another concrete example. On some theological issues of very great importance I am resolutely opposed to the theology of Hans Urs von Balthasar, and he to mine even more so. For the time being, I believe, he has not accused me to Rome of being a heretic. I have not done it either. The Church's leadership keeps quiet, thank God. We are both of us deeply intent to think according to the faith of the one Church, so we may concelebrate and do not have to send each other to the stake. But, as mentioned above, the rationale for such situations has not yet been clearly thought through. Instead, one stumbles through history with some kind of rule of thumb, without knowing precisely why one acts this way in one case and that way in another. Why does one tolerate differences here that are very fundamental, and why is one so touchy about other questions that are much less important?

How representative are your bishops for the faith of your faithful?

On both sides church leaders behave as if that which they proclaim as their faith were the faith of God's flock for whom they care. In general, that is not true at all. Now I do not say that when the flock does not agree with the doctrine of the magisterium, the latter is automatically wrong. However, the far-reaching question of the importance of people's actual faith and its difference from the official faith of the church leadership has not yet been thought through. When a Catholic bishop says that Protestant Christians do not believe in the infallibility of the pope, he is probably right. But the strange thing is that the fact that probably a large part of his own faithful does not believe in it either does not upset him. We need a theology of the "sociality" of the knowing mind. More research is needed here—especially for ecumenical purposes.

How long will it take to make progress in the union of Christians? Can we still afford much delay when we keep in mind the erosion of faith in the so-called Christian countries?

We cannot. What we are actually doing is another question. And how God in his providence reacts to this is once more a quite different question. The Church—in all denominations—has already done much in its history it should not have done. And lo and behold, Christianity has not perished as a result, nor will it perish in the future.

Professor Rahner, you are a Jesuit. Is Protestant thought, is the theological impulse that comes from Luther, not necessarily alien and strange to you, because of your religious upbringing?

I am not a Luther expert. Because of my Catholic upbringing and my theological training, I cannot say that I am really at home in Lutheran theology. Yet I would like to distinguish three things in Luther. First, that which should clearly be ascribed to his own character and to the mentality of his time would not today be considered by any Protestant Christian as especially nice, gratifying, or worthy to be imitated nowadays—such things should quietly be forgotten by both sides. What do I care, when reading Nietzsche, that he did or did not die from paralysis? That is a private concern of his. And to derive many conclusions from it about what he has to say is simply nonsense. Second, among the great figures of church history, to whom, of course, Luther belongs, there exists a specific mentality that, although not simply identical with the common self-awareness of the Church, means nonetheless a positive contribution to the universal Church. I am, for instance, convinced that Ignatius Loyola might have in what is really his own theology a great significance for the religious life of Christians, at least of Catholic Christians, a significance that has not yet been fully put to use. And in that way I attribute to Luther a great significance, one that can still be alive and that, let us hope, will not vanish.

And that has not been fully put to use by Catholics?

Yes, to be sure. This does not mean, however, that every Christian has to live from the charismatic peculiarities of another great Christian. And the third point about Luther: With all the great ones of the history of the churches and theology and of the living faith of the Church, there is always the living witness of the really common Christian heritage. We find this also in Luther.

At what points would you yourself today critically challenge Protestant theologians and Protestant churches?

Especially in this. At first you have told us deservedly that the ecumenical movement stagnated among us. I think that today it is necessary to address the same remark to the Protestant leadership.

For more than fifty years you have been doing and teaching theology. What is beyond theology? When words no longer will do, when one ceases to talk theology—then what is the most important idea for your faith?

For me the incomprehensibility of God is not just one statement among others. It is absolutely fundamental. In reality, all Christian dogmas as well as all church dogmas basically forbid any definitive conclusion and any conviction that one might have that everything is comprehensible.

When one is old one thinks of death and one hopes that it is a sudden fall into the incomprehensibility of a God who says yes to us. From that angle—without, of course, giving up single dogmas—the perspectives and the comparative importance of official church doctrines often look quite different.

Translated by Joseph Donceel, S.J.
Fordham University

50 · Spirituality Requires a Certain Educated Ignorance

Interview with Louis Ter Steeg for Radio KRO,
Hilversum, Holland (October 5, 1981)

What problems are associated with your having been called "a theological atomic physicist"?[1]
Professional theology, in its thought world, with the sublimity of its questions and the aggregate of its problems, is at such a distance from ordinary Christians that they get nothing out of it. The assumption is, of course, that the Christian ought to get something at least out of theology, and the assumption is correct. A theology that would, as a general rule, dispense itself from any concern for serving the Church's proclamation, for serving the life of Christians would no longer be Christian or Catholic theology. We are faced with the question of just how far apart professional theology and the immediate needs of Christians ought to be. A certain distance is naturally necessary.

1. See page 204.

When an atomic power plant is built (the morality of this we pass over for now), atomic physics, which made the plant possible, is serving the people who turn on their lights and plug in their refrigerators. It is, however, perfectly clear that the atomic physics immediately involved is not understood by the person who turns on the light switch. This distance between use and understanding is legitimate, and ultimately is of service to the ordinary user down the line. And there is something comparable to this in theology.

What do I have to tell a Christian of today when I want to tell him of the Real Presence in the Lord's Supper? That can perhaps be quite simple, perhaps simpler than it has ever been. But one has to think over such things very carefully, taking into account the history of dogma, exegetical considerations, and questions of systematics, for ordinary Christians to hear anything that will be meaningful and intelligible. The subtleties of theology may be unintelligible to believers, yet they serve them. In other words, I think we can go right ahead and have our "theological atomic physicists," and their production should then be passed on in appropriate ways. The notion of the popularizer is not quite justified, since it can be, in some cases, very difficult and demanding of deep insight to say something simply. For example, one who wants to preach on Trinity Sunday about the Trinity and not the Third World must be able to speak in plain and simple terms about this ineffable mystery. But in order to do that, not only the work of speculative theology is needed, also the very hard work of translating that theology. This happens not just by popularizing; it demands a special theological reflection. The popularizer is not the simple, stupid primitive pastor; rather, the real popularizer is one who, with great intellectual labor, tries to think through Christian dogma and then asks: What does it mean, not just for the "dummies down there" below the pulpit but for me? In that moment, when he changes from the theologian to the one who must pray, who must work out his own salvation in fear and trembling, his theology, with all its necessary and preparatory speculation, becomes humble and simple. Then he can also preach it. We must have "atomic physicists" in theology, but they must know their proper function, and understand that finally the most they can say is also simple, so that the listener below the pulpit can understand. And then Jesus must be able to listen and say, "I understand."

You once wrote about the inevitability of heresies among the faithful in the Church: Many Christians and Catholics who live in and value the Church cannot be completely protected from holding opinions that are objectively heretical, given the intellectual pluralism of our day and the excessive number of offered opinions.

Yes, I would say the more balls the juggler has to play with, the greater the danger that one ball may fall. The same happens in theology. If one does it simply, that is, if one plays with only two or three balls, naturally one can see to it with relative ease that none fall. But given the tremendous differentiation of sciences today, anthropology, exegesis, history, cultural history, and all the other branches of human sciences, it is extraordinarily difficult to say all *that* in such a way that it all fits together. You catch one ball, and suddenly another one gets away on you, without your even noticing it. That happens in theology too.

Let's suppose some theologian says: Pius XII solemnly declared that the human soul is created by God. Fine, and I am convinced of that. But what does that mean now, in the face of today's theory of evolution, the possibility of simulating consciousness with computers, perhaps even someday to produce it; what crossover or noncrossover is there between human and animal consciousness, and so on? If I do not know about all these things, which one really could and should know, then it can happen to a theologian who teaches that the human soul is created by God that he or she says something that is quite correct in the intended sense, but expresses simultaneously something stupid and false.

If I want to say with the Council of Trent, "The substance of the bread after the consecration is no longer there," then I would like to know what the "substance of bread" is supposed to mean today. If I presume modern physics here, it can well happen that I say something about the Real Presence of Jesus in the sacrament that is objectively false. All the more is this what happens to the ordinary faithful who hear what they get from the pulpit. And now, what the preacher says doesn't drive into an empty barn of the hearer's consciousness, but into one that is stuffed full of thousands of opinions and bits of knowledge, and how all of that is supposed to fit together is a most difficult matter.

For example: Suppose I were to undertake to examine a pious, orthodox Catholic bishop on the Real Presence of Christ, taking questions from modern physics, to the point where he would either have nothing to say or he would make a philosophical or theologically false statement. Today something like that is unavoidable. One should avoid errors, I would say, that one recognizes, or can recognize, that one with a bit of hard work can foresee, that with some respect for the sense of the universal Church one can avoid; but one must also sometimes have some patience with oneself and try also with patience to live in a peaceful co-existence with those errors of theologians that cannot be avoided.

When you were ordained back in 1932 did you already look forward to theology as your priestly work, or would you then rather have worked in directly pastoral work?

At the time I had a so-called assignment from superiors, which I had not sought out, to teach the history of philosophy at Pullach. It didn't come to that, as I was switched to the chair of dogmatic theology at Innsbruck. But in fact, I was quite indifferent about all these things, as became a good Jesuit. They could have made me this or that as far as the specific work goes. At bottom, a pastoral interest was always the common element in all the possibilities.

Today there is a great shortage of priests. What could be done to cure this?
That is, of course, a difficult question to answer, simply because there are so many factors influencing the shortage. An external and not insignificant reason, but by far not the only one, is the insistence of the Latin Church on the celibacy of the clergy. But many other factors contribute: the complete change in the spiritual climate; a much clearer pluralism in today's mentality; the decline of a closed Catholic society in which especially the diocesan clergy could live more easily than today. In today's society they are very much isolated; greater problems in theology come to them than formerly; and there are other possibilities for having a theological or ecclesial, pastoral career outside the priesthood. These and many other reasons work together to produce this shortage of priests. How to change this is another question. Last evening, a professor from Budapest told me that in the diocese of Egar in Hungary there was only one applicant. I have heard also that in Austria the monastery of Kremsmünster has more young people who want to be Benedictine priests than the huge diocese of Vienna. This is perhaps connected with the fact that in the community of a monastery one can more easily experience a protective, supportive atmosphere of life than can a diocesan priest living alone in a metropolis where there are perhaps 6 to 8 percent practicing Catholics.

Priestly celibacy could be changed; could women also be ordained?
You know, of course, that Rome is against such a move, and has declared, not as definition but as teaching, that this exclusion of women from ordination has dogmatic reasons and cannot be changed by the Church. Nonetheless, I remain of the nondeterminative opinion that there is no principle of divine right involved, and it could be changed by the Church. Whether and when such a change is possible and opportune, where and when the societal relations between men and women reach a point where there would be no problem with entrusting leadership functions to women in the Church—all these are naturally questions to which I have no answer. I hope that for Europe and North America such a change will soon occur in the total climate of relation-

ships between men and women in the world and in the Church that one will entrust such offices in the Church to women.

Would you regard the spirituality of Ignatius of Loyola as the unifying element of your life?

I hope it is the case that spirituality intends to be a relationship to God. One does not know about a relationship to God, whether one has it, how one has it, what is decisive in it. I have a certain "educated ignorance" about myself which is appropriate to spirituality.

Translate that please.

It is wise, educated ignorance about oneself, which must be entrusted to God, without knowing how it is. Paul says, "I do not judge myself. I am not conscious of any guilt, but he who judges me is God alone."

And so a part of human existence, in spite of all psychology and psycho-analysis and all that stuff, is an ultimate nonreflectiveness about oneself that cannot be overcome. And the one who knows that, and knows that one knows nothing about oneself, such a person entrusts himself or herself to God and hopes, as we say in Christian terms, to find a merciful judgment at the hands of God. We have to work our own death into our daily lives and try so to live as we would wish to be at our death, peaceful and tranquil. It is in daily life that God is present with his liberating grace. There is a mysticism of daily living, the finding of God in all things, the sober drunkenness of the Spirit mentioned by the Fathers of the Church and ancient liturgy, which we dare not reject or disdain just because it is sober.

You have spoken before in this connection of a "wintry piety"?

We need not take the frightfully enthusiastic or the dreadfully ardent as a guideline if we are not really that kind. We have to take our own skepticism as an experience of grace, up to a point. We live in a sober era, and in that sense a wintry time, when in religious life there are not all too many blossoms about which one could wax enthusiastic. But I think even a wintry time can be a time of grace. Will we die, sick with cancer on our deathbed, with a char-ismatic enthusiasm, or painfully and nonetheless hoping beyond all hope, "Lord into your hands I commend my spirit"? If the second is the style of our dying, then I think there is also a legitimately analogous way of living, also a life of grace, for grace can also be the sober hope against all hope.

This sober hope would then be more your personal piety?

I do not reflect much on my own personal piety, because at bottom one

really does not know anything about that. If you like, I would say: The sober-
ness of daily living as a true presence of the liberating Spirit is what I wish my
piety to be.

*You let me page through your photo album. Could you explain some of the pic-
tures to me?*

These are my parents as I remember them from my childhood, and here are
my brother Hugo, my brother George, my last living sister, and this one with
the peaked cap and the horn—that's me; it was a Mardi Gras costume. I would
say that by and large, apart from external political and societal events, my life
has run along in an unobtrusive, continuous fashion. I had a normal family
life, with good parents and six siblings. After secondary school I entered the
Society of Jesus right away, and with that there came a certain normal continuity up to the present day, for I am still a Jesuit.

How did you come to be a Jesuit?

Let's put it formally and in the abstract: I was religiously interested and
wanted to become a priest. I don't know exactly why, but it was understood
right from the start that I wanted to be in an order, and so, again I don't know
just why, the Jesuits were the only ones considered. I did not want to enter a
contemplative order since I had no frightfully intense attraction for liturgy, as
would be proper for a Benedictine, and I was interested in studies and apolo-
getics. And so it turned out that I became a Jesuit, although I cannot give detailed and determinative reasons why. For example, I had never made a retreat
before I was in the order. I was a member of the Fountain of Youth Catholic
youth movement, slightly left, so to speak, of the more legally oriented New
Germany movement. Those were the two Catholic youth groups for Gym-
nasium students of the day. So I was with Fountain of Youth, and became a
Jesuit in spite of it. Other young people at that time probably experienced or
considered the Jesuits very much as relatively reactionary soldiers of the pope,
but I did not—I don't know why.

*Was it perhaps that, since you were intellectually very active, you had an early
glimmering of the renewal of theology and of the Church with the help of the intensive theological and especially patristic work that, for example, your brother Hugo
later got underway with other Jesuits?*

I would say, first of all, I was and I remained an ordinary teacher who fulfilled his obligations and did not have any great experiences. The great experiences came in connection with and just before and after the Second Vatican

Council. The possibility of a genuine renewal seemed closer and more realistic, and my theological activity became more intense. Take a look at this picture for example: Here is Monsignor Höfer kneeling humbly and devout, here is chief editor Remigius Bäumer, and here I am, in such a large papal audience, where we certainly played an important role. Monsignor Höfer and I together had published a huge theological dictionary [*Lexikon für Theologie und Kirche*] in eleven or twelve volumes (depending on how you count them), with more than two-thousand collaborators. Here we are handing over one of the volumes to Pope John XXIII. This one is a fine picture, taken shortly after the Council at an international congress of theologians. Karl Barth was in Rome too, having some dealings with Willibrands's secretariat. In conjunction with that there was a discussion and a celebration in which Barth, Eduard Dhanis, also a Jesuit, and I took part. In this picture you see one of my students and friends, Professor Metz, Cardinal Döpfner, and me, and here are several pictures of the synod at Würzburg. Here again are pictures from the meeting of the order *Pour le mérite* at Villa Hammerschmid belonging to the then [German] president Scheel. This picture was taken at an award ceremony in Vienna with Cardinal König.

Have you influenced the Church and society with your theology principally through your students or also through the magisterium, for example, as adviser to bishops?
I think that in time there were a good number of theologians who were my students and brought something of that with them in their later activity, but the greater influence was naturally simply through the *Schriften zur Theologie*, these fourteen [later sixteen] volumes which have been translated into Italian, English, and Spanish. These have had the greater part in the influence my theology has had in the world. Add to that a certain influence through the Council, to which I accompanied Cardinal König, and during which I had close contact with Cardinal Döpfner, since he lived in the same house with me. So yes, I had an opportunity of having a certain influence on the theology of the Second Vatican Council. I have to tell you a little story about that. Sebastian Tromp, a well-known and important Dutch theologian, was in Rome at the time as secretary to the Theological Commission I was on. He remarked once, "This Rahner is remarkable—when he starts talking *Latin*, then you can understand him."

Better than when you would talk German?
Better than when I write or would write German; he didn't much like me with his neoscholastic, conservative mentality.

Do you have the impression that relations between theologians and the magisterium were much better then than now?

By and large I believe relations during the Council really were a lot better, at least for our central European situation. There was immediate contact: We saw each other; you could perhaps give a lecture some evening before the German, Brazilian, and Austrian bishops' conferences on a specific theological question that was up before the Council; we knew each other; we could talk together reasonably before and after the sessions, where bishops and theologians were together in the Theological Commission. At that time I had a very good relationship with Cardinal Ottaviani and with the Irish Cardinal Browne.

And also with Pope Paul VI?

Pope Paul VI was not in our commission, but I got to know him better through a private audience after the Council, when he was already pope and received me.

Might I ask what you spoke about with him?

We spoke Latin, since I do not speak Italian. He spoke fluently and intelligently in Latin with me about all kinds of things, not terribly important things; that theology can be pluralistic but should not become chaotic, as the pope has said. Once I said to him, "Look, Holy Father, ten years ago the Holy Office forbade me to say another word about concelebration, and today you concelebrate yourself." He chuckled ever so quietly and said, "There is a time to weep and a time to laugh." What that is supposed to mean in the context is not so clear to me, but he apparently meant to say that times and mentalities change, even in the Church of God, and there is no escaping that.

After the Council you were named to the international commisison of theologians. I take it your experience there was not positive?

I will have to say honestly, no. That was a commission in which theologians from all over the world and from all schools of thought were represented in very democratic fashion, learned and peaceful people, and to that extent it was a very good theological affair. But what is the use of it, when smart theologians with all their good will discuss any number of theological themes, and then remain of no import to the church leadership? The Holy Office and the Congregation for the Doctrine of the Faith never asked us for advice on a single topic. In other words, the whole Roman theologians' commission was a discussion among theologians in exactly the same way that other meetings are held; people sit down and talk intelligently about theological matters. It is true Cardinal Séper and his secretary were there, but that was all. I once said expressly, "I do not understand why I come here, since we are of no use." Cardinal Séper answered, "We don't give you or ask you anything because we want to leave you your freedom. Of course we in the Congregation for the Doctrine of the Faith ask theologians outside of Rome, but when we ask there, that is our own affair and has nothing to do with this Roman commission." That didn't enlighten me at all.

So then you resigned?

I quit the commission because, though I enjoyed discussing with theologians, I saw no point in coming to Rome to do it when nothing purposeful came of it. Now when I go to Rome I converse gladly with officials there who wish to speak with me on various occasions.

Hans Urs von Balthasar once said of your theological work, "Karl Rahner is like an ox that does not step out of the harness until he has moved the cart of tradition to which he is hitched a jolt forward." Have you really been able to help the cart of tradition to make this jolt forward, or had you expected more?

Ultimately, I cannot judge that of course, but I think that I have remained continually in a positive relationship with the Church's tradition, not just perforce, but freely and gladly. Naturally, any theological work is always the striving to move forward from out of the tradition and within it within a specific time. Whether and to what extent I have succeeded in this is hard to say. I do believe that in one way or another I have made a contribution. If I may formulate it somewhat pretentiously: Today there is no neoscholasticism anywhere in the Catholic world such as we had in the nineteenth and the first half of the twentieth centuries, and neither the popes nor the Church's teaching has remained what they thought in the days of neoscholasticism they would always remain. And in this movement and change to a contemporary theology, which is closer to us and our world, I believe I have made a contribution. Finally, neither conservatism nor progressivism are important, but rather that people really experience the nearness of God and get on with their lives toward God. Theology is not a science for its own sake, but it is in the service of humankind seeking to find God, trying to pray to him and love him. Only where one loves God for himself and not for some personal advantage can one become a Christian and a saint. To that extent, all the important and unimportant things in the history of theology are finally to be judged by whether they have performed this service to humanity for the sake of God. Everything else passes and is not so terribly important. This one thing can be accomplished in any age, whether the ecclesiastical political atmosphere is good or bad, joyful or less joyful, That is not important; ultimately, I am really quite indifferent to that. But the single finally determinative thing in theology that I did want to work on and contribute to was the one ultimate and encompassing quest for God.

Translated by Thomas A. Caldwell, S.J.
Marquette University

51 · The Language of Science and the Language of Theology

Interview with Joachim Schickel of North-German Radio (NDR), Hamburg (November 22, 1981)

While Hans-Heinz Holt and I were discussing the language of philosophy a month ago, we came across the phenomenon of a double relationship on the part of philosophy: (1) to its object and (2) to its manner of speaking about the object—a relationship of a kind that we thought peculiar solely to philosophy. I would like to elaborate briefly on that with an example. A scientist in a particular field can speak about his or her object directly; the botanist, for example, can speak about a plant, the biologist about an animal. The philosopher, of course,—when talking on a specific topic, like God, the world, humanity, being, and the like—also speaks directly about his or her object on the one hand; but, on the other hand, so we thought, at the same time the philosopher is necessarily speaking as well about the expression of this object; he or she is unable to separate the one from the other. The Göttingen philosopher Joseph König once called this the specific forte of the philosopher. If a philosopher wants to say something well, both of these aspects have to be considered and discussed simultaneously, and König clarified that with an example from geography: "Mount Everest is the highest of all mountains,"—taken as a statement—, and with a second statement (a sentence from Aristotle): "Eudaemonia, happiness, is the highest of all goods." In regard to the first statement (Mount Everest is the highest of all mountains), he says that the linguistic statement, which makes the assertion, is a pure adjunct; it can also be expressed by means of a method of physical measuring, whereas in philosophy it is not possible to find out anything about eudaemonia *without this linguistic expression. König even says that what* eudaemonia *is is accessible to the philosopher only in the predicate.*

It seems to me, however, that theology is also in this peculiar situation. When it speaks, for example, about God or about Being (both of which it does do), it has access to the object solely in the predicate. But isn't there still something missing to render it capable of theological language?

They certainly do have what you are pointing to in common, since ultimately the theologian can speak of God only by including, to express it in my terminology, the human being's absolute transcendence toward absolute being or toward the mystery—or however one wants to name it. Consequently, every theological statement, if it is directed toward God, is naturally always necessarily a statement about the human person, who possesses this special relationship to God. To this extent, of course, the authentic humanities, especially philosophy and theology, have a common structure. But you are quite right: Above and beyond this common trait theology definitely has in its language a quite precise peculiarity that derives both from the speaking, theologizing person and from its "object," God, in a manner that is common to both and ultimately indissoluble. Theological language is, at least for a normal Christian understanding, God-talk, but God-talk understood insofar as God has revealed himself in a true sense extending beyond the created world; and in this sense we already have a linguistic peculiarity of theology in contrast to philosophy. Theology appeals to the speaking God, repeats his speech—at least that is the intention—whereas philosophy once again, even though it be submitted to other conditions, speaks, as it were, the first sentence itself.

Can that still be said in view of a philosopher like Aristotle, in whom both are entwined each in the other in an original manner, with the result that many philosophers and philologists speak of a theology when they are talking about first philosophy?

For a Christian theology—at least according to a Catholic understanding— the philosopher can and even ought to speak of God; but then God is an object in this philosophical theology in a way different from that in theological theology when it speaks of God. Theological theology—if I may express it like that —speaks of God as of him whose word it has heard, whereas the philosophical theologian, an Aristotle if you will, speaks of God insofar as he is the ultimate primary ground of being in general, which the philosopher studies. Naturally, the matter is somewhat more complicated in view of the fact that a really radical separation between pure theology and pure philosophy is presumably not at all possible.

If I may interrupt you at this point—perhaps it depends upon the philosopher's position? I would probably have to agree with you for a man like Heidegger, even if it is very difficult to differentiate in his thought. Actually he does not speak of God, he speaks more of gods.

It is all the same whether someone wants to speak as a philosopher explicitly of God or gods or of the divine or of a numinous being or anything like that—wherever a philosopher wants to consider philosophically the whole of reality qua whole, he or she cannot get around, and cannot avoid, standing (speaking now theologically) under the influence of God, who wants to communicate himself to humanity. Whether one reflects upon this is quite another question.

The theologian will appeal to Sacred Scripture as God's word; the theologian will work with an understanding of revelation that presupposes a revelation that occurs in history and in space-time. This the philosopher will not do, even when thinking about absolute being, about God, about the ultimate primary ground of all reality. But human nature's most interior movement, which in our philosopher does not perhaps even reach reflective expression but is nonetheless present, is a most interior movement, originating from the God who is communicating himself, as Christians say, in grace. And to that extent, of course, the question can be raised as to whether essentially Aristotle, regardless of his pure philosophy, permits elements to enter into his thought which, without his noticing it, actually originate from the event that I refer to as "God's self-communication to the human person's spirituality."

Perhaps, being a theologian, Father Rahner, you are forced to speak like this. But are you not giving a theological interpretation to a philosophical question that is not absolutely necessary?

Yes, of course that is the case. But, look, even a philosopher, if reasonable, will admit that elements flow into his or her talk, that there are conditions and motives involved that he or she does not expressly reflect upon and perhaps is even unable to reflect upon.

That is correct; then it does not have to be God.

No, it does not have to be God; but on the basis of this fact no one can object a priori to my supposing that this sort of divine inspiration—if I may call it that—is also possible in philosophical language.

Are you not then defining reason in a way that is somewhat overly broad, in view, say, of the great tradition of the European Enlightenment?
Now, to begin with, all modern philosophy from Descartes up to and including German idealism undoubtedly continues to be a philosophy that is concerned with God.

But then the great deterioration begins!
And does that then still hold true for Heidegger?

In the case of Heidegger it no longer holds true; he returns to quite old traditions.
But then we already have a dispute among the philosophers themselves as to which of the many philosophical languages best measures up to the demands of the subject matter. And of course I am going to join sides with the theologizing philosophers and say: Your dynamic of an absolute transcendentality toward absolute being is in truth already radicalized toward the immediacy of God, whether or not you reflect upon it; and for that reason your language always virtually contains—even if you do not know it and do not reflect upon it—a slight overstepping of the border into the properly theological realm.

Perhaps we may employ another parallel as a point of departure. I recall the sermons of Buddha, which I would not absolutely consider to belong to the realm of theology, for in strict Buddhism God does not play such a role. It could be said that Buddha is a metaphysician who preaches metaphysics. His preaching is a valid form of philosophical speaking, it seems to me, just like the tractate or also the discourse or the critique or the like have also become valid forms of philosophical speaking; maybe even the essay, which Montaigne wrote. Theology with all its forms has perhaps evolved more richly; I recall to mind apologetic speaking, catechetic, liturgical, prayerful speaking. Yes, does prayerful speaking belong to theology; is that not a kind of religious speaking?
Of course I can and must distinguish between a religious language and a truly scholarly theological language; but they both condition each other reciprocally; both languages can never occur unmixed in absolute purity, for in every intelligent, genuine theological reflection there is included, to be sure, an ultimate impetus, an ultimate yearning, an ultimate will in the religious person; otherwise, theology, even as scholarly reflection, dissolves.

There probably have been times when this danger ...

Surely, there have been times, beginning with scholasticism and extending on into the present, when this became rather the case; but it is also the case vice versa that in the religious language of a hymn, or a prayer, or doxology an element of reflection necessarily always occurs, in other words, an element of true theology.

In proportion to the capacity to reflect of the person praying?

To be sure, it can have different degrees, but it can never be completely absent, for even the most immediate, unreflected religious language pays attention, in a sort of accompanying phenomenon, to whether it is correct, whether it remains within the required limits, whether it can reach the other person to whom it is directed, and so on. In other words, even the most immediate religious language always remains a language that is accompanied by a certain element of reflection, and for this reason one is unable to separate these two things, theological language and religious language, from each other absolutely; they condition each other reciprocally, without, for this reason, simply coinciding.

Let us speak once again about philosophy, and in particular about the great attacks directed by philosophers of our century against the language of theology, against religious or even theological statements. Naturally, I am thinking first of all of the Vienna Circle, that is, of a logical positivism, a Wittgenstein, who was very strict, who permitted one language only, namely, the language of logic, a point perhaps that at the time was ahead of the narrow-minded positivists of the Vienna Circle. I believe that even the young Wittgenstein was more careful than, say, Carnap. If one reads his tractate-diaries, that will probably become clear. But at that time a criterion for meaningful statements was being demanded, so that they could be verified, and this criterion for meaningfulness was seen in empirical verification. That was really the first great attack, on the basis of which, that is, on the basis of this hypothesis, the attempt was then made to eliminate something like religious, theological statements, as well as metaphysical statements in philosophy, to dismiss them as wrong, false, meaningless.

On this point, we as theologians find ourselves naturally in good company with traditional metaphysics and with a metaphysics that is raising its voice again today in the wake of this positivism, even in America. And my opinion is that it goes without saying that to begin with I can propose the sentence: Meaningful sentences should be verifiable.

Or as Popper later corrected it: falsifiable.

Good. But then the question would still be: Can this sentence, which I do not now want to call in question, be verified or falsified in the manner required? And then I would say that it would not be possible. In other words, the thinking of thought has other laws and other legitimations than purely empirical verification or falsification, which is what is demanded by this positivism. I can also say that the language of love, the language of ethics, and so on, are in fact languages that establish their own legitimation absolutely and prove their own worth themselves, and that cannot really be verified in the positivistic manner of the Vienna Circle or perhaps of the young Wittgenstein as well.

They were always speaking of scientific sentences; nobody ever disavowed the right of lovers to express sentences or disavowed the right of people who hate one another to hurl accusations against one another.

But along with that they elevated science to the highest norm, nonetheless, as the final, unsurpassable court of appeals for every kind of speaking, and that is nonsensical. The natural scientist can speak about empirical objects with this method of verification, but about the essence of natural science, about the meaningfulness of carrying on science, about himself or herself as the responsible human being carrying on science he or she is unable to speak in the manner of natural science. At that point this language simply comes to an end, and it is revealed to be a regional language. There exists a language that does go just beyond that and has the courage to talk about reality as a whole, in spite of the fact that as a particular instance we ourselves acknowledge within our own radius only this reality. Speaking *above* the real as one and whole is for us, philosophically and theologically, impossible.

Of course you know as well as I do, Father Rahner, that individuals who have said something like that have become traitors in their own camp. Bertrand Russell, whenever he wrote about culture, morality, and the like, did not pay the slightest attention to what he had previously said in regard to scientific sentences. In any case, Wittgenstein (we shall probably come to that later) became disloyal. But in a quite different and fundamental way Whitehead, who together with Russell published the Principia Mathematica, *in his own philosophizing spoke a metaphysical language that actually should have been forbidden to him by his own position.*

Yes, that is surely unavoidable.

Presumably. It has never been admitted. Whitehead does not admit it, Russell does not admit it, whereas Wittgenstein does admit it.

Yes, he is more likely to admit it, at least in his later writings. It is also unavoidable; when one person says to the other, "I love you," then I would just like to know how, without destroying the meaning of this sentence, this simple and unavoidable sentence, how one can reduce it to an empirical (in the sense of natural science) and verifiable language. That does not work.

Maybe it does work. But a great deal is lost, the essential is lost, the main thing, love, is lost.

But, Father Rahner, as a result of these heavy attacks by the early logical positivists something has indeed happened, namely, some theologians went so far as to search for a new verification method for theology. And it was believed to have been found in the so-called eschatological verification. That is a very strange theory indeed.

To tell you the truth, that is somewhat beyond me. It goes without saying that I can modify and extend the notion of verification so that it can also be applied to theological statements. Why not?

But if I shift everything that involves some content into the afterlife, then surely I am actually contradicting what was earlier....

Yes, I would maintain that it is not a matter of whether this verification method is necessarily the only one possible; there exist very many other possibilities to overcome modern positivism right at its very foundational principles and to develop a verification method for theology, which works with the use of the conception and language of present-day Anglo-Saxon epistemology on the one hand, and, nonetheless, attempts to establish a justification for theology on the other. My pupils in Münster, Helmut Peukert and Kuno Füssel, for example, have certainly made attempts of this kind. The argumentation and the method of so-called political theology are also an attempt to demonstrate the meaningfulness and justification of theology from the perspective of the question of sociopolitical and sociocritical relevancy. If I were to say that without Christian theology I would really be abandoning and betraying those killed in Auschwitz, I would be abandoning the past in favor of a utopian future (something I am not permitted to do), and so on: If I say remembering the dead belongs essentially to human existence, and if I then say in addition that all that is from the outset basically theology, then in a certain sense I have also really suggested and at least indicated a verification process for theology. And naturally the scholarship and meaningfulness of theology does not lie in certain methodological presuppositions.

Translated by William Hoye
University of Münster, Germany

52 · Interdisciplinary Dialogue and the Language of Theology

Interview with Joachim Schickel of North-German Radio (NDR), Hamburg (November 22, 1981)

The philosophers of "ordinary language" at Oxford and Cambridge as well as in the United States, working in Wittgenstein's wake, appear to be more open now toward religious language.

Modern philosophers, linguistic philosophers, are currently studying the existent languages and posing questions not in regard to their justification, but rather in respect to their use.

Of course, on this point I am of the opinion that—remaining within the sector of pure linguistic philosophy—I can justify neither the language itself nor theology. When I ask why it is that language expresses something meaningful, then of course I can put what I am now thinking into language, but the fact remains that I am expressing something that is not simply identical with language as such. I would like to put it this way: Language is always simultaneously the language of something distinct from the language itself and is not contained in it. And to this extent, of course, I can also justify theology, I believe, even at the level of an intelligent linguistic philosophy. And if they say that these languages exist and I have no choice but to recognize the fact of their existence— yes, why then do linguistic philosophers speak of a mere reprieve granted to us poor theologians?

It's not originally linguistic philosophers who speak of it; it's a theologian who does that.

Granted, but then that is a theologian who has himself been infected by this Anglo-Saxon positivism.

That seems to be just as much the case with him as it is with many other theologians; at any rate, they are surely flirting with many of the basic principles of this positivism!

This phenomenon of a theology betraying itself and permitting itself to be slain, as it were, by an external opponent is simply a matter of course. I mean, what theologian does not have to expect in his or her theology qua theology that there are people who fundamentally challenge his or her theology and the meaningfulness of its statements? It stands to reason that there exist more philosophies than merely those that are compatible with a Christian theology; and there exist theologies that want to eliminate themselves, as it were; in a certain sense, these two facts no longer upset me. It stands to reason that something like this exists and must exist. Of course, as a theologian I then have to reflect once more upon how I in a world that is contained and supported and willed by him whom I call God, how in such a world something like that can exist. Atheism is not just the denial of theology, it is also an object of theology, to which theology has to devote some positive thought. In the past maybe it did too little of that or simply presumed, with too little afterthought, that anything like atheism cannot exist in a meaningful way.

But surely it is nothing new in itself that theologians permit themselves to be affected, infected by extratheological approaches and thus expose themselves to danger.

Yes, to reinforce my health, after all, I have to let myself be infected—as in the case of a vaccination—but theology itself doesn't have to let itself be called in question. Theology will always be contested, called in question in its language and in its substance; but it will never, at any rate that is my conviction, be that which in an historical process will someday have totally come to an end.

Now theology has surely assimilated impulses from another important philosophy, perhaps the most important philosophy of the present century, from Heidegger. You were really very strongly impressed, I believe, in many regards by Heidegger (as was Bultmann). Has not a great deal been set into motion through Heidegger, including what involves the language of theology?

Now that you bring this up explicitly then naturally I have to say that I sat in on Heidegger's seminar for two years, that even later on not all contact was terminated. I would also say that I am indebted to Heidegger for whatever little bit of philosophy is contained in my theology; but whether, becoming specific, the truly theological subject matter and work is so very much influenced by Heidegger and dependent upon him I really have to doubt. Of course it is the case that in what he calls "demythologizing" Bultmann explicitly demanded that through it the true intention of Christianity and its biblical message can be expressed, can be better expressed, and therefore today must be thus expressed; this is acceptable up to a certain point. But the question, of course, is what is existial philosophy, what categories are therewith given and what categories are therewith abolished. All of these are surely questions with regard to which no uniform notion of existential philosophy can be presupposed, and to that extent, of course, the thesis that theology should and must express itself in accordance with existential philosophy is a rather inexact and unclear matter.

Without hesitation one can always pose the question: In which specific existential philosophy does it have to express itself? Heidegger himself was, of course, convinced that after the pre-Socratics from Plato on up to and including German idealism a philosophy was being carried on that was based on an ultimate misunderstanding of being. I cannot share this opinion. I consider it false; and to this extent, of course, the question as to which language is employed in theology is more a question of historical relativity as well. One necessarily talks in the language of one's time. But perhaps it is also a question, to a certain degree, of free choice, and it is certainly a question that cannot at all be answered solely in favor of a quite specific philosophy. I feel thoroughly at home with Thomas Aquinas and hence. . . .

. . . And hence with Aristotle as well?
With Aristotle as well; and on the other hand, I have no inhibitions whatsoever about following Heidegger's thought in some respects. Hence, I refuse to be condemned as a theologian to being subject exclusively to a completely determined philosophical system.

It probably cannot be denied—the influence that Heidegger exerts on some theologians demonstrates it—that in his own philosophy he has come close to theological thinking in some matters; for that reason, he is also easily susceptible to exploitation by a few theologians.
Heidegger did begin as a theologian. Furthermore, he always worked on Kierkegaard and never got quite free, if it can be put like that, of his theological Christian past. That is not an objection against him, but simply what goes without saying in a philosopher who thinks deeply and radically; but then he never did want to express it clearly. Heidegger spoke in a language that, in part, can also be employed just as well in a theology.

But perhaps the reason is his metaphysical phraseology, which is very strongly conditioned by antiquity and sometimes also by scholasticism.
He once worked on a medieval philosopher, whom he confused with Duns Scotus (that was not his fault). But thanks to this work he always had some added understanding of Christian metaphysics and theology. He always regretted (I know this for a fact) that Christian theologians, especially Catholic ones, did not show enough interest in entering into discussion with him.

In contrast to scientists, like Weizsäcker, for example.
In contrast to some scientists, in contrast to some theologians outside of Europe. Zen Buddhism in Japan is almost more interested in Heidegger than the usual Christian theologians. To a certain degree that is regrettable, but of

course it will always remain the case that Christian theologians, as long as they desire to be theologians of the Church, will never be able to detach themselves absolutely from their past. They cannot behave as though they were to make an absolutely new beginning; repeatedly, they will feel necessarily and justifiably called upon to talk in the language of the Church tradition. And they should also like doing that. Hence, they cannot embrace, such as it is, the tendency that is noticeable in Heidegger of saying everything in a way different from the way it has thus far been done, and, moreover, they do not even desire to do this.

We neglected earlier, when we were speaking of the differences between theology and philosophy, to say expressly that a theology—including a theology à la Schleiermacher and even more so one à la Barth—quite desires to be an ecclesial theology, meaning the scholarly reflection upon the previously given faith of the community, of the Church, as well as, if you will, speaking as a Catholic, of the Church's teaching office. For that reason, then, it also has a connection with the language of the past, which a modern philosopher proudly ignores.

You mentioned Bultmann and Barth; they have both clearly followed quite different paths, as far as language and theology is concerned.

Barth wrote a church dogmatics, in which he begins first of all by coming to terms with Scripture as an absolutely unquestionable norm and then goes on to do the same with church teaching—regardless of whether it is a question of the Middle Ages or Calvin or Luther. Barth, therefore, more than Bultmann, used a language that in some way or other was already being practiced by the Church. Whether that prevented him from saying the most real and ultimate of what is at all capable of being said or whether that can indeed be accomplished in this language, that is to be sure, once again, quite another question.

Bultmann had the impression that the Church, including the New Testament, is speaking in a mythological language that is no longer really understood, such as it is, and for this reason one has to explain what is really meant by it. He was of the opinion that what has to be said as the real meaning could be examined with the help of modern existential philosophy.

Of course, the two of them were involved in terrible arguments and bitter confrontations with each other. The truth may well be that not only is the controversy between them passé but also that they simply overestimated their differences.

In the literature there are also allusions to that; it really is a fundamental problem how it is possible for a human being to be able to speak or to echo God's word in his or her natural language. Barth considers it possible only by way of grace, an act of grace stemming from God. In Bultmann that seems to work in a completely different way; here human beings do not need this act of grace.

Perhaps for Barth, in contrast to Bultmann—but I do not want to make such an apodictic assertion on that now—the word of Scripture was the word of God that bound him absolutely. I believe that a Christian theologian should not deny this sentence and may not deny it, but it is a tremendously difficult question how a sentence like that can be made more precisely understandable in its meaning and in the nature of its content. With Barth it was the case that he went so far as to emphasize something like an absolute power of faith, in comparison to which rational considerations would actually have nothing more to say, whereas I think both of these, metaphysics and theology, could be brought to a more positive, more reconciled relationship in a strict, genuine sense.

That would certainly also correspond to the tradition?

That would also correspond to the tradition, because genuine Christian theology never really had such fear of rational legitimation in the way it announces itself in Barth. Maybe in Bultmann's case, on the other hand, it is just the opposite, and philosophy is, in spite of everything, too powerful in his thought. But the extent to which a theology can come solely from above and the extent to which it can also come from below (that too would then be relevant for the understanding and interpretation of theological language)—this is a controversy between Brunner and Barth and also between Barth and Bultmann. With that I return again to what I was saying: Covertly and unreflectively, philosophical language is ipso facto highly charged theologically. . . .

It can be charged in this sense, but must it be so?

Ultimately, that is simply not within the control of the persons speaking, even if they believe that for themselves and in their reflection nothing more is to be found in their language than what they *reflectively* regard as, and accept as, content.

I mean, every human language contains willy-nilly more within itself than the person speaking explicitly realizes in a reflective manner. When a Tirolian farm boy says ''I love you'' to his girl friend, and you ask him what he means by that, then maybe something quite stupid, something quite inadequate or quite false emerges in his reflection, occurring subsequently; but with this sentence he has nonetheless said something that goes immensely far beyond his reflection and nevertheless is contained in this language. And of course, something like that also occurs with philosophers in regard to theology.

Certainly. But essentially it is not our topic to discuss the fact that philosophy is charged with theology. That is altogether possible, but I believe that there are philosophers with whom you could perhaps show that philosophical thinking does not move very far in the theological direction. But you mentioned earlier the problematic of philosophy and theology in Karl Barth; now it is probably in connection with this that he dismisses the analogy of being, the analogia entis . . .

He dismissed that at an earlier time during his Münster and Bonn period; I believe that later on he did not do so any more. At that time, naturally, he branded the analogy of being as the devil's own invention, because he was of the opinion that by means of the analogy of being the thinking, speaking, theologizing, and philosophizing person would be, as it were, getting a hold on God, rendering this object subservient; and thus theology would be transformed through the backdoor into essentially a human tour de force. In reality, however, a correct understanding of the analogy of being consists precisely in the fact that human concepts are all essentially open to the mystery which is no longer comprehensible and which for us is decidedly incapable of being reduced to subservience, being at one and the same time the *ens realissimum* (the most real being) and the absolute mystery, which we then call God.

Father Rahner, let us spend some time with analogous speaking as one of theology's great traditional modes of speech.

Naturally, I would say that wherever this analogous openness of human concepts and statements toward the incomprehensible mystery is seriously denied philosophy and theology cease to be themselves. From then on one can speak only of individual beings within this infinite horizon, but no longer about the horizon itself. One will be able to speak of conditioned things and no longer of the condition of all reality in God, which remains incomprehensible for us and no longer susceptible to further questioning. And in my opinion, that would result precisely in the changing of philosophy back, perhaps, into a subsequent reflection upon scientific methods, upon a pure philosophy of science, which then, essentially speaking, does not really make any more progress. And that would imply theology's own utter self-annulment. No, analogous language is the primary condition for the very existence of something like theology at all; for it speaks of God, and it can of course speak of God only analogously. That is, it always says something (to express it quite simply for once) with the consciousness that what is really being meant is not encompassed in this statement, but instead must be left unmastered by us. To this extent it is clear, of course, that theology always remains essentially the science of human beings—just as religious talk in the true sense occurs on the border of silence.

But that is just as valid for philosophy, I would think, which is also by essence dependent upon analogous speaking about being.

Exactly. I believe that when Wittgenstein says that one should not speak about that about which one cannot speak clearly, then with this statement, no doubt, he has virtually spoken once more about something, and, furthermore, he had no choice but to speak. It is true what Augustine said at the beginning of the *Confessions*: "Woe to him who would simply be silent in regard to that about which one cannot speak clearly and univocally!" No, the belief in the legitimate existence of such a language, which by its very speaking, as it were, renders itself mute, is the fundamental presupposition for philosophy and theology.

And nonetheless there remains indeed a difference between the two.
Certainly, yes.

Even in the act of speaking, even in analogous speaking?
Yes, even in the case of analogous speaking, because theology (at the scholarly level) presupposes as such the analogous speaking of Jesus' Church, of the prophets, of revelation in general as God's valid word, and reflects upon it, whereas the philosopher naturally does not admit this presupposition and is not required to; but he is also not permitted to deny its instrinsic justification, at any rate insofar as he is a Christian philosopher or theologian.

Translated by William Hoye
University of Münster, Germany

53 · Aggiornamento Is Not Finished

Interview with Gerhard Ruis for *Süddeutsche Zeitung*,
Munich (January 6, 1982)

Pope John Paul II has named the archbishop of Munich and Freising, Joseph Car-
dinal Ratzinger, the new prefect of the Roman Congregation of the Faith. Cardinal
Ratzinger thereby becomes, after the pope, the most important authority of the Catholic
hierarchy in all questions of faith and morals. As theological advisor to Cologne's
Cardinal Frings, Ratzinger was among the progressive theologians at Vatican II.
He worked together with you, Professor Rahner, although you also felt close ties with
the later rebel against Roman magisterial authority, Tübingen theologian Hans
Küng. Wicked tongues say that Ratzinger has gone from a courageous reformer to a
cautious conservative. . . .

Whether the words *reformer* and *conservative* really express anything clear
and exact in the domain of the Church is on principle open to doubt. But prescinding from such a general question, opinions do point, with some justice,
to a certain change in Ratzinger's theology.

At the Council we both worked together almost from the beginning on a
Latin text concerning the revelation of God and of human being in Jesus Christ.
Even though this text soon almost disappeared from conciliar discussion (which
was no great loss), still this small fact itself shows that indeed the two of us
were then a lot closer theologically than we are today.

Cardinal Ratzinger himself clearly indicates, in the foreword to his eschatology, this "turn" in his theology. On the other hand, one must not exaggerate
this change in Cardinal Ratzinger; otherwise, he would not have been able, for
example, to speak so positively on the whole about my *Foundations*, as he
recently has.

And ultimately, after all, all theologians have the right to revise their opinions,
whether that brings them closer to or farther away from traditional teachings.
Then the question always remains open whether the earlier or later position is
the correct one.

If you ask me for the reasons behind the pope's appointing Cardinal Ratzinger, actually I know no more than anyone could pick up from the news-
papers. The Congregation of the Faith needs a cardinal as its head, and a cardinal
he is. The congregation needs a theologian as its head; Ratzinger is certainly
an important, well-informed theologian with significant publications.

I don't know whether anyone has ever stood at the head of this congregation who had better credentials within the area of academic theology. Cardinal Ratzinger also enjoys, thanks to several meetings with John Paul II, his personal *sympathie*, which also has surely contributed to his appointment.

As a theologian Cardinal Ratzinger seems to have distanced himself from you. Now he says that through thoughtless conversations with modern ideas the Church, by adapting to the world (aggiornamento), has not won followers but rather is more in danger of losing itself. Do you share this view?

Some things about the second question I have already answered when dealing with the first. I myself feel that he correctly sees many a danger and defect in the Church, which became clearer after the Council, but that the aggiornamento that began in the Church with the Council is still not nearly finished. And obviously this situation cannot simply be repaired by a return to what was good at one time in the Church and in theology.

The undesirable dangers of our contemporary situation in the Church cannot be met with a sterile conservatism. The norm of correct adaptation is of course not just any current opinion, but rather is that radical understanding of the gospel from which not just the usual modern notion but also the traditional practice and mentality of the Church are far removed. Whether Cardinal Ratzinger himself will act merely restoratively in his new ministry—to prophesy that or to fear it do not fall within my competence.

Along with the Polish pope Cardinal Ratzinger links the Christocentricism of faith and theologizing. It is from here that he gets to his position against Western consumerism as well as Eastern Marxism. He contrasts this with the "culture of intuition and of the heart." What do you think about that?

If he really must label his goal as "the culture of intuition and of the heart," then that is his right. Whether his task as prefect of the Congregation of the Faith can be encompassed with this description is another question for me, especially since everyone will admit that "intuition" and "heart" are very ambiguous concepts and Cardinal Ratzinger certainly cannot be tied down to a popular understanding of these words.

Obviously, the truth of revelation, which the Congregation of the Faith must protect if it really be in accord with its own preaching must also be a thing of the heart and contain an element of unanalyzable "intuition." But Cardinal Ratzinger's new task cannot be described with these two words alone. I don't believe he meant to do so.

Pope John Paul II has expressed the wish that the new prefect of the Roman Congregation of the Faith not understand his ministry to be "defensive" only but rather to strive to be "positively stimulating." Do you think this speaks to your wish that the relation between the Roman teaching office and the theologians always be rather vague?

This description of the task of the Congregation of the Faith points to a difficult problem. I thoroughly agree with the pope and Cardinal Ratzinger if they mean that the Congregation of the Faith should not only censure, condemn, and work defensively, but instead should seek to be much more "positively stimulating."

But now, just when an important professional theologian takes up the leadership of the Congregation of the Faith, one needs perhaps even to underscore the caution that such a head of the congregation must obviously guard against bringing his own personal position into the decisions and measures taken by the congregation. The task of theology remains different from that of the Congregation of the Faith and should not be confused with it.

Given this presupposition one can indeed say: In the future the Congregation of the Faith should make its contribution to a dialogue with the theology of our time and especially with the intellectual and spiritual currents of the present, so that the message of the gospel and of the Church can reach today's world intelligibly and convincingly.

According to the view of the new prefect of the Congregation of the Faith the great epoch of theology was before Vatican II. Shortly thereafter if was lost because of a certain fatigue. At the moment there are hardly any more great names. To be sure, there are more faculties and more writers. But along with that there is still an inner weariness, a growing mediocrity, and the problem of people going their separate ways. This seems basically one messy situation. . . .

For me it's interesting to hear how you say Cardinal Ratzinger characterizes the contemporary situation of theology. I wish it were not the case but I have no objection against it. Though why this contemporary situation of theology should be "one messy situation" I don't understand. I would rather say that this situation is a fact that is as understandable as the change of seasons; what one needs to ask is whether in the Church, even if its history and that of theology cannot be directed in isolation or autonomously, something can be done so that theology can flourish again.

That with its new expanses the Church as world-Church needs to and should seek to make its own theological impression, with a good unity in theology, is a view of Cardinal Ratzinger with which I fully agree. I would not say that the Congregation of the Faith has up to now clearly and practically done justice to this intention. So I can only hope that now it will do better in this regard.

According to Cardinal Ratzinger's recent view theology needs its space of freedom. The limits are, of course, there where theology so interferes with church life that it would be a concrete threat to unity. Have I understood you correctly that theology has the right and sometimes even the duty to contradict an interpretation of the teaching office?

Obviously theology needs an area of freedom. No doubt theology's free space was often unduly restricted in the years of the "Pian era" (as I would name the era of Pius IX to Pius XII). Naturally, there are limits to its range of freedom wherever theology denies head on and decisively a defined truth of church faith.

Of course it can also happen, which is again and again something ever to be avoided, that a church authority asserts that a theological view is incompatible with a dogma of the Church where, in fact, such is not the case at all. Within the free space of theology there is room for differing opinions. An opinion within this free space should not be censured by a church authority who personally considers it false.

Translated by Andrew Tallon
Marquette University

54 · The Courage to Make Decisions

Interview with Norbert Steidl for *Kirche, Wochenblatt der Diözese Innsbruck*, Innsbruck (January 24, 1982)

Professor Rahner, is there anything you would like to say to young people?[1]
First, young persons today should not give in to the temptation to become crudely skeptical or, more basically, to resign themselves timidly to their fate.

1. See Karl Rahner, *Is Christian Life Possible Today?* (Denville, New Jersey: Dimensions, 1984). This volume contains letters from young people to Rahner about their problems and Rahner's instructive replies.

They should truly set a goal in life for themselves, regardless of what this might be. They should be committed to something. They should have the courage to resist falling prey too easily to the comforts of life offered in a consumer society. In my opinion as a Christian, priest, Jesuit, and old man, a young person should also be asking the question about life's ultimate meaning; and he or she shouldn't try to pretend that the answer to this all-encompassing question is just a helpless shrug of the shoulders.

A young person should clearly realize that postponing a reply or being skeptical about a reply is itself an answer to the question of life's meaning—and a bad answer, at that! There are people who think that everything is so terribly uncertain and who state that humans basically know nothing for sure, so that we simply have to resign ourselves to our fate without a decisive opinion on anything. But this view itself is an opinion, and it is by no means self-evident that it is the right one. Whoever claims that we know nothing for sure is expressing an opinion that is just one among many; and this abstention from decision-making is not really an abstention but is, in fact, itself a decision. Accordingly, we should at least find the courage to make decisions of our own about something and to keep our minds on it, rather than be helpless or skeptical when faced with problems. I think that a young person today can do this, in spite of all the confusion over world views and in spite of the undeniable uncertainty of contemporary life.

Isn't part of the answer for young people today an ability to let oneself be really "fascinated" by things?
You know, I really believe that in the old days people could more easily become enthusiastic and excited about something, whether one's homeland or some cause or a political trend or even some religious community or church.

In those days, people could be uninhibited in their enthusiasm. But this is hard for us today—whether for you or for me, an old man. We shouldn't however try to solve this puzzle by forcing some sort of tearful enthusiasm on people. Many modern youth movements seem to me to be a flight into some kind of emotionalism that's basically inauthentic. It's possible for people to be decisive and truly committed to something, yet remain cool and not overly emotional. As a Christian I don't have to get horribly excited about every bishop or every pope. This really has nothing to do with Christianity, so why bother? Nor do I have to find everything wonderful and exciting in some group, even the Church. In spite of this, I'm still able to be decisive with a down-to-earth sobriety: decisive about Jesus Christ, about God, about holding firm to a conviction regarding an eternal responsibility to the eternal God, and about eternal life. In such matters, we don't have to get horribly excited and gush forth with tears of emotion; rather, we can `say to ourselves: In my unique situation, this is the decision that is possible for me and meaningful to me —a decision that I can carry through with patience, confidence, and decisiveness in spite of the wintery era we live in.

Translated by Michael C. O'Callaghan
Marist College, Poughkeepsie, New York

55 · The Election of Bishops Today

Interview with the *KSÖ Nachrichten und Stellungnahmen der Katholischen Sozialakademie Österreichs*, Vienna (February 6, 1982)

What are the possible ways of electing bishops according to the dogmatic principles of the Roman Catholic Church?
From a dogmatic standpoint one can say that there are a number of ways of appointing bishops, if the nominated, elected, and appointed bishop receives his post through the approval of the entire episcopate as represented by the Roman Pontiff. In other words, from a strictly dogmatic position, various ways are possible under certain conditions, and these are also indicated in the decrees of Vatican II.

In effect, therefore, a bishop could be elected by all the people in the diocese, the priests in the diocese, a cathedral chapter, or by a priests' senate. He could also be elected by neighboring bishops, through a bishops' conference, or even by the Roman Pontiff. Thus, from a dogmatic standpoint as well as the very nature of the Church, a direct appointment by the pope is not the only method of election.

This is supported by the declaration in *Lumen Gentium*, the Dogmatic Constitution on the Church of Vatican II, no. 21:

This Holy Synod teaches that by episcopal consecration the fullness of the sacrament of Orders is conferred . . . the episcopal consecration, together with the office of sanctifying (i.e., with the full sacramental powers), *also* confers the offices of teaching and *governing*. These, however, of their very nature, can be exercised only in hierarchical communion with the Head and members of the College. . . . It (therefore) devolves on the bishops to admit newly elected members into the episcopal body by means of the Sacrament of Orders.

What is desirable?

One would have to say that the nomination, election, and appointment of a bishop must take place in such a manner that the qualifications of the person appointed to administer the episcopal office, possess the necessary ability, and the confidence of his diocese, especially of his fellow-priests. These conditions can be examined from a variety of angles, and this happens wherever and in whatever way a bishop is elected today in our countries. Obviously, one can assume that when a bishop is nominated from Austria, Rome seeks to determine whether the conditions for the appointment are fulfilled. Whether this always happens in practice is a question that can be asked over and over again. In Austria, therefore, the process is one in which the qualifications of the candidate are usually reviewed in secret. One should not forget that the reasons for this anonymity stem from the very nature of the situation itself.

For example, a bishop must possess qualities with respect to his past life, education, and experience which do not easily lend themselves to public review. In so far as this is true, one cannot simply dismiss the traditional method. However, it would certainly be desirable to solicit the cooperation of those affected by the appointment, that is, the representatives of the diocese, especially the priests and others serving in official positions. They should be permitted to participate fully in the process of the episcopal search. This is not only consonant with today's democratic processes, but this would also offer the bishop the greatest measure of trust, willingness to cooperate, and so on, from the diocese in order to be successful. It is, therefore, desirable that, to an appropriate extent, the diocese itself be permitted to participate in the search for a suitable candidate.

How this happens—or can happen—is, naturally, a question that is not easily answered. But there are priests' councils, cathedral chapters, committees, and individuals who could contribute in a practical way toward the search for such a candidate, which to a certain extent does happen today. Bishops' conferences, perhaps the ordinary of a diocese, and even priests' councils (unfortunately this seems to have fallen out of practice), do offer Rome recommendations. Then, with the cooperation of the papal nuncio, Rome selects the candidate it deems most acceptable. However, the preparatory procedures could probably be conducted in a simpler and more public manner.

What is practical?

This question can naturally be divided into the following: How should a prospective episcopal nomination be juridically established? What is in fact practical under the present legal norms? We have already attempted to answer the first question elsewhere. The second question can possibly be answered as follows: If, in the search for a suitable candidate, the priests' council would be more significantly and publicly invited to participate, and Rome would evaluate its recommendations in a more satisfactory way and not lightly shove them aside, then, under the present legal norms, bishops could be found who, with respect to their human qualities, their spirituality, and their pastoral experience, are suitable. Moreover, they would be extended the greatest measure of trust and cooperation from the diocese and the priests. Under the present laws, therefore, one can certainly find the best candidates. The only assumption is that the present laws be observed, and the present norms be actually and fairly applied. With this observation I do not mean to say that although the present procedures may conceivably be the best, there are not other, perhaps more democratic, procedures that should be acknowledged and tried. In conclusion, it should be repeated: That every Roman Catholic bishop requires the approval of the pope in Rome is not to say that such episcopal appointments must be undertaken simply and solely through Roman channels.

In this connection one can naturally expect a change in the future only if the Roman officials and the bishops in their own countries are informed and influenced by the environment of an open society to such a degree that, of their own accord, they would look into the possibilities for making legitimate changes.

Translated by Richard W. Rolfs, S.J.
Loyola Marymount University, Los Angeles

56 · Theological Thinking and Religious Experience

Interview with Rogelio García-Mateo and Peter Kammerer
for *Entschluss*, Innsbruck (1982)

*Professor Rahner, in contrast with the religious movements of our time the image
presented by contemporary theology is one of weakness and diffusion. There is even
talk of a standstill in theology. It is not clear even to professional theologians how
theology should proceed. You have often been concerned in your theological work with
the question of theology's understanding of itself. So what job does theology have today as science and as preaching?*

I suppose that it has the same job today as always. As a science theology is a
reflection upon revealed Christian faith, which has been undertaken with scientific means and methods. This reflection stands in the service of the Church
so that it can fulfill its job of preaching that reaches, as well as it can, the
understanding of the contemporary person. Of course, to the extent that the
situation of preaching is other than before, the job of theology is somewhat
changed despite all its unchanging nature. Today the Church lives in a pluralistic society, and it has a worldwide job; it has become in the course of the last
century a world-Church. Consequently, theology has the job of a dialogue
with the contemporary person's understanding of self and world; that means
an interdisciplinary dialogue with the contemporary sciences as well. Beyond
that it has the job of being a worldwide theology, that is, not only a theology
suited to European and North American cultures, but it must develop theologies of the different cultures and situations in the world. At least it must develop
a Latin American, East Asian, and African theology. That also means, of
course, that contemporary theology must be a theology that itself develops as
well as accepts the modern scientific methods and the results coming from them.

What concrete consequences follow from this?

There must be a historical-critical exegesis, and honest and genuine history
of dogma, and a dialogue with the modern sciences. In present-day theology a
single neoscholastic philosophy simply cannot be at the basis, such as had been
developed in the nineteenth and the first half of the twentieth century. Rather,
a philosophy has to include a really genuine dialogue with modern philosophies,
namely, Kant, Descartes, German idealism, modern existentialism, but beyond
that also with modern logic, with contemporary linguistic philosophy, and with
all the philosophies that have been developed in the Anglo-American world.

What does that mean for philosophy done by Catholics?

Modern Catholic philosophy, which represents an inner moment of the Christian, ecclesial theology, should not try to be modern indiscriminately and in a false sense. It should preserve its independence; it should be a philosophy with which a convinced Christian can really live. Still it can no longer be the homogeneous philosophy of the neoscholasticism of the last 150 years—simply because the problems, the methods, and even in part the results have changed. Today there is, for example, a modern theory of science which has an importance for philosophy as well. Earlier there was either no such thing at all in scholastic thought or only in minute beginnings. Today it exists, and consequently present-day theology cannot ignore all these things.

What role do the other great world religions play in this?

Dialogue with the present-day or still surviving world religions ought to be a major area of modern theology. The Second Vatican Council marked a considerable change of attitude in the relation of the Church to the other world religions. Hinduism, Buddhism, and Islam cannot be considered simply as human inventions that have gone bad or as a deterioration of human religiosity that has to be judged merely negatively. But how they are to be more exactly interpreted, what can be learned from them, what differences and what common characteristics there may be already existing—all that has to be investigated much better so that there really can be a dialogue of Christianity with the other world religions.

In your doctrine of God the human person plays a fundamental role as the being of transcendence to the world and to the infinite. Is there not the danger of ultimately speaking only about the human person? Does not the central position of the human person bespeak an anthropological diminution of the theological? Your theology has been described as anthropologically oriented.

There is, first of all, the question whether such a description of my theology is correct. It has received such a characterization. However, in the first place, I do not want to develop a special theology all my own. Any such thing for a Catholic theologian would be nonsense from the start. I want to develop an entirely normal Catholic Christian theology that deals with problems which perhaps had not existed so explicitly before. But I want a normal Catholic theology without ambitions for a special originality all my own.

But does not anthropology have a central importance in your theology?

The fact that the human person appears in a theology, that there is a theological anthropology, and that, furthermore, in a certain sense theology must always begin with the human person, seems to me to be self-evident. It was precisely the neoscholastic theology of the nineteenth century that always stressed the rationality of faith against radical fideism as well as against Protestant theology. It had postulated that there is and must be a genuine, rational fundamental theology that starts from the person and the person's questions. Today such a fundamental theology must, of course, stand in a closer reciprocal relationship to systematic theology. If there is at all such a fundamental theology as a true, inner moment of dogmatic theology, then in a true sense the human person is obviously the starting point. Even if the supernatural, divine origin of the genuinely Christian revealed theology is stressed radically in the style of a Karl Barth, it still remains true for Catholic theology that it must reflect upon the human person as the receiver of divine revelation.

How far this receiver of divine revelation is made fit for it only by revelation and by grace itself may well be an important question that is not so easily answered. In any case, theology has to talk about the human person who is a potential hearer of the word by nature, but all the more so by grace and the historical event of divine revelation. In other words, a theological anthropology has to be done. Besides, if the human person is understood from the start as radically related to God in nature and grace and cannot be thought without this relationship, then an anthropocentric and a theocentric theology is no contradiction or inconsistency but ultimately the same thing: a unity, in which neither God nor the human person can be left out. If it is, moreover, true, that God became flesh and remains so for eternity, then there can be no theology in which anthropology need not be done, since in the Incarnation God himself did anthropology for himself and does anthropology for all eternity. This is the sort of thing that I have always wanted to do to a certain extent in my reflections, but I don't see why such a starting point, which is quite obvious for Catholic theology, is now supposed to be a special peculiarity of my theology.

How can specific focal points emerge for individual theologians?
The concrete individual theologian obviously will never be able to handle with equal thoroughness every imaginable theological question.

Obviously, there are differences in theological work that have their effects on the results of theology. If someone, for example, has studied the history of Christological dogma and Christology as thoroughly as Alois Grillmeier in Frankfurt, then obviously, when he develops his own systematic theology, his theology will look practically and concretely somewhat different from a theology like mine, since I do not understand so much about matters of the history of dogma. And if an exegete does exegesis in a great, sublime, and laborious work, his or her own theology will inevitably look somewhat different at the very point where another—simply because of the division of human work and the limitations of human capacity for insight and work—cannot do such exegesis. But for me there basically cannot exist a fundamental difference between my theology and another normal Catholic theology.

Where do the focal points of your theological reflection lie?
In contrast with other theologies there may be a certain difference in some particular point or from some particular starting point. I stress, first of all, what is quite typically Catholic, namely, the close connection between grace and revelation. I believe that grace itself already effects a change in the human person's consciousness that has to be appreciated and understood as a beginning, as a start of something like revelation. I am merely referring to what is obvious for a good Thomist, that genuinely supernatural grace gives a formal object befitting the spiritual person in knowledge and freedom—which, as the standard traditional theology of the schools says, cannot be attained by knowledge and freedom that are purely natural in their formal object.

If this thoroughly Thomistic theology of the schools is presupposed and if, moreover, because of the universal salvific will of God, supernatural elevating grace can be offered to every person, then one gets a concept of a fundamental revelation, whose scope in the history of the world and of religion does not simply square with that anthropological and geographical area that we normally consider as the area of positive supernatural revelation. So on this point, of course, I represent a theology that is not that of simply every Catholic theologian, but I think that it is a theology that can be defended and that is also important for the basic conception of the relationship of Christianity to the other religions.

In the sixties religion, meditation, and prayer were more and more shoved into the background—recall the death-of-God theology and the wave of secularization. As a countermovement to this Enlightenment attitude, we are experiencing today a rediscovery of the religious sphere and of meditation. Often a neglect of critical reason or even its rejection has been pointed out in this regard. How do you evaluate this rediscovery of the religious sphere?
That is hard to say. A few years back an American Methodist bishop sat on the chair on which you are seated, and I asked him what he thought of the pentecostal movement. He answered, "Not much!" I replied that others, such as Pope Paul VI or Cardinal Suenens, had a very positive attitude toward charismatic movements. Then the bishop said, "Just wait, this time the pope

has got on the wrong horse." Now I do not think that that is so. Obviously, there are religious and charismatic movements that have to be taken seriously. I have previously said, even if it sounds dramatic and exaggerated, that the Christian of the future has to be a mystic or he or she won't be at all.

Does the religious and mystical then take precedence for you over rational consideration?

For me in my theology the givenness of a genuine, original experience of God and his Spirit is of fundamental importance. This precedes logically (and not necessarily temporally) theological reflection and verbalization and is never adequately overtaken by this reflection.

What Christian faith teaches is never communicated merely by a conceptual indoctrination from without, but is and can basically be experienced through the supernatural grace of God as a reality in us. That does not mean that the linguistic representation and interpretation of the religious experience is not something that has to occur within the Church under the supervision of her magisterium. But I believe, it is true, that an awakening, a mystagogy into this original, grace-filled religious experience is today of fundamental importance. Now there arises, of course, the question of how and where there has been a Christian mystagogy into such an experience that can be called genuine. There are, of course, exercises, courses in and practices of meditation, even from non-Christian religions, that are extraordinarily useful and perhaps even necessary for such an introduction.

It is no longer necessary to think that such mystagogy takes place only in absolute isolation and interiority. The Ignatian Exercises need no longer be viewed as the be all and the end all for accomplishing such a mystagogy.

To what extent can the site of religious experiences be community?

I am convinced that there is a modern flight into the communal that really only runs into emptiness. But it cannot be doubted that there can also be a communal religious experience that up to now has been fostered too little within the modern Church. The Church has always celebrated the liturgy; people have in this liturgy, as a matter of fact, always realized the genuinely personal, inner, and mystical. But one did not explicitly pay much attention to it.

If one is convinced that liturgy, the Office, and the sacrifice of the Mass are not merely external ritualism, which one can perform on the side, but can mean a total religious actualization of the person toward God, then a Catholic Christian cannot deny that there both are and can be the possibility, the ways, and the methods of a communal religious experience. Something of the sort has not really been fostered. However, if charismatic groups recently are trying something of the sort, if Christians are praying in common, if there really can be something like communal deliberation that is more than a common rational testing, pondering, and planning, then there can be no objection if people as Christians live today a charismatic religious life as a community. How that should be done in detail is another question. I, for example, do not think very highly of speaking in tongues, and I think that Paul fundamentally agrees with me, even if he was tolerant of such marginal religious phenomena. I also believe that, in the American charismatic movement with its healing miracles and so on, there has been a tendency toward and a belief in such fringe phenomena—a belief that a sober Western European, now in the age of late rationalism, neither has nor will have nor need have in order to be a radical Christian.

What positive impulses do you see in the charismatic movement?

These charismatic movements as well as their theological self-interpretations must be tested in terms of the different tendencies and goals toward which they move. One has to grant Christians in the European countries a sufficient freedom of the Spirit and of their religious practice. These charismatic groups should not feel that they alone are simply the only true and living Christianity. They should selflessly and humbly recognize other shapes and forms of both common and individual religiosity. But there should be no objection if it should be shown in the further history of the Church that it simply does not have to continue in the same way it has for the last 150 years. If then there are basic communities whose coherence requires certain charismatic preconditions and foundations, there should be no objection to that.

In this matter the official, episcopal side in the Church ought to be broad-minded and ought not to quench the Spirit, but test all and keep what is good, as Paul says; then there is no objection to such a charismatic movement. One ought not in this matter to act as though all this had never previously existed. In the piety and spirituality of non-Catholic Christianity there have always been such charismatic movements. Previously, they were found among us in the houses of religious orders, but that does not always have to remain so. Lay groups can also have charismatic phenomena. In any case, if the Church and her spirituality moves more in the charismatic direction, let there certainly be, nonetheless, a continuity preserved in the life of the Church.

Could you in conclusion sum up what being a Christian today means for you?

To be a Christian means to adore God, to love him, to entrust oneself to his incomprehensibility and to the incomprehensibility of his governance. It means to know that there is an eternal life that consists in the immediacy of the vision of God. All this relationship to God is carried and legitimated by Jesus Christ, because we—in view of him, of his cross and his resurrection, in view of the unsurpassably given unity between God and the human person—can trust that our life's task of entering into immediate relation with God, will be blessed by God's victorious grace. That people venture before God because of Jesus Christ to build a faith community that is called the Church, that this faith community has a history and has a social structure that binds the individual, along with everything that even the ordinary Christian knows about his or her Church— then all that is really obvious. Obvious too is it that Christians and the Church must by the power of the Holy Spirit enter and work for justice, love, and peace in a world considered as God's creation.

Translated by Roland J. Teske, S.J.
Marquette University

57 · The Church's Angry Old Men

Interview with Paul Imhof for Radio Saarland, Munich (April 3, 1982)

Don't you sometimes have the desire to criticize the Church's critics?
Yes. People always expect me to be an angry old critic. Criticism of the Church is entirely normal and basically legitimate. At Vatican II the Church confessed that it was always in need of reforming, and again and again it has to say what needs reforming. But today an angry old man should also criticize the critics.

In what ways?

It just isn't so that the critics themselves are above criticism. But they often act as if they are. Sometimes they behave as if they're especially wise and holy, and suffer the most from the Church's defects and failings to which they haven't contributed to in any way. They often lack the self-critical eye that should belong to everyone, and especially those who set themselves up as the judge of others and of the Church.

As I've already said, I'm not opposed to criticism in the Church, it's necessary—surely I've done my share of it—even when afterwards one wonders whether one always hit the nail on the head or feels one would have formulated the criticism differently had the facts been better known.

A Christian critic of the Church must really be critical, and, at the very least, practice the modesty and caution which must be shown everyone with whom one finds fault. Theological criticism must obviously be supported by the factual data necessary to engage in theological discourse. A respectable criticism must know the valid criteria for criticizing theological opinions, otherwise it talks foolishly at cross-purposes with its opponents. A real critic should proceed as though the person or issue involved were already at fault because of the critic's unsympathetic attitude. The real critic of the Church must always calculate that he or she will also be criticized. After all, the critic is a member of this Church, a myopic sinner, who, directly or indirectly, contributes something to the Church's outward image.

A good critic also knows how to distinguish between what can actually be improved in a society of finite and sinful people, and what is part of society's baggage—a society composed of people (including the critics) who are not geniuses and saints. Criticism should only be spoken or written when critics are in a good mood, when they can laugh and show loving good will to those they criticize, when they know that those criticized are also not geniuses or saints, but on closer examination are as lovable, friendly, and reasonable as the critics consider themselves to be. Naturally and justifiably, the Church also has its angry prophets, who, like John the Baptizer and Jesus, make terrifying threats. But caution is necessary before assuming such a call—it requires as much repentance as John and as much prayer as Jesus. It's seldom that such critics appear in the Church.

But the justification for criticism of the Church, its officeholders, institutions, and structures lies still deeper: in the Church's essence.

Do you distinguish between critics who are members of the Church and those who are not?

Yes, indeed. The criticism of a Christian who has actually made a faith commitment is the criticism of a Christian in the Church. This criticism is, or at least should be, entirely different from that of someone who stands outside the Church, someone whose faith is lukewarm and whose relationship to the Church is, at best, conventional. The two proceed from entirely different presuppositions.

It is entirely conceivable that a radically believing Christian in the Church suffers more and reacts more bitterly than someone who considers the Church irrelevant.

One should be able to tell from such a Christian's criticism that one comprehends the Church as an unconditional reality at the heart and center of one's Christian existence and of one's relationship to God, who is eternal salvation. In all honesty, the statement, "Why I remain in the Church," strikes me as abominable. Faith can be attacked; I can also imagine someone losing this ecclesial dimension of faith without feeling any guilt before God. But the real Christian believer can't possibly have a patronizing attitude toward the Church that allows him or her to weigh staying in the Church against getting out of it. Relationship to the Church is at the very essence, an absolute of Christian faith. And one should be able to detect this when people who claim to be people of the Church, members of the Church, criticize their Church. Those who stand outside the Church or for whom the Church is not an integral part of faith but only an enormous sociological accident which they entered by chance, may judge the Church differently. One should be able to tell from the criticism whether it is formulated by someone who does or does not have a real relationship to the Church.

One often gets the impression from the criticism that comes from Catholics who are "on the rolls" that they do not really grasp the Church's unique essence—indeed, have not incorporated it into their personal faith consciousness. As far as I'm concerned, people can energetically, fiercely, bitterly, even rabidly criticize much in the Church. But if it is the criticism of a Catholic, one should be able to see that here's someone who wants to find eternal salvation as a member of the Church. Remember, the Catholic critic argues in the Church against the "Church" on the basis of an intimate understanding of it. The critic knows that the Church, ultimately, is not merely a dubious religious organization satisfying people's needs but—yes, it has unavoidably a societal structure—the community which believes that Jesus Christ the crucified and risen one is God's irrevocable promise to us. Of what great importance is anger with pastors, bishops, possibly even the papacy, when one knows that in this Church God's tangible word of grace was promised through baptism for a lifetime; when in the Eucharist one can celebrate Jesus' death and resurrection as the event of the holy God; when one knows that in this Church, despite all the problems of theological discourse and idle chatter, one can always hear the pure word of God's eternal self-communication; when one is promised forgiveness of all life's guilt; when in this Church, as nowhere else, in life and in death, one can hold on to Jesus, the trusted witness of the eternal God?

As I've said, there is criticism of the Church other than that of a true Christian and Catholic. For this reason, one should remember that the Christian and Catholic critic is speaking from the standpoint of an intimate understanding of the Church's essence. Thus, the critic doesn't always have to give explicit, long-winded, and unctuous witness to one particular understanding of the Church. Among brothers and sisters such professions of orthodoxy are superfluous and only make a bad impression. All criticism should flow from the innermost core of our understanding of the faith. It should be presumed that those criticized (from the pope right down to the janitor) are inspired by the very same faith and love of the Church. What right do we have not to presume this?

Naturally, this means that every just and concrete criticism of the Church will involve a certain discrepancy between this fundamental understanding of the faith and what the criticism factually does or says, or even teaches. But since such discrepancies are possible with people generally, they are also possible with critics specifically.

What does this mean for the critics?

It presupposes that every "insider" who criticizes the Church has an understanding of the faith in general and the Church in particular, and that this understanding challenges the critic to see the contradiction between this understanding and his or her specific words and actions. When criticism flows from the center of the Church's common life, it is justified, even a necessary and sacred responsibility. But only then. We should leave criticisms of another kind to those who have rejected the Church. We should not flatter them.

Translated by Bernhard A. Asen
St. Louis University

58 · I Am a Priest and a Theologian

Interview with the editorial staff of *Dom, Sonntagsblatt für das Erzbistum Paderborn*, Paderborn (February 29, 1982)

Professor Rahner, if there were a short formula for what you propose to accomplish with your theology, with your thinking—what would it sound like?

You see, to find a short formula for what I have done in theology in these last decades—I haven't looked for something like that myself. My life work, if we can call it that, has had no plan, proposed in advance, but was strongly influenced by the needs of the day, by the tasks I had as a professor, and so on. If you look at the twenty volumes of my *Theological Investigations*, you will see that they are made up of individual articles, which were mostly lectures originally. And so even I don't know how to characterize my theology, if we want to summarize it in a short formula.

I would plainly and simply say that I am a Catholic Christian, I am attempting to reflect on my faith and relate it to the questions, needs, and difficulties, which confront me as a man and a Christian. From this everything else follows. Of course, I pursued one thing or another in scholarly theology in the strict sense and in historical theology—this follows from my office as professor. But in general, I really have endeavored to pursue a theology that looks to concrete proclamation in the Church, to dialogue with people of today. Perhaps some will believe that this is just the opposite of what I have done, for there are, of course, many people who say that my writings are not understandable, that I write sentences that are too long, and so on. I believe, however, that the pastoral concern of proclaiming the Christian faith for today has been the normative aspect of my work.

People have found many titles to characterize you and your work. From "architect of the new theology" to "intellectual of our era," as you have been called. Which encomium pleases you most?

To your second question I should first like to say very soberly that such titles and slogans are advertising phrases, which publishers use to market books. We mustn't hold it against them, but I don't feel that these epithets describe me or honor me. If you ask me which is my favorite encomium, I would tell you: I am a priest and theologian, and that's it, isn't it? Those are the real designations that say something.

Whoever is in the spotlight is watched carefully and also creates critics. What do you believe is the best way to meet critics?

Of course I have known very many critics in my life, important critics, and perhaps even absurd ones. Some time ago an important philosopher, a Catholic, a man who belonged to the Lefebvre-group, wrote to one of my assistants that he should leave me because I belonged to the people who make dog kennels out of tabernacles and have betrayed Christ, not for thirty pieces of silver but for nothing. Such critics are gullible and unjust.

But naturally in theology there are opinions, that one holds, that are criticized, or added to, or rejected. About such opinions one must dialogue quietly and reasonably and examine whether one is right or whether the other is. There are also, of course, many things in theology about which one expresses a view, thinking it quite significant and good, while questioning whether one has hit it correctly.

When Hans Urs von Balthasar criticizes my theology of redemption in his book or others perhaps find my theology of the Trinity not quite correct, then naturally questions are raised that must be reconsidered. What seems to be correct now? Has something perhaps been overlooked? Can anything be done differently? Or after such criticism and after detached examination can we still remain set in our opinion? There are many other questions, more of the nature of church politics or pastoral care, where criticism is, by the nature of the thing, of quite a different type again. Such are questions of discretion, where it is not so much that one person is 100 percent right and the other, absolutely wrong. If one says two and two are five, then one is absolutely wrong. If someone says, I could conceive of the election of bishops of Rome or the choosing of bishops otherwise than the way they are now chosen, then this inquiry is not about an absolutely wrong view, but an inquiry where one must weigh the most varied aspects of an apostolic task or about a decision in Church policy. Accordingly, we have different opinions, so that one can try to ground a point of view in the joint decision of the Church or in its collective consciousness, which is neither true nor false, but better or less good. In such cases, who is right always remains an open question.

If there were a more intimate spirit of brotherhood, wouldn't there be a new, entirely different form of brotherly criticism from that which we feel in many places today?

I recently wrote a small book, *The Love of Jesus and the Love of Neighbor* [New York: Crossroad, 1983]. And I think the theme that love of God and love of neighbor belong together is a theme which must always be considered anew, a theme that has very practical consequences. I'd like to remark here, in passing, that I was once attacked, and it was said that my understanding of the inter-dependence of the love of God and the love of neighbor—or a certain unity, correctly understood, of the love of God and love of neighbor—was heresy. I don't believe that, and I'm still of the opinion that here and there, where someone approaches his or her neighbor in a truly ultimate radicalism of self-lessness (let's say it cautiously), he or she is on the way to God himself; for the last power and possibility to get out of oneself and really to love one's neighbor can only come from the eternal, secret mystery which alone guarantees mean-ing to each one, the mystery we call God.

Translated by John J. O'Neill, S.J.
Loyola Marymount, Los Angeles

59 · Autobiographical Reflections, Anonymous Christianity, Reincarnation

Interview with Leonhard Reinisch for Radio Bayern (BR #2), Munich (April 29, 1982)

Our conversation is not just a conversation with professional theologians, but above all with Karl Rahner, and especially about the way he has approached the question, For what do I live? when he was asked. Let us begin therefore with the year 1904, or with the time, when in your parents' house you suddenly became conscious yourself of the question; For what do I live, really?

This question of yours reminds me first of the old question in the catechism: Why am I on earth? With this question and its answer I grew up in a Catholic family with seven children. And in all interests about the world, in all problems and all intellectual movements, which existed between 1915 and 1925, I was a very normal Catholic Christian with an ordinary religious education. In our family there existed an interest in religious questions, in questions about our world view. I had a thoroughly Christian father and a very religious mother who lived to the age of 101; that's the way I grew up. Right after World War I my brother Hugo, who was four years older, entered the Jesuit order, when he was still a soldier. I can't remember exactly that this was an important inducement for me to do the same. But it did set the tone of the atmosphere in which I grew up and I would like to say frankly and simply that from this point I was convinced that one must love God and neighbor and, by this means, win eternal life with God; in this I could see the meaning of my life decisively and unaffectedly.

It is, of course, clear—if I now reflect philosophically or theologically or psychologically—that my life, in my first twenty years, was also filled with many other spontaneous, innocent, meaningful experiences of joy, trust, and comradeship, of interest in science, and also in metaphysics and theology; and so, I would not like to give the impression that I grew up in this terrible, tortuous period in world outlook, suffering attacks of pessimism or agnosticism or even atheism.

How did you come to write your dissertation on Saint Thomas Aquinas or choose him as your subject?

You see I became a Jesuit at the age of eighteen and went through a spiritual training period of two years—we call it the novitiate. Then I took, partly in Feldkirch and partly in Pullach near Munich, a three-year course of neoscholastic philosophy, during which I had naturally become familiar with scholastic philosophy, especially with Thomas Aquinas. I was then sent by my religious superiors, after four years of theology, to study philosophy and to take a doctorate at Freiburg. I chiefly studied under Martin Heidegger, who was already well known and becoming famous. Now he had just been made the first university rector there in the Nazi period, and we two young priests, J. B. Lotz and I, were not anxious to throw in our lot with him for good or ill; so we enrolled with the professor of Catholic scholastic philosophy, Martin Honecker. On the other hand, our meeting with Martin Heidegger was the truly decisive, impressive experience. So I arrived at a dissertation, which dealt with Thomas on the one hand and attempted to view Thomas, I might say, from the point of view of a modern philosophy on the other—whether that would be German idealism or the existential philosophy of Martin Heidegger; but in any case such a dissertation was obvious. I can let you in on something, if you are interested; I had to be finished in two years on the instructions of my Jesuit superiors. I therefore completed this dissertation, *Spirit in the World*, after two years and turned it in. I was then to go to Innsbruck as an instructor in theology, beginning in October, 1938. When I arrived there, the precious mentor of my dissertation informed me that he rejected my philosophical *opus*. That was all right with me, for I had already landed on another track, theology; but it is nevertheless interesting that a work that went through three editions in German and was translated into French, English, Spanish and, I believe, also into Italian, was rejected by a German university professor as unsuitable as a modest doctoral dissertation in philosophy.

Was that your first annoyance with the official Church or wasn't it the official Church?

No, it wasn't the official Church, but official university work; but perhaps we're getting too far away from the real subject. May I say something now? You see, when you asked what I live for, then I had to say, naturally, as a theologian, a Christian, and a normal man, I live, first of all, because I found myself to be alive. I did not choose this. I was, therefore, without being asked, set in a situation—and if you would like to put it somewhat philosophically— with this given situation and not with a situation determined by myself beforehand. I had to live as a free subject and clarify for myself whether I should protest having this entrance ticket pressed into my hand, or whether I should accept it and see it as really very nice, very significant or at least as very hopeful.

I admit to you that for me and my theology, the experience of God as the incomprehensible entered more and more strongly into the foreground—as well for my own existence as also for my theology. If you now ask, "What do you live for, or where can you recognize the meaning of your life?" then I, of course, must now say, "I feel myself from the outset confronted with the incomprehensible mystery that embraces, holds and penetrates me, which we call God." I say that, naturally, a thousand complexes of meaning are given before this last perspective, that I loved my mother—independently of such ultimate metaphysical questions—that I enjoyed scholarly work, giving myself to Jesuit ideals, and in all things like this found meaning and hence lived—all that is self-evident. But all these particular, meaningful experiences, experiences of joy, love, being sheltered, of hope, also experiences of anxiety, nearness of death, and so on, are all integrated in this ultimate whole of a huge risk—to entrust oneself to the incomprehensibility of God as self-concealing Love.

You had in your life also many dark hours, I believe. When people in Rome wanted to put your writings under a special censure, surely you weren't very happy. There were certain points that often made life somewhat dark and gray and shadowy.

Yes, that is of course correct; only here I would like to see myself, if I may say so, as an old-fashioned Christian, and as an old-fashioned theologian. You see, these quarrels, these censures, these threats to one's professorship or of the possibility of publishing something, were experienced by us older people as more or less not as life-threatening troubles. They belong in a similar way to every human life.

Dear Lord! Two people get married. They really love one another in a serious and honorable way, but in certain circumstances they can quarrel or in many respects they don't understand themselves so well, or someone starts a business and it doesn't flourish as magnificently as he originally expected, and so on—and so a reasonable, somewhat normal person ascribes all these things to what is unavoidable in life. Earlier we ascribed to the unavoidable things of life all these eccelesiastical, professional troubles.

Take the example from the most recent period in my life. Perhaps you learned from the newspaper how the present pope imposed a special delegate on the order.[1] All right, it's not very pleasant, perhaps one gets angry, perhaps one wonders; one doesn't understand so well why that should be a good thing. One doesn't easily see that the measure taken by the highest church authorities was justified by the situation. But do you believe that I was so terribly shaken? If I think that tomorrow I might be dead—in any case I shall not live much longer—that the curve of life inexorably and unceasingly and ever faster moves away to a zero-point, then such an encroachment by the pope finally doesn't shake me. I can't say that I have lost sleep because of this matter. We did write a letter from Munich to the pope, which was answered by the secretary of state in a very friendly and courteous manner. But what difference does all this make?

You brought an important catchword into theological discussion with "the anonymous Christian." You use it to understand the person, who is not a baptized Christian, whom you defend perhaps with greater courage than anyone has done before.

You see, there are, of course, in the development of the Church's consciousness of faith extraordinarily great developments and changes. What I wanted to say, however, with this problematic catchword, the anonymous Christian, is in itself at least today, looking at the reality, if perhaps not in this terminology, an understandable, accepted reality in Catholic Christianity. This whole problematic is in reality unavoidable. I am a Christian: I would like to be uncondi-

---

1. On October 5, 1981, Paolo Dezza was entrusted, as a papal delegate, with the leadership of the Jesuit order. Rahner's judicious comments on this situation can be found in, "Zur Situation des Jesuitenordens nach den Schwierigkeiten mit dem Vatikan," *Schriften zur Theologie XV* (Zürich-Einsiedlen-Köln: Benziger, 1983), pp. 355–72.

tionally a Roman Catholic Christian, and at the same time I see that there are so many people whom I appreciate, who have a different opinion, a different view of life. Then I must ask myself as a Catholic Christian: How is it with these others who are encompassed by the love of the one and the same God, whom I attempt to serve? In this way, I come to these realities which in themselves today are a part of the Catholic heritage: everyone who follows his or her conscience and is true to it—even when believing oneself an atheist or belonging to another Christian Church or to another great culture-religion —is and remains—as we said, if one does not sin mortally against one's own conscience—encompassed by the salvation of the one, eternal God, whose absolute promise for me has come in Jesus Christ, the crucified and risen one.

It is clear that your relationship to life and death and therefore also to the meaning of life and death is formed by Catholicism. You have just described your relationship and your understanding of the anonymous Christian. What is then your understanding of those who can't stand their life and, for this reason, end their life?

Yes, first of all, I'd like to distinguish clearly between people, who without guilt of their own, go to pieces. You see, if, for example, some alien power would seize me and submit me to brainwashing or to such torments that I would simply be broken, that I simply couldn't bear any more, then, of course, the threshold of human responsibility is passed, just as if through cancer or something similar I should be unconscious in the hospital. What comes after that has nothing more to do with responsibility for my life before God, and so there can be those who, although they are fully intact physically, are so broken through internal or external influences that they really have no more responsibility to bear for their lives before God, if they die by their own hand.

In the course of my life I have intimately experienced such cases in every generation of my family. Do you believe, then, that I have the impression that these men in some way—to use the Christian expression—as mortal sinners before God are destroyed and lost? By no means! I hope that they have nevertheless found the God of eternal love, of understanding and faithfulness. Fundamentally and theoretically, I must say: Whoever in a final, truly guilty despair ends his or her own life in a last protest against meaning, truth, and good fortune, and therefore, against God, would be theoretically speaking, lost. Whether there are *de facto* such persons, *that* I do not know as a Catholic Christian. I hope that *de facto* there are no such people, although, to uphold the seriousness and responsibility for my life before God, I must uphold the fundamental thesis, that something like this is in itself possible.

In your meditations on world religions, what do you make of the idea of rebirth, of eternal rebirth or of reincarnation, which hardly finds any support in the Catholic Church?

Naturally, I know a German woman poet who told me that she had once been in Ireland and realized there that she had existed there once in a former life. Thus, there are of course many examples which seem to bespeak such a migration of souls, reincarnation or whatever you want to call it. Leaving more exact distinctions aside, one must say crudely that from a Catholic Christian standpoint one can't hold fast to such an idea.

How such true or supposed phenomena like a reminiscence of past lives can be explained is naturally another question, a dark question, although there are possibilities for an explanation into which I cannot now enter, for which, however, the assumption of a real migration of souls does not seem necessary. For myself as a free subject, I must accept my present course of life, which is granted to me, as the decisive story, which I continue to its final completion; and I can't console myself with the thought that, if things go wrong, I can find a further opportunity to improve the whole business, and so make my life cheaper.

Even Buddhists must finally have the will to find their way out of the eternal wheel of life and death. My affirmation as a Christian is that I hope rightly that, through ways which finally only God knows, I really succeed in this my present concrete life, that I shall find my way out of the eternal to and fro, out of the eternal return of all things and find the eternal happiness of God, his eternal grace, his eternal love face to face.

Translated by John J. O'Neill, S.J.
Loyola Marymount, Los Angeles

60·Salvation and Liberation

Interview with Gerhard Ruis for Landesstudio Salzburg of Radio Austria
Salzburg (April 7, 1982)

Today there is little doubt that some people are attempting contemporary interpre-
tations of the Christian truth of salvation in terms of a program of social freedom. In
this view, evolutionary or revolutionary changes of external structures, solidarity with
the oppressed, and the actual utopia of a complete humanizing of the world promise the
development of an immeasurable realm of freedom. Could it be that "liberation" is
contrary to the Christian view of salvation?

No! If liberation, freedom, and earthly happiness are understood properly
and without illusion, then the Christian message of God as the unique, singular,
and definitive goal of humankind is not contrary to this: rather, the Christian
message is oriented toward a completely different dimension. Freedom and happiness cannot be denied to people. Everyone must strive for these goals. It is
even that through all work for earthly happiness, for justice, and for the overcoming of social egoism the Christian is the one who awaits eternal life in God
and knows of course that he or she can obtain this eternal life promised by God,
and thus salvation, only through this attitude of ultimate love of neighbor. To
this extent, the modern institutional, social, and individual movements to struggle for freedom, happiness, and justice join inseparably with the Christian message of salvation. On the one hand, this world's liberation and, on the other,
eternal life with God are two separate realities which are not necessarily contradictory, though eternal life cannot be replaced simply by this world's liberation.

This would mean that a theology which knows both history and theology's contem-
porary task may not dismiss the attempt to provide a new interpretation of the concept
of "salvation" nor may theology discredit such attempts as phenomena which are
simply peripheral to the proper Christian belief in salvation.

What I have said can be worked out and explored with more precise and
profound links between the Christian idea of salvation on the one hand and
liberation movements of an earthly sort on the other. For example, someone
might say: Only in the experience of political freedom and in the struggle for
this freedom can a person gain a new understanding of the message of eternal,
definitive, and limitless freedom which is God himself and which God has
promised us. If someone said this, there would be nothing to object to. To
this extent, one can of course totally and rightly speak of a political theology,

and for this position *even* the message of Christianity—though not seen exclusively in horizontal terms—can be effective. However, this theology still implies that the definitive, eternal redemption, the absolute salvation from guilt, suffering, and death, occurs not in this life but through our death in union with the death of Jesus through which alone we break into the eternal life of God himself.

Can the idea of salvation, understood as the death and resurrection of Christ, incorporate the stimulus of the "modern pathos" for freedom without, at the same time, being sucked into an accommodation to the times? Is liberation theology—understood as an anthropological-social category—suited to take up the entirety of the Christian message of salvation without clarifying for people where its own limitations lie and from which transempirical powers these limitations must be loosened?

You see, Christianity's message of salvation cannot be enriched through non-Christian content. Yet every age with its own set of ideas and specifically contemporary experience can again challenge Christianity to understand itself anew. In this perspective one can understand today's message which is socially critical and presses for more freedom as a legitimate challenge to be addressed to Christianity to understand itself in more adequate, multifaceted, profound, and radical terms. Freedom in the Pauline sense and freedom in the modern sense are not identical. The one cannot replace the other. Nevertheless, a person can attain a deeper and more radical understanding for the modern language of freedom through the Christian language of freedom—as the freedom for the infinite God through his grace. Conversely, from the modern talk of liberation a person can better understand what an actually vast, radical, utterly definitive reality has occurred through Christianity and its message of redemption and is to be proclaimed by Christianity.

Are you as a theologian concerned about the reduction of the efficacy of Christianity? There can be no doubt that this is at least the case in Europe.

Christianity's effects are not established by means of statistics. I could just as accurately say that Christianity never has had such a great impact on the world as it has today. If human rights are being proclaimed today throughout all the world, this is actually an effect of Christianity. What is the source of the doctrine of an absolute respect for everyone who bears a human countenance? Today's enlightenment and what occurs within this milieu of enlightenment is nothing other than secularized Christianity, which has not ceased to be in the last analysis Christian. I would only stress this: One must proceed very cautiously with the claim that Christianity has lost its impact on the modern world.

Further, it is understandable that a Christian who wants to represent and proclaim the message of the gospel, that a theologian who reflects on the essence of Christianity, must be concerned about those experiences of which you speak, if you speak of the increasing ineffectiveness or of the declining effectiveness of Christianity. All of these experiences are challenges for the Church and its representatives, for the preacher of the gospel to consider freshly, radically, courageously, and self-critically, even valiantly, how one must convey the message of the gospel today. The Church should take up this challenge more radically. It must not flee into a small clerical ghetto or into the ghetto of folklore Christianity, and abandon the rest of the world to itself. The Christian is, then, only a true Christian when he or she believes fearlessly in God's salvific will and love, and does not make his or her faith dependent upon the tangible effects of faith. I believe in God, not in the institutional-political, tangible power of the Church. I trust in God, but in no one else. Moreover, when I know that I find the eternal God of the blessed life even through disillusionment, illness, and death, then I realize that the issue of the institutional efficacy of Christianity is, to be sure, a thoroughly legitimate, important, vexing question. But for me it is still not the final issue. It may indeed be that God will ask me in judgment: How have you broken through all the powers of this earth and of history to my eternal life? God may also ask me: Have you been a Christian as the first-century Christians who offered their lives without any tangible institutional-political consequences? The question is whether we believe unconditionally in God and his power—that is, without having the consequence already in hand—or whether we hanker after the earthly, rational-calculable consequences of Christianity. The true Christian cannot make his or her Christianity dependent upon whether Christianity will have or not have an impact on the next twenty or one hundred years.

Right to the present Christians firmly hold to the claim of the absoluteness of Christianity. May one deduce from that Christianity's superiority over the other great religions of salvation?

Of course, I hold fast to the claim of the absoluteness of Christianity, insofar as Christianity in its proper reality and center, thus in the redemption through Jesus Christ, recognizes the salvation of all people, and insofar as Christianity is the invitation to grasp explicitly in Jesus Christ this true final reality of the grace of eternal life. I have nothing significant to say about whether, to what extent, in which perspectives, and in which time periods the message of Christianity is actually comprehended by all people, that is, by all cultures and historical periods. One can nevertheless demonstrate that Christianity's presence in the world today has yet to be equalled by the great world religions.

Of course, Christianity must continue to learn from its encounters with other religions—not as though it is learning something that is being imported into Christianity from the outside, rather as learning to come to itself in a radical, decisive manner. If there is a modern ideology of freedom, why should Christianity not discover how it can proclaim its own message of freedom more energetically and radically than it has yet managed to?

Of course, today there is a situation for Christianity that has never before existed. Until our time, even though Christianity wanted to become and to be a world religion, a message to all people, it could live solely out of its concrete, historical origins—whether it was the Christianity of the cultural sphere of Judaism or the Christianity of the cultural sphere of the Hellenistic-Roman West does not matter. Now however, without denying its historical origin, Christianity must really become a world religion, taking root in mutually different cultures—cultures that presumably remain different from each other. This is something Christianity never had to do before, and to this extent Christianity faces an entirely new situation for its message of redemption through Jesus Christ. This contains a vast opportunity for Christianity really to become what, from the outset, it always wanted to be. Now historical Christianity must historically become in a certain sense transregional and we must wait to see how Christianity will meet this extraordinary opportunity.

Translated by Robert A. Krieg, C.S.C.
University of Notre Dame

61 · What Does It Mean to Be a Priest Today?

Interview with Gerhard Ruis on the occasion of
Karl Rahner's fiftieth jubilee as a priest for *Landesstudio Salzburg*
of Radio Austria, Salzburg (April 7, 1982)

For the past few years one has spoken of a crisis in the Catholic priesthood, at least in the Western industrialized nations. This is certainly not a crisis caused simply by talking much about it, even if opinions expressed in public completely overlook the fact that a broad spectrum of priests remain who attempt to perform their service in peace and with the conviction of their vocation. These remain in spite of all the identity problems, difficulties, and threatening breaks within the Church. How do you see this, Father Rahner? Is there a crisis in the Catholic priesthood?

One can certainly speak in many ways of a crisis in the Catholic priesthood without falsifying reality or creating a crisis through much discussion. If for no other reason than the undeniable fact that the number of priestly callings, the number of those who allow themselves to be ordained, has fallen greatly. There are a few weak tendencies toward a reversal, but, for the most part and even in those dioceses where the number of seminarians has risen, it is a major problem in contrast to earlier times. There are fewer priests.

On the one hand, we live in modern society, under certain conditions which are simply detrimental to faith, to preaching faith, and therefore to the service of the Church. On the other hand, we come from a society in which faith, Christianity, baptism, church attendance, a church burial, Easter communion, and similar things were all taken for granted. Today it is different. The number of practicing Catholics has declined considerably. Hence, it is very understandable that a young man will have different problems in studying for the priesthood today than in past years.

Earlier, a young priest had a career to look forward to—even if he didn't strive for this in an immoral or profane sense—first as a chaplain, then as a pastor. He was a respected man in his community. He belonged to those people in a normal society who were looked up to, even if no one called upon his services very often.

In other words, one can speak of a complication of the will to become a priest and therefore of a crisis in the Catholic priesthood. One must be careful here, however, because this refers only to our environs. It can certainly be very different in India or Indonesia, if only because of the different spiritual and sociopolitical conditions. It could well be that the lack of priestly callings from the native populations in South America was much greater thirty years ago than it is now. In any case, this remains: There are complicating circumstances regarding the priestly calling so that one can, in a way, speak of a crisis.

How one is to judge such a crisis when one is a practicing Christian or even a priest is a whole other question.

You said that a main reason for the lack of priests which we experience could be that becoming a priest no longer means a career. But is not the situation more propitious the other way around, as seen from the Bible. I read recently a new translation of a letter of Paul: "publicly we have become dirt—pushed to the edge by everyone." One can think of this translation what one will; however, if this is now the situation, wouldn't it be a more believable decision to become a priest?

When I said earlier that the priestly calling no longer means a career, I did not want to suggest that the priests of centuries past had bad or earthly motives for their priesthood. The possibility of being a respected person in an open society was, we hope, not the reason for their priestly lives. However, this created an atmosphere, a dimension, within which something like the priestly call with its absolute religious motivations offered itself much more understandably.

Earlier, there were many pious and hardworking brothers in the Society of Jesus who worked with their hands. They entered our ranks and were truly holy, selfless men. One must say they had a career inside the Society. In the order they had a low-level, yet respected position which gave an ambiance in which the true religious motivation could more easily grow when compared with today's situation. It is also similar in the priestly calling.

Now you can rightfully say that the priestly calling in its true religious meaning is something which fits into today's secularized and profane situation. The priest should not be one who lives as a respected pastor in a lovely rectory and who is counted among those most truly honored in the community. Rather, he should proclaim the implausible message of Jesus Christ, the one crucified and risen. Then, contradicting the world, the folly of the cross, as well as other specifically Christian motivations will play their respective roles in the priestly calling.

The question still remains: How many people today and tomorrow would hear such a radical and confrontational calling with the concomitant folly of the cross and God's inconceivability? This is again a totally different question. One could very easily say that today's spiritual situation is very similar to that at the time of Paul. The question is: How many can hear such a calling? Naturally, that will depend in large part upon how well the people of today can hear the message of Jesus Christ and how well they will implement it. I do not believe that the number of priestly callings proportional to the number of practicing Catholics has declined. . . . The real question is how the Church should *efficiently* proclaim her message to all humanity.

The profile of the priest within the Church has become somewhat hazy. For example, the inclination of the Church to turn to the cultic-sacral area, which has been connected with the service of the Catholic priesthood for a few centuries now, has also faded to the background. In my opinion, however, the priestly-sacral work and the form of life so foreign to the world, celibacy, have lost much of their meaning as you have already said.

Yes, there are other reasons in addition to those just given by me which have contributed to the so-called crisis in the priesthood. There are changes in the ways of thinking of everyday Christians (some justified and some unfortunately not) and, consequently, in the mentality of the Church and those who represent her concerns. It follows then that this will affect, in time, the offices of the Church. It is completely justified nowadays to take sociopolitical duties in the Church more seriously than before.

Earlier, when it took centuries for things to change within society, social structures were of unquestionable importance; there were kings and officeholders, wars and the corresponding rituals of the adjutants. There were the poor (who were accepted matter-of-factly) and the rich who were of the opinion that God's providence saw to it that they could never lose their money, could pass it on to their children, and the like. We live today in a society with different duties with many more rash tendencies to change and also to real possibilities. It is understandable, then, that Christians—and these include, to be sure, the Church's officeholders and their official pronouncements—must also take part in these changes.

The duties of the Church, which were earlier under the auspices of officialdom, were more or less identical with those of the priest. In this way, perhaps we can shed a different light on the problem of priests.

There were naturally women who cleaned the Church; there was a sacristan who lit the candles and brought water for the baptism. For the most part, all the important and high-ranking duties of the Church were also, as a matter of fact, the duties of the priests. For example, let us look at the Catholic schools of Belgium. Until a decade ago, the clerics working there taught math, writing, Latin, and Greek. But now we have the following situation: On the one hand, the duties of the Church have grown, to a degree shifted; on the other hand, however, these cannot all be fulfilled by priests. This hides the danger, as you already mentioned, that today's young priest has the impression that what he has to do as a priest is foreign to this world: a ceremonial concern which does not necessarily interest him nor the people. He does not have the impression that he is being hemmed in by the power of the state or by those persecuting the Church. Rather, he feels pushed by social developments into the sacristy or choir loft. These additional duties, which a priest understandably accepted and which somehow fulfilled him, can no longer be executed by him. There are nowadays an enormous number of religion teachers who are not priests. There are also social workers in the service of the Church who are not priests. This raises the question whether the priesthood is attractive as it is. May or should a young man say (we do not address here the problematic question of celibacy): I will enter the service of the Church which will fulfill my whole life, but I don't want to be a priest. You see, when I was young I came to know an Italian youth who lived with us. His father was an Italian diplomat in Berlin at the time. This young man, an engineer by training, died of polio which he contracted from the poor of Turin. Perhaps he will be canonized later. By the way, on John Paul's trip to Turin, he celebrated Mass in honor of Don Bosco and my young friend. My mother even asked him why he did not become a priest, to which he replied that one can do more for the salvation of souls in Italy if one is not a priest. Naturally, this example is a bit extreme and onesided, but it shows the reason for the identity crisis in which young men thinking of priesthood can get caught up.

Let me interrupt here. A while back, a pastor in Vienna, respected by parishioners and colleagues alike, said to me concerning his understanding of his office: "I do not want to be a representative of Christ. I do not want to be an intercessor between God and man. I am simply one of the community and I serve this community." It seems to me that a new aspect is being introduced. One speaks today of a horizontal and vertical understanding of the priestly office. In a large poll, many priests preferred the word service *and do not want to hear anything further about the* office. *Conversely, others, mostly older priests, still hold tight to the preconciliar understanding of the office.*

I would also say that there are many misunderstandings on both sides. Perhaps we can leave the word *office* aside and speak of a mission in the service of the Church for the accomplishment of her duties; a mission which one cannot make exclusively one's own. It would be one which imparts certain obligations as well as certain possibilities, but these are not shared by everyone, not even in the Church. Such a lasting mission, however, can be called an office. Now the pastor from Vienna may say of himself that he serves his community. He is baptized and so are the others; all are truly children of God with an eternal destiny.

It is a matter of how he serves the community. Is he only a social worker who cares for the poor of his parish and who cares fraternally for the down-and-outs? Is he only a good marriage counselor? Is he only the one who tries to teach morals to those who have none? Is he only the representative of an inner-worldly, horizontal humanity or is he something completely different? I am of the opinion that where there is a critical attitude toward the priesthood, despite true Catholic belief, be it among priests or seminarians, one is missing what the priest, in the true sense of the word, can and should be.

He has, of course, thousands of duties. He has to care for the poor in his community; he must work for peace; he is to awaken a critical spirit toward society in his community. Now I would like to say something about the real heart of the priesthood, even if I have to use seemingly odd terminology. . . . A priest is one sent by Christ, an apostle of the eternal God with one message that far surpasses any and all earthly duties and possibilities. This message is: There is a God and he, in his inexplicable way, wants to be a part of our lives. Even if he caused a cosmos to explode which may be ten thousand light years away, he is still with me, still loves me, still surrounds me. He wants to make my existence eternal and wants to reward me with his presence and his eternal life. The word in which God commits himself to us must be spread. It must be witnessed to: It is eternal through the crucified and risen Jesus. And there must be people who do this.

Naturally, God works in the freedom of his unending love, in the depths of people, and in the atheist who stands by the banality of his or her earthly existence. But God's grace and irrevocable promise of fuller self-disclosure to us has corporeally, definitely, and irreversibly appeared in the person of Jesus of Nazareth. This message must be spread. The word carries a stated reality which one should receive as challenging, redeeming, and satisfying. This word is the reality. That is why we call it a sacramental word of grace. If because of this the priest is also the dispenser of sacraments, the administrator of Christ's Last Supper in which the crucified Jesus and his power are present, then he is not a performer of various antiquated magical rituals about which a modern person knows nothing. He is much more the one who proclaims the incomprehensible, eternal, and sanctifying mystery of God to us. If a priest cannot understand this, then perhaps he should have become a social worker instead.

I freely admit that today's priest does not have it easy proclaiming the message of the New Testament and that of the Church. It is difficult for him to understand what an incredibly blessed message he has to proclaim. It is difficult for him to announce this in a way that others understand it. If he knows only to repeat boring catechism formulations or if he takes refuge in homilies that contain only social and political critique, then it is difficult for him to comprehend that he is the guru of the loving God. He is not this by his own doing; he is one, rather, who has been graced and empowered by God. Many people feel a need to aim for more on earth than just making money and being able to take trips.

There are people who yearn for the incomprehensibility and eternity of God. To these people the priest says that the most inconceivable optimism, which you cannot even comprehend, is actually your possibility, yes, even your most holy duty. You are a person of eternity, of absolute yearning, of unlimited hoping. You can be this because we have experienced the love of God in Jesus Christ.

I do not see why a priest of this vision could not overcome the crisis in today's priesthood. Naturally, all these things have been overshadowed by the triviality and the habitual nature of our life from which the priest also suffers. He is necessarily also the one who must constantly pray: I believe, Father, help my unbelief. He too must accomplish a breakthrough in hope—out of the banality of the mundane and into God's eternity. He cannot be a priest and be happy if he is not a spiritual person, if he does not always begin again— he need not do more than try. He must be a man of God, a man of experience with the Holy Spirit and a man of eternity. If he is not this, then the priesthood will be a terrible burden for him. But even if he is such a spiritually oriented person, it is also clear that he will experience disappointment in himself and in those to whom he preaches the word of God.

But this burden is not taken from laypeople and from those who think they would be freer and happier if they were to leave the priesthood. Disappointment, death, hardship, and the like are part of human life. It would indeed be sad if a priest were not to experience these as well. However, he should not be quick to blame all the above on the priesthood as such. He should rather ask: Where is there one who does not experience disappointments in our time here on earth, ultimately at death?

It seems to me correct that today's priest no longer has certain functions which earlier perhaps made his life a bit easier and cheaper to live. Many of a priest's earlier duties have now disappeared, be it because others have taken them over, or be it because the priest no longer has the time and energy. He should not be disappointed in his priesthood because of this. He should reflect much more upon the real heart of the priesthood. There certainly must be men in our dreadfully banal and brutal society who nurse the fire of praise and love of God and who initiate others in the experience of God's mystery. Each one will be successful in his own way. Of course, a priest's religious potential and dynamic force is going to depend upon his talents and personal history. One should not turn up one's nose or look down upon even the smallest servant in God's kingdom who, true and faithful, proclaims the message of the New Testament through his priestly calling, even if this is done in a common, banal, traditional, and somewhat "burnt-out" manner. Every priest should always say to himself: Within the limits given you by God, you should be truly a prophet, a man of God, one moved by the fire of God. You should love God and your fellow man. You should proclaim the message of Jesus Christ in our time, as Paul said, be it convenient or inconvenient.

Translated by Jeffrey Seeger, S.J.
Loyola Marymount University, Los Angeles

62 · Horizons of Thinking in Theology

Interview with Manfred Waldenmair-Lackenbach and Thomas Untersteiner, Innsbruck (1982)

Professor Rahner, you can look back on an enormous effort in theology. Is there such a thing as a legacy from Karl Rahner?

I have no theological legacy to leave; I have no particular message to formulate, no statement I can give to coming generations with the authority of the Church—for that, my theology is too insignificant. It fits easily and modestly into the total picture of Catholic theology as it is today, despite all the changes of the last thirty years.

If I have to say what my theology is, then I only have to point to the *Foundations of Christian Faith*, a book translated into English, French, Italian, Spanish, and Dutch (it is scheduled to appear in Hungarian and is in the process of being translated into Swahili by two theologians in Tanzania). In this book, in general, one can read what I have attempted to say in theology. Whether it is particularly original or not is a secondary and useless question. A Catholic theologian ultimately cannot strive to be particularly original: to say something which no one else has ever said. Rather, the theologian's obligation, duty, and intent aim at guarding and interpreting the message of Jesus, the revelation of God, and the teaching of the Church, and to make it intelligible and accessible to one's contemporaries. If I have achieved something in this regard, I'm happy; but I don't have a particular message. (I could mention that for my seventy-fifth birthday a collection from my works appeared as *Rechenschaft des Glaubens* [untranslated] which is a systematic collection of what I have said in my theology; and then later *The Practice of Faith* [New York: Crossroad, 1983] appeared which presents texts touching upon spirituality and praxis, piety and life.)

Cardinal Ratzinger, who is now the prefect of the Congregation of the Faith, wrote that *Foundations* would have a significance when most of today's theological literature is forgotten. Naturally, one can ask—with or without modesty— whether such a theology as mine does not have a particular style, certain tendencies, and patterns which are not simply drawn from the normal, exhausted scholastic texts.

But if I can ask this question, still I am not particularly suited to answering it. As an example I can emphasize (and this might not be what is most important) that I advocate and work at a theology in which thinking, philosophical thinking, has a position which is not arbitrary. Today that is no longer taken for granted. I grew up as a neoscholastic theologian; then biblical theology was not prominent; also one did not think and live charismatically and spiritually in an immediate way. One thought in a sober and, in a sense, clean conceptuality, reflecting upon the content of revelation, in a synthesis or a confrontation with human knowledge about oneself in the way that this consciousness —above all in philosophy—had long expressed itself.

Certainly this neoscholastic theology was too cool in is rejection of modern philosophy, too imprisoned in medieval theology. It received modern philosophy from Descartes to Kant and German idealism up to modern existentialism as the opponent against which everything must be protected and defended. Neoscholasticism was still a little colored by the trauma which theological work at the beginning of the twentieth century in the battle with modernism went through. One was careful, thought rather fundamentalistically, was too reserved vis-à-vis modern biblical criticism and historical-critical theology. I do think that this period in which I grew up has today come to its end. We have in theology a more open relationship to the modern world.

Now we reflect a plurality of philosophies; look for points of view, concepts, perspectives from modern consciousness in a clearer, more courageous, more open way than in the time of neoscholasticism, and we try to bring, with the new, the theology of the tradition into a synthesis. Today's systematic theology is more or less closer to biblical theology, to exegesis, and has a richer relationship to the history of doctrine.

In this period of retrieval and renewal, transcending the ghetto mentality of neoscholasticism in the nineteenth and in the first half of the twentieth century, I have developed my theology . . . and perhaps have made a contribution. But on the other hand, I would want also to be a theologian who—as much as possible—watches over the good and the venerable from traditional theology.

I hope that my theology has inner, authentic and living connections with the theology of Thomas Aquinas and respects simply and clearly the teaching ministry of the Church. Naturally, the theologian must, in terms of this ministry, discern whether this office is expressing itself in a final, defining, binding way, or whether it is giving teaching and direction (and they too might have an authoritative character) which, a priori, are not immune from the danger of erring. A theologian may and must, with regard to the binding expressions of the Church's magisterium (to delineate particularly the Roman magisterium), stand apart precisely in order to work toward an understanding which will place certain expressions in a new, more encompassing connection than one can reach immediately in these Roman statements. But again, my theology intends to stand in an unbroken unity with the magisterium.

Naturally, there are people in the Church of God, for example, Cardinal Siri of Genoa, who picture me inevitably as a heretic, as a warrior against the true teaching of the Church, as a relativist and a skeptic who can't distinguish between grace and nature. But I think that such labels (even if one concedes that one can err in individual questions) are nonsense. I would tell Cardinal Siri to read the telegram which Cardinal Höffner in the name of the entire German bishops' conference sent me on the occasion of the fiftieth anniversary of my ordination.[1] I can also fall back on Cardinal Döpfner, Cardinal Volk,

---

1. Very reverend and dear Father Rahner. In the name of the German bishops' conference and personally, I sincerely wish you the Lord's blessings on your fiftieth anniversary as a priest. Serving the gospel and with that promoting the unity of the people of God and their perfection in the eucharistic celebration—these fundamental New Testament priestly tasks—are not only theological topics to you. Above all, they have been the way you have labored in personal, priestly service these fifty years, with God's help. I am most grateful to you for this. May God continue to grant you many more years of your extraordinary productivity.

Joseph Cardinal Höffner
July 26, 1982

Cardinals Höffner and Jäger with whom I was on very good terms, as well as Pope Paul VI and Pope John Paul II (with whom I had a private audience in which we had a wide-ranging exchange of views). Neither pope ever attacked my modest theological efforts and these popes would have had the courage to express any objections which were justified.

Naturally, there are points of view which are characteristics of my theology. For me and for my theology the universal will of God, which from the beginning encloses and bears the totality of humanity and its cultural history, and which—through divine self-communication, divine grace—has as its goal the immediacy of God, is a more fundamental, a more significant point of view than would have been the case in ordinary scholastic theology. At first, what was considered was baptized Christians with their faith and with their express confession in God and Jesus Christ, but then later the issue of how others came to salvation called for reflection. Did God really have a general will of salvation which reaches out effectively through all people? Thus, the man and woman of today who profess atheism more or less explicitly are present in my theology. At least that was my goal.

Naturally (and this is a further characteristic of my theology), there is also a universal salvation-history acted out in space and time and a universal history of revelation effected in space and time, both of which stand in an indissoluble relationship to each other. Naturally, I know and confess that Jesus is the one mediator of salvation for all people and has a unique, irrevocable, all-encompassing significance for the salvation of all people. And of course I recognize and confess a history of revelation which (as Vatican II says) began in paradise and moves through the Old Testament history of revelation from Moses through the prophets to Jesus Christ as the unsurpassable high point of revelation. But I think that one can link the conviction that the entire history of humanity is finalized and —if you wish—divinized with the knowing belief that our history is a history in which God is always at work in the power of his salvific will toward all human beings. From that results a perhaps more positive and flexible evaluation of the history of religions which naturally are also a history of human wandering and moral depravity.

I think that from this perspective my theology is quite different from the perspective of an Augustine (if you will excuse my boldness), but is very much in conformity with the intentions of Vatican II. For Augustine the history of humanity was the history of the *massa damnata*, out of which God—in a judgment which was impenetrable and by a grace effective for some individuals— saved only a few. For me the history of humanity—despite all the horrors committed by people, despite Auschwitz and all the catastrophes we have to fear from atomic weapons and the exhaustion of natural resources—is a history of salvation, a universal history of the power of grace and divine love, a history we can want in hope for *all* and not just for a few.

Naturally there are, at a closer glance, perspectives which one could make clearer. Since the end of the Second World War, I have have frequently worked in ecumenical circles. I think that I, in absolute solidarity with the Church's magisterium, have said this or that for our Protestant brothers and theologians which made something more understandable than it had been in neoscholastic theology and in the statements of the magisterium.

In light of the letter that was sent to the Holy See at the beginning of this year concerned in a critical way with the issue of freedom of speech within the Church, are you a man of the "reform wing," a man of novelty?

No, that letter had nothing to do with novelty. You see I was one of those who took a critical and negative view toward many of the positions of Hans Küng; but I also belong to those who value the positive significance of Küng and his honorable efforts to bring genuine Christianity to our liberal, bourgeois, and skeptical contemporaries. And so it was understandable that along with other theologians like Heinrich Fries and Rudolf Schnackenburg I wanted the conflict between Rome and Küng to be resolved. That is why we wrote the Holy Father that this affair should not be let rest but everything should be done to resolve the conflict.

The secretary of state, Cardinal Casaroli, answered me concerning this letter at length and with every kindness. It was not a question of a controversy with Rome but the issue of our right, obvious and disputed by no one, to present our wishes, views, and concerns to the highest office in the Church in a plain, honorable, and open manner. Whether and how this situation continues is naturally another question, something which depends not only upon Rome but upon Küng. We will have to wait and see.

But this has nothing to do with any kind of critical, bellicose, rebellious mentality; that is something I have never had. But I do have, in the past and now, the obvious right and indeed the obligation of a Catholic theologian to ask about the statements of the magisterium, to look behind them and to express myself in a critical way, not in order to want to display myself as someone smarter than everyone else but in order to work along with the efforts of making the message of the gospel attractive and meaningful today and to preserve it from ecclesiastical difficulties which are superficial and capable of solution.

Cardinal Ratzinger, the new prefect of the Congregation of the Faith, indicated in December, 1981, a very optimistic path for the Church in the future: a council of union with Orthodoxy, a new evaluation of the local churches in the Third World and—even if farther in the future—chances for a common path with Protestants. Do you agree with his prognosis?

Fortunately or unfortunately, depending upon how you see it, there are in religion and the Church as in politics many questions that come up simultaneously, for example, ecology, thermonuclear war, unemployment, electronic media, and communications. They appear at the same time but they can't all be solved at once. So there has to be a priority without simply forgetting about the problems which are of lower priority. We have the same thing in the Church. There is the task of a definitive and full reconciliation with the Eastern churches (this is harder to do than perhaps the present Holy Father in his optimism thinks). There is the ecumenical question of a union with Protestants at the level of theology and then at the level of church constitution and ecclesial reunion.

And naturally, in a Church which is now little by little becoming worldwide, a worldwide Catholic Church, there is the problem that Latin American, African, and Asian churches are achieving greater self-responsibility and working toward their own theology, a responsibility and a theology more suited to their needs and aspirations than what previously existed in their countries where, formerly, ecclesiastical life and Catholic theology were simply nice, useful imports. And beyond this there is also the necessity of larger and more intensive encounters with modern science, with psychology, with political science and sociology, with the individual natural sciences. The issues of evolution, of the length of human history, of our apparent position as an abandoned island in an enormous cosmos, of the possibility of a spiritual (that is, a cultural and human) history which nourishes a relationship to God—these must be pondered.

There are then thousands of theological questions and problems, and it is hard to arrange their priority. Perhaps that is not so important; perhaps we need only to open up all these problems with greater intensity and courage, and each of us (who can only touch a small piece of the whole) must see where one can best labor—in theology, in preaching, in discerning the form of Christian life for our time and our world.

A strong ecumenical consciousness pervades your entire work.[2] Do you think ecumenism will be the decisive theological area for the coming decades, perhaps up to the turn of the century?

2. Heinrich Fries and Karl Rahner, *Unity of the Churches*, tr. Ruth Gritsch and Eric Gritsch (Ramsey, N. J.: Paulist Press/Philadelphia: Fortress, 1985).

You know the Catholic (socially structured as Roman) Church faces in a very clear way two counterparts today, opponents or potential friends: on the one hand, Christianity which is not Catholic and which poses the ecumenical question; but on the other hand we also live in a world in which there are not only Catholics and other Christians (so that we can just let the rest of the world alone). The Church stands before an atheism and a skepticism which is worldwide, and before a strong relativism. These are movements which are organized at times in a social and aggressively political style as in communist countries. Also in Western nations there is an anti-Church consciousness. We live with Protestant and Orthodox Christians in a world which is not Christian, and this non-Christian world is no longer a world outside of Western boundaries, but it exists in our midst. So the serious, burning ecumenical question is not simply the differences between Christian confessions and churches, but is occupied much more vitally, intensively, and radically with this culturally widespread, expressly or implicitly atheistic world.

We can add to this the recent unexpected restoration of Islamic fundamentalism which is also politically organized and powerful in a way which twenty, thirty years ago we could not imagine. The Church should of course not become involved in politics in this area (it has no battalions or divisions), but it must converse intensively with the Islamic world of faith so that it reaches a better understanding for this faith of hundreds of millions of human beings and learns thereby to make its own message more intelligible to this world.

I will not say that we have three fronts here, but you see that beyond ecumenism there are burning questions; they exist because in the world today we have not only Christians but also Moslems and the entire secularized, positivistic, relativistic, skeptical, atheistic world in which the message of Christianity must be preached in a new way.

And I haven't even mentioned the religions of Africa and South America or the great cultural religions of Asia; they too must be brought into a new dialogue with the Church and with the Christian gospel. Here we have the question: To what extent in those Asian countries are those of the traditional spirituality, tradition, and religion or those men and women already secularized and threatened by atheism the partner in dialogue for Christianity? In Japan is the modernized, technological Japanese or the old Japanese of Shintoism and Buddhism the true partner? This is hard to answer. And then you have almost a billion people in China where, for the moment, for all practical purposes, Christianity is banned, but where a potential partner, a potential space for a later preaching of Christianity exists, a possibility for which the Church must prepare itself right now.

The Church has an enormous number of tasks. Any one of them would be beyond its capabilities. Practicing church members do not exhaust the world addressed by and responding to the Church. It was astonishing to see how many hundreds of thousands of people in England expressed interest and enthusiasm over the visit of Pope John Paul II. He is today certainly one of the few, if not the only, key figure to whom those many bring trust, who have been made skeptics by the deception of their political leaders.

But all that is encouraging in the Church should not distract us from the fact that the Church today stands before enormous, innumerable, extraordinarily difficult questions (almost beyond human measuring) so that it is capable of daring to move into an unknown future only by trusting in Jesus Christ, in his cross and resurrection.

Translated by Thomas F. O'Meara, O.P.
University of Notre Dame

63 · The Catholic Church and the Peace Movement

Interview with Horst Wünsche for West Germany's Channel 2 (ZDF), Mainz (August 29, 1982)

Professor Rahner, as a Catholic theologian you are counted among the most significant dogma professors of your Church. Now, in revelation the duty of peace and of love of one's enemy stands out clearly. The peace movements, which today are spreading everywhere, believe, therefore, that the Church must nourish and represent them, and, as far as possible, must march along at the head of the movement.

The Catholic Church cannot identify itself absolutely with a definite peace movement and its postulates. The moment the Church knows that this concrete peace movement did nothing but draw consequences from the gospel, the Church would naturally have to embrace such a peace movement. The Church, for example, at the Second Vatican Council completely and unambiguously condemned atomic war—not only the first strike, but also a second strike. But the concrete peace movements go even beyond this, beyond the self-evident Christian peace mentality—self-evident to the Church. Perhaps they do this rightly, but with demands that are not based on any unanimity among Christians that these demands necessarily follow from the gospel. And so the Church can observe, in my opinion, a certain distance and neutrality in the face of certain defined demands of certain peace movements.

Armament is not yet war. Is armament already an offense against the obligation of peace? There is the opinion we arm to save the peace, since in this way we can frighten the opponent.

I believe that it is impossible to draw clearly, here and now in concrete situations, such a conclusion from the gospel, so that the Church could oblige all its members to this definite conclusion. Therefore, nothing else remains for the Church, as I see it, with regard to concrete demands, that is, armament to secure the peace or disarmament to guarantee peace, no definite position to enjoin upon its members in an authoritative way.

Could a unilateral disarmament based on a Christian motive then not be inferred to be compulsory?

I should think that as a concrete, individual Christian, I have the right to plead for a unilateral disarmament from Christian motives. But I can't deny to the other person who does not believe that he can answer for this disarmament—I can't deny that he has intelligence and good will and a positive Christian attitude.

How would you explain to yourself that the leading Christian party in the German Federal Republic has a rather negative stance on the peace movement?

That is a position to which I cannot deny good will and intelligence, but at the same time I can explain from Christian motives that I am of a different opinion. Cardinal Höffner, for example, has expressly said, and I quote: "In the field of securing peace, there are questions in which Christians with equal conscientiousness can come to various judgments, and to these questions," says Höffner, "belong armament and the exportation of weapons." In other words: I can represent another opinion than that of the Central Committee of German Catholics and their declaration. The Christian Democrats and the Central Committee have no right to deny me this freedom.

In closing, we would still like to know from you how it happens that the Catholic Church and the Protestant Church have a different picture with regard to the peace movement?

I must first say, of course, that we are only speaking of the German Catholic Church—that is not the same as the Catholic Church all over the world. In the German Catholic Church there is really a certain tendency toward a peaceful homogenizing of opinions. Such a tendency, for historical and theological reasons, occurs less in the Protestant Church. Among Protestants, quarrels, differences of opinion are found to be clearer and stronger. In questions like the securing of peace, the Catholic Church in Germany need not necessarily take the position she has in the past.

There is no theological foundation, therefore, for this difference?
No, I don't think so.

> *Translated by John J. O'Neill, S.J.*
> *Loyola Marymount University, Los Angeles*

SIGNIFICANT DATES IN THE LIFE OF KARL RAHNER

March 5, 1904	Born in Freiburg in Breisgau, West Germany.
1913–1922	University-oriented primary and secondary school education at the Realgymnasium in Freiburg in Breisgau.
1922	Entrance into the Society of Jesus at the Jesuit novitiate in Feldkirch/Voralberg, Austria.
1924–1927	Philosophical studies at the Jesuit philosophates at Feldkirch and Pullach (near Munich).
1927–1929	Teacher at the Jesuit house of studies (juniorate) in Feldkirch-Tisis.
1929–1933	Theological studies at the Jesuit theologate in Valkenburg, Holland.
July 26, 1932	Ordained a priest at St. Michael's Church in Munich.
1933–1934	Tertianship (final year of Jesuit training) at Saint Andrä in Lavanttal (Kärnten), Austria.
1934–1936	Doctoral studies in philosophy at the University of Freiburg in Breisgau. Here he wrote *Geist im Welt* (ET: *Spirit in the World*, tr. William Dych, S.J. [New York: Herder and Herder, 1967]).
1936	Doctoral studies in theology at the University of Innsbruck, Austria.
December 19, 1936	Received the Doctor of Theology degree from the University of Innsbruck.
July 1, 1937	Completed postdoctoral work (*Habilitation*) required for university teaching. Lecturer in dogmatic theology at the University of Innsbruck.
1939	*Geist im Welt* is published.
1941	*Hörer des Wortes* (ET: *Hearers of the Word*, tr. Michael Richards [New York: Herder and Herder, 1969]).
1939–1944	University lecturer in Vienna. Colleague at the Vienna Pastoral Institute. On the bishop's advisory board. Lecture circuit.
1944–1945	Pastoral work in Mariakirchen, Lower Bavaria.
1945–1948	Professor of Dogmatic Theology at the Jesuit theologate in Pullach. Also gave theology courses in priestly formation programs in Munich.

August, 1948	Returned to the theology faculty at Innsbruck.
June 30, 1949	Promoted to Ordinary Professor of Dogma and the History of Dogma at the University of Innsbruck.
March 31, 1954	Associé de la Société Philosophique de Louvain, Belgium.
1954	Publication of the first volume of *Schriften zur Theologie* (ET: *Theological Investigations* I, tr. Cornelius Ernst, O.P. [Baltimore: Helicon, 1963]).
1975ff.	Editor of the second edition of *Lexikon für Theologie und Kirche* and the *Quaestiones Disputatae* series.
1961	Publication of *Kleines theologisches Wörterbuch* (ET: *Theological Dictionary*, tr. Richard Strachan [New York: Herder and Herder, 1965]).
1962	*Peritus* at the Second Vatican Council.
February 20, 1964	Medal in honor of his scholarly achievements bestowed by the government of Tirol, Austria.
March 25, 1964	University Professor of Christian Philosophy and the Philosophy of Religion at the University of Munich.
May 13, 1964	Doctor of Theology, honoris causa, from the University of Münster/Westfalen, West Germany.
November 21, 1964	Doctor, honoris causa, from the University of Strassburg.
1964ff.	Editor of *Handbuch der Pastoraltheologie*.
June 26, 1965	Recipient of the Reuchlin Prize from the city of Pforzheim.
March 23, 1966	Doctor of Law, honoris causa, from the University of Notre Dame's Law School.
April 1, 1967	Professor of Dogma and the History of Dogma on the Faculty of Catholic Theology at the University of Münster/Westfalen, West Germany.
October 12, 1967	Doctor, honoris causa, from Saint Louis University.
April 1, 1968	Recipient of the University of Helsenki Medal in Finland.
April 27, 1969	Member of the Papal Theological Commission.
June 9, 1969	Doctor of Theology, honoris causa, from Yale University.
March 18, 1970	Recipient of the Romano Guardini Prize from the Catholic Academy in Bavaria (Munich).
May 6, 1970	Recipient of West Germany's Distinguished Cross of Merit with Star.
June 6, 1970	Doctor of Philosophy, honoris causa, from the University of Innsbruck.
June 23, 1970	Member of the West German Order of Merit for Arts and Sciences.
September 3, 1971	Professor emeritus.
October 1, 1971	Honorary Professor of Interdisciplinary Questions Relating to Theology and Philosophy at the Jesuit philosophate in Munich.

February 2, 1972   Doctor of Theology, honoris causa, from the University of Louvain, Belgium.

May 10, 1972   Honorary member of the American Academy of Arts and Sciences in Boston.

June 18, 1972   Honorary Professor of Dogma and the History of Dogma in the Department of Catholic Theology at the University of Innsbruck.

1972   Publication of *Strukturwandel der Kirche* (ET: *The Shape of the Church to Come*, tr. Edward Quinn [New York: The Seabury Press, 1974)].

October 20, 1973   Recipient of the Sigmund Freud Prize for Scholarly Prose from the German Academy for Language and Literature.

May 19, 1974   Doctor of Humane Letters, honoris causa, from Georgetown University.

May 31, 1974   Doctor of Theology, honoris causa, from the Pontificia Universitas Comillensis, Madrid.

July 10, 1974   Corresponding Fellow of the British Academy.

July 15, 1974   Recipient of the Lorenz-Werthmann Medal from West Germany's Caritas Society.

November 6, 1974   Campion Award from the Catholic Book Club of America Press.

November 8, 1974   Doctor of Humane Letters, honoris causa, from the University of Chicago.

November 9, 1974   Doctor of Law, honoris causa, from Duquesne University.

1976   Publication of *Grundkurs des Glaubens* (ET: *Foundations of Christian Faith*, tr. William V. Dych, S.J. [New York: The Seabury Press, 1978]).

September 4, 1976   Recipient of the Cardinal Innitzer Prize.

1978   Publication of *Ignatius of Loyola*, together with P. Imhof and H. N. Loose (ET: *Ignatius of Loyola*, tr. Rosaleen Ockenden [Cleveland: Collins, 1979]).

March 1, 1979   Honorary Member of the Commonwealth of Kentucky, in Frankfort, Kentucky.

March 27, 1979   Recipient of the Père Marquette Discovery Award from the University of Marquette in Milwaukee.

April 1, 1979   Honorary Member of Alpha Sigma Nu, the National Jesuit Honor Society.

April 3, 1979   Keys to the city of Louisville, Kentucky. Also made a "Colonel of Kentucky."

April 6, 1979   Doctor of Humane Letters, honoris causa, from John Carroll University.

April 18, 1979   Doctor of Humane Letters, honoris causa, from the Weston School of Theology in Boston.

May 16, 1979	Cultural Prize of Honor from the city of Munich.
1979	Publication of *Was sollen wir noch glauben?*, with K. H. Weger (ET: *Our Christian Faith*, tr. Francis McDonagh [New York: Crossroad, 1981]); *Rechenschaft des Glaubens*, ed. K. Lehmann and A. Raffelt.
May 25, 1980	Doctor of Law, honoris causa, from Fordham University.
1981	Publication of *Theologie in Freiheit und Verantwortung*, with H. Fries.
May 14, 1982	Recipient of the Dr. Leopold Lucas Prize from the Faculty of Protestant Theology, Tübingen.
1982	Publication of *Was heisst Jesus lieben?* (published in English with *Wer ist dein Bruder?* [1981] as *The Love of Jesus and the Love of Neighbor*, tr. Robert Barr [New York: Crossroad, 1983]); *Karl Rahner im Gespräch, Bd. 1: 1964–1977*, ed. P. Imhof and H. Biallowons; *Mein Problem—Karl Rahner antwortet jungen Menschen* (ET: *Is Christian Life Possible Today?*, tr. Salvator Attanasio [Denville, NJ: Dimension, 1984]); *Praxis des Glaubens. Geistliches Lesebuch*, ed. K. Lehmann and A. Raffelt (ET: *The Practice of Faith: A Handbook of Contemporary Spirituality* [New York: Crossraod, 1983]).
1983	Publication of *Schriften zur Theologie 15: Wissenschaft und christlicher Glaube*, ed. P. Imhof (ET forthcoming as *Theological Investigations XXI*); *Karl Rahner im Gespräch, Bd. 2: 1978–1982*, ed. P. Imhof and H. Biallowons.
1984	Publication of *Schriften zur Theologie 16: Humane Gesellschaft und Kirche von Morgen*, ed. P. Imhof (ET forthcoming as *Theological Investigations XXII*); *Erinnerungen im Gespräch mit Meinold Krauss* (ET: *I Remember: An Autobiographical Interview*, tr. Harvey D. Egan [New York: Crossroad, 1985]); *Gebete des Lebens*, ed. A. Raffelt (ET: *Prayers for a Lifetime* [New York: Crossroad, 1984]).
March 5, 1984	Eightieth birthday. Establishment of the Karl Rahner Prize for the furthering of theological development.
March 30, 1984	Death in Innsbruck, Austria.

INFORMATION ABOUT THE INTERVIEWS

The number given in the margin corresponds to the interview number as found in the table of contents. The date for the television and radio occasionally refers to the first transmission date. Many interview titles and questions in the texts have been slightly emended or completely changed in this volume. Some of the English translations have been abridged, as noted below.

1. See: Patrick Dom Granfield, O.S.B., *Theologians at Work* (New York: Macmillan, 1967), pp. 35–50.
2. *America*, New York, 24/112 (June 12, 1965), pp. 860–63.
3. *Sonntag*, Olten, West Germany, 38 (September 22, 1968), pp. 18–19.
4. *Der Spiegel*, Hamburg, West Germany, 39 (September 23, 1968), pp. 166–76.
5. *America*, New York, 13/123 (October 31, 1970), pp. 356–59.
6. Radio West Germany (WDR), Cologne (November 1, 1970).
7. *Treffpunkt*, Magazine of the KSJ-Schwaz, Widum, West Germany, 1/1971, pp. 35–36.
8. *Nürnberger Nachrichten*, Nürnberg (December 24–26, 1971), p. 17.
9. "Questions for the Theologians," on West Germany's Channel 2 (ZDF), Mainz (April 4, 1971). Slightly abridged.
10. As number 9 (May 16, 1971).
11. As number 9 (September 19, 1971).
12. As number 9 (February 20, 1972).
13. As number 4, 9 (February 21, 1971), pp. 112–19.
14. *Münchener Katholische Kirchenzeitung* (MKKZ), 1 (January 2, 1972), pp. 3–4, and 2 (January 9, 1972), pp. 12–13. Slightly abridged.
15. As number 14, 45 (November 5, 1972), pp. 3–4. Slightly abridged.
16. *Neue Züricher Nachrichten*, 132 (June 9, 1973), no page numbers given. Abridged.
17. Radio Saarland, Saarbrücken (December 9, 1973).
18. As number 17 (April 14, 1975).
19. Coproduced by Radio Free Berlin (SFB) and Radio Southwest (SWF), Baden-Baden (July 28, 1974). Slightly abridged.
20. Unpublished manuscript for the closing session of Dr. Albert Raffelt's seminar, "Introduction to Karl Rahner's Theology," Theology Department at the University of Freiburg in Breisgau (summer semester, 1974).

21. *Evangelische Kommentare,* Stuttgart 8/1975, pp. 483–86. Abridged.
22. *Welt am Sonntag,* Munich 37 (September 12, 1976), no page numbers given.
23. *Presse,* Vienna (June 5–6, 1976), p. 1.
24. *Caritas,* of Nordrhein-Westfalen, Cologne 2 (March/April 1976), pp. 105–9. Abridged.
25. As number 6 (July 25, 1976). Abridged.
26. "Katholisches Tagebuch," on West Germany's Channel 2 (ZDF), Mainz (November 21, 1976). Abridged.
27. "Theologie im Gespräch," of Radio Austria (FS 1), Vienna (December 26, 1976).
28. *Herder-Korrespondenz,* Freiburg in Breisgau, 12/1977, pp. 607–14.
29. *Saarbrücker Zeitung,* Saarbrücken (July 14, 1978), p. 6.
30. *Entschluss, Zeitschrift für Praxis und Theologie,* Vienna, 5/1978, pp. 8–11.
31. As number 31, 8/1978, pp. 17–18 and 23.
32. *America,* New York, 9/140 (March 10, 1979), pp. 177–80.
33. Original production, Munich (January 27, 1979). As "Feature," in Radio West Germany (WDR III), Cologne (February 21, 1979).
34. Taped for study group of the public-legal radio institution of West Germany, ARD; broadcast by South German Radio, Stuttgart (April 14, 1979).
35. Taped for North-German Radio III, Hamburg; used by Radio Austria (FS 2), Vienna (March 2, 1979). Slightly abridged.
36. Taped for *Dienstagredaction* of South-German Radio, Stuttgart (March 19, 1979). Slightly abridged.
37. As number 36.
38. As number 35. Slightly abridged.
39. "Report," in South-West Radio (SWF), Baden-Baden (November 13, 1979). Abridged.
40. Original taping: Editors of the Catholic News Service, Munich. Reprinted in *Publik-Forum,* Frankfurt 22 (October 31, 1980), pp. 27–28.
41. *Die Furche,* Vienna 14 (April 2, 1980), p. 1.
42. Radio Saarland, Saarbrücken (October 21, 1980).
43. *Süddeutsche Zeitung,* Munich, 31 (February 6, 1980), p. 11. Summary of an interview on "Night Studio" of Radio Salzburg, no date given.
44. *Münchener Katholische Kirchenzeitung* (MKKZ), 21 (May 25, 1980), p. 3. Abridged
45. "Night Studio" on FS 2 of Radio Austria, Vienna (July 11, 1980).
46. As number 45.
47. Abridged. For the complete text, see: *Civitas, Zeitschrift des Schweizerischen Studentenverein* 5/6 January 1981, pp. 288–308.
48. *France Catholique Ecclesia,* Paris, 1799 (June 5, 1981), pp. 7–8, and 1800 (June 12, 1981), pp. 3–4.
49. *Lutherische Monatshefte,* Hannover (April 1980), pp. 211–14.

50. "TV Profile," Een onverstoorbare bernieuwer im Katholike Radio Omroep (KRO), Hilversum (October 5, 1981).
51. Original tape. Also transmitted by North-German Radio III, Hamburg (November 22, 1981).
52. As number 51.
53. As number 43, 1 (January 6, 1982), p. 3.
54. *Kirche, Wochenblatt der Diözese Innsbruck*, Innsbruck, 4 (January 24, 1982), p. 6.
55. *KSÖ, Nachrichten und Stellungnahme der Katholischen Sozialadakemie Österreichs*, Vienna 3 (February 6, 1981), p.7.
56. As number 30, 5/1982, pp. 31–34.
57. Appeared as an essay in: *Geist und Leben*, Würzburg, 5/1982, pp. 336–39. From a text in the series, "The Angry Old Men," by Norbert Stammler, broadcast in the *Studio-Welle Saar* of Radior Saarland III, Saarbrücken (April 3, 1982).
58. *Dom, Sonntagsblatt für das Erzbistum Paderborn*, 9 (April 29, 1982), pp. 11.
59. "Night Studio," in Radio Bayern II, Munich (April 29, 1982).
60. Original tape. Abridged like number 43, 14 (April 7, 1982), p. 11. Also in *Landesstudio Salzburg* of Radio Austria, Salzburg.
61. Original tape. Also in *Landesstudio Salzburg* of Radio Austria, Salzburg. Slightly abridged.
62. Original tape: published for the first time.
63. "Questions of our Time," on West Germany's Channel 2 (ZDF), Mainz (August 29, 1982).

INDEX

Translators

(Numbers after the name refer to the number of the interview)